85-19600

The Establishment of Human Antiquity

Dieu est éternel, mais l'homme est bien vieux.

Jacques Boucher de Perthes, 1857

The Establishment of Human Antiquity

Donald K. Grayson

Department of Anthropology
and Burke Memorial Museum
University of Washington
Seattle, Washington

1983

ACADEMIC PRESS

A Subsidiary of Harcourt Brace Jovanovich, Publishers

New York   London
Paris   San Diego   San Francisco   São Paulo   Sydney   Tokyo   Toronto

The design stamped on the front cover of this volume and used in the chapter headings is taken from a depiction of a woolly mammoth, *Mammuthus primigenius,* at the late Pleistocene site of Font de Gaume, southwestern France.

ACADEMIC PRESS, INC.
111 Fifth Avenue, New York, New York 10003

United Kingdom Edition published by
ACADEMIC PRESS, INC. (LONDON) LTD.
24/28 Oval Road, London NW1 7DX

Library of Congress Cataloging in Publication Data

Grayson, Donald K.
    The establishment of human antiquity.

    Bibliography: p.
    Includes index.
    1. Anthropology, Prehistoric--History--18th century.
2. Anthropology, Prehistoric--History--19th century.
3. Archaeology--History--18th century. 4. Archaeology--
History--19th century. 5. Man--Origin. I. Title.
GN720.G73 1982   930.1   82-11571
ISBN 0-12-297250-3

PRINTED IN THE UNITED STATES OF AMERICA

83 84 85 86   9 8 7 6 5 4 3 2 1

To Barbara

Contents

List of Illustrations

Preface

"God is eternal, but man is very old." So ended the second volume of Jacques Boucher de Perthes's *Celtic and Antediluvian Antiquities,* published in 1857. At the time he wrote these words, few influential scientists agreed with him; just 2 years later, few influential scientists disagreed. This book deals with the events that led to, and were involved in, that great shift in view concerning the antiquity of humankind on earth.

The establishment of an extensive human antiquity was a crucial event, perhaps *the* crucial event, in the attempt to understand our origins. Not only did the recognition that people are ancient provide, as Darwin said, "the indispensable basis" for understanding human origins, but this recognition also played a major role in the establishment of prehistoric archaeology as a discipline and thus fueled the growth of an increasingly detailed knowledge of our past.

Archaeologists fully recognize the historical importance of the new consensus on human antiquity that was reached in 1859. Nearly all introductory archaeological texts include a section that briefly describes the events that were involved in the recognition of a lengthy human history, usually focusing on Boucher de Perthes and the discovery of the Neanderthal skull. Given this acknowledged importance, it is somewhat surprising that no detailed chronicle or analysis of the full sequence of events that led to the new consensus and that is based on the primary literature has previously appeared. This is not to say that the years during which the new consensus was reached have not been the subject of excellent studies: Jacob W. Gruber's "Brixham Cave and the Antiquity of

Man'' (1965) and Kenneth P. Oakley's ''The Problem of Man's Antiquity'' (1964) provide detailed and insightful analyses of those years. Nor is it to say that general histories of archaeology have in any way ignored the establishment of a great human antiquity. Glyn Daniel's *A Hundred and Fifty Years of Archaeology* (1976) and *A Short History of Archaeology* (1981), the best general surveys of the history of archaeology available, treat the issue, as does Annette Laming-Emperaire's superb *Origins of Prehistoric Archaeology in France* (1964). There has, however, been no attempt to combine the detailed chronicle and analysis found in Gruber or Oakley with the broad historical sweep provided by Daniel or Laming-Emperaire. It is this gap that I have attempted to fill.

As an archaeologist, I have written with archaeologists as my primary audience, but I have also tried to provide an analytic review that can be read and followed by anyone interested in life and earth history. At a time when there are those in the United States who are suggesting once again that humankind is no more than 6000 years old, it seems appropriate to provide a discussion of the complete and powerful rejection of this view made by highly religious scientists over a century ago and to provide it in such a way that it is available to anyone with a general knowledge of scientific approaches to the history of our planet and of the life it supports.

Any historical study makes heavy demands on libraries and librarians, and I gratefully acknowledge the assistance provided by the staffs of the libraries of Columbia University (Rudolph Ellenbogen), New York University, the New York Historical Society, the New York Public Library, the Library of Congress, the Academy of Natural Sciences of Philadelphia (Sylva Baker), the University of California, Berkeley (Steven Speier), the University of Washington (Karen Hedelund and Adrienne Stevens), and, especially, the American Museum of Natural History (Nina J. Root, Red Wassenich, and Sandy Jones). Much of this book was written while I was on leave from the University of Washington; I thank David Hurst Thomas for making my stay at the American Museum of Natural History both possible and pleasurable and Nina J. Root for introducing me to the wonders of the museum's library. Margot Dembo, Robert C. Dunnell, Barbara E. Grayson, Pamela Haas, V. Standish Mallory, Deborah Mayer, David J. Meltzer, Dennis J. O'Brien, Nan A. Rothschild, Stanley A. Shockey, and Trudy C. Thomas provided help in many ways. The initial draft of this volume was penetratingly reviewed by James R. Sackett, and Jacob W. Gruber and Peter J. Bowler provided equally penetrating critiques of earlier work that led to parts of Chapters 4, 5, and 6. All maps were drawn by Margaret A. Davidson. To these friends and colleagues, my sincere thanks.

1

Introduction

Most of us were taught as we grew up that our ancestry extends back into the extremely remote past. Scientists accept as fact that the human species has been on earth for tens of thousands of years, that morphologically similar and closely related kinds of beings have been on earth for a span of time measured in millions of years, and that our early ancestors lived and died on an earth different in many ways from that which we now occupy. We are accustomed to this view of our place on earth, and most of us are comfortable with it.

We now learn of our long existence almost as casually as we learn of the Crusades, so it is easy to forget that the antiquity of people on earth had to be discovered. It is even easier to be unaware that agreement that the human species is ancient and had existed long before our globe took on its modern form did not occur until the second half of the nineteenth century. The 1959 centenary of the publication of Darwin's *Origin of Species* was also the centenary of the recognition that people are ancient on earth.

Prior to about 1859, there was widespread agreement in the Western world that people had appeared on earth very recently. As I will discuss, what "recent" meant differed from person to person and from time to time. For some, recent meant some 6000 to 8000 years ago, the date suggested by tallying the genealogical information presented in the Bible. For others, recent meant geo-logically recent, after the earth had reached the state it now displays. For still others, human recency carried both of these meanings. But no matter which of these meanings was adopted, before about 1859 most Western natural historians and philosophers were as certain that the advent of the human species was a fairly modern event as they are now quite certain that it was a fairly ancient one.

The recognition of a deep human antiquity is one of the most important contributions made by those who have studied the debris that people leave behind. That study is now called archaeology, but those who made and published the initial discoveries of human bones and artifacts in a context that strongly suggested tremendous antiquity were not archaeologists. They were, instead, natural historians whose prime interests lay in geology or paleontology, and who happened to discover ancient human remains while pursuing those interests. Routinely, they stressed the geological and paleontological context of their dis-coveries, but placed very little emphasis on the nature of the human relics they had found. At the same time, the antiquarians, whose studies were artifact-oriented, generally did not work in ancient deposits since human remains were not expected there. If they did work in such deposits, they paid as little attention to the geological and paleontological context of their finds as the natural histo-rians paid to their artifacts. It was not until the 1840s that these separate ap-proaches toward the distant human past were combined in the work of a single individual, Jacques Boucher de Perthes, although combined in such a way that the results were anything but compelling.

The real fusion of these two different sets of interests developed out of the reexamination of the question of human antiquity that occurred during the late 1850s. Indeed, the *discipline* of prehistoric archaeology in large part developed out of this reexamination, as Jacob W. Gruber and Annette Laming-Emperaire have suggested.[1] As a result of those events there arose a set of people whose research focused on questions about the prehistoric human past, questions that were generated by those researchers themselves, and whose studies used tech-niques and methods suggested by those questions. It was not accidental that the first journal of prehistoric archaeology was founded by the archaeologist Gabriel de Mortillet (1821–1898) in 1864, a year after the first synthesis of the evidence for a lengthy human antiquity appeared. Nor was it accident that the decision to hold an annual International Congress of Prehistoric Anthropology and Archae-ology was made in 1865.[2] Both events reflect the impact of the demonstration of a deep human antiquity on the development of prehistoric archaeology as a discipline.

That the establishment of human antiquity played a major role in the devel-opment of prehistoric archaeology and of anthropology as a whole reflects just one aspect of the impact that this establishment had on the Western mind. This volume, however, deals with the recognition of the fact that people are ancient on earth, and not with the effects of that recognition. As a result, my historical coverage goes no further than the middle 1860s. The real debate did not begin until about 1810, when wide acceptance was given to a set of time markers by which human antiquity could be empirically assessed; my detailed examination begins with the acceptance of those time markers. I have provided some of the crucial pre-1810 historical background in the second and third chapters, in which I review the development of the principles of stratigraphic analysis and the incorporation of those principles into studies of life and earth history and also survey eighteenth-century views of the antiquity of the earth and its human inhabitants. These two chapters are presented for those who have had little introduction to these matters and, with the possible exception of a few subjects relating to human antiquity, provide little that has not been discussed in detail elsewhere.[3]

Although the possibility that our species might have been derived by transmutation from some earlier, nonhuman form played a role in arguments against a lengthy human existence on earth, this is not a book about evolutionary theory. I stress this at the outset because of the connection made today between questions of human antiquity and questions of human evolution. This connection is now so intimate that it might be surprising that the establishment of human antiquity and the publication of Darwin's *Origin of Species* were not causally connected events, even though they occurred at virtually the same instant in time. Many of those who, before 1859, were arguing for a deep human past were very much opposed to transmutationist theory of any sort. After 1859, many who were involved in extending the human lineage back into the Tertiary were also not very taken with Darwin's notions. As I discuss in the closing chapter, questions of the length of the human existence on earth immediately became caught up in questions of the evolution of our species. However, a deep human antiquity was then, and still is, compatible with creationist views. Thus, Charles Darwin could suggest in 1871 that the earliest members of the human lineage might have walked the earth during the Eocene, while antitransformationist French investigators were simultaneously pushing human history back into the Miocene. It is sometimes difficult to recognize today that questions of human antiquity and questions of human evolution are separable, but they are; that they could be treated separately was well recognized during the last half of the nineteenth century. This is not to say that evolutionary views did not gain much more from a vast human antiquity than creationist views gained, for they did. Indeed, had Darwin published his *Origin of Species* a few years earlier, the debate over the antiquity of people on earth would likely have been much more protracted. The length of the human existence and the transformation of species were the burning issues of life history during the late 1850s and early 1860s, but at the time that a deep human antiquity was established, they were fully separable issues.

That human beings were ancient on earth could have been concluded from a variety of approaches. The sheer magnitude of human knowledge could have been found to be incompatible with a short chronology for the existence of our species. Darwin could have come first, and the conclusion followed as transformationist thought became more popular. Scientists could have concluded from modern human physical or linguistic diversity that people had been around for an immense number of years (see Chapter 7). But none of these approaches would have been convincing. We can be sure, since most were tried.

The argument based on the magnitude of human knowledge is the oldest of these approaches, and illustrates the problem well. The heart of this means of assessing human antiquity is very simple. If all major inventions and discoveries have already been made, that might be because people have been in existence for a vast period of time, perhaps even eternally. On the other hand, if significant inventions and discoveries are still being made, the clear implication is that people are recent, unless such knowledge is simply being relearned. Were people ancient, then these things would have been known before. The basic question was asked in Ecclesiastes 1:10: ''Is there any thing whereof it may be said, See, this is new?''

The argument from invention and discovery has an impressively long history. Plato provided the seeds of the argument in the *Timaeus,* the same work that provided the Atlantis legend. Through some 20 centuries the analysis of the magnitude of human knowledge, and of how much of this knowledge might merely represent rediscoveries of things once known but subsequently lost, was used to argue that people were either recent or ancient on earth.[4] Most frequently, such analyses were used to combat Aristotelian eternalism, the idea that the world and its human occupants have always existed. They were often used simply to argue that people are recent arrivals on earth, without eternalism as an explicit target. Occasionally, these analyses were used to posit an immense human antiquity. The magnitude of human knowledge could be used to argue for or against human recency because there was no accepted approach to calibrating whether we knew a lot or a little, and no means of knowing how much had been lost of what people once knew. It was a reasonable way to try to tell time without an archaeology, but it could not provide an empirical demonstration one way or the other. As a result, it was always called upon to support positions originally taken for very different reasons.

Assertions of human recency or human antiquity based on assessments of the amount of knowledge people had amassed were similar in an important way to such assertions made on the basis of human physical or linguistic diversity. The results provided by all of these approaches were equivocal unless they could somehow be linked with securely dated time markers from the distant past. Thus, it was no accident that the great age of our lineage was decided on the basis of the discovery of human remains—stone tools—in geological settings that the crucial players agreed could not be considered recent, no matter how one defined recency.

That stone tools represented the work of human hands also had to be discovered, but this recognition came during the late 1600s and early 1700s. Before that time, all but the most obvious of stone artifacts were included along with other distinctively shaped, stony objects that came from in or on the ground in the general category of fossils, or things "dug up." Descriptions of stone tools, often under the name *ceraunia,* were routinely inserted into discussions of minerals, where the artifacts took their place next to such items as agate, chalcedony, turquoise, diamonds, and potter's clay. Often they were posited to have either grown in the ground or fallen from the sky, just as meteorites were known to do. Indeed, the name *ceraunia* was often translated as thunderstone, in line with its derivation. In Greek, *keraunos* means thunderbolt; in Latin, *ceraunius* means pertaining to thunder.

It was not until the middle and late 1600s that the categorization of fossils as things "dug up" began to fall apart. As Martin Rudwick has discussed, until that time there were adequate explanations, drawn from Aristotelian and Platonic philosophies, that accounted for the attributes shared by all those things treated as fossils.[5] During the last half of the seventeenth century, this broad conception of fossils began to be weakened from two separate directions. The first wedge was driven by increasingly detailed observations of the objects themselves. Such observations underscored the differences and similarities among kinds of fossils. In addition, they also underscored the similarities between some of the objects included as fossils and their modern counterparts. Nicolaus Steno (1638–1686), for instance, analyzed the formation of crystals and compared their structure to that of the shells of fossil and living molluscs, showing that the fossil and modern shells were much more similar to one another than they were to the inorganic crystals. In his *Forerunner to a Dissertation on a Solid Naturally Enclosed within a Solid* (1669), Steno concluded that the fossil shells did not represent objects that had grown in place in the earth, but were instead the remains of actual, once-living animals now buried beneath the surface.[6] Observations of this sort were also made of stone tools, with comparisons made between the fossil objects and stone tools still in use by non-Western peoples.[7] Ethnographic analogies of this sort played the same role for stone tools as Steno's observations of modern molluscan shells played for their fossil counterparts. Yet the ethnographic analogies could have been made long before. Not only had non-Western stone tools been known well before the late 1600s, but some analogies were made to modern European tools as well.[8] The role of analogy in the recognition of stone tools as stone tools was secondary. More important was the fact that natural historians were losing faith in the traditional explanations of the similarities possessed by all those things classed together as fossils.

Thus, the second and more important wedge was driven by shifts in approaches to the explanation of natural phenomena. These shifts, Roy Porter has noted, saw the metaphysical underpinnings of Classical and Renaissance philosophies give way to more mechanical approaches. The remarkable successes of

Newton and Newtonian physics gave rise to the possibility that similar approaches might yield similar successes in more earthly arenas. If the great Newton could demonstrate the laws the Creator had impressed on the heavenly bodies, then the same kind of approach should work for the things of the earth, and, in fact, for earth history itself. With the demise of earlier philosophies, in Porter's words, "theories of figured stones geared to metaphysical foundations such as the creative and sportive powers of Nature, the continuity of Nature, the virtues and tendencies of the mineral world, lost their main props."[9] With that loss, explanations of the shared attributes of fossils derived from Aristotelian and Platonic concepts no longer sufficed to account for the nature and origin of these objects. Coupled with the results of detailed observations of the objects themselves, the coherent concept of fossils was shattered during the late 1600s and early 1700s, leaving separate categories of items to be accounted for in different ways.

Among others, the fallout categories included organic fossils and stone tools. The history of the recognition of stone tools as stone tools runs exactly parallel to the history of the recognition of organic fossils as organic fossils. Arguments that stone artifacts were the handiwork of some earlier set of people did not become common until the latter decades of the seventeenth century, the same decades during which the possible organic origin of some kinds of fossils was coming under heated debate.[10] At times, the same individual pondered the meaning of both sets of items. The natural historian Robert Plot (1640–1696), for instance, did so in his *Natural History of Stafford-shire* (1686). Here Plot illustrated and discussed a small series of stone tools, items that he argued showed that the makers of these implements "sharpen'd their warlike instruments rather with stone than metall."[11] Plot's illustrations of these objects are as important as his discussion of them, because he displayed them adjacent to other items of human manufacture, including metal implements, figurines, and stone monuments. The contrast between these illustrations and those in Ulysses Aldrovandi's *Musaeum Metallicum* (1648) is striking, because Aldrovandi depicted stone tools alongside organic fossils. Plot was speaking the same visual language as modern archaeologists; Aldrovandi, only 40 years earlier, was not.[12]

After about the year 1700, arguments that stone tools were stone tools became almost routine[13]; by 1728, the natural historian John Woodward (1665–1728; see Chapter 2) could make active fun of those who had treated those items as anything but the results of human fabrication. In his *Fossils of All Kinds Digested into a Method* (1728), Woodward noted that although stone weapons and instruments

carry in them so plain Tokens of Art, and their Shapes be such as apparently to point forth, to any Man that rightly considers them, the Use each was destin'd to; yet some of the Writers of Fossils, and of great Name too, have been so sanguine and hasty, so much blinded by the Strength of their own Fancy, and prepossessed in Favour of their Schemes and Notions, that they have set forth these Bodies as natural Productions of the Earth, under the Names of *Cerauniae*.[14]

Woodward then presented what had become a common argument:

The Stone-Weapons, and Instruments were all cut out; and made, before the Discovery of Iron. But, when once this Metal was brought to Light, and its Uses known, 'twas found so much preferable in every Respect, that those Stones were presently cast away: And they are those which we still sometimes find Abroad in the Fields, not only here in England, but in Scotland likewise, and Ireland, and Germany, and several other Countries; where they serv'd, in the most early Ages, for Axes, Wedges, Chizels, Heads of Arrows, Darts, and Lances. Nay, among Nations yet barbarous, and unacquainted with the Manufacture of Iron, and that have not been discover'd by the European Navigations, till of late Years, these Stone-Weapons and Instruments are in Use to this day.[15]

By 1758, Antoine Yves Goguet (1716–1758), in the course of his lengthy and popular consideration of the origin of arts and sciences, could simply note about stone tools that "it is evident from inspection alone, that these stones have thus been wrought by the hands of men."[16]

The most famous discussion of stone tools published prior to Goguet's work is certainly John Bagford's account of the discovery by John Conyers of a handaxe near the remains of an elephant in London. Bagford's presentation is of interest for a number of reasons, including the fact that it has so often been misinterpreted during modern times. Bagford (ca. 1650–1716) seems to have been raised a shoemaker, but he made his living as a book dealer; he was also active in reforming the Society of Antiquaries in 1707, published on the history of printing, and was an avid collector of antiquities. Little is known of his friend John Conyers other than that he was a London apothecary and that he was also an active antiquarian. Both men knew John Woodward well, and supplied him with antiquarian items for his own collection.[17]

Conyers died without publishing his discovery. That job fell to Bagford, who published his account in 1715 in Thomas Hearne's edition of John Leland's *Collectanea*. Bagford's paper was offered as a review of the Roman antiquities of London. The handaxe and elephant form but a small part of that discussion:

Mr. John Conyers, an apothecary . . . who made it his chief Business to make curious observations, and to collect such Antiquities as were daily found in and about London . . . discovered the body of an Elephant, as he was digging for Gravel in the Fields . . . not far from Battlebridge, and near to the River of Wells. . . . How this Elephant came there? is the Question. I know some will have it to have layn there ever since the Universal Deluge. For my own part I take it to have been brought over with many others by the Romans in the Reign of Claudius the Emperour, and conjecture . . . that it was killed in some Fight by a Britain. For not far from the Place where it was found, a British Weapon made of a Flint Lance like unto the Head of a Spear, fastned into a Shaft of a good length, which was a Weapon very common amongst the Ancient Britains, was also dug up, they not having at that time the use of Iron or Brass, as the Romans had.[18]

Bagford also provided a drawing of the implement involved: it was a classic handaxe.

What is telling about this presentation is that it is introduced into a discussion of the Roman antiquities of London, and that the real focus of the paragraph is the elephant, not the stone tool. Far from being something surprising, the implement was of a sort that was known to be common, and whose artifactual nature required little comment in 1715. The source of the bones, however, was quite a different matter. The tool became important for Bagford because he could use this item of known origin to account for the elephant of unknown origin. It is quite possible that Bagford had Woodward in mind when he noted that some might attribute the elephant to Noah's Flood. Whether or not this was the case, Bagford used the implement to make the beast Roman, and thus included both tool and animal in his review of London's Roman past. It has often been argued that Bagford tried to make the tool recent by attributing the elephant to Claudius,[19] but such an explanation is anachronistic. As will become clear, Bagford would have been amazed at the notion that an artifact associated with the Deluge-deposited elephant would have made the human species too old, and even more amazed that his elephant could have been of an extinct species. Such possibilities were nearly a century away. Bagford was simply trying to account for an elephant in London.

In retrospect, the establishment of human antiquity can be visualized in terms of a series of discrete steps, each of which made the discovery of truly ancient human beings more likely. Stone tools became widely recognized as such during the early 1700s. At about the same time, the order of deposition of strata began to be used to extract sequences of events in earth history, opening the door to placing human remains in that sequence. In the early 1800s, it became widely recognized that the fossil content of strata could be used to link those strata together across wide expanses of the earth. When it became recognized as well that the superficial strata of western Europe and many other regions of the earth contained the remains of extinct mammals, including such creatures as the woolly mammoth and woolly rhinoceros, and that the remains of these animals were often associated with a set of distinctive gravels and clays, geological markers became available for assessing the antiquity of people on earth. Fifty years later, stone tools were found tightly associated with those time markers, and general agreement was reached that people were, in fact, ancient on earth.

But this sequence does come in retrospect. There was little reason that things had to happen this way; they just happened to. It would be wrong to view this history as the unfolding of something that, sooner or later, had to occur, and even less correct to think that the way these things occurred was the way they had to occur. This was no inexorable rise to the truth caused by the continuing conquests of the human mind. It could have happened sooner, it could have happened later, it could have not happened at all, and it certainly could have happened very differently.

In addition, viewing the establishment of human antiquity solely as a series of such discrete steps does not do justice to the complexity of the theoretical contexts in which the arguments over human antiquity were made. While I have organized my discussion generally in terms of the events I have just described, I have tried to indicate what those theoretical contexts were and how they molded the way in which things from the earth were viewed. I have also tried to indicate why some older accounts of the establishment of human antiquity, which tended to picture the issue as one in which conservative theological views were pitted against progressive scientific ones and often against the facts themselves, provide an inappropriate characterization of the questions involved. In England, for instance, the influential geologist William Buckland was not the stultifying force regarding the establishment of human antiquity that he has been painted to be, and the geology of the even more influential Charles Lyell was not the key to the answer. Instead, what characterized the issue was the increasingly implicit nature of the theological assumptions of the scientists themselves, a situation no different from that which characterized approaches to other major questions of earth and life history during the eighteenth and nineteenth centuries.[20] Of particular importance was the assumption by some that the details of human history contained in Scripture provided the revealed Word of God and were literally true, and the assumption made by most that the history of the earth had been guided by a superintending and caring Creator in such a way as to provide an appropriate receptacle for God's highest work, the human species.

Notes and References

1. Gruber 1965, Laming-Emperaire 1964.
2. De Mortillet 1865; see the general discussion in Laming-Emperaire 1964.
3. Excellent introductions to these matters are found in Haber 1959, Greene 1959, Porter 1977, Toulmin and Goodfield 1965, Rudwick 1972, and Zittel 1901.
4. Early uses of the argument to support human recency are found in Lucretius' *De Rerum Natura*, Macrobius' *Commentary on Scipio's Dream*, and Saint Augustine's *The City of God*; later uses are found, among many other places, in Hale 1677, Burnet 1684, and in Turgot's *On Universal History* (in Meek 1973). The argument was used to support human antiquity by La Peyrère 1655, Diderot 1875[1754], Voltaire 1963, and White 1896.
5. Rudwick 1972.
6. Steno 1968[1669].
7. For instance, Plot 1686, Lhwyd 1713 (written in 1699); for a general discussion of Plot, Lhwyd, Dugdale, and the antiquarians as a whole, see Piggott 1976.
8. For instance, Dugdale 1656.
9. Porter 1977:52–53.
10. Valuable discussions of stone tools as ceraunia are found in Peake 1940 and Laming-Emperaire 1964.
11. Plot 1686:396.
12. Piggott 1978 provides an important discussion of the history of archaeological illustration.

13. See, for instance, de Jussieu 1725, Mahudel 1740, and Montfaucon 1722 and reviews in Hamy 1906a,b.
14. Woodward 1728, Part 2 (Letters):37–38.
15. Woodward 1728, Part 2 (Letters):39–40.
16. Goguet 1761, Volume 1:156.
17. Biographical information on Conyers and Bagford is drawn from Nichols 1812, Fletcher 1898, and Levine 1977; Hunter (1971) discusses Conyers' antiquarian activities; Woodward (1744) provides a discussion of Conyers' contributions to Woodward's collection. Bagford has been vilified by book lovers because he amassed a huge collection of title pages by removing them from the books themselves (see, for instance, Hunter 1978). Bagford's thoughts on the invention of printing are in Bagford 1707.
18. Bagford 1770:lxiii–lxiv.
19. See, for instance, Daniel 1963, 1976; Heizer 1962.
20. See, for instance, Gillispie 1959, Porter 1977.

2

Sequence and Stratigraphy: Documenting Change in Earth History

The recognition that there had been a time in Europe when tools were fashioned from stone was accompanied by the realization that these tools must have been used at a time when their makers did not possess the art of working metal. Such European tools were, as a result, relatively ancient. Many often interrelated lines of evidence were used to support the relative antiquity of European stone tools. The very fact that they were found there and seemed to have been used as cutting, chopping, and piercing implements bespoke a great antiquity: no Europeans would now make stone tools for these purposes. It seemed self-evident that stone was inferior to metal for tools of this sort, and it followed that people who used these implements must not have had access to metal. If the self-evident superiority of metal were not sufficient, then one could turn to examples of the rapid replacement of stone by metal among non-Western peoples after contact with Europeans. The written testimony of ancient authors also concurred; Lucretius and Hesiod were often cited. Finally, one could also turn to evidence drawn from the earth itself. Stone axes, wrote Cornelius de Pauw (1739–1799) in 1768, are often found in Sweden and Germany "at great depths, and . . . must be extremely ancient, having been used before the invention of iron and copper."[1] In addition, there had been discoveries of stone tools associated with human burials and pottery, but without metal implements of any sort; such discoveries supported the notion that these tools had been used prior to the time that metal was available.[2] "Fashioned by men who had not yet the use of metals" became, in one version or another, the stock phrase used during the late seventeenth and eighteenth centuries to encapsulate this view.

The argument was not that stone tools were everywhere more ancient than metal ones. The example provided by the Americas showed that people who used stone implements could exist at the same time as those who used metal ones, and it was also commonly believed that the western European users of stone tools had probably been contemporary with classic Greek and Roman civilization. As a result, Bagford was on firm ground when he attributed his stone handaxe to a British native during the time of the Roman occupation of his homeland. The argument was instead that in some places there had been a progression in the raw materials used for stone tool manufacture from the more easily discovered and worked, but less useful, stone to the less easily discovered and worked, but more useful, metal. By the time that stone tools became recognized as such, it was also felt that the use of such tools in Europe must have occurred during early times.

For some, this recognition posed a problem similar to that posed by the much earlier discovery that many non-Western peoples lacked metal tools. Genesis clearly indicated that metal tools were in use prior to the Deluge, naming Tubal-Cain as one who forged tools from both bronze and iron. Such use was, of course, well prior to the confusion of tongues and dispersal of people across the earth associated with the building of the tower of Babel. How, then, could one account for both the discovery of stone tools in Europe and the lack of metal ones among many non-Westerners, while still not violating the certainly trustworthy historical information presented in Scripture?

The answer was not hard to find. It lay in combining the idea of sequence with the psychological trauma caused by the Deluge. Clearly, metal tools were known before the Flood, but so great was the shock and confusion caused by this event, so great the need to concentrate on the basics of life, that the use of iron was simply lost. Those who survived made their tools from stone. It was not hard to find support for this position in the Bible itself, since the sacred writings describe the use of stone tools after the Flood. Exodus 4:25, for instance, relates that the son of Moses was circumcised with a flint knife during the return of Moses to Egypt.

Thus, John Woodward pointed out that although Noah and his sons certainly remembered the use of iron, the effects of the Deluge were such that they were "reduced to the greatest Distress, Exigence, and Necessities. . . . In this so calamitous a Condition, Iron might be perfectly forgot, and the Knowledge of it quite worn out."[3] The dispersal of peoples to the far reaches of the earth took place prior to the rediscovery of metal tools; as a result, both the presence of stone tools in Europe and the lack of iron ones in the Americas matched the historical records well. The French physician and antiquarian Nicolas Mahudel (1673–1747) went further, positing two sequences of stone to metal, one before and one after the Flood.[4]

Woodward and Mahudel were not alone in such reconstructions. In his much reprinted *Origin of Laws, Arts, and Sciences* (1758), Antoine-Yves Goguet made a similar, though much more detailed, argument some 30 years later:

> Metals were discovered, and they understood the art, even of working iron, before the deluge. But that dreadful calamity deprived the greatest part of mankind of this, as well as of other arts. All antiquity agrees in saying that there was a time, when the use of metals was unknown to mankind. . . . We see that people used stones, flints, the horns of animals, the bones of beasts and fishes, shells, seeds, and thorns for all the purposes for which civilized nations use metals at present. The savages set before us a striking picture of the ignorance of the ancient world, and the practices of primitive times. They have no idea of metals, and supply the want of them by the means I have just now mentioned.[5]

Goguet's speculations were more detailed than those of Woodward and Mahudel, since he argued that the full sequence of raw materials involved an initial post-Deluge use of stone, followed by the use of those metals easiest to discover and work—gold, silver, and especially copper, this last perhaps hardened by tempering and alloying. Because it was hardest to find and to shape into tools, iron came last in Goguet's sequence.

Woodward, Mahudel, and Gouget thus explained the presence of stone tools in Europe in terms of the history of humankind provided by Scripture, the only reliable written history of those times available. For those concerned with the interrelationship between early stone tools and scriptural history, the results were of great importance: the new evidence as to the nature of the human past was indeed in line with the biblical narrative.

I have noted that the evidence supporting the stone-to-metal sequence included two kinds of information taken from the position of stone tools in the earth itself: the great depth at which they had been found, and the fact that they had been discovered in European sites that also contained pottery and burials but not metal tools. Of these two sources of information, the second, associational argument was by far the more frequently employed. When arguments as to relative age based upon such data went further than this, they were usually drawn from the degree of preservation of materials associated with the stone or metal tools themselves. Thus, Bernard de Montfaucon (1655–1741) included a letter in his *Antiquity Explained, and Represented in Sculptures* (1719) that supported the chronological priority of brass over iron in a stone–bronze–iron sequence by noting that European sepulchres "that are of the greatest Antiquity, and the Urns of which are most decayed by Time, have most frequently Brass; and those that are of a later Age have commonly Iron" tools.[6]

It was not until the nineteenth century that Scandinavian workers, who used the stone–bronze–iron sequence to organize entire museum collections, were to use stratigraphic principles to support the chronological nature of this sequence. That demonstration depended upon excavations in archaeological deposits that paid close attention to the order in which the strata that composed these deposits had been laid down, and to the contents of those strata as well.[7] Ultimately, the demonstration of the great antiquity of the oldest known stone tools was to depend upon the stratigraphic correlation of archaeological materials with events in earth history whose great age had been previously established.

The stratigraphic tool used in the nineteenth century to give further credibility to the chronological nature of the stone-to-iron sequence in Europe was the principle of superposition: that in any pile of undisturbed strata, the oldest is at the bottom and the youngest at the top, that the order of undisturbed strata from deepest to most superficial is also the order of deposition of those strata. This principle had been fully enunciated by Nicolaus Steno in 1669, but the reaction to John Woodward's work helped spur the incorporation of the analysis of stratigraphic order into the study of earth history.

As I have discussed, Steno (who was then physician to the Grand Duke of Tuscany but later dropped natural history to become an ascetic Catholic cleric) was intrigued by fossils whose form implied that they might have been the remains of once-living organisms. He demonstrated in his *Forerunner* that the structure of fossil shells was more similar to that of modern ones than it was to the structure of modern crystals, and concluded that his fossil shells must be fossil shells.

Steno fully recognized the interconnected nature of questions relating to the form of organic materials on the one hand, and to their position in the earth on the other:

> The first question was, whether *Glossopetrae Melitenses* ['tongue-stones from Malta'] were once the teeth of sharks; this, it was at once apparent, is identical with the general question whether bodies which are similar to marine bodies, and which are found far from the sea, were once produced in the sea. But since there are also found on land other bodies resembling those which grow in fresh water, in the air, and in other fluids, if we grant to the earth the power of producing these bodies, we cannot deny to it the possibility of bringing forth the rest. It was necessary, therefore, to extend the investigation to all those bodies which, dug from the earth, are observed to be like those bodies which we elsewhere see growing in a fluid. But many other bodies, also, are found among the rocks, possessed of a certain form; and if one should say that they were produced by the force of the place, one must confess that all the rest were produced by the same force. And so I saw the matter

finally brought to the point that any given solid naturally contained within a solid must be examined in order to ascertain whether it was produced in the same place in which it is found; that is, the character not only of the place where it is found, but also of the place where it was produced, must be investigated. But no one, in truth, will easily determine the place of production who does not know the manner of production, and all discussion concerning the manner of production is idle unless we gain some certain knowledge concerning the nature of matter. From this it is clear how many questions must be solved in order that a single question may be set at rest.[8]

This remarkably broad conception of the problem led Steno directly to a consideration of the structure of the earth. The strata of our globe, he argued, had been formed by sedimentation from a fluid, and much could be learned by observing the materials of which those strata are composed. A stony stratum whose particles were all of an identical and fine consistency, for example, must have been deposited from the primordial fluid at the time of the Creation. If, on the other hand, the stratum contained fragments of another stratum, or the remains of plants and animals, it had clearly been formed at some later point in earth history. If a stratum contained traces of sea salt, ship's timbers, or the remains of marine animals, it must have been formed in the sea, no matter where it is now. Similarly, the presence of charcoal, ashes, and calcined material implied that a fire had occurred in the area in which the stratum had formed. One could, in short, begin to decipher earth history through empirical observations of the layers of the earth.

Having considered the contents of strata, Steno proceeded to examine their position. Because the strata had originally been laid down in a fluid, several interpretive principles seemed to follow with certainty. At the time of formation of an upper stratum, no stratum could have lain above it, while a more solid stratum must have lain beneath it. In addition, at the time it had been formed, any given stratum must either have been bounded by other solid substances or have extended across the entire surface of the globe. Concerning original form, Steno argued that because they had been formed in a fluid, all strata must have been deposited horizontally. Any departure from horizontality must, therefore, have occurred after the original deposition and solidification of that stratum. How could this happen? Steno suggested that changes in position could come about in two major ways: through upheaval, as a result of the burning of subterranean gasses or the explosion of air due to nearby violent subsidence, or through downfall, as a result of the withdrawal of supporting strata. As a result of such events, all kinds of jumbled strata could be observed, even though every stratum had originally been laid down horizontally.

Steno presented a brilliant analysis of the structure of the earth, ultimately directed toward understanding the nature of fossils. He argued that since all major strata were originally laid down horizontally, the deepest ones must also be the oldest ones. He argued that deposition in a fluid also implies that any given stratum should continue unless obstructed by some solid, and thus that stratigraphic continuity should be sought over vast expanses of the earth. He argued that the contents of a stratum could provide information on the nature of the environment of the area where that stratum had formed. And he argued that departures from original horizontality must have resulted from the postdepositional histories of the tilted strata. Steno not only provided the principle of superposition, but also incorporated that principle into a wide-ranging and dynamic picture of the structure of the earth. Observe the strata, he was saying, and they will tell you of the history of the globe.

After discussing the structure of the earth, Steno turned to a discussion of organic fossils, and then to an analysis of the geology of Tuscany. He held that the strata of this region had been laid down horizontally; fire or water then created huge cavities beneath the upper strata, causing their collapse; an incursion of the sea followed, creating new strata in the valleys; lower strata in these newer beds were then destroyed, and a second episode of collapse followed.

He felt that this picture, derived from observations in Tuscany, applied to the entire earth. It also seemed in accord with Scripture: the earth was at first covered by water, then dry, then flooded by the Deluge, then dry once again. In addition, he noted, the earliest strata lacked the remains of organisms, just as the Mosaic account would lead us to believe. Indeed, Steno concluded, even the timing of the Deluge suggested by Genesis is confirmed by empirical observation, since cities built on strata deposited during the Deluge have histories that go back no further than 3000 to 4000 years.

Steno thus put into action his theory of the formation of strata and his conclusion that some fossils were the remains of once-living organisms. He provided a history of the earth by combining his interpretive principles with observations of the strata themselves, and also provided an empirical approach to the development of life on earth. This was, as Martin Rudwick observed, the first published work in which organic fossils were used to build such a life history.[9] As immense as the research program outlined in the *Forerunner* was, Steno had carried much of it off, and in a remarkably small volume. It is no wonder that some of Steno's scientific contemporaries regretted his decision to abandon science for religion.[10]

In 1644, in his *Principles of Philosophy,* René Descartes (1596–1650) had speculated on the mode of formation of an earth. Steno's earth history drew heavily on Descarte's theory that a body like our earth would originally have been a smooth sphere covered by a hard crust, and that topographic unevennesses would have resulted from the collapse of that crust into an underlying liquid. While Descartes had built his speculative earth without supernatural assistance, Steno showed that an empirically derived earth history was congruent with the Mosaic account of that history. Soon, others were to make similar demonstrations, and in so doing were to spread some of Steno's ideas widely.

The late 1600s and early 1700s saw the publication of many theories of the earth, a number of which were produced by scholars of the first rank. Examples include Thomas Burnet's *Sacred Theory of the Earth* (1680, 1689)[11]; John Ray's *Miscellaneous Discourses Concerning the Dissolution and Changes of the World* (1692) and his *Three Physico-Theological Discourses* (1693); John Woodward's *An Essay toward a Natural History of the Earth* (1695); and William Whiston's *A New Theory of the Earth* (1696). These theories all differed greatly in detail—differences that sparked published debates among the supporters and detractors of each—but they also shared common thematic ground. All, for instance, took for granted the Divine Creation of a designed earth whose major purpose was the provision of a place for human beings. The most influential of these theories also examined in some detail the major changes that had taken place in the nature of the earth from its creation to modern times and beyond, with special attention paid to the two undeniable scriptural touchstones: the Creation and the Flood. Burnet noted that he called his theory "sacred" because it dealt only with "the great Turns of Fate, and the Revolutions of our Natural World; such as are taken notice of in the Sacred Writings, and are truly the Hinges upon which the Providence of this Earth moves; or whereby it opens and shuts the several successive Scenes whereof it is made up."[12] The Flood, in particular, played a major role in these theories as a means of accounting for global changes that had occurred since the Creation. The detailed differences among the theories are exemplified in their explanations of the causes of the Deluge. Burnet, for instance, called on crustal collapse, Whiston suggested the effects of a passing comet, while Woodward called on the direct intervention of God and on the "Cessation and Suspension of the Laws of Nature."[13]

These theories also had an important impact on the idea that the earth's history was both knowable and worth knowing, since they all contained historical pictures that were consistent with Genesis. In large part, these pictures coincided with the Mosaic account because the interpretations that led to them were preconditioned by Scripture. As the brilliant and prolific John Ray (1627–1705) said in his *Three Physico-Theological Discourses,*

> in things of this nature, to the giving an account whereof whatever Hypothesis we can possibly invent, can be put meerly conjectural, those that are to be most approved that come nearest to the Letter of Scripture, and those that clash with it to be rejected, how trim or consistent soever with themselves they may seem to be: this being as much, as when God tells us how he did make the World, for us to tell him how he should have made it.[14]

But observations of the earth itself also played a significant part in constructing these theories. Thus Burnet used evidence drawn from the nature of caves, earthquakes, and volcanos as support for his theory, and pointed out the need for topographical and civil maps in order to understand the nature of the earth more fully. Woodward considered not only these things, and in more detail, but also provided an analysis of springs, rivers, and other surficial waters in the context of a discussion of hydrological cycles.

In demonstrating that the facts of the earth provided a history that was in line with Genesis, these theories provided a powerful stimulus for learning more of the earth itself.[15] This is not to say that all the theoreticians got their hands dirty. Burnet and Whiston, for instance, were not fieldworkers, whereas Edward Lhwyd (1660–1709), who was, did not publish a theory of the earth. But empirically based theorizing was important to all of these systems, whether or not the theorizers were the ones doing the fieldwork, both in the sense that the theories were at least ostensibly based on empirical observation and in the sense that debates about their accuracy tended to depend heavily on such observation.

John Woodward was one of the theorizers who had obtained first-hand knowledge of both organic fossils and the deposits in which they occurred. Although he taught medicine at Gresham College in London and ran a successful medical practice, Woodward found the time to take geological excursions in England, to increase his geological knowledge of other areas by circulating questionnaires, and to amass a large paleontological collection. His involvement in two sword fights and his expulsion from the Council of the Royal Society of London suggests that John Ray's characterization of him as a "rude and insolent fellow"[16] was accurate, but it is probably also true that these attributes, once translated into his often acerbic writing style, gained him a wider and much more critical audience than he might otherwise have had.[17]

Because of his field observations, Woodward knew that any adequate history of the earth had to take into account both the stratification displayed by that body and the position of organic fossils within the strata themselves. These were things that Burnet had completely ignored in his widely read work. In *An Essay toward a Natural History of the Earth* (1695), much of which was aimed directly at Burnet, Woodward dealt with both of these phenomena.

Unlike Burnet, who had argued that the pre-Deluge earth had been a smooth, round globe, Woodward asserted that the world before the Deluge was very much like the contemporary world. He did not feel that the Deluge had been caused by a secondary, natural cause, as Burnet had argued, but saw it instead as the result of the direct intervention of a wise and supernatural power. At the time of the Flood, he argued, the laws of nature were suspended, waters flooded the earth, and all solid materials—except organic fossils—were dissolved and thrown into suspension in those waters. Even though organic fossils were not dissolved into their constituent particles at this time, they were nonetheless thrown into suspension:

> During the time of the Deluge, whilst the Water was out upon, and covered the Terrestrial Globe, All the Stone and Marble of the Antediluvian Earth: all the Metalls of it: all Mineral Concretions: and, in a word, all Fossils whatever that had before obtained any Solidity, were totally dissolved, and their constituent Corpuscles all disjoyned, their Cohaesion perfectly ceasing. That the said Corpuscles of these solid Fossils, together with the Corpuscles of those which were not before solid, such as Sand, Earth, and the like: as also all Animal Bodies, and parts of Animals, Bones, Teeth, Shells: Vegetables, and parts of

Vegetables, Trees, Shrubs, Herbs: and, to be short, all Bodies whatsoever that were either upon the Earth, or that constituted the Mass of it, if not quite down to the Abyss, yet at least to the greatest Depth we ever dig: I say all these were assumed up promiscuously into the Water, and sustained in it, in such manner that the Water, and Bodies in it, together made up one common confused Mass.[18]

So suspended, the rock particles and organic fossils then settled in order of their specific gravity. The layers formed in this manner became solid as they were deposited, producing a spherical globe with a deep series of concentric strata covered by water. Toward the end of the Deluge, the strata were disrupted; they collapsed into the earth, allowing the water to retreat into the underlying abyss, and reached their modern positions. Woodward's depiction of the scale of this whole process was accurate:

Here was, we see, a mighty Revolution: and *that* attended with accidents very strange and amazing: the most horrible and portentous Catastrophe that Nature ever yet saw: an elegant, orderly, and habitable Earth quite unhinged, shattered all to pieces, and turned into an heap of ruins: Convulsions so exorbitant and unruly: a Change so exceedingly great and violent, that the very Representation alone is enough to startle and shock a Man.[19]

Any explanatory power that Woodward's theory had lay in the fact that it contained an account of stratification and an explanation for the position of organic fossils. Modern strata had formed by sedimentation from a fluid, and marine organisms dispersed by the Deluge had become incorporated into some of these strata; the strata, at first horizontally distributed over a spherical earth, had subsequently collapsed to form the rugged earth as we see it today, with marine fossils in otherwise inexplicable places.

If any of this sounds like Steno, that is because much of it is Steno. John Arbuthnot (1667–1735) pointed out the similarities in his *Examination of Dr. Woodward's Account of the Deluge* (1697). Nearly half of the 63 pages of Arbuthnot's book were dedicated to the presentation of selections from Steno's works adjacent to corresponding selections from Woodward's *Essay*. To take one example, Arbuthnot provided this passage from Steno's *Head of a Shark Dissected* (1667):

That the Bodies which made the Water turbid, the violent motion ceasing, must have sunk to the bottom. That they were not all of the same gravity: whence it came that the heaviest subsided first; the less heavy subsiding next after; and the lightest floating longest of all nearest the bottom, before they joyned themselves to it: whence, from the same Sediment there would be formed different strata.

He then gave this from Woodward's *Essay:*

That at length, all the Mass that was thus born up [in] the Water, was again precipitated, and subsided toward the bottom. That the Subsidence happened generally, and as near as possibly could be expected in so great a Confusion, according to the Laws of Gravity: that the Matter, Body, or Bodies which had the greatest quantity or degree of Gravity subsiding first in Order, and falling Lowest: that which had the next, or still Lesser Degree of Gravity, subsiding next after, and settling upon the precedent: and so on their several

Courses, that which had the least gravity sinking not down till last of all, settling at the surface of the Sediment, and covering all the rest. That the Matter subsiding thus, formed the Strata of Stone, of Marble, of Coal, of Earth, etc.[20]

Arbuthnot, however, was not interested in attacking Woodward for plagiarism. Instead, his interests lay in determining which of the two accounts provided better explanations of earth history. The comparison, he felt, was not to Woodward's benefit. He noted that Woodward had "baulk'd our Expectations in the most material Points"[21] by not explaining such things as why the metals had dissolved but the organic fossils had not, and how the strata once formed had come to be disrupted. The only major aspect of his earth history he had attempted to explain, Arbuthnot emphasized, was the order of the strata. And here the facts of the earth did not support him, for observation shows that the strata, and the contents of single strata, are not ordered according to their specific gravity. If Woodward's theory were correct, he asked, how could both heavy stones and light shells have been deposited in the same stratum, as the examination of strata shows them to be found?

In calling on facts drawn from observing the layers of the earth to disprove Woodward's theory, Arbuthnot's critique was fully characteristic of the attacks made on this theory.[22] Here, in fact, lies one of the contributions Woodward made with his *Essay*. He had borrowed much of Steno's approach to the analysis of strata, an approach that does not seem to have attracted much direct attention during the eighteenth century,[23] and had built much of his theory around the order and content of strata. His *Essay* proved very popular, as is shown by the fact that eight editions appeared, three in English (1695, 1702, 1723), one in Latin (1704), two in French (both in 1735), one in Italian (1739), and one in German (1744, reissued in 1746).[24] This popularity spread the recognition of the importance of stratification in understanding earth history, as did the fact that either to support or refute Woodward required that the order and content of strata be examined. Although Woodward attempted to answer some of his critics[25] and retained his theory to his death,[26] the theory itself was generally rejected. It demanded that strata be organized in terms of specific gravity, and observations showed that this was simply not the case. Nonetheless, as Roy Porter has pointed out, Woodward's theory "irreversibly required that all future theories address themselves to the facts of stratification."[27]

Whereas the theories of the earth published in the late 1600s and early 1700s focused attention on major events in earth history and led to the use of the stratigraphic record preserved in the earth in deriving that history, the eighteenth century also saw the publication of detailed stratigraphic sequences for areas that contained economically important minerals. Mining surveyors wanted to show that their skills formed a predictive science in which a knowledge of the strata could be used to locate economically important minerals. Mining activities also opened up deep sections of the earth in which the order of strata could be readily observed.[28] Thus, the first published vertical section showing the disposition of strata across a region dealt with the important coal-mining area of Somerset, in southwestern England. Published in 1719 by John Strachey (1671–1743), this section diagrammed the position of seven coal-bearing strata across an area about 6.5 kilometers in extent,[29] and was followed in 1725 by a pair of profiles showing a lengthier sequence across a 30-kilometer section of Somersetshire.[30] In 1723, Benjamin Holloway (1691?–1759), who also translated John Wood-ward's *Natural History of the Earth, Illustrated* (1726), published a discussion of the order and continuity of strata in Bedfordshire, a sequence he was able to describe (although he did not include a drawn profile) because it had been exposed by quarrying activities. Written in the form of a letter to Woodward, Holloway's reason for publishing the description was explicit: "it confirms what you say of the regular Disposition of the Earth into like Strata, or Layers of Matter, commonly through vast Tracts."[31] In 1695, Woodward had said that many, including miners, assumed that little of value could be learned from the strata because they possessed no order; a few decades later, this was no longer true.

Many of the published discussions of the order and nature of strata that appeared during this time were purely descriptive, with no attempt to derive history from the described sequence. Indeed, Strachey's discussion of the Somerset strata implied that they had all been deposited at once "whilst in a soft and fluid state."[32] But these descriptions were crucially important in refining knowledge of stratigraphic sequences in particular areas, be those areas large or small. And, during the eighteenth century, observations of superposition and of the interpretation of superposed strata in terms of the historical development of the earth became common.[33]

The 1700s also saw the growth of a large group of surveyors, miners, prospectors, engineers, and other professionals whose work required detailed, first-hand knowledge of the structure of the earth. These professionals were a product of the industrial revolution and of the large-scale engineering ventures that characterized it. Many of these men had scientific ambitions, which they attempted to satisfy by publishing what they had learned on the job.[34] It can, of course, be noted that acquiring a scientific reputation could only have been good for business, but that is only to point out that the reasons for doing science are numerous. Many of these men also labored under severe practical limitations when it came to doing science that was acceptable to the general scientific community—an important matter since that community controlled the scientific journals and was often influential in determining what science was published by the commercial houses. In particular, these professionals often had little formal education; their knowledge of the earth came from the earth itself. Such a lack of education could prove disastrous in attempting to produce a work meant for consumption by scientists with a wealth of formal training. In addition, these men typically lacked strong ties to the scientific community as a whole, and were often insulated from recent theoretical developments in their field. Finally, the positions they held did not allow them much leisure time to write. If they wrote, they did it during those relatively rare moments when they were not on the job. These were formidable obstacles to overcome.

William Smith (1769–1839) was one such professional. He was the son of an Oxfordshire farmer whose formal education consisted of what he was taught in his village school. As Smith himself said, that was not very much. In 1787, at the age of 18, he became assistant to a surveyor and then became a surveyor himself. For 6 years, from 1793 to 1799, he worked as surveyor and engineer for the construction of the Somersetshire Coal Canal, in the same region for which Strachey had provided his stratigraphic profiles some 60 years earlier. (Smith was familiar with Strachey's work, and had annotated his 1719 profile.[35]) His association with the coal canal came to an end in 1799, after which he made his living in association with engineering and surveying projects throughout England, becoming much in demand because of his success in draining wet regions and in irrigating dry ones.[36]

By the mid-1790s, Smith had recognized that not only were the strata he had seen superposed in predictable fashion, but also that each of these strata possessed its own characteristic assemblage of organic fossils by which it could be recognized. Thousands of people who have collected fossils, he noted in 1796, have done so without "the least regard to that wonderful order and regularity with which Nature has disposed of these singular productions and assigned to each Class its peculiar Stratum."[37] This generalization, often called the principle of strata identified by fossils, forms one of the foundations of modern stratigraphic analysis.

Smith was sketching plans to publish his insights as early as 1797. In 1799, and with the assistance of two friends, he produced a handwritten table of the "Order of the Strata and their imbedded Organic Remains" for the region of Bath. This table provided a list of the strata of the area ordered by depth, along with the thickness and a description of each, and a list of the fossils that were known to characterize each.[38] But while the table became well circulated and a prospectus for his work on the strata of England and Wales appeared in 1801, Smith did not publish his work on British strata until 1815. The intervening time was spent in making a living, in making more stratigraphic observations, and in putting his manuscripts in order.

In 1815, Smith's colored map of the strata of England and Wales appeared, issued in 16 separate sheets.[39] In 1816, his *Strata Identified by Organized Fossils* began to appear, providing "a general account of those organized fossils, which I found imbedded in each Stratum, and which first enabled me to distinguish one Stratum from another."[40] *Strata Identified* was supposed to have been issued in seven separate parts, but only the first four appeared: two in 1816, one in 1817, and one in 1819. In the four numbers that were completed, Smith presented a description of each stratum he considered and a list of characteristic fossils of each. In addition, he provided illustrations of some of the diagnostic fossils for each stratum on paper colored to match the color used to designate that stratum on his 1815 map. In 1817, he published his *Stratigraphic System of Organized Fossils,* a partial catalogue of his own collection of fossils, a collection he had sold to the British Museum to raise funds. "The identification of Strata by the help of organized fossils," he noted in this work, "becomes one of the most important discoveries in Geology. It enables the Geologist clearly to distinguish one Stratum from another in Britain, and also to trace their connexion with the same Strata on the continent. Thus it is capable of the most extensive or the most local use."[41] The bulk of this volume provided lists of fossils, primarily invertebrates, by stratum and two summary tables of his results. The catalogue was to be issued in two parts; only the first appeared.

Thus between 1815 and 1819 Smith published the results of the considerable knowledge and insights he had gained from his geological observations during the previous 30 years; a lengthy list of county maps followed during the next decade. The handicaps under which he labored are clear not only from the available descriptions of his life, but also from his work itself. He was never rich; much of what he earned was spent in travelling to increase his geological knowledge. He also suffered a failed business venture in the years just before his 1815 map appeared. Indeed, in 1819 he spent 10 weeks in prison because of his indebtedness. He was not well versed in invertebrate paleontology. As he noted himself in 1817, his *Stratigraphical System* was offered in spite of the fact that he had to write it "without much knowledge of Conchology,"[42] and the descriptions of fossils published in this catalogue were prepared by his nephew, John Phillips. He was clearly not familiar with theoretical developments in his field, and his discussions of the value of his work underlined the importance of his discoveries to the landowner: "the organized Fossils which may be found, will enable him to identify the Strata of his own estate with those of others; thus his lands may be drained with more certainty of success, his buildings substantially improved, and his private and public roads better made, and repaired at less expense."[43] His work had to be produced as he could find time to do it, and in spite of his financial situation, his lack of a broad education, and his insulation from current theoretical developments in geology. It took him decades to do, but he did it.

By the time Smith published his insights, they were, in fact, already well known. "It was his misfortune," Joan M. Eyles has observed, "that as knowledge of his discovery spread, without any real recognition that he was its discoverer, so its novelty was diminished and anything he chose to publish about it seemed less remarkable."[44] This was certainly true, and Smith himself knew it.

His contribution was, nonetheless, fully recognized by his contemporaries in Great Britain. In 1831 he was awarded the first Wollaston Medal of the Geological Society of London, "in consideration of his being a great original discoverer in English Geology; and especially for his having been the first, in this country, to discover and to teach the identification of strata, and to determine their succession by means of their imbedded fossils."[45] In his presentation of the award, Adam Sedgwick (1785–1873), president of the Society, called Smith the "Father of English Geology."[46] In 1832 he received a pension from the Crown; in 1835, an honorary LL.D. from Trinity College in Dublin.

The first "in this country," the award read, and that was certainly true, since by the time Smith had actually published his observations the principle of strata identified by fossils had been described, used, and published in France. That feat was accomplished by Georges Cuvier (1769–1832) and Alexandre Brongniart (1770–1847) in their brief *Essay on the Mineral Geography of the Paris Region,* published in 1808. In this paper, they described and discussed seven Tertiary formations, the Cretaceous chalk beneath them and the Quaternary deposits above, in the area surrounding Paris. Within the second of their Tertiary formations, Cuvier and Brongniart described a series of individual strata, strata they were able to trace across large expanses of the Paris basin. They were able to identify these strata in different parts of the basin not only because of the structure of each, but also because of their fossil mollusc content, and they used both the kinds of species and the frequencies of species of these molluscs to construct a stratigraphic sequence for the Paris region. As they noted,

> The constancy in the order of superposition of the thinnest beds, and for an extent of at least 12 myriameters [120 kilometers] is, we feel, one of the most remarkable facts that we have established in our research. . . . The means we have used to recognize, in the midst of so many calcareous layers, a bed already observed in a far-removed district, is taken from the nature of the fossils incorporated in each bed: these fossils are always generally the same in corresponding beds, and present sufficiently marked differences of species from one system of beds to another. It is a method of recognition that to the present has not deceived us. It is not necessary to believe, however, that the difference from one bed to another is as well marked as that from the chalk to the limestone, i.e., from the Cretaceous to the Tertiary deposits. . . . the fossils characteristic of one bed become less numerous in the succeeding bed, and disappear entirely in others, and are gradually replaced by new fossils that had not appeared before.[47]

The 1808 *Essay* was followed in 1811 by a much longer and more detailed monograph on the stratigraphy of the Paris basin, one which provided lists of the characteristic invertebrate fossils by which various strata or groups of strata could be distinguished. This monograph then appeared in Cuvier's *Researches on the Fossil Bones of Quadrupeds* in 1812, guaranteeing it wide recognition.[48] Here was the first detailed, published use of the fossil content of strata as a means of recognizing those strata and as a means of constructing the order in which they had been deposited across a region.

Cuvier and Brongniart not only published their analysis before Smith, but they also used their insight into the relationship between strata and the fossils they contained in a very different way. For Smith, the value of this relationship was a practical one: being able to recognize a stratum from its fossils meant that one could generalize from fossil content to such things as the water retention capacity of the embedding material. For Cuvier and Brongniart, however, superposition and fossil content provided a means of unraveling earth history, and their essay stressed the derivation of such history from the strata and their contents. These were two very different uses, and reflect not simply different interests but different backgrounds as well. Unlike the isolated Smith, Cuvier and Brongniart were at the heart of their scientific community. The question of who gets the credit for discovering that fossils can be used to identify strata is unimportant, although a debate later arose between the English and the French as to whether Smith or Cuvier and Brongniart were to be so honored; a similar debate later took place over whether it was the English or French who first convincingly demonstrated the great antiquity of the human species. What is important is that by the end of the first decade of the nineteenth century it was well recognized that different strata or groups of strata contained different and characteristic assemblages of fossils, and that these assemblages could be used to recognize the strata that contained them. Along with the much earlier recognition that the order of undisturbed superposed strata was also the order of deposition of those strata, this realization soon supported the definition of a set of time markers by which human antiquity could be assessed and also provided the means by which this assessment could proceed. It was no coincidence that the person who provided these markers, and who showed how they could be used, was Georges Cuvier. To understand fully the significance of Cuvier's achievement, however, it is necessary to understand the chronologies of earth and human history that were widely accepted during the eighteenth century prior to the definition and acceptance of these time markers.

Notes and References

1. [de Pauw] 1771, Volume 2:396.
2. See, for instance, Montfaucon 1722, Book 1, Part II, Chapter 9, and the general discussion in Laming-Emperaire 1964.
3. Woodward 1728, Part 2 (Letters):42.
4. Mahudel 1740.
5. Goguet 1761, Volume 1:140–141.
6. Montfaucon 1722, Book 1:135.
7. Klindt-Jensen 1975; see Rodden 1981 for a perceptive discussion of the Three Age System; see also Gräslund 1981.
8. Steno 1968[1669]:211–213.
9. Rudwick 1972.

10. G. W. White, Introduction, in Steno 1968[1669].
11. I have used the English edition of Burnet's *Theory* (Burnet 1684, 1690c).
12. Burnet 1684:[vii].
13. Woodward 1695:277.
14. Ray 1693:34–35.
15. See Porter 1977, Rudwick 1972.
16. Lankester 1848:332.
17. Eyles 1971; see Levine 1977 for a general discussion of Woodward's life and a detailed account of the events that led to his expulsion.
18. Woodward 1695:74–75.
19. Woodward 1695:82.
20. [Arbuthnot] 1697:52–53.
21. [Arbuthnot] 1697:7.
22. See Levine 1977 for a brief review of responses to Woodward's *Essay*.
23. Rudwick 1972.
24. Eyles 1971; Jahn 1972.
25. Woodward 1726.
26. Woodward 1728.
27. Porter 1977:80.
28. Porter 1977.
29. Strachey 1719.
30. Strachey 1725.
31. Holloway 1723:421.
32. Strachey 1725:397.
33. See the discussions in Berry 1968, Davies 1969, and Porter 1977.
34. Porter 1977.
35. Cox 1942.
36. Biographical information on Smith is drawn from Cox 1942, Eyles 1969a, and Phillips 1844.
37. Cox 1942:13.
38. Phillips 1844.
39. See the discussion of the publication of Smith's map in Eyles 1969b.
40. Smith 1816:[ii].
41. Smith 1817:vii–viii.
42. Smith 1817:vi.
43. Smith 1817:v.
44. Eyles 1969b:143.
45. Sedgwick 1834a:271.
46. Sedgwick 1834a:279.
47. Cuvier and Brongniart 1808:436–437.
48. Cuvier and Brongniart 1811, 1812.

3

Chronologies of Earth and Human History during the Eighteenth Century

During the late 1600s and early 1700s, while the production of new theories of the earth was flourishing, there was widespread agreement that the earth had been created about 6000 years ago. This date had been reached by tallying the biblical genealogies and then combining these tallies with analyses of other historical documents and with various astronomical calculations. The famous conclusion of Archbishop James Ussher (1581–1656) that the Creation had occurred "upon the entrance of the night preceding the twenty third day of *Octob.*"[1] in the year 4004 B.C. was but one of many such estimates of the date of Creation that had been, and were to be, forwarded. The precise date reached differed according to which version of the first books of the Bible were employed, with variations in the dates taken from other sources and with different methods of performing astronomical calculations, but the results from the best of these efforts—and Ussher's was accepted as one of the best—were generally the same. The use of Scripture in determining the age of the earth stemmed primarily from the fact that it was felt to represent the revealed Word of God, to be taken as literal truth. But even outside this framework, the Bible was also seen as a written history of early times, compiled by people who had either been present at the events involved or who, if not present, still had access to information that allowed them to record earlier events with accuracy. " 'Tis the Sacred writings of Scripture that are the best monuments of Antiquity,'' said Thomas Burnet in 1684, " and to those we are chiefly beholden for the History of the first Ages, whether Natural History or Civil.''[2] Either as the revealed Word of God or as a more straightforward historical document, the Bible presented reliable facts that could be used to study early history.

The 6000-year date for the creation of the earth actually applied to the creation of human beings, since the heart of the chronology was formed by the genealogies from Adam onward. The extension of the date to all of earth history followed from a literal reading of Genesis and of its statement that Adam had been created on the sixth day. It also followed, however, from the widely held assumption that the earth had been fashioned for humankind by a caring, even if wrathful, Creator and that without people the earth had no purpose. It followed that if people had been created some 6000 years ago, the earth had not been created long before.

There was a flexibility inherent in this chronology, a flexibility stemming from the fact that although the chronology for the human existence on earth was based upon the biblical geneaologies, the application of the same chronology to the entire history of the earth was founded upon a literal reading of the first verses of Genesis. As a result, any doubts that might develop over the meaning of the word *day* as it was used for pre-Adamic times did not affect the chronology once Adam had appeared. The fact that the 6000-year chronology for all of earth history was constructed by adding the first, prehuman days of Creation to the roughly 6000 years calculated for human history on the basis of the genealogies meant that the two could be unhooked and treated separately. Because the genealogies were generally felt to be secure, any separation of the chronologies required that the beginning of human history would remain fixed at approximately 4000 B.C. while the prehuman epochs of earth history became longer.

Such decoupling was rarely done during the seventeenth and eighteenth centuries, however, because of the twin beliefs that the words of Scripture were to be taken literally, including the word *day* in Genesis, and that the earth without people would be an earth without purpose. Thus, one of the things that the theories of Burnet, Whiston, Woodward and others had in common was the belief that the earth had been created about 6000 years ago. Burnet, for instance, spent a section of his *Sacred Theory* supporting the view that the impressive lifespans of the ''Ante-Diluvian Patriarchs'' provided in Genesis were to be reckoned in actual solar years and not, as some had suggested, in months. To take any other approach, he observed, "perverts all Chronology."[3] This chronology could then be applied to all of earth history because "the Sublunary World . . . was made for the sake of Man."[4]

That these theories took the 6000-year date for the creation of the earth as fact does not mean that the chronology went unquestioned. To some, observations of earthly phenomena suggested that the earth might be much older than this and that the biblical chronology might, in fact, apply only to the human species. Thus, in a letter written to Edward Lhywd in 1695, John Ray observed that if some fossils really were of organic origin, then their form and position were such as to "shock the Scripture-History of ye novity of the World," but went on to note that even if the earth were older than the 6000-year chronology allowed, "ye race of mankind is new upon ye earth, & not older then ye Scripture makes it."[5]

Ray never published such a critical view, but the less cautious Burnet did, and he did it in a way that cost him his theological career. Burnet was well aware that his theory took many liberties with Genesis, and was careful to explain that "it is no fault to recede from the literal sense of Scripture, but the fault is when we leave it without a just cause."[6] Where his theory receded, Burnet felt, his causes were just. At first, he also felt the conventional chronology for earth history quite adequate for his purposes, and when Erasmus Warren attacked him in 1690 for discussing the Creation in terms that seemed to demand more than 6 literal days,[7] Burnet was not moved:

> To this Exception the general answer may be this; either you take the Hypothesis of an ordinary Providence, or of an extraordinary, as to the time allowed for the Formation of the Earth; If you proceed according to an ordinary Providence, the Formation of the Earth would require much more time than Six days. But if according to an extraordinary, you may suppose it made in six minutes, if you please.[8]

To defend other aspects of his theory, however, Burnet had to defend as well his often liberal modification of what Genesis seemed to say. In 1690, he did this by arguing that Scripture was couched in terms that could be understood by the masses of the time, and that "this vulgar style of Scripture in describing the natures of things, hath often been mistaken for the real sense, and so become a stumbling block in the way of truth."[9] In 1692, he developed this position further. Much of Genesis, he argued, represents "Parables, and . . . Hypotheses adapted to the Vulgar";[10] Moses did not mean to give the beginning of the world "exactly according to Physical Truth . . . but . . . after such a method as might breed in the Minds of Men Piety, and a worshipping of the true God."[11] Burnet no longer regarded his earlier answer to Warren's criticism of his chronology as fully satisfactory. Some of the things described in Genesis as having happened in a single day, he observed, involved "truly a very considerable and numerous piece of business,"[12] and it was clear from the nature of Genesis itself that it was meant to be an allegory. While the biblical chronology applied to human history, it clearly could not be taken to apply to the Divine Creation as a whole. It was this attack on Genesis that went too far, an attack that even allegorized the Fall, and Burnet saw himself removed from his theological office as a result.

Burnet and Ray were not the only philosophers and natural historians during this period who saw difficulties with a literal interpretation of the biblical chronology as it applied to the entire creation. Unlike Burnet, who was spurred into his attack in order to defend his own theory, most who wondered about the accuracy of this chronology wondered as a result of empirical observations of the earth itself. The astronomer Edmund Halley (1656–1743), then Secretary of the Royal Society of London, outlined the problem concisely in 1715:

> There have been many Attempts made and Proposals offered, to ascertain from the Appearances of Nature, what may have been the Antiquity of this Globe of Earth; on which, by the Evidence of Sacred Writ, Mankind has dwelt about 6000 years; or according to the Septuagint above 7000. But whereas we are told that the Formation of Man was the last Act of the Creator, 'tis no where revealed in Scripture how long the Earth had existed before this last Creation, nor how long those five days that preceeded it may be to be accounted; since we are elsewhere told, that in respect of the Almighty a thousand Years is as one Day. . . . Nor can it well be conceived how those days should be to be understood of natural Days, since they are mentioned as Measures of Time before the Creation of the Sun, which was not till the Fourth Day.[13]

In his *Short Account of the Saltness of the Ocean,* Halley suggested a method whereby the age of the world might be assessed. Noting that enclosed lakes must receive their salt content from the streams entering them, and therefore must grow saltier through time, he suggested that it was probable that the ocean became salty in the same way. If this were the case, then if one knew the present salt content of the ocean and the rate at which that content was increasing, the age of the ocean—and therefore of the world—could be determined by extrapolating this rate back through time. Halley's purpose was not to determine this age, since neither the current salt content nor the rate of increase was known, but was instead to encourage the acquisition of such information so that future generations might be able to use the salt clock to answer this crucial question. This approach, he hoped, would "refute the ancient Notion, some have of late entertained, of the Eternity of all Things," but he also knew that "by it the World may be found much older than many have hitherto imagined."[14]

Nonetheless, the 6000-year date for the origin of the earth remained well accepted in England until late in the eighteenth century. It was much earlier in the same century, however, that the biblical chronology for earth history came under a more general and direct attack in France. The French Enlightenment saw the Creator recede into the background as a continual influence in determining the direction and nature of earth history. For some French writers, in fact, God drifted out of the picture entirely. More commonly the Creator simply remained offstage, leaving an earth that marched along very much on its own, an earth whose history had been a dynamic and active one. In such a world view, the scriptural account of earth history played a greatly diminished role, and for many the 6000-year date for all of earth history played little or no role at all. The earth became a body with great antiquity and with a past that had been marked by continual change.[15]

It was, then, no coincidence that *Telliamed* was written by a Frenchman and went through three editions in French between 1748 and 1755. Published ten years after the death of its author, Benoît de Maillet (1656–1738), *Telliamed* (the author's name in reverse) proved quite objectionable to the orthodox, objections that added to the popularity with which the book was received. The universe that de Maillet portrayed in *Telliamed* was eternal, its history directed not by God but by chance. Adopting many of Descartes' views, de Maillet argued that the heavenly bodies alternated between being luminous suns and dark planets. The earth, currently a dark planet, had a surface that had been formed under the sea— a sea that has been continually diminishing in size and that will ultimately disappear entirely. Such a process took billions of years; in manuscript, de Maillet suggested that the diminution of the sea has been going on for 2 billion years, a figure his posthumous editor removed. His ideas on human antiquity were scaled to match his notions on the history of the earth. "The earth was inhabited by men," he suggested, "nearly 500,000 years ago and perhaps more."[16] Perhaps much more, in fact, since he also suggested that seaside habitations might be found 6000 feet (1830 meters) above the current sea level. Since de Maillet felt that the rate of decrease of sea level was 3 inches (7.5 centimeters) per century, such habitations would be over 2 million years old.[17]

De Maillet also argued that different groups of people originated from different varieties of sea men, that the more savage of modern peoples might represent those who had most recently made this transition, and that such transitions might still be occurring. As widely read as *Telliamed* was, much of it appeared fantastic. It was good Enlightenment reading in France, but little of it was compelling.

The same cannot be said of the 36-volume *Natural History* of Georges Buffon that appeared between 1749 and 1789. Keeper of the Jardin du Roi and a member of the Académie Française (1753), Buffon (1707–1788) was a man whose talents and accomplishments as a natural historian and literary stylist were well recognized during his own time. Certainly the major natural historian of the French Enlightenment, and perhaps of the entire eighteenth century, Buffon viewed earth history as dynamic and as operating according to a set of laws impressed on matter by the Creator. Buffon viewed himself as a disciple of Newton, and felt that these laws could be discovered by the application of reason and observation, in the same way that Newton had discovered the laws determining the movements of matter in a larger realm. In this view, shared by many Enlightenment natural historians, not only did the continued intervention of the Creator play no role in earth history, but Scripture became little more than a historical document, the days of Genesis to be treated allegorically if they were treated at all. To be sure, in his search for the laws that had governed earth history and in his assumption that this history was not to be interpreted by calling on Divine intervention, Buffon did not differ from many other naturalists who worked at or after the time of Newton's great accomplishments. As much as he depended on Scripture, for instance, Burnet used secondary causes to account for major events in earth history, while Woodward was roundly criticized for explaining the Deluge through the suspension of such causes and thus, it was pointed out, not explaining it at all. But Buffon did differ from these earlier naturalists in that the evidence of Scripture played only a token role in his search for an explanation and description of the history of our globe and of the things on it. As Ernst Cassirer noted many years ago, Buffon's silence on the matter of the biblical version of the creation of the earth was more telling and effective than direct disavowal would have been.[18]

Indeed, theological concerns had drifted so far out of Buffon's *Natural History* that the Faculty of Theology at the Sorbonne censured the first 3 volumes of the work, which had appeared in 1749, "as including principles and maxims that do not conform to those of religion,"[19] itemizing 14 offending sections from the first 2 volumes. Buffon thanked the Faculty for allowing him to express "the integrity of my intentions,"[20] and declared

> that I had no intention of contradicting the text of Scripture; that I believe very firmly all that it says about the creation, whether as to the order of time or as to the circumstances of facts; and that I abandon that which, in my book, deals with the formation of the earth, and in general all that might be contrary to the narration of Moses. . . .[21]

Nonetheless, the later volumes of the *Natural History* proceeded to present an earth history that could not be recognized from Genesis.

Buffon's approach to interpreting events in earth history was uniformitarian, both in the sense that it attempted to explain those events only in terms of processes that can now be seen in operation (actualism), and in the sense that he saw those processes generally operating in the past at the same rates at which they now operate. To understand the earth, he argued,

> It is necessary to take it as it is, to observe all of its parts well, and to argue inductively from the present to the past; in addition, causes whose effects are rare, violent, and sudden must not affect us, since they are not found in the ordinary course of Nature, but effects that occur everyday, movements which follow one another without interruption, operations that are constant and always repeated, these are our causes and our reasons.[22]

Although Buffon did not always tightly adhere to these stated principles, the massive and catastrophic deluges that played so heavily in earlier theories found no place in Buffon's earth history. Indeed, there is no universal deluge in Buffon at all, and, except for the event that led to the formation of the earth, little role for any catastrophes.

Buffon derived the mass that composes the earth from a collision between a passing comet and the sun, which produced a body of incandescent matter that eventually cooled to become the earth as we know it. Such a history, Buffon knew, demanded a lengthy period of time, but he also felt that the same processes that operate today would have produced more rapid change during the early stages of earth history.

In 1749, Buffon did not say how long it would have taken for his molten, incandescent globe to have become the modern earth. In 1775, however, he became explicit about his chronology. Following his belief that the earth had reached its present temperature as a result of having cooled from a molten mass, Buffon had conducted experiments on the length of time it took balls of various sizes and various materials to cool from an incandescent state. Extrapolating these data to a body the size of the earth, he now presented absolute dates in years for several important events in earth history. The earth, he argued, would have taken 2,936 years to become solid to the core, 34,270.5 years to become cool enough to be touched, and 74,832 years to reach the temperature it now has. In addition, he suggested that life would have appeared on earth 35,983 years after the earth had been formed, while our ever-degenerating home would become so cool that it would no longer support life 168,123 years after its formation. Thus he felt that life on earth will last 132,140 years. He made similar calculations for other planets and other satellites, making the then-common assumption that they were all occupied by living organisms.[23]

Buffon's use of such exact values had an important function. Not only did they provide the appearance of the same kind of accuracy that one expected from a system that meant to do for the earth what Newton had done for the heavens, but they also helped dispel the notion that Buffon was spinning the same kind of webs that Woodward and others had spun during earlier decades. Buffon's earth history came not from baseless speculation, but from reason, careful observation of the earth, and detailed experimentation; the precision of his chronology was meant to convey these facts. Although he presented his values to the nearest half-year, Buffon himself felt that much greater amounts of time were necessary to account for the origin of the earth and the changes it had undergone since that origin.

Buffon expanded his ideas on the history of the earth in his *Epochs of Nature,* published in 1778. Here he organized earth history in terms of seven epochs—epochs that could, if one wished, be analogized with the days of creation outlined in Genesis. Although his history had little in common with Genesis, he suggested that the two were not in conflict, since Genesis, expressing Divine words in a poor language and in such a way as to be intelligible to the vulgar, was not to be taken literally. As a result, the length of time his theory required was not a problem:

> What can we understand by the six days that the sacred Writings designate so precisely in counting them one after another, if not six spaces of time, six intervals of duration? And these spaces of time indicated by the word *day*, in the absence of other expressions, can have no connection with our actual days, since three of them had passed before the sun was placed in the sky. . . . These are but six intervals of time.[24]

If you cannot accept my reasoning, Buffon asked, then simply accept my history for what it is—hypothetical.

Buffon's first epoch saw the molten earth take its rounded form after having been struck off from the sun. In the second epoch, the consolidation of the earth led to the formation of its rocky interior, while the vitrified rocks of its surface were formed as well. By the third epoch, the earth had become cool enough to allow water to fall without becoming vaporized; water came to cover all but the highest peaks, and the first organisms—marine invertebrates and plants—came into being. The fourth epoch saw the slow withdrawal of the waters from the earth's surface and the appearance of the first land animals. The fifth epoch was marked by the presence of such large land mammals as the hippopotamus, rhinoceros, and elephant in the north, reflecting the fact that this area had yet to cool to its current temperature and that areas to the south were still too hot for them. During the sixth epoch, the continents separated from one another and slowly took on their modern forms; toward the end of this epoch, but while the earth was still more geologically active than it is now, human beings appeared. The seventh and final epoch saw the rise of human power as a force in modifying the surface of the earth.

This whole process, he argued, had taken about 75,000 years, a figure derived from his earlier experiments on the cooling of incandescent masses. He felt, however, that the years he had allotted for his epochs were inadequate: "far from having unnecessarily lengthened the timespan, I have perhaps shortened it too much."[25] In response to those who would think he had been too generous with his years, Buffon asked, and answered, a simple question:

> And why does the human mind seem to lose itself in the space of time more readily than in that of extension, or in the consideration of measures, weights and numbers? Why are 100,000 years more difficult to conceptualize and to count than 100,000 pounds of money? Whether it is because the sum of time cannot be felt or realized in visible form, or rather that our short existence accustoms us to seeing 100 years as a huge span time, we have difficulty in forming an idea of 1000 years, and can form no representation of 10,000 years, or even conceive of 100,000.[26]

As long as one agreed with the allegorical interpretation of the Mosaic account of creation, one could, with some strain, reconcile Buffon's epochs with the days of Genesis. Indeed, it was no coincidence that his last epoch—the world as it is now—began about 6000 years ago. Buffon was explicit about retaining the biblical chronology as it applied to human history:

> It is correctly said that . . . since the end of the works of God, that is to say since the creation of man, only six or eight thousand years have passed, because the different genealogies of mankind since Adam indicate no more: we owe this faith, this mark of submission and respect, to the most ancient, to the most sacred of all traditions.[27]

Buffon's treatment of the chronology of earth and human history was important in several respects. First, he denied the applicability of the biblical chronology to earth history and substituted in its place a very different and empirically derived set of dates. Buffon, of course, was not the first to abandon the biblical chronology for earth history, as we have seen. Nor was he alone in making this rejection at the time he wrote. Such rejections were commonplace during the French Enlightenment, and some were in works that reached a wide audience. But even though a number of works that attributed a great age to the earth were widely read by continental Europeans, none were written by a natural historian of Buffon's stature.

Second, Buffon popularized a means of retaining Scripture and the Mosaic chronology, even while arguing for a lengthy earth history. This he did by taking advantage of the flexibility inherent in the biblical chronology, splitting earth history from the history of its human inhabitants and applying the 6000 year chronology to people alone. Again, Buffon was not novel in taking this approach. Halley, for instance, had done it in 1715, and Buffon had praised Halley's suggestions for a salt chronology in the first volume of his *Natural History* (1749). But Buffon was now providing a detailed account of earth history and was carefully relegating people to the tail end of that history. No natural historian of major reputation had ever done this. By treating the chronology of Moses as applying only to people, and the days of Genesis as allegory, Buffon had allowed himself free movement in dealing with the history of the earth up to the time of the creation of humankind, and gave to Scripture the task of dealing only with the history of our own species. That history covered the last 6000 to 8000 years, and was marked at the outset by the appearance of people on a physically modern, or nearly modern, earth.

These three themes—an ancient earth, the origination of people some 6000 years ago, and the correlation between the appearance of people and the appearance of a physically modern earth—were to play crucial roles in the interpretation of human antiquity for the next 8 decades. Buffon's *Epochs of Nature* was the first substantial work by a scientist of major reknown in which this combination of themes appeared. The combination proved to be a particularly powerful one. It removed a major stumbling block by joining the much older belief that earth history had been directional with the growing belief that it had also been much longer than Scripture seemed to allow, and it did so while retaining the accuracy of Scripture on what was, after all, the most important point: the early history of human beings. Humankind had, indeed, been God's last creation, some 6000 years ago, and had not appeared until the rest of the Creator's work had been completed and the earth had become modern in form. All this was just as Scripture suggested.

The power of this resolution can be seen by the popularity it gained during the closing decades of the eighteenth century among natural historians with extremely different goals and interests. While Buffon was allegorizing Moses in Paris, for instance, the Swiss-born naturalist Jean André de Luc (1727–1817) was taking a very different approach to earth history in London. De Luc was interested in showing the literal accuracy of most of the scriptural account of earth history. His five-volume, 3000-page *Physical and Moral Letters on the History of the World and Man,* which appeared in 1779, had as one of its goals the demonstration that the facts of the history of the globe did not clash with Moses, that Genesis "contains the true history of the World."[28] Nevertheless, de Luc also confined the biblical chronology to human history.

De Luc's earth history was built largely around the fact that the surface of the earth everywhere seemed to show the effects of having been inundated at some time in the past. Calcareous rocks, invertebrate marine fossils in terrestrial deposits, massive gravel beds, and a wide range of other phenomena suggested to him that the present continents had once been covered by water. The time at which the waters had retreated from modern land surfaces could be judged by using the effects of terrestrial geological processes as chronometers, since those processes would not have begun until the modern continents became dry. Observing such things as the amount of material rivers had deposited in the sea and the magnitude of talus accumulation in mountainous areas, de Luc concluded that such processes had only begun to operate relatively recently. Thus, the retreat of the waters must have been a comparatively recent event. As a result, de Luc concluded from this set of facts that

> all the phenomena of the Earth, thus of the history of Man, lead us to believe, that by a sudden revolution, the Sea changed its bed; that the continents occupied today, are the bed it occupied before; and that a great number of centuries have not passed, since these new lands were abandoned by the waters.[29]

In de Luc's primordial world there had been a very different set of continents, while the modern land surface formed the bed of the sea. His revolution saw the sea cover the entire earth, with the exception of the highest mountains of the ancient world, and then retreat into a new bed formed by the collapse of the primordial continents. All organisms, including human beings, were destroyed by this process, except for those lucky enough to have survived on mountain tops. The lucky ones formed the stock that colonized the new land surfaces.

De Luc equated his revolution with the biblical Deluge, and used the details of his system to explain why no pre-Deluge human remains had been found: "this is another of those Circumstances, which appears contradictory in the Mosaic account, but that my Natural History explains. . . . the ancient Earth was destroyed, and the Sea covered the Bodies of Men and of Animals that had perished in the Revolution."[30]

De Luc's revolution was unlike anything that Buffon would allow in the earth's past, and de Luc's use of geological phenomena to confirm the literal accuracy of much of Genesis was far different from Buffon's depiction of Genesis as allegory. Buffon was a French Enlightenment *philosophe,* and viewed the world in dynamic terms, with God well in the background. De Luc's *Physical and Moral Letters* was an antagonistic response to such views, including Buffon's, written in Protestant England and presenting a history in which an essentially stable earth had been disrupted and reformed by a massive deluge equated with Noah's Flood.

Here were two very different outlooks, yet de Luc's approach to the biblical chronology was identical to that of Buffon. De Luc viewed the history of the earth as lengthy, the days of Genesis as indeterminately long periods of time. "The succession of days" described in the Mosaic account, he felt, "expresses only a succession of periods, in which different parts of the sensible Universe had their beginnings."[31] While he allegorized the days of creation, and thus allowed a lengthy earth history, de Luc also applied the biblical chronology to human history: "men occupied the earth much later than the animals . . . about 17 centuries before the Deluge."[32] Thus, while disagreeing with Buffon on so many crucial issues, he agreed with him on the issue of absolute chronology. The Mosaic days represented lengthy epochs, and the biblical chronology was to be applied to the history of people on earth. He was also very close to Buffon's position on the issue of the geological antiquity of human beings, although the reasons de Luc associated the earliest remains of people with a geologically modern earth were very different from those that led Buffon to this position. Since de Luc's pre-Deluge human beings lived in places that are now at the bottom of the sea, today's continents must lack pre-Flood human remains; all human relics on these continents must be associated with deposits laid down by those processes we now see in operation around us, and thus indicative of a geologically modern earth. As vastly different as their outlooks and earth histories were, Buffon and de Luc were in full agreement concerning human antiquity and the remains of our more distant past. People had existed for some 6000 years, and their remains were to be found associated only with deposits characteristic of the modern world.

The speculations of Buffon and de Luc on the history of the earth were part of a waning scientific tradition, and had closer ties in many ways with the theories of Whiston and Woodward than with approaches to earth history that were to follow in a few decades. James Hutton's concerns with denudation, however, led him to couple the Enlightenment view of a dynamic earth history with a fully uniformitarian approach to the interpretation of that history. The result was a picture of an active earth that had little in common with earlier systems. Still, the general structure of Hutton's chronology was similar to that of both Buffon and de Luc in that it denied the applicability of the Mosaic chronology to all of earth history while applying it to the history of our own species.

Born in Edinburgh and trained as a physician, Hutton (1726–1797) became sufficiently wealthy to spend much of his time pursuing intellectual matters, including geology. His *Theory of the Earth* was published in 1788 in the *Transactions* of the Royal Society of Edinburgh, 3 years after he had presented it to that society.[33] Viewing the earth as a wisely designed system, Hutton noted the pervasiveness of erosional processes that tended to level the earth's surface and to wash the eroded materials into the sea. Such erosion, he felt, was necessary, since life would be impossible on a rock-hard globe, but might also lead to the destruction of the habitable earth. This consideration of the denudation dilemma, as Gordon L. Davies has called it,[34] led him to ask if there were not some mechanism built into the earth to ensure its continued operation through time. If no such mechanism existed, he pointed out, it would imply that the earth "has not been the work of infinite power and wisdom."[35]

Hutton argued that the earth did, indeed, renew itself. While land surfaces were constantly being worn away and the eroded materials deposited into the sea, the action of heat at the bottom of the sea consolidated these materials into new, massive strata. The same heat that caused the consolidation of these strata also caused their uplift, forming new land surfaces while the older surfaces were disappearing into the sea. He did not feel that these processes counterbalanced one another perfectly, but was certain that the proportion of land and water was always sufficient to allow the continuation of life on earth.

This was a truly dynamic system, with continual erosion of old land surfaces and continual creation of new ones. Hutton had no way to gauge the actual amount of time such processes would take, but he did think that the only way the magnitude of time could be judged was by observing the pace of modern erosion. The slow operation of erosional processes revealed by such observation clearly implied "the immense amount of time necessarily required for this total destruction of the land,"[36] though he was not clear about the speed with which new land surfaces might appear.

Continual slow erosive destruction of the land and continual replacement of those lands by new ones uplifted from the sea, followed by the slow loss of the newly formed lands in anticipation of future uplifts, all this formed a picture of a self-renewing earth spinning around the sun for immense periods of time. Hutton closed his 1788 essay with what has become a famous observation: "the result, therefore, of our present inquiry is, that we find no vestige of a beginning,—no prospect of an end."[37]

Hutton's uniformitarian, steady-state system implied a globe that might as well have been in existence forever, although Hutton was no eternalist. Yet, while expanding the time scale of earth history far beyond what either Buffon or de Luc had suggested, Hutton also felt that the Mosaic account provided trust-worthy information on human history:

> If we are to take the written history of man for the rule by which we should judge of the time when the species first began, that period would be but little removed from the present state of things. The Mosaic history places this beginning of man at no great distance; and there has not been found, in natural history, any document by which a high antiquity might be attributed to the human race.[38]

For Hutton, while the origins of the earth receded far into the past, people remained biblically recent in terms of both the number of years they had been on earth and in terms of the nature of the globe, "but little removed from the present state of things" at the time of their appearance. Here, Hutton was on common ground with Buffon and de Luc.

The initial publication of Hutton's theory met with a critical response.[39] He answered his critics with a ponderous two-volume *Theory of the Earth* in 1795, a work that was also roundly attacked. The Irish mineralogist Richard Kirwan (1733–1812), for instance, included a caustic analysis of Hutton's theory in his *Geological Essays* (1799), an analysis whose goal was to "subvert the funda-mental principles upon which his system is constructed, and occasionally to point out the absurdities that flow from it."[40] The answer to all these criticisms did not come from Hutton, who died in 1797, but from his friend John Playfair.

In 1802, Playfair (1748–1819), professor of mathematics at the University of Edinburgh, published his *Illustrations of the Huttonian Theory of the Earth,* a volume that both summarized Hutton's theory in a concise, readable fashion and responded to Hutton's critics. Here Playfair provided a more detailed defense of Hutton's lengthy earth history and of Hutton's restriction of the Mosaic chronol-ogy to human history. Playfair's defense was, in fact, strongly reminiscent of Buffon:

> On what is now said is grounded another objection to Dr Hutton's theory, namely, that the high antiquity ascribed by it to the earth, is inconsistent with that system of chronology which rests on the authority of the Sacred Writings. This objection would no doubt be of weight, if the high antiquity in question were not restricted merely to the globe of the earth, but were also extended to the human race. That the origin of mankind does not go back beyond six or seven thousand years, is a position so involved in the narrative of the Mosaic books, that any thing inconsistent with it, would no doubt stand in opposition to the testimony of those ancient records. On this subject, however, geology is silent; and the history of arts and sciences, when traced as high as any authentic monuments extend, refers the beginnings of civilization to a date not very different from that which has just been mentioned, and infinitely within the limits of the most recent of the epochas, marked by the physical revolutions of the globe. . . . The authority of the Sacred Books seems to be but little interested in what regards the mere antiquity of the earth itself; nor does it appear that

their language is to be understood literally concerning the *age* of that body, any more than concerning its *figure* or its *motion*. The theory of Dr Hutton stands here precisely on the same footing with the system of Copernicus; for there is no reason to suppose, that it was the purpose of revelation to furnish a standard of geological, any more than of astronomical science. . . . It is but reasonable, therefore, that we should extend to the geologist the same liberty of speculation, which the astronomer and mathematician are already in possession of; and this may be done, by supposing that the chronology of Moses relates only to the human race.[41]

Playfair did not have to worry much about the critical acceptance this argument might have. He was, in fact, defending Hutton's chronology by simply summarizing how most natural historians then viewed the relationship between the history of the earth and its human occupants on the one hand, and the biblical chronology on the other. It was the eternity of years implied by Hutton's theory that was the prime chronological concern,[42] not his general belief in an ancient earth, his restriction of the biblical chronology to the human existence, and his view that people had not appeared until the earth had come to look very much as it does now. For most, those ideas had become accepted as facts.

This is not to say that there was full agreement on the issue. Some still argued that both earth and human history had been biblically short. Indeed, much of Playfair's defense was directed toward Richard Kirwan who, in his attack on Huttonian geology, had argued against the possibility that Mt. Etna might be 8000 years old because he realized "how fatal the suspicion of the high antiquity of the globe has been to the credit of the Mosaic history, and consequently to religion and morality."[43] On the other end of the scale, some late eighteenth-century continental philosophers argued that both people and their planet were ancient, as the Baron d'Holbach argued in 1770 (see Chapter 6). Although there were those who disagreed from one perspective or another, disagreements that were usually associated with strong theological opinions, the last few decades of the eighteenth century nonetheless saw a general consensus reached by natural historians on this issue: the earth was ancient, and people had come into being about 6000 years ago and at a time when the earth was fully modern or nearly so.

At the beginning of the eighteenth century, it was widely accepted that both the human species and the earth had been created about 6000 years ago. This belief was in turn associated with the beliefs that the words of Genesis were to be read literally, and that since the earth had been created for people, an earth without people was an earth without purpose. By the last decades of the century, the first few days of Genesis had become allegory and earth history had been greatly lengthened. It was realized that during the course of its long history the earth had undergone major changes in form—changes that some, including de Luc, saw as catastrophic in nature, and that others, such as Hutton, saw as milder in form. The human species, God's last creation, had not appeared until these changes were complete or nearly so. The only exception possible was the Deluge, an event witnessed by many but survived by few. However, the scope and nature of the Deluge was also a matter for debate.

For some, especially in England, the history of the earth had become a history of the earth as it developed into a fit habitat for mankind, a history that had been superintended, at one degree of remove or another, by a Creator who cared for all of His beings. An earth without people was no longer an earth without purpose, and this view was still firmly in line with Scripture. For those who subscribed fully to this belief, the discovery of human remains in deposits that could not be considered to belong to the geologically modern world would have tremendous implications. Since the appearance of people was seen to have postdated the onset of modern geological conditions, such a discovery would put in doubt the accuracy of the biblical genealogies, and thus of Revelation itself. Since the human species was God's last creative work, as Scripture made clear, such a discovery would conflict with God's Words in this way as well. By showing that people had appeared before the world had been fully prepared for their arrival, such a discovery would shed doubt on the belief that the history of the earth had been superintended by a caring Creator.

Even for those unconcerned with the direct reconciliation of the facts of geology with Scripture, these beliefs formed a significant background for the reception of the relics of possibly ancient peoples. And even without this background, it was nevertheless widely accepted that each kind of organism had been created in one place from which it had subsequently spread, and that each kind had been adapted from the beginning to a certain set of environmental conditions. This view was applied to our own species as well, with western Asia routinely considered a homeland, as both Scripture and the records of the most ancient civilizations suggested. In such a view, the creation of humankind prior to the onset of modern environmental conditions simply did not seem possible.

By the end of the eighteenth century, then, a conceptual framework was in place that required that all human relics be recent in both absolute years and in terms of geological age. In this constellation of beliefs, the recency of the human appearance on a much more ancient earth had taken on great importance with respect to our place in the scheme of things. Since no human remains had been found within the ancient strata of the earth, the facts of geology concurred with the belief in human recency, as Hutton was careful to note. Lacking, however, was a set of widely accepted time markers that could be used to assess the antiquity of the superficial strata of the globe, and it was, of course, precisely those strata that contained the remains of early people. The year after Hutton's massive *Theory of the Earth* (1795) appeared, however, work began to be published in France that was soon to support the definition of such markers.

Notes and References

1. Ussher 1658:1.
2. Burnet 1684:4.
3. Burnet 1684:217.

4. Burnet 1684:314.
5. Gunther 1928:260.
6. Burnet 1690a:84.
7. Warren 1690.
8. Burnet 1690a:2.
9. Burnet 1690b:45.
10. Burnet in Blount *et al.* 1693:32.
11. Burnet in Blount *et al.* 1693:74.
12. Burnet in Blount *et al.* 1693:48.
13. Halley 1715:296.
14. Halley 1715:300.
15. See discussions in Burchfield 1975, Davies 1969, Gay 1966, and Porter 1977.
16. De Maillet 1748, Volume 2:54. See the discussion in Carozzi 1968. De Maillet's chronology was shortened to 5000 years in the English translation (de Maillet 1750).
17. See the discussion in Carozzi 1968.
18. Cassirer 1951.
19. Buffon 1753:v.
20. Buffon 1753:x.
21. Buffon 1753:xj.
22. Buffon 1749:98–99.
23. Buffon 1775.
24. Buffon 1778:34.
25. Buffon 1778:67.
26. Buffon 1778:67–68.
27. Buffon 1778:35.
28. de Luc 1779, Volume 1:24.
29. de Luc 1779, Volume 1:8–9.
30. de Luc 1779, Volume 5:660.
31. de Luc 1779, Volume 5:638–639.
32. de Luc 1779, Volume 5:661.
33. The publication history of Hutton's presentation is discussed in Eyles 1970; see also Dott 1969.
34. Davies 1969.
35. Hutton 1788:216.
36. Hutton 1788:215.
37. Hutton 1788:304.
38. Hutton 1788:217.
39. See Davies 1969, Dott 1969, Gillispie 1959, Porter 1977, and Rudwick 1972 for discussion of the responses to Hutton's *Theory of the Earth*.
40. Kirwan 1799:433.
41. Playfair 1802:125–127.
42. Rudwick 1972.
43. Kirwan 1799:433.

4

Extinct Mammals and Diluvium: Arriving at Time Markers

As long as the most superficial strata of the earth lacked known attributes indicative of a great age, the belief in human recency was secure from being questioned on geological grounds. Human remains were not present in undoubtedly ancient strata, such as those that provided coal. Those few human, or ostensibly human, bones that had been found in the upper strata could all be assigned to the time of the Deluge or to times just preceding that event (see Chapter 6). In fact, lacking any evidence to the contrary, the very presence of human remains implied the recency of those deposits.

At the end of the eighteenth century, this situation began to change dramatically. A set of geographically widespread time markers, linked with what were seen as major and geologically relatively recent events in earth history, were defined for the superficial strata. These markers allowed the uppermost layers of the earth to be placed securely in the general framework of earth history, whether or not they contained human remains. Indeed, as was soon demonstrated, these time markers could also be linked with the biblical chronology.

There were two related aspects to this development. The first involved acceptance of the fact that animals could become extinct, and, along with this acceptance, the recognition of a set of distinctive animals that had existed in the relatively recent geological past but that no longer existed. The second involved the analysis and interpretation of the superficial boulders, gravels, clays, and related materials that are now attributed to the action of Pleistocene glaciers. These two aspects were integrally related because the extinct animals were often found tightly associated with the superficial gravels and clays, and because the event that was at first thought to have caused the placement of those deposits was also felt to have caused the extinction of many or all of the animals. The extinct animals and superficial debris quickly became indicators of the last major event that had occurred in a directional earth history, and provided a means whereby the antiquity of humankind could be assessed empirically.

Although we are now surrounded by the reality of extinction, two centuries ago it was not at all clear that organisms could actually disappear from the face of the earth. Before the late 1700s, most of those who dealt with the history of life found the idea that an organism could become extinct to be an affront to the guardianship that the Creator maintained over His creations, and an attack as well on the principle of plenitude, of the fullness of the Creation and all that that implied. "The sacred phrase of the eighteenth century," Owen Lovejoy has said, was the "great chain of being,"[1] a phrase encapsulating the view that life consisted of a huge chain composed of vast, or infinite, numbers of links from the lowliest forms to the most perfect. The place that human beings were felt to occupy in this chain was such that they could look down to the amoeba and beneath, or up to the angels and beyond. The continuity among links in this chain also implied that removing a piece of that chain threatened the whole with destruction. Pope's famous lines express the concept well:

> Vast chain of being, which from God began,
> Natures aethereal, human, angel, man,
> Beast, bird, fish, insect! What no eye can see,
> No glass can reach! from Infinite to thee,
> From thee to Nothing!—On superior pow'rs
> Were we to press, inferior might on ours:
> Or in the full creation leave a void,
> Where, one step broken, the great scale's destroy'd:
> From Nature's chain whatever link you strike,
> Ten or ten thousandth, breaks the chain alike.
>
> [*Essay on Man,* 1733–1734].

This framework was strongly in place up to the 1790s. Thomas Jefferson's discussion of the remains of the extinct ground sloth *Megalonyx* from West Virginia, for instance, took place well within the bounds provided by this framework. Jefferson was no great paleontologist, and there can be no doubt that he pursued the study of the bones of large mammals for reasons that were as nationalistic as they were scientific.[2] Buffon, for instance, had argued in his *Natural History* that the productions of nature were weaker and smaller in the New World than they were in the Old, a view that Jefferson attempted to prove wrong not only by sending Buffon a moose, but also by studying and describing the huge animals known only from their bones and only from North America.

No matter what Jefferson's motivations and scientific skills, his approach to the question of whether this huge animal, which he thought was a carnivore but that was immediately recognized to be more closely allied to the sloths,[3] still existed displays the pervasiveness of the feeling that extinction could not occur. Although such an animal had never been seen alive in North America, Jefferson argued in 1799 that

> in fine, the bones exist: therefore the animal has existed. The movements of nature are in a never-ending circle. The animal species which has once been put into a train of motion, is probably still moving in that train. For if one link in nature's chain might be lost, another and another might be lost, till this whole system of things should evanish by piecemeal. . . . If this animal then has once existed, it is probable on this general view of the movements of nature that he still exists.[4]

Basing his argument on the continuity that characterized the relationships among organisms, Jefferson thus denied the possibility of extinction on the assumption that the chain of being would be disrupted "whatever link you strike." His denial was, in turn, similar to many others that appeared prior to the end of the eighteenth century.[5]

Many arguments for the reality of extinction made during the 1700s were made on the basis of fossil invertebrates that seemed to have no living counterparts. Given the prevailing theoretical framework, which denied the possibility of extinction, these arguments were easily countered by noting how poorly known the molluscan fauna of remote regions of the ocean floors were. In his *Essay toward a Natural History of the Earth* (1695), for instance, Woodward attempted to avoid the problem of extinction in the course of an argument that fossil shells were the remains of once-living organisms by noting that "there are many kinds of Shell-fish which lye perpetually concealed in the Deep, skreen'd from our Eyes by that vast world of Water, and which have their continual abode at the bottom of the Ocean, without ever approaching near the Shores."[6] If this approach were not sufficient by itself, it could be powerfully augmented by citing discoveries of existing populations of organisms that had first been described on the basis of fossil shells. Indeed, nearly a century after Woodward wrote his *Essay,* Jean-Guillaume Bruguière (1750–1799) used such discoveries as a reason to include fossil shells in his discussion of living molluscs, published in 1792: "having given the general history of shellfish, I must not neglect to describe the fossil shells, since it has been proven that all these shells have their marine analogs, and that many of them were long known in the fossil state before individuals of the same species were discovered living in the sea."[7]

It was Georges Cuvier who put an end to arguments against the possibility of extinction. Cuvier had been attracted to the study of natural history by reading Buffon as a child; he came to the National Museum of Natural History in Paris in 1795 as an anatomist, where he remained for the rest of his life. A brilliant scientist, Cuvier has been called the founder of both modern comparative anatomy and vertebrate paleontology, and it is certainly true that descriptive vertebrate paleontology emerged almost full-blown with Cuvier's work.

Cuvier took the argument against extinction based on invertebrates and turned it around, basing his arguments for extinction on animals so large that their future discovery on the hoof could not be used as a counter to his position. On the one hand, he noted, "we are still very far from being acquainted with all the testaceous animals and fishes belonging to the sea, and as we probably still remain ignorant of the greater part of those which live in the extensive deeps of the ocean, it is impossible to know, with any certainty, whether a species found in a fossil state may not still exist somewhere alive."[8] On the other hand, regarding large terrestrial quadrupeds, "there is little hope of one day finding those which we have seen only as fossils."[9] Beginning in 1796 with ground sloths and mammoths, Cuvier published detailed demonstrations, based on comparative osteology, that no living representatives of these animals were known to exist. These demonstrations quickly ended opposition to the concept of extinction. Indeed, the opposition had ended long before Cuvier gathered together the various separately published reports on vertebrate fossils and issued them, along with a lengthy *Preliminary Discourse,* as *Researches on the Fossil Bones of Quadrupeds* in 1812.

It proved easy to reconcile the power of the Creator with the fact of extinction. Soon after Jefferson's denial of the likelihood of extinction, many argued that it was a measure of God's omnipotence to have created a world in which pieces could be removed without the whole tumbling into a shambles.

James Parkinson was one such author. Parkinson (1755–1824) was a physician who was also active in political matters, at one time under suspicion of having been involved in an attempt to assassinate King George III. His name is in common use today as a result of his 1817 description of what is now called Parkinson's disease. Parkinson also published the first general summary in English of fossil vertebrates after the notion of extinction had become accepted. In the first volume of his *Organic Remains of a Former World* (1804), he had no trouble reconciling the fact of extinction with the goodness of the Creator:

> Some very good and learned men have regarded the loss of a single link, in the chain of creation, as inadmissible: it implying, they say, such a deviation from the first plan of creation, as might be attributed to a failure in the original design. But such an inference does by no means follow; since that plan, which prevents the failure of a genus, or species, from disturbing the general arrangement, and œconomy of the system, must manifest as great a display of wisdom and power, as could any fancied chain of beings, in which the loss of a single link would prove the destruction of the whole.[10]

By about the year 1800, then, it had become widely accepted that extinction not only could, but did, occur. The animals that Cuvier used to make his argument for extinction covered a broad period of time, many millions of years. But a large number of them, including ground sloths, mammoths, and mastodon, were Pleistocene in age. These animals had been discovered in the most superficial strata and were, therefore, the most recent of the extinct organisms he had described.

What had caused the extinctions? Cuvier carefully considered the kinds of processes he saw operating in the world today, and concluded that such slowly operating processes could not account for some of the major changes evidenced by the geological record. Inclined strata containing salt water molluscs, alternating sequences of terrestrial and marine deposits, frozen mammoth carcasses in Siberia, and a wealth of other well-described phenomena could, he felt, be explained only by calling on forces working more powerfully and more rapidly than any that had ever been seen in operation. Cuvier concluded that the extinction of the species of elephant, rhinoceros, and other quadrupeds that he had so carefully described had occurred as a result of some major, rapid change, some revolution as he called it, that had affected the surface of the earth.[11]

Unlike some later scientists, who called upon universal catastrophes to account for the extinction of Pleistocene mammals, Cuvier called on more localized events. Although he suggested that Siberian mammoths may have been terminated by rapid refrigeration, he placed major emphasis on localized floods caused by changing relationships between land and sea to explain the destruction of the mammoth and of the extinct quadrupeds with which they were so often associated. "If there is anything established in geology," he wrote in 1812, "it is that the surface of our globe was the victim of a great and sudden revolution that can date to no more than five or six thousand years ago,"[12] a revolution that saw low-lying areas inundated and the former seabed exposed. This rapid, but relatively local and transient, incursion of the sea caused the extinction of those species of mammals caught in its way. Recolonization of flooded areas then occurred from regions that had not been so affected. However, such modern animals as elephants and rhinoceroses could not have descended from the extinct European forms he had described, because those species had been totally exterminated. Had this not been the case, he asked, why do we not find elephants in places like Mexico or South America, places that seem well suited for them?[13] The causes of such revolutions were unknown but were, he felt, knowable.

Why did Cuvier lay such stress on flooding? The reason was not that he was explicitly concerned with demonstrating the reality of the biblical Deluge and the fate of the animals that had not made it onto the ark. There was, in fact, a great deal of evidence to suggest that the kind of flooding Cuvier had posited had occurred. Not only had some of his fossil bones come from deposits that also contained the remains of marine organisms, but many came as well from the superficial gravels that are now explained in terms of Pleistocene glaciation. De Luc had recently used the same kinds of superficial deposits to support his argument that the modern continents had recently been beneath the sea, and Cuvier cited de Luc's opinion in making his own argument. Cuvier, however, accepted the notion of flooding while remaining aloof on the issue of theological reconciliation, although he later noted the similarity between the teachings of science and the teachings of Genesis.[14] At the time, the best mechanism to account for the widespread, superficial gravels was, in fact, flooding. It was not until the late 1830s that an alternative cause was to be advanced in terms of glaciation, an argument made most influentially by Louis Agassiz in his *Studies on Glaciers* (1840).[15] And not until decades later did most geologists attribute low-elevation gravels in Europe and America that occurred far from major mountain masses to anything other than flooding. To call on floods to account for the gravels was good and convincing science.

For Cuvier, then, the superficial gravels and the extinction of such animals as the mammoth and the hippopotamus in Europe became chronologically linked to one another in tight fashion, since both had been caused by the same event. Since this event was also felt to have occurred some 5000 to 6000 years ago, a date based in part upon de Luc's natural chronometers, the gravels and extinct mammals provided a well-defined time marker that could be used to assess the date of the appearance of human beings in various parts of the earth. Cuvier was explicit about the relationship between these chronological markers and human antiquity:

> The human race did not exist in the countries in which the fossil bones of animals have been discovered, at the epoch when these bones were covered up; as there cannot be a single reason assigned why such men should have entirely escaped from such general catastrophes; or, if they had also been destroyed and covered over at the same time, why their remains should not now be found along with those of the other animals. I do not presume, however, to conclude that man did not exist at all before those epochs. He may have then inhabited some narrow regions, whence he went forth to repeople the earth after the cessation of these terrible revolutions and overwhelmings. Perhaps even the places which he inhabited may have sunk into the abyss, and the bones of the destroyed human race may yet remain buried under the bottom of some actual seas; all except a small number of individuals who were destined to continue the species. However this may have been, the establishment of mankind in those countries in which the fossil bones of land-animals have been found, that is to say, in the greatest part of Europe, Asia, and America, must necessarily have been posterior not only to the revolutions which covered up these bones, but also to those other revolutions, by which the strata containing the bones have been laid bare. Hence it clearly appears, that no argument for the antiquity of the human race in those countries can be founded either upon these fossil bones, or upon the more or less considerable collections of rocks or earthy materials by which they are covered.[16]

Cuvier thus argued that the absence of human remains in deposits that had yielded the bones of extinct mammals strongly implied the absence of people in these areas at the time the deposits had accumulated. Since this time was taken to be no more than 5000 or 6000 years ago, human beings must have appeared in these areas subsequent to that date. This temporal correlation made sense to Cuvier for a number of reasons. It was obvious, he felt, that the affected areas took on their modern appearance only after the last retreat of the sea. It was at this time as well that the nature of the surface of the earth in these regions began to be determined solely by the operation of the processes that can be seen in action today. The spread of people into western Europe, and into other previously inundated areas, thus coincided with the onset of modern geological conditions. A modern environment saw· the arrival of a modern fauna in these areas, a fauna that migrated in from elsewhere and that included human beings.

Cuvier's conviction that people existed somewhere prior to the last revolution can be seen throughout his *Preliminary Discourse,* including his discussion of the chronological implications of the magnitude of human knowledge. He examined these implications not simply because they had been used to support the notion of tremendous human antiquity, but also because he saw that they could be used against his arguments for a relatively recent catastrophe. "It may be objected," he observed, "that the advanced state of astronomy among these ancients is a striking proof of their high antiquity, and that it must have required a vast many centuries of observations by the Chaldeans and Indians to enable them to acquire the knowledge which they certainly possessed nearly three thousand years ago."[17] But such detailed astronomical knowledge did not imply any "prodigious" antiquity to Cuvier. Attainments of this sort, he pointed out, were fully possible in a short period of time for peoples who had no other sciences to attend to. Even two or three exceptional individuals could have taken astronomy this far in a few centuries. Even had this not occurred, however, the implication was only that astronomy was one of the sciences that had survived the last catastrophe, not that that catastrophe had not occurred.

For Cuvier, then, the last revolution was evidenced by the bones of extinct mammals or by the presence of the matrix that usually enclosed them. Empirical evidence suggested that in areas affected by this revolution, people appeared only after the transient incursion of the sea had ended. This appearance coincided as well with the appearance of a fully modern fauna and with the operation of only those geological processes that operate today. People had clearly existed somewhere prior to the last revolution, though where was not known. They certainly had not existed in the geologically known portions of Europe, Asia, and America; these regions they had entered, like all other mammals, after the waters had retreated.

Cuvier had a number of reasons for stressing the fact that the most recent episode of mammalian extinctions and the deposition of the gravels and clays had occurred prior to the arrival of human beings. To a large extent, his position could have been inductively derived from the fossil record itself. In 1812, there was no compelling evidence for any association between human relics and either the extinct mammals or the gravels. Nonetheless, in 1774 Johann Friedrich Esper had described such an association on the basis of discoveries he had made in Gailenreuth Cave in Germany, and Cuvier was fully familiar with the fossil bones that had come from this cave (see Chapter 6). Had Cuvier any reason to make the argument, he could have used Esper's work to do it. Cuvier's position on human recency was primarily theoretical in origin. Although his arguments were well supported by the paleontological record available in 1812, he maintained this position until his death in 1832, by which time a number of apparent associations between extinct mammals and human remains had been published.

Because Cuvier viewed a species as a group of organisms of common descent and functionally integrated to meet the demands of the environment in which they existed, he also saw each species as having appeared in any given area only when the environments to which they were adapted had appeared. Cuvier's reconstructions of many extinct species of vertebrates, his knowledge of fossil invertebrates, and his use of stratigraphic analysis to place those animals in an ordered scheme of earth history allowed him to show that the history of life on earth had not only been directional, but also that the nature of this direction had apparently been determined by the nature of the changing environments of the earth itself. In such a view, human beings would not be expected to appear until modern environmental conditions appeared. Cuvier's position on the recency of the human species in all areas that had been both affected by the last revolution and that were geologically known was fully consistent with this view. People, and the modern land animals with which they are now associated, had migrated into these regions after the last revolution had been completed.

But while human recency in these areas may have been consistent with Cuvier's general theoretical position, such consistency was not the reason for his careful arguments that no human relics had been found associated with the remains of the extinct mammals. Instead, his argument for human recency stemmed from his concern for documenting the reality of extinction itself. Such concerns had arisen because of contemporary speculations dealing with the possibility of the transformation of species through time, and in particular because of the transformationist hypotheses of Jean-Baptiste Lamarck (1744–1829).

Lamarck's evolutionary views had stemmed in part from his consideration of the possibility of extinction. A leading expert on both fossil and modern shells, Lamarck was fully aware that many fossil shells had no counterparts among living organisms. Only three explanations were available to account for these differences: the ancient organisms were extinct, or they still existed but had yet to be discovered, or they represented the ancestors of modern, transformed animals. Lamarck firmly rejected the first of these possibilities, since the general design and balance of nature seemed to preclude extinction for most kinds of organisms. Major catastrophic events of the sort that Cuvier called upon to account for extinction seemed to Lamarck to provide no explanation at all. Nature's processes worked uniformly through time, and catastrophes had played no important role in earth history. With no natural means of accounting for extinction, Lamarck denied the possibility for most kinds of animals, and adopted instead the two remaining explanations to account for the morphological differences between ancient and modern forms. Some of the animals represented in the fossil record still existed, awaiting discovery. Others represented the ancestors of transformed descendants.

Lamarck did not totally deny the possibility that organisms could become extinct. On the one hand, the simplest forms of life directly exposed to the harshness of nature's elements might succumb entirely. On the other hand, human predation might have caused the extinction of some large, slow-breeding mammals, including those Cuvier had described.[18] Lamarck and Cuvier thus differed over the general importance of extinction in life history, and, because of their very different views of the nature of earth history, over how the few extinctions Lamarck might be willing to admit were to be explained. They also differed over the possibility of transformation. Lamarck viewed life as organized into continuous categories and viewed species as fully mutable. Cuvier, viewing life as organized into discontinuous and fully integrated units called species, denied the possibility that one of these discrete units might be transformed into another. To Lamarck, ancient animals whose morphology differed from the most similar modern ones represented potential ancestors. To Cuvier, they represented animals that had become extinct because of changed conditions of life.

These were profound differences, and Cuvier's discussion of extinction and of the recency of the appearance of people in Europe, Asia, and America must be seen in their light. By arguing that the species of hippopotamus, rhinoceros, elephant, mastodon, and other animals he had described had been totally destroyed, Cuvier was removing a possible set of ancestors for a number of modern mammals. More importantly, since Lamarck was willing to concede this one point, by pointing out the absence of human remains with the bones of those extinct mammals Cuvier was also removing the only cause of extinction that Lamarck had allowed for these creatures. These were extinct forms, people could not have caused their extinction because people were simply not there, and some other, natural cause must have been involved. It was precisely those natural causes whose existence Lamarck had denied.[19]

Uppermost in Cuvier's mind, however, was the need to deny that the morphological distinctiveness displayed by the most recent extinct mammals could have been caused by the most powerful known cause of variability within a species: domestication. Lamarck had stressed this source of variability in his *Zoological Philosophy* (1809), and had used it to support the possibility of transformation. Now Cuvier had to demonstrate that this undoubtedly potent agent could not account for the characters that distinguished his extinct mammals from similar modern species. Therefore, Cuvier inserted his argument that "there are no fossil human bones" immediately after his discussion of variability within species, including variability caused by domestication. And he began his argument against the existence of human fossils by observing that the lack of human bones among the remains of extinct animals provides "more proof that the fossil races were not varieties [of modern species] since they could not have been subject to the influence of man."[20]

Cuvier was on very firm ground in taking these positions on human recency. In observing that in those areas that had been geologically explored, the arrival of people seemed to postdate 5000 to 6000 years ago and to be associated with the onset of modern geological conditions, Cuvier was repeating two chronological themes that were already widely accepted. People were recent in both the absolute sense of the biblical chronology and in the relative sense of having appeared only after the earth had become modern in form. Prior to Cuvier, however, these assertions had been based directly on the biblical chronology on the one hand, and on the absence of human remains in the ancient strata of the world on the other. Now Cuvier had provided a means of assessing human antiquity relative to the uppermost deposits of the earth. Deposits dating to 5000 to 6000 years ago were marked by a distinctive set of extinct mammals and by an equally distinctive set of gravels and clays, both of which had been deposited just before the onset of modern geological conditions in the affected areas. In concluding that "no argument for the antiquity of the human race in those countries can be founded either upon these fossil bones, or upon the more or less considerable collections of rocks or earthy materials by which they are covered," he had shown precisely how this chronological assessment could be made.

Cuvier's arguments were compelling, his influence on the scientific world deservedly vast. After his *Researches on the Fossil Bones of Quadrupeds* appeared in 1812, the extinct mammals and superficial gravels and clays were almost routinely treated as time markers against which human antiquity was to be assessed. This was true even though many who followed Cuvier proposed very different mechanisms for the deposition of the superficial gravels and for the extinction of the mammals whose remains were found in them. While the causes of deposition and extinction, and the speed with which those causes had operated, came to be the focus of much debate during the first half of the nineteenth century, it was nonetheless generally agreed that there was a temporally distinct set of units involved. Early in the century, prior to Agassiz's demonstration that at least some of the superficial gravels and related materials were glacial in origin, the usual mechanism called upon to explain them was flooding; the debate centered on the cause, extent, and speed of the flooding, not on whether the deposits formed a stratigraphically distinct unit. Indeed, William Buckland's term for these deposits, *diluvium*, referring to "those extensive and general deposits of superficial loam and gravel,"[21] became widely adopted after the appearance of Buckland's *Reliquiae Diluvianae* in 1823 (see Chapter 5) and continued in use long after the advent of glacial theory. But no matter what the term used to refer to these materials, and no matter what the mechanism called upon to explain them, they were recognized as a set of deposits differing in age from those above and below them, and the general relationship of such mammals as the woolly rhinoceros and woolly mammoth to them was recognized as well.

Superficial glacial deposits—diluvium—occurred in both the Old World and the New. During the early nineteenth century, these far-flung deposits were temporally correlated on the basis of general morphological similarity and because of their stratigraphically superficial position. This correlation also implied, using what by now was standard stratigraphic reasoning, the general temporal correlation of the fossils associated with the diluvium. Extinct Pleistocene mammals found outside of glaciated areas, and not associated with diluvium, were correlated through association with extinct mammals that were found in the diluvium—an extension of the principle of strata identified by fossils—and by the fact that they, too, were found in deposits close to the earth's surface. In addition, but even more generally, the animals were seen as forming a rough chronological group because they either belonged to extinct species of genera that still survived, or belonged to extinct genera with closely related survivors *and* were not found stratigraphically associated with more ancient animals belonging to genera now completely unknown. Thus, in 1812 Cuvier supported the recency of the extinct mammals of the superficial deposits by observing that "the most celebrated of the unknown species, which belong to known genera or to genera very near those that are known, such as the elephants, rhinoceroses, hippopotamuses, and fossil mastodons, are not found with the most ancient genera. It is only in the alluvium that they occur."[22]

In this fashion, the principles of stratigraphic correlation allowed the reconstruction of an entire fauna, although the proper placement of some animals routinely found in bog deposits (including the giant Irish deer and the American mastodon) posed problems throughout the century. But soon after the concept of extinction became generally accepted, it began to be accepted as well that there was a set of mammals generally associated with diluvium that must have become extinct at roughly the same time this material had been deposited.

Some felt the deposition of the diluvium and the extinction of the mammals incorporated in that material had occurred relatively rapidly. Since the cause of deposition was also felt to have been the cause of extinction, the temporal correlation between emplacement of the diluvium and the extinction of the mammals was seen as very tight. Cuvier, Buckland, and Agassiz, among many others,[23] treated diluvium and extinct mammals in this fashion. But even for those who argued that the diluvium had accumulated over long periods of time, and who argued as well that the extinctions had occurred slowly and one by one, the diluvium and fossil remains provided a time marker against which human antiquity could be assessed. The superficial gravels and extinct mammals, even if they did not mark a fairly precise point in time, still marked a series of events that had occurred in the geologically relatively recent past, but long enough ago that they seemed to most to predate the time allotted the human existence on earth by the biblical chronology. By their very nature they also marked a time when modern environmental conditions had yet to be established.

Thus Cuvier's demonstration of the extinction of numerous large quadrupeds, and his association of the most recent of these extinctions with the deposition of what soon came to be known as diluvium, provided for the first time a widespread set of time markers for the superficial deposits of the earth against which human antiquity could be judged. Cuvier himself showed how this could be done, using the markers to argue for human recency in a way that was fully consistent with accepted views of the age of humankind and in a way that also supported his position on the reality and nature of extinction. While interpretations of the extinct mammals and the superficial gravels were to vary across investigators and through time—variations that greatly affected the implications for any associated human relics—the question of the antiquity of our species could now be addressed in a much more precise way than had been possible before. Because of this very precision, however, for the first time it was now also possible for human remains in superficial deposits to be controversial.

Notes and References

 1. Lovejoy 1964:184; Rudwick 1972 contains a valuable discussion of eighteenth-century treatments of the possibility of extinction; see also Davies 1969.
 2. Osborn 1935 and Simpson 1942 discuss Jefferson's paleontology; Hindle 1974 places Jefferson's science in the broader framework of revolutionary America.
 3. Wistar 1799.
 4. Jefferson 1799:255–256.
 5. See the general discussion in Burkhardt 1977 and Rudwick 1972.
 6. Woodward 1695:26.
 7. Bruguière 1792:472.
 8. Cuvier 1812a:38–39.
 9. Cuvier 1812a:39.
10. Parkinson 1804:469–470. The first two volumes of *Organic Remains*, published in 1804 and 1808, dealt with plants and invertebrates; vertebrates were discussed in the third volume (1811). For a discussion of Parkinson's paleontological work, see Thackray 1976.
11. Cuvier 1812a.
12. Cuvier 1812a:110.
13. Cuvier 1812b, Volume 2:140; Cuvier 1806a.
14. Cuvier 1841.
15. Agassiz 1840.
16. Cuvier 1813:131–132.
17. Cuvier 1813:167–168.
18. See Lamarck 1801, 1809.
19. I have drawn on Burkhardt 1977 in my discussion; see also Rudwick 1972.
20. Cuvier 1812a:82.
21. Buckland 1823:2.
22. Cuvier 1812a:71.
23. See the general discussion in Grayson 1980 and 1983.

5

The Treatment of Human Antiquity in Early Nineteenth-Century Great Britain

In 1797, John Frere (1740–1807), at one time high sheriff of Suffolk and later a member of Parliament, wrote a brief letter describing his discovery in eastern England of a series of flint implements buried beneath deposits whose nature and faunal content suggested tremendous antiquity. (See Figure 5.1 for location of sites mentioned in the text.) Three years later, his letter was published in *Archaeologia*, the journal of the Society of Antiquaries:

> Sir,
>
> I take the liberty to request you to lay before the Society some flints found in the parish of Hoxne, in the county of Suffolk, which, if not particularly objects of curiosity in themselves, must, I think, be considered in that light, from the situation in which they were found. . . .
>
> They are, I think, evidently weapons of war, fabricated and used by a people who had not the use of metals. They lay in great numbers at the depth of about twelve feet, in a stratified soil, which was dug into for the purpose of raising clay for bricks.

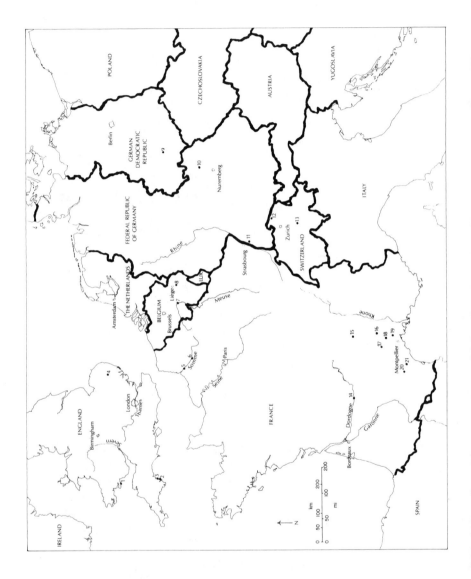

The strata are as follows:

1. Vegetable earth 1½ feet.
2. Argill 7½ feet.
3. Sand mixed with shells and other marine substances 1 foot.
4. A gravelly soil, in which the flints are found, generally at the rate of five or six in a square yard, 2 feet.

In the same stratum are frequently found small fragments of wood, very perfect when first dug up, but which soon decompose on being exposed to the air; and in the stratum of sand . . . were found some extraordinary bones, particularly a jaw-bone of enormous size, of some unknown animal, with the teeth remaining in it. I was very eager to obtain a sight of this; and finding it had been carried to a neighbouring gentlemen, I inquired of him, but learned that he had presented it, together with a huge thigh-bone, found in the same place, to Sir Ashton Lever, and it therefore is probably now in Parkinson's Museum.

The situation in which these weapons were found may tempt us to refer them to a very remote period indeed; even beyond that of the present world; but, whatever our conjectures on that head may be, it will be difficult to account for the stratum in which they lie being covered with another stratum, which, on that supposition, may be conjectured to have been once the bottom, or at least the shore, of the sea. The manner in which they lie would lead to the persuasion that it was a place of their manufacture and not of their accidental deposit; and the numbers of them were so great that the man who carried on the brick-work told me that, before he was aware of their being objects of curiosity, he had emptied baskets full of them into the ruts of the adjoining road. It may be conjectured that the different strata were formed by inundations happening at distant periods, and bringing down in succession the different materials of which they consist. . . .

If you think the above worthy the notice of the Society, you will please to lay it before them.

I am, Sir,
with great respect,
Your faithful humble servant,
John Frere[1].

The Society of Antiquaries did, in fact, think it was worthy of notice, for they published it. Here was an efficient, careful presentation of archaeological data. Frere had provided a brief description of stratigraphy, a note on the fossil remains contained in the stratum immediately overlying the human relics, illustrations of two of the artifacts (Figure 5.2), and his opinion that they were to be referred to "a very remote period indeed; even beyond that of the present world." Although there had been earlier presentations of human remains in stratigraphic contexts suggesting a substantial antiquity (see Chapter 6), Frere's

---

Figure 5.1. Location of major sites discussed in text. 1. Paviland Cave; 2. Brixham Cave; 3. Kent's Cavern; 4. Hoxne; 5. Abbeville (l'Hôpital, Menchecourt, Moulin Quignon); 6. Amiens (St. Acheul, St. Roch); 7. Chauvaux; 8. Engis, Engihoul, Chokier, Fond-de-Forêt; 9. Köstritz; 10. Gailenreuth Cave; 11. Lahr; 12. Oeningen quarries; 13. Altdorf; 14. Badegoule, Combe Grenal, Pech de l'Azé; 15. Le Puy (Denise); 16. Durfort; 17. Nabrigas; 18. Mialet; 19. Lunel-Viel, Pondres, Souvignargues; 20. Fauzan, Pontil; 21. Bize, Sallèles.

Figure 5.2. One of the two Hoxne handaxes illustrated by Frere (1800). Lacking any convincing demonstration of antiquity, the Paleolithic site at Hoxne was not rediscovered and placed in proper chronological context until 1859.

short letter provides the earliest published description of such a discovery in a clear and undeniable stratigraphic setting.

For all this, his discussion did not demand agreement with the assertion that the artifacts were truly ancient, belonging to a time when the geography of England was vastly different. Had he convincingly established an incursion of the sea, his arguments might have had impact, since Hoxne is some 30 kilometers from the shore, and Frere's pit some 35 meters above sea level.[2] However, his prime evidence for such an incursion came from the shells, and he had not identified these: he simply asserted that they were marine. Indeed, it was later shown that they were all of freshwater species.[3] In addition, he left the remains of the large quadruped unidentified: these came from an unknown animal, not an extinct one. Had he identified the shells accurately, or had he tracked down the bones in Parkinson's Museum (located in London; this was not the Parkinson of *Organic Remains*) and identified them accurately, things might have been different. However, as it stood, Frere attributed great antiquity to his discoveries, but had not provided the stratigraphic and faunal evidence that would have supported such antiquity. This is really not surprising because in 1797 Cuvier had just begun his work and his time markers were not yet developed.

In retrospect, the importance of Frère's discovery is clear. At the time, however, it was not at all clear, and it is no surprise that his brief publication caused no contemporary stir. It has often been asserted that Frère's work was neglected because the intellectual climate was firmly against the notion of great human antiquity.[4] This characterization of the intellectual climate is certainly true, as I have discussed, and in this regard it is important to note that the key phrase in Frère's presentation is ''beyond that of the present world.'' Frère was suggesting the possibility of people in a world not yet modern in form. Especially in England, this suggested in turn a world not yet fully prepared for our species by the Creator; this had a meaning far beyond what the words themselves might seem to imply. Since Frère had not made a convincing case for such unparalleled antiquity, it is not surprising that his paper generated no interest at the time. His publication went unnoticed for some six decades. It was only in the turmoil of the mid-nineteenth century arguments over human antiquity that his letter, and the data presented in it, reemerged to be discussed in the light of new, and more convincing, evidence for the extreme age of humankind on earth.

One can only speculate what might have happened had Frère returned to Hoxne armed with Cuvier's work, since Hoxne was to become one of the sites used at the end of the 1850s to confirm the great antiquity of our species. But Frère did not return, and Cuvier did not have to contend with Hoxne in any of his many critiques of the data that might support a substantial human antiquity.

Cuvier's first general critique of this sort was published in his *Preliminary Discourse* in 1812. That work was immediately translated into English, appearing in 1813 as an *Essay on the Theory of the Earth*. The same translation was published in the United States in 1818, with an added discussion of North American fossils by the New York physician Samuel Latham Mitchill (1764–1831).[5] In English, however, Cuvier's work took on a very different tone from that which he had given it. The new tone was provided by Robert Jameson (1774–1854), professor of natural history at the University of Edinburgh, who supplied the preface and a lengthy series of geological notes for the translation. Jameson's preface presented Cuvier's work as if it were a piece of British natural theology, the interpretation of the earth and its history as the Book of God's Works to be used as a supplement to the Book of His Words.[6] As part of this approach, Jameson explicitly equated Cuvier's last revolution with the biblical Deluge. The value of the work for an English reader was clear:

> Although the Mosaic account of the creation of the world is an inspired writing, and consequently rests on evidence totally independent of human observation and experience, still it is interesting, and in many respects important, to know that it coincides with the various phenomena observable in the mineral kingdom. The structure of the earth, and the mode of distribution of extraneous fossils or petrifactions, are so many direct evidences of the truth of the scripture account of the formation of the earth; and they might be used as proofs of its author having been inspired. . . . The deluge, one of the grandest natural events described in the Bible, is equally confirmed, with regard to its extent and the period of its occurrence, by a careful study of the various phenomena observed on and near the

earth's surface. The age of the human race, also a most important enquiry, is satisfactorily determined by an appeal to natural appearances; and the pretended great antiquity of some nations . . . is thereby shewn to be entirely unfounded. These inquiries, particularly what regards the *deluge,* form a principal object of the Essay of Cuvier. . . . Subjects so important . . . afford the highest pleasure to those who delight in illustrating the truth of the Sacred Writings, by an appeal to the facts and reasonings of natural history.[7]

Cuvier's *Preliminary Discourse* was, in fact, quite conformable with Scripture; Cuvier himself felt that all of science was so conformable.[8] Nonetheless, Cuvier's object was not the reconciliation of the facts of geology with the words of the Bible, nor does the *Preliminary Discourse* read as if this were his goal. Such direct reconciliation was a British, not a French, concern. Jameson had taken Cuvier's work and had, quite literally, converted it. Even before the translation had begun, however, and even before the *Preliminary Discourse* had been published in France, Cuvier's labors had made their mark in England and the process of reconciling Cuvier's science with revelation was well under way.

That process had been initiated in earnest by James Parkinson, whose survey of fossil vertebrates appeared in 1811 as the third volume of his *Organic Remains of a Former World* (Figure 5.3). Parkinson's discussions depended heavily on Cuvier's published accounts of ancient vertebrates, but Parkinson was intimately concerned with theological issues, and his work was fully within the British tradition of natural theology. Indeed, to Parkinson, the fact of extinction itself affords "a direct proof of the Creator of the universe continuing a superintending providence over the works of his hands."[9]

Although the bulk of his discussion was descriptive, Parkinson's conclusions directly addressed the issue of the relationship between the fossil record and the Mosaic account of earth history. He found that this entire record, from the earliest known rocks to the late appearance of human beings, was fully in accord with Genesis. "So close indeed is this agreement, that the Mosaic account is thereby confirmed in every respect, except as to the age of the world, and the distance of time between the completeness of different parts of the creation."[10] Not even this apparent chronological problem was crucial, however, since it disappeared as soon as the Mosaic day was taken as allegory: if "the word day be admitted as figuratively designating certain indefinite periods, in which particular parts of the great work of creation were accomplished, no difficulty will then remain."[11] Cuvier's localized revolution that had caused the last episode of extinction became, for Parkinson, the Noachian flood; the sporadic but repeated appearances of new kinds of organisms during earth history, including our own species, became evidence for the direct and repeated intervention of the Creator in that history.

When Cuvier discussed the lack of human fossils in 1812, he did it without any stated concern for its potential biblical meaning. For Parkinson, the issue of human antiquity had a very different import: "the creation of man, we are informed, was the work of the last period: and in agreement with his having been

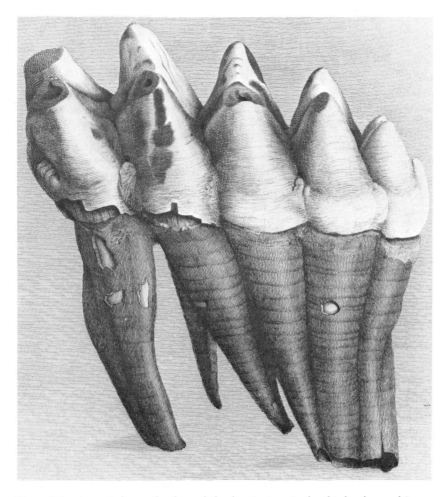

Figure 5.3. A mastodon molar formed the frontispiece to the third volume of James Parkinson's *Organic Remains of a Former World*. This volume provided the first general review of vertebrate paleontology in English after Cuvier's demonstration of the reality of extinction, and began the incorporation of Cuvier's approach to earth and life history into British natural theology.

created after all the other inhabitants of the earth is the fact, that not a single decided fossil relic of man has been discovered.''[12] By ''we are informed,'' Parkinson meant the informing agency to be Genesis, and he cited Genesis 1:26: ''And God said, Let us make man in our image, after our likeness: and let them have dominion over the fish of the sea, and over the fowl of the air, and over the cattle, and over all the earth, and over every creeping thing that creepeth upon the earth.''

But the Bible provided Parkinson with two items of information, only one of which was welcome. Genesis stated that human beings were created last, and this statement was in line with Parkinson's interpretation of the paleontological record that Cuvier had provided. No human remains had been found in or beneath debris attributed to the Deluge. This was the welcome information. But Genesis also stated that people had been created before the Flood. If this were the case, why were there no human remains in or beneath Flood deposits or found with the extinct mammals? Parkinson was aware of the problem, but did not deal with it directly:

> Not a single fossil relic of man has been discovered. This last circumstance will be considered by many as contradicting the account of the Deluge, by which the earth, with man, was said to have been destroyed; since in the remains of the deluged world man might be expected to be found in subterraneous situations. The fact, however, is, that although no remains of man are found, the surface of the earth, which is inhabited by man, displays, even at the present day, manifest and decided marks of the mechanical agency of violent currents of water. Nor is there a single stratum of all those which have been mentioned which does not exhibit undeniable proofs of its having been broken, and even dislocated, by some tremendous power, which has acted with considerable violence on this planet, since the deposition of the strata of even the latest formation.[13]

By equating Cuvier's last revolution with the Deluge, Parkinson had created a real dilemma. Either people had existed with a fauna, and therefore in a region of the earth, that was anything but modern in form, or the correlation of the extinctions and the superficial deposits with the Deluge was incorrect. But even if the human species could have existed in such a different, pre-Deluge environment, placing them there left open the possibility that even more ancient peoples might have existed. To Parkinson, one of the values of paleontological evidence was that it showed theories such as Hutton's to be wrong, that it falsified "that system . . . which considers the form and structure of the surface of this planet, as resulting from a regularly recurring series of similar mutations."[14] Here was a prospect even less welcome than the appearance of our species in environments not quite prepared for it. If people existed in such environmentally different regions at such relatively remote times, what was to guarantee that even older relics of our species from even more different environments would not be found, or that others might not take the opportunity to build the human species into a Huttonian system of endlessly recurring similar mutations? It was the need to deny such a possibility that led Parkinson to deny in turn the coexistence of people with the mammals whose extinctions had been caused by the Deluge. He was fully aware of Esper's discovery of human bones at Gailenreuth Cave, since he had discussed both the cave and its extinct mammals in some detail and had extracted parts of Esper's monograph in the course of that discussion. Yet he chose to pass by those bones in silence in order to avoid placing people in environments not yet modern, and in order to stress the recency of our species.

The possibilities inherent in the other choice were simply too great for him to accept any of the shaky evidence for pre-Deluge human remains in or beneath the Flood deposits of Europe. His solution to the dilemma posed by that denial was to evade the problem by simply stressing the magnitude of the evidence for the Deluge. The geological record having provided such clear indications that the Flood had occurred, the absence of human remains from within or beneath Flood debris was a problem, but not a major one. Later authors were to deal with this difficulty in a much more convincing way, but for Parkinson the most important point was the recency of the evidence for the appearance of people on earth, "the last and highest work appearing to be *man*."[15]

Parkinson's arguments were important, for they laid the groundwork for the English approach to human antiquity during the first part of the nineteenth century. He had taken the paleontological evidence for the history of life on earth, shown that it meshed with the Mosaic account, and built human history into that picture, with our species appearing as the last in a progressive sequence of organic creations. Cuvier had provided the tools by which to assess human antiquity; Parkinson had shown that these tools could be linked to events described by Genesis and that, as a result, the paleontological record provided a means of demonstrating the accuracy of Genesis insofar as it applied to *all* of human history. This was, of course, all very different from Cuvier's approach. While it was certainly no accident that Cuvier's results matched Scripture so well, Cuvier's arguments for human recency had much more to do with his defense of extinction than they had to do with Genesis, and Cuvier was careful to argue that people had existed somewhere before the last revolution. Parkinson had begun the process of conversion that Jameson was to help along after the appearance of the *Preliminary Discourse* in 1812, and in so doing had clearly demonstrated the contribution that studies of the superficial deposits of the earth could make to this aspect of natural theology. Indeed, it is possible that one of the reasons Jameson felt so secure in offering the *Preliminary Discourse* as confirmation of Scripture was the reconciliation that Parkinson had already offered in the third volume of *Organic Remains*. Jameson had certainly read it by the time he prepared his preface, since he borrowed, but did not cite, Parkinson's description of Gailenreuth Cave (which Parkinson had taken directly from Esper) for his notes to the translation.[16]

Although Parkinson laid the groundwork, it was William Buckland (1784–1856) who solidified Parkinson's modification of Cuvier's approach. Trained as a minister, Buckland spent much of his life doing geology and paleontology. In 1813, he accepted an appointment in mineralogy at Oxford; 6 years later he took the newly created readership in geology at the same institution, and became the influential teacher of many of Britain's young geologists.

Buckland's inaugural lecture at Oxford in 1819 was meant to illustrate the powerful role that geology could play in natural theology, a role in which

"Philosophy becomes associated in its Natural and just office, as the faithful auxiliary and handmaid of Religion."[17] For Buckland, one of the wonders of geology was not only that it provided evidence for the wise design of the earth by a superintending Omnipotent Architect, but that it also provided evidence that the Creator continually exerted His will through secondary laws that guided the history of the earth toward beneficial ends. Like Parkinson, Buckland was concerned with the specter of eternalism and felt that through the study of the facts of earth history, "the hypothesis of an eternal succession of causes is thus at once removed."[18] Further, the study of geology showed, just as it had for Parkinson, that the Mosaic account of Creation and subsequent events was correct in all its major points, including "the two great points . . . of the low antiquity of the human race, and the universality of a recent deluge."[19] These points, he felt, were "most satisfactorily confirmed by every thing that has yet been brought to light by Geological investigations."[20]

Buckland's inaugural lecture was published in 1820 as *Vindicae Geologicae, or the Connexion of Geology with Religion Explained*. He followed this in 1823 with his greatest work, *Reliquiae Diluvianae (Relics of the Flood)*. This classic book was written explicitly to deal with the second of Buckland's two great points, the universality of the Deluge. In it, he attempted to

> throw new light on a period of much obscurity in the physical history of our globe; and, by affording the strongest evidence of an universal deluge, leads us to hope, that it will no longer be asserted, as it has been by high authorities, that geology supplies no proofs of an event in the reality of which the truth of the Mosaic records is so materially involved.[21]

Buckland thus wished to show that the paleontology and geology of western Europe in specific, and of many other parts of the world in general, supported the biblical accounts of the Noachian flood. Although his aims and concerns were much the same as Parkinson's, his ammunition and skills in this area were much more powerful. He proceeded by examining the paleontology and geology of a number of cave and fissure sites in Western Europe, in particular from England. In addition, he reviewed a wide range of evidence for diluvial action from many other parts of the world, with most attention paid to Europe. From this review, he concluded that "we may for the present rest satisfied with the argument that numberless phenomena have already been ascertained, which without the admission of an universal deluge, it seems not easy, nay, utterly impossible, to explain."[22] He had, in fact, reached the identical conclusion several years before, prior to gaining much of the evidence presented in *Reliquiae Diluvianae*, and had published that identical conclusion in *Vindicae Geologicae* in 1820.

Buckland's arguments were carefully and tightly made. Much of the evidence that he amassed in support of a universal deluge—for instance, valleys out of proportion to the streams they now contain, grooved and striated rocks, huge boulders far from their source, and deep gravel deposits—was later to be accounted for by glacial theory. It is all too easy to read Buckland now and dismiss his brilliance, but that would be a mistake. Buckland was a superb scientist, a superb natural theologian, and a superb writer; his *Reliquiae Diluvianae* was an important and influential contribution to paleontology and geology.

To Buckland, the relationship of Pleistocene mammals to diluvial deposits left little doubt as to the cause of their extinction:

> How is it possible to explain the general dispersion of all these remains, but by admitting that the elephants as well as all the other creatures whose bones are buried with them, were the antediluvian inhabitants of the extensive tracts of country over which we have been tracing them? and that they were all destroyed together, by the waters of the same inundation which produced the deposits of loam and gravel in which they are embedded.[23]

As had Parkinson, Buckland relied heavily on the great Cuvier as an authority; as had Parkinson, Buckland transformed Cuvier's last revolution, producing a universal deluge where Cuvier had posited something much less. How, then, did Buckland treat the first of his two great points, the antiquity of the human race?

By the time Buckland wrote, a number of associations between extinct Pleistocene mammals and human remains had been discovered. Many of these, in fact, had resulted from Buckland's own work. Buckland discussed in some detail the nine cases of which he was aware. All nine of the possible associations had been provided by evidence from caves or fissures, six in England, the remaining three in Germany. All involved human bones, though in some cases artifacts had been found as well, and Buckland had examined a number of the sites personally. Buckland came to the same conclusion for all of these sites: "the human bones are not of the same antiquity with those of the antediluvian animals that occur in the same caves with them."[24] The associations were apparent only, and had resulted from the accidental intermixture of materials of very different ages.

The most famous of these sites today is Paviland Cave, or Goat's Hole, a limestone cavern overlooking the sea near Swansea in Wales. Buckland was told of the discovery of fossil bones in this site late in 1822, and he quickly visited the cave and took part in the excavation of its deposits. Those excavations revealed not only further remains of extinct mammals, but also the presence of scattered human bones and "a small flint, the edges of which had been chipped off, as if by striking a light."[25] In addition, Buckland himself discovered a partial human skeleton located some 15 centimeters beneath the surface of the cave floor, a skeleton that had been covered with red ocher and was accompanied by bone and ivory artifacts. Although Buckland at first felt the skeleton to be that of a male, he was soon convinced by the presence of the apparently decorative ivory cylinders and rings that he was dealing with the remains of a woman. As the illustration in *Reliquiae Diluvianae* makes clear, the bones of extinct mammals did not lie far away (Figure 5.4).

Here, it seemed, was yet another relic of the Flood. Had Buckland wished

Figure 5.4. Buckland's schematic profile of Paviland Cave (1823). Buckland's illustration shows the close physical relationship between the Red Lady and the remains of a mammoth. Nonetheless, the association was rejected not only by Buckland, but by others until long after a great human antiquity had been established.

to further his argument that the diluvium had really been deposited by the Deluge, he certainly could have used this skeleton to do so. Instead, he took a very different approach and argued that the skeleton represented a postdiluvian intrusive burial. He noted the presence of the remains of a British camp on the hill above the cave, and suggested that this camp threw "much light on the character and date of the woman under consideration; and whatever might have been her occupation, the vicinity of a camp would afford a motive for residence, as well as the means of subsistence, in what is now so exposed and uninviting a solitude."[26] Although Buckland did not publish his speculations on her possible occupation, in his correspondence he suggested that she may have been "a dealer in Witchcraft."[27] He concluded that the bones in question were contemporaneous with the occupation of the British camp and either predated or were coeval with the Roman occupation of Britain.

The Red Lady of Paviland, as the skeleton became known because of its associated red ocher, was in fact a male, as W. J. Sollas showed in 1913. Whether or not the skeleton was precisely contemporary with the extinct mammals of the cave cannot be known today, although it certainly could have: a radiocarbon date of approximately 18,500 years ago has been obtained from it. Even in the wake of the acceptance of a great human antiquity, however, the Red Lady was felt to postdate the extinct mammals of the cave.[28]

Buckland used similar arguments to conclude that all known associations between human remains and extinct mammals or diluvium were spurious, involving the chance association of postdiluvian human bones or artifacts with earlier debris. He could not have been more explicit about his stand on this issue: "human bones have not been discovered in any of those diluvial deposits which have hitherto been examined."[29] In addition, the very number of extinct mammal bones that had been found in the diluvium implied to him that those animals must have been abundant at the time of the Flood. Had human beings been present, he observed, the animals would not have been so common; so many wild beasts were incompatible with a human presence. As a result, not only had human remains not been found in those parts of the world in which the diluvium had been explored, but it was "highly improbable that they ever will be found."[30]

In concluding that no human remains had been found securely in or beneath the diluvium, Buckland was as aware as Parkinson had been of the strain that this created with his equation of the diluvium with Noah's Flood. Buckland's position against admitting the evidence for pre-Deluge peoples resulted from his hesitation to place the human species with a fauna that was anything but modern in form, and from his desire to demonstrate human recency as best he could. To allow antediluvian peoples in places that were geologically known, such as Europe, was to leave open the possibility of vastly early peoples. Denying all evidence for antediluvian peoples in geologically known areas allowed him to establish that as far as such areas were concerned, the human species was recent. All of these concerns were very similar to Parkinson's.

Where, then, were pre-Deluge peoples to be found? Buckland gave a much more satisfactory answer to this question than Parkinson. The remains of antediluvian peoples were to be found in central or southern Asia, the cradle of the human race and a region in which the extinct mammals of the diluvium of other areas were as yet unknown. Because Buckland also saw the presence of large numbers of the extinct creatures as incompatible with the presence of people, he had good reason to doubt that the animals would ever be found here in number, if at all; lacking extinct antediluvium creatures, the fauna would be much more modern in form. Indeed, the only diluvial mammals that Buckland mentioned for central or southern Asia were horse and deer, fully modern forms. All this formed a consistent picture. People were very recent in Europe, but, as Scripture suggested, more ancient in Asia; nowhere were they known from an earth not yet modern in form.

Buckland tackled head-on the issues he had laid out 3 years earlier in *Vindicae Geologicae*. He hung the truth of the Mosaic account of human history on "two great points" and argued forcefully for the accuracy of both these points: the Deluge had occurred, and people were recent. Buckland, of course, was not original in intertwining the recency of people and the reality of the Deluge with the truth or falsehood of the Mosaic account and in using empirical observations of the time markers Cuvier had provided to prove the case. Parkinson had done that before him. Buckland, however, did a far superior job. Indeed, in *Reliquiae Diluvianae* he argued the case in such a scientifically meticulous way that even when stripped of its biblical overtones, and even when stripped of the Deluge itself, his cautious treatment of the age of human skeletal remains and artifacts from British and German diluvial deposits and his argument that people postdated the diluvium still made sense. Buckland took the accepted British view of human antiquity that people were created last, relatively recently, and in an environmentally modern world, demonstrated that the available facts from the earth were in accord with that view, and accomplished this demonstration in a work of great scientific merit. While Parkinson had laid the groundwork, Buckland built the structure itself. His general approach and specific arguments provided the mainstay of the treatment of potentially ancient human remains in Britain until late in the 1850s. Much of that influence, however, was to be transmitted by an individual whose positions on many theoretical issues were very different from Buckland's.

Reliquiae Diluvianae proved very popular. The initial publication of 1000 copies sold quickly, and a second edition, identical to the first except for title page details, appeared in 1824. Even this edition was nearly half sold before it appeared.[31] This success spurred Buckland's plans to produce a sequel, but the sequel never appeared because British geologists as a whole soon came to realize that the phenomena attributed to a single flood by the diluvialists could not be adequately explained by that event. By the late 1820s, it began to seem clear that diluvial deposits of different regions were not of the same age, that the diluvium of a given area had been deposited at different times, and that such things as the sinuous morphology of deeply incised stream channels could not have been caused by a single, violent rush of water. These and other facts were inconsistent with the Deluge hypothesis.

The abandonment of the Flood by British geologists as a cause of the deposition of diluvium was symbolized by the presidential addresses of Adam Sedgwick (1785–1873) to the Geological Society of London in 1830 and 1831. In the first of these addresses, he pointed out that many of the phenomena that had been attributed to the Deluge seemed to belong to "many successive periods."[32] In the second, he abandoned the Deluge entirely:

> Bearing upon this difficult question, there is, I think, one great negative conclusion now incontestably established—that the vast masses of diluvial gravel, scattered over the surface of the earth, do not belong to one violent and transitory period. It was indeed a most unwarranted conclusion, when we assumed the contemporaneity of all the superficial gravel of the earth. We saw the clearest traces of diluvial action, and we had, in our sacred history, the record of a general deluge. On this double testimony it was, that we gave a unity to a vast succession of phenomena, not one of which we perfectly comprehended, and under the name diluvium, classed them all together. To seek the light of physical truth by reasoning of this kind is, in the language of Bacon, to seek the living among the dead, and will ever end in erroneous induction. . . . Having been myself a believer, and, to the best of my power, a propagator of what I now regard as a philosophic heresy . . . I think it right, as one of my last acts before I quit this Chair, thus publicly to read my recantation.[33]

Parkinson's dilemma, the lack of human remains in or beneath diluvium, was no longer a problem. Indeed, for Sedgwick this lack became part of the proof that the diluvium had not been deposited by the biblical Deluge. "We ought," he observed, "to have paused before we first adopted the diluvian theory, and referred all our old superficial gravels to the action of the Mosaic flood. For of man, and the works of his hand, we have not yet found a single trace among the remnants of a former world entombed in these ancient deposits."[34] These conclusions, Sedgwick was careful to note, were not opposed to the sacred records: the foundations of moral and physical truths are independent of one another, and science, by documenting undoubted instances of paroxysmal change in earth history, had shown that the biblical Deluge was a physical possibility, even if the evidence for it had yet to be discovered.

Buckland himself gave up the universal Deluge during the late 1820s, and a decade later adopted Louis Agassiz's equally catastrophic glaciers to account for the deposition of much of the diluvium.[35] In 1839, the geologist Roderick I. Murchison (1792–1871) argued that the term diluvium should be dropped because of its association with the Flood. In its place, he suggested the term *drift*, since much of the diluvium was now felt to have been deposited during periods of marine submergence, during which icebergs had drifted over submerged portions of the continents, ultimately dropping their rocky loads to produce the gravels and boulders that made up so much of the diluvium.[36]

The general abandonment of the equation between Noah's Flood and both the mammalian extinctions and the deposition of the diluvium completely altered the chronological and environmental implications of these events with regard to human antiquity. First, if the diluvium had not been deposited by the Flood, it could not be linked in any clear way with the biblical chronology. The loss of this absolute time marker meant the loss of any immediately convincing scientific support for the biblical chronology derived from the fact that human remains were not associated with either the mammals or the diluvium. As a result, explicit references to the Mosaic chronology become very difficult to find after about 1830, although they were not uncommon before that time. Those that did discuss the biblical chronology after this time had primarily theological, not scientific, interests. Indeed, such discussions were mostly produced by theologians who happened to do natural history, rather than by individuals who, no matter what their training, had a major orientation toward science. It is telling that many of these people also continued to equate the diluvium and the extinctions with Noah's Flood. The biblical chronology remained important to many of the scientists who dealt with human antiquity after 1830, as the discussions of this issue after a great human antiquity had been established clearly show (see Chapter 9). However, once the diluvium and extinctions on the one hand, and the Deluge on the other, were decoupled, direct scientific access to the absolute time of the human appearance on earth was lost, and explicit concern with the biblical chronology receded far into the background.

Second, if the diluvium had not been deposited by the Deluge, it appeared that it must be much older than the Deluge equation had suggested. The fauna alone now bespoke a great antiquity. The increased age of the diluvium and its extinct mammals thus made an association between either the deposits or the creatures far less likely and far more dangerous. So did the fact that it was now fully clear that the earth had not become modern in form until after the diluvium had been deposited and the mammals had become extinct. There could be no doubt that these were, as Sedgwick said, "the remnants of a former world." As Sedgwick also observed, the lack of human remains in or beneath the diluvium, previously something of a problem, now became precisely what one would in fact expect. All fit together much better than it had before. The diluvium was much older than had been thought, it marked in an unequivocal way a period of time before the earth had become modern in form, and the lack of human remains in or beneath it either confirmed these new facts or followed from them.

The changed interpretation of the diluvium and of its extinct mammals thus made any associated human relics pregnant with unwelcome meaning, unless the associations were somehow accidental. Much more so then when Buckland had written his *Reliquiae Diluvianae* only a few years earlier, such an association would implicate the accuracy of revelation through its implication of the biblical chronology. Even more important, given the secondary role of that chronology in the moral lessons of Scripture, such an association would question the very notion of the designed history of the earth. "Geology," Murchison wrote in 1839, "in expounding the former conditions of the globe, convinces us, that every variation of its surface has been but a step towards the accomplishment of one great end; whilst all such revolutions are commemorated by monuments, which revealing the course and object of each change, compel us to conclude, that the earth can alone have been fashioned into a fit abode for Man by the ordinances of INFINITE WISDOM."[37] The implications of human beings on an earth before it had been so fashioned are clear.

It was to produce one or more works demonstrating "*the Power, Wisdom, and Goodness of God,*"[38] in fact, that in 1829 the eighth Earl of Bridgewater left £8000 and its proceeds. Eight authorized Bridgewater Treatises appeared, including Buckland's *Geology and Mineralogy Considered with Reference to Natural Theology* (1836). Buckland's contribution focused on the evidence provided by geology and mineralogy for "prospective wisdom and design"[39] in the structure and history of the earth. It was thus fully appropriate that he took this opportunity to reexamine the question of human antiquity, a question integrally related to the development of a designed earth.

Observing that the diluvium could no longer be taken as providing evidence for the Deluge, Buckland observed as well that if human remains had been found in secure association with the remains of extinct mammals, this fact would be difficult to reconcile "with our received chronology."[40] Although a number of such associations had by now been reported from France and Germany (see Chapter 6), Buckland argued that none of them were valid. In passages that encapsulated the British view of the causes of the co-occurrence of human relics with both extinct mammals and diluvium—and whose message was to be repeated again and again during the coming decades—Buckland argued that

the occasional discovery of human bones and works of art in any stratum, within a few feet of the surface, affords no certain evidence of such remains being coeval with the matrix in which they are deposited. The universal practice of interring the dead, and frequent custom of placing various instruments and utensils in the ground with them, offer a ready explanation of the presence of the bones of men in situations accessible for the purpose of burial. . . . Frequent discoveries have also been made of human bones, and rude works of art, in natural caverns, sometimes enclosed in stalactite, at other times in beds of earthy materials, which are interspersed with bones of extinct species of quadrupeds. These cases may likewise be explained by the common practice of mankind in all ages, to bury their dead in such convenient repositories. The accidental circumstance that many caverns contained the bones of extinct species of other animals, dispersed through the same soil in which human bones may, at any subsequent period have been buried, affords no proof of the time when these remains of men were introduced. Many of these caverns have been inhabited by savage tribes, who, for convenience of occupation, have repeatedly disturbed

portions of soil in which their predecessors may have been buried. Such disturbances will
explain the occasional admixture of fragments of human skeletons, and the bones of
modern quadrupeds, with those of extinct species, introduced at more early periods, and by
natural causes.[41]

The disturbances created by people themselves, then, provided a likely explanation of many apparent associations between extinct mammals and human remains. But in the case of caverns there was yet another powerful cause of such
associations. Because many caverns are subject to sporadic flooding, while
others routinely contain running water, deposits of very different ages can easily
become intermixed and mislead the unwary investigator. Buckland concluded
that there was no evidence that people had coexisted with the extinct beasts.
Although the issue could not as yet be regarded as completely settled since so
much of the superficial deposits of the globe were unexplored, "the fact of no
human remains having as yet been found in conjunction with those of extinct
animals, may be alleged in confirmation of the hypothesis that these animals
lived and died before the creation of man."[42]

Although Buckland may have regarded the fact as incompletely settled,
however, it is also true that he lent his hand wherever he could to ensure that
when it was, it would be settled in the most likely direction. Kent's Cavern is a
case in point.

A series of solution chambers formed in limestone, Kent's Cavern is located
on the southern coast of Devonshire, southwestern England. It is one of the more
frequently excavated sites in England. In addition to unrecorded diggings, more
than 15 different organized excavations have taken place here since the first
recorded holes were dug in 1824. In that year, two small, separate excavations
took place, followed by a third that was, in part, conducted by Buckland. Recent
excavations in the cavern have been archaeologically oriented, since the first
human occupations here date well into the Pleistocene. Indeed, it is possible that
the site contains the earliest known archaeological deposits in England.

The early work that Buckland conducted here did not come to much; he
concluded that ancient deposits were not to be found in the site. John B. Campbell and C. Garth Sampson have suggested that Buckland may have reached this
conclusion because his excavations involved only the superficial deposits near
the entrance of the cavern—deposits that contain only iron age material—and the
excavators failed to penetrate the hard travertine layer beneath this material,
perhaps thinking that they had reached the floor of the cave.[43]

In 1825, 1826, and then again in 1829, further excavations were conducted
in Kent's Cavern by Reverend John MacEnery (1796–1841), chaplain at nearby
Tor Abbey.[44] MacEnery's work was fairly extensive. Unlike the earlier digging
in which Buckland had participated, MacEnery's excavations penetrated the hard
travertine layer. "Perceiving that it was in vain to look for the fossils without
first piercing the crust, which stood between them and the mould under-foot,"[45]

MacEnery noted, he went to a spot that appeared disturbed, and, sorting through the materials in that disturbance, found fossil teeth:

> They were the first fossil teeth I had ever seen, and as I laid my hands on these relics of distinct races, and witnesses of an order of things which passed away with them, I shrunk back involuntarily; though not insensible to the excitement attending new discoveries, I am not ashamed to own, that, in the presence of these remains, I felt more of awe than joy.[46]

MacEnery did not share this initial discovery with others working in the cave with him, fearing that his discoveries might be damaged or lost. He was, he continued, "anxious to send them in a state in which they were found to Oxford,"[47] that is, to Buckland.

MacEnery's letter and specimens reached Buckland, who in turn urged him to continue his work. This MacEnery did, and the list of fellow excavators he provides is telling, since it indicates the tremendous interest that had been generated in the study of fossils. This list included, among others, Sir Thomas Acland (1787–1871), a member of Parliament at the time; Dr. Henry Beeke (1751–1837), Bishop of Bath and Wells and an authority on finance; and Sir Walter Trevlyan (1797–1879), an Oxford-trained naturalist. These were not eccentrics following some odd fashion; they were members of British high society pursuing what had become a passion for natural history, directed toward fossils by the work of Buckland. Buckland himself, in fact, assisted with the work on several occasions.

In continuing his search, MacEnery penetrated beneath the hard travertine layer and discovered the remains of extinct mammals intermixed with undoubted stone tools. "I dug under the regular crust, and flints presented themselves to my hand,—this electrified me."[48] He then excavated further in the presence of his assistant to ensure that the discovery could be repeated and observed by a second party, which it was. What he had discovered, he noted, was the presence of stone tools "in indurated masses consisting of decidedly antediluvian or diluvian materials, viz., fossil bones and rolled pebbles."[49]

Here, then, was the end of the search for antediluvian human remains. MacEnery had doubtless found the results of human activities in the form of stone tools, in association with both extinct mammals and diluvium. Or had he?

There can be no doubt that MacEnery had found what it appeared he had found. Later excavations at Kent's Cavern show that this is so.[50] In addition, MacEnery was quite explicit—electrified, in fact—about the association between stone tools and extinct mammals here. He also held the opinion that, since modern mammals are found associated with the extinct ones, there is no reason why the remains of our own species, who are "allowed to have lived before the last catastrophe that destroyed animal life on the globe,"[51] should not be found with extinct animals as well. Yet even though this was the case, MacEnery concluded that man did not, at the epochs alluded to, co-exist in this country with the animal population, and that the latter held sovereign and undivided dominion over the tract above and the regions beneath. From hence, and from the different circumstances of the flints in the loam, we are also justified in concluding that these instruments owe their introduction to the era when the wild tenants of the woods and caves had ceased to exist, and were inhumed in the loam, and were succeeded by savage men in the possession of both . . . and that man consequently became the allocated inhabitant of this region immediately after the deluge; which is assigning him a higher antiquity in this country than has hitherto been admitted.[52]

MacEnery provided a number of reasons for considering the association between the tools and the extinct mammals and diluvium to be fortuitous. He noted, for instance, that no human bones had been found along with the flint implements, that stone tools had not been found with the remains of extinct mammals throughout the deposit, and that the "enormous multitudes of ravenous wild beasts which swarmed through the surrounding plains"[53] and contributed their bones to Kent's Cavern were themselves incompatible with the presence of humans here. This last argument, of course, came directly from Buckland. MacEnery thus concluded that while he had discovered the remains of early people, earlier than had ever been found before in England, they were not *that* early: they were immediately post-Deluge. This was a respectable antiquity, since he followed the biblical chronology in dating the Flood to between 4000 and 5000 years ago. But it was an antiquity fully compatible with the notion that people and the extinct mammals had not coexisted.

Why did MacEnery take this step? He took it because of Buckland. In the course of his discussion of the materials from Kent's Cavern, MacEnery enumerated and discussed a series of sites from which human remains of supposed great antiquity had been reported; he then concluded this discussion by quoting the critique Buckland had provided of such assertions in his Bridgewater treatise. In the very next sentence, MacEnery stated that

had I not devoted so long a period to personal examination of all the circumstances attending this delicate question, I should have fallen in common with others into the error of supposing human remains to be contemporaneous because conjoined with the deposit of mud and bones.—Into this opinion I fell at first from the discovery of flint blades in contact with both in several parts of the cavern and the alternation of stalagmite, and I communicated my impression to Dr. Buckland with all the earnestness of sincere conviction.[54]

It was only as a result of his extended observations in the cavern, he ended, that he realized that his initial opinion was mistaken.

There is no need to guess the role that Buckland played in convincing MacEnery of the relative recency of his artifacts. MacEnery was quite clear about that role. He noted, for instance, that he had pointed out to Buckland that the travertine layer was unbroken over many of the places where artifacts had been found associated with diluvium. Buckland responded that "the fact of an unbroken crust of stalagmite over any given spot in which a knife has been found is not decisive to show that the Dil[uvium] at that spot had not been broken into at some early Post dil[uvian] period and subsequently sealed over."[55] This argument, MacEnery conceded, was a "just dissertation."[56] Such comments are scattered throughout MacEnery's manuscripts on Kent's Cavern. It is clear that he first concluded that the associations were real, then communicated this opinion to Buckland, and then concluded with Buckland that they were accidental.

MacEnery did not agree completely with Buckland, for the latter was unwilling to give the human remains from Kent's Cavern even the relatively low antiquity that MacEnery had settled on. Buckland's opinion was that ancient Britons had dug ovens in the travertine, and that stone artifacts had found their way through these openings into the diluvium beneath. MacEnery disagreed, both because of the difficulty in breaking through the hard crust and because there was absolutely no evidence of such prehistoric excavations: "I am bold to say that in no instance have I discovered evidence of breaches or ovens in the floor but one continuous plate of stalagmite diffused uniformly over the loam."[57] Nonetheless, MacEnery had given way on the most important point. The cavern provided no evidence for the contemporaneity of stone tools, extinct mammals, and diluvium.

MacEnery left Torquay in 1830 and conducted no further excavations here,[58] although others did. He had always planned to publish his results and had prepared a manuscript to that end, but died without having accomplished his goal. A greatly edited version was published in 1859; 10 years later, the geologist William Pengelly published the complete version of the manuscript.[59] By 1859, however, the issue had been resolved by others.

How is all of this to be taken? Did MacEnery, as has been suggested, simply give in to the prestigious Buckland and reinterpret his results in line with Buckland's views? That does not seem likely. MacEnery did, after all, attribute a much greater antiquity to his archaeological materials than Buckland was willing to admit, and took a strong stand against Buckland in doing so. The cause of the shift in MacEnery's interpretation goes deeper than this. It must be recalled that MacEnery had the misfortune to have excavated Kent's Cavern during precisely those years when the interpretation of diluvium was undergoing major change. When he began his work, the diluvium was widely equated with the Deluge; by the time he was digging his last, in 1829, this equation was in serious doubt; by the time he began to prepare his results for publication, the equation was gone. He began with *Reliquiae Diluvianae* as his guide; he ended under the influence of *Geology and Mineralogy Considered with Reference to Natural Theology* and its careful denial of any identification of diluvium with "the comparatively tranquil inundation described in the Inspired Narrative."[60] It was MacEnery's fate to have the chronological ground on which he stood drop from beneath him, to shift from indicating a time when people might have been in existence in western Europe to indicating a time when they should not have been. Here was a powerful incentive to take another look at the facts. What seems likely, then, is that

MacEnery, confronted with the growing possibility that he was wrong, reexamined the situation with that possibility in mind, and found that there was
sufficient reason to doubt his initial conclusions. Given that sufficient reason,
given the changing interpretation of diluvium, and given Buckland's very informed opposition, MacEnery reevaluated his conclusions. Although during the
same years in France Marcel de Serres and Paul Tournal were to see their way
through these difficulties, MacEnery could not. It is, perhaps, no wonder that he
was unable to produce his planned volume on Kent's Cavern.

While MacEnery's manuscripts went unpublished for several decades, the
evidence for human antiquity provided by Kent's Cavern did not. In 1842, the
same year that the late Reverend MacEnery's paleontological collections and
manuscripts were being auctioned off in Torquay,[61] R. A. C. Godwin-Austen
(1808–1884; at the time, he was still R. A. C. Austen) published the results of
his own excavations in this site. Unlike MacEnery, Godwin-Austen did not
believe that the diluvium had been deposited by the Deluge, and he argued that
the Kent's Cavern deposits must have accumulated over many years. He was,
however, convinced that the association between human remains and extinct
mammals here was real:

> Human remains and works of art, such as arrow-heads and knives of flint, occur in all parts
> of the cave and throughout the entire thickness of the clay; and no distinction forwarded on
> condition, distribution, or relative position can be observed, whereby the human bones can
> be separated from the other reliquiae. The obvious inference from this fact is at variance
> with the opinions generally received, and the circumstances of the Paviland Cave will
> doubtless be adduced as a solution of the difficulty. The two cases have nevertheless
> nothing in common. . . . There is not a single appearance which can suggest that the cave
> has been used as a place of sepulture.[62]

Such conclusions, he observed, required care, and he emphasized that ''my own
researches were constantly conducted in parts of the cave which had never been
disturbed, and in every instance the bones were procured from beneath a thick
covering of stalagmite. . . . As far as evidence is to be our guide (and that is all
we should look to), there is no ground why we should separate man from that
period, and those accidents, when and by which the cave was filled.''[63]

Care taken in excavation or not, Godwin-Austen's statements had no impact. He included them as a small part of a large memoir on the geology of
southeastern Devonshire, and he did nothing more than simply assert the association. It was clear that much more was needed to make the argument, since
Buckland had already stressed the very valid point that caves are particularly
treacherous places in which to unravel secure stratigraphic sequences. Without a
detailed discussion of the stratigraphy of the site, and without a careful presentation of the exact nature of the associations involved, there was little reason to
believe him. Certainly, Buckland did not believe him, for Buckland knew the
site well, and also knew of MacEnery's conclusions. When, at the eleventh
meeting of the British Association for the Advancement of Science in 1841,

Godwin-Austen observed that "at Kent's Hole, near Torquay, arrows and knives of flint, with human bones, in the same condition as the elephant and other bones, were found in an undisturbed bed of clay, covered by nine feet of stalagmite,"[64] Buckland was unimpressed. The artifacts and human bones, he maintained, had been "found in holes *dug by art,*"[65] just as had happened at Paviland Cave, and Buckland "considered the occurrence of human remains in caves no greater proof of their equal antiquity with the other bones, than in the churchyards of Dorchester and Oxford, where they are often dug up together with the bones and grinders of the elephant."[66] Kent's Cavern changed no one's mind.

In the archaeological literature, Buckland has been seen as a retrograde force, retarding the progress of prehistoric archaeology at least in England.[67] Buckland, the believer in catastrophes, slowed the recognition of a great human antiquity because of his stubborn insistence that people postdated the catastrophe that caused the extinctions. Only the ascendance of uniformitarian geology rectified this situation, leaving Buckland's notions behind. That position not only provides an incorrect assessment of Buckland's approach to science and to his accomplishments, but, in opposing Buckland's beliefs on human antiquity to those of the uniformitarians, is entirely untrue. Many of the cave excavations in both Britain and France after the very early 1820s occurred because of the interest Buckland had aroused in the fossil contents of such sites. Kent's Cavern is a perfect case in point. It was a result of Buckland's work that so many associations began to be discovered, and that is hardly retrograde. Buckland was also correct in stressing the treacherous and often misleading nature of cave deposits, and his caution in this regard was fully warranted.

In addition, the decline of the catastrophist star makes it all too easy to overlook the fact that many of the early nineteenth-century British catastrophists, including Buckland, were the ones who were interpreting the evidence of earth history in rather straightforward fashion. If something looked like it had happened rapidly *and* they could not find a known process operating at a known rate to account for it, they interpreted that event in terms of unknown processes, or, far more frequently, unknown rates. If some alternative, superior explanation became available, they used it. The abandonment of the Deluge by Buckland (one of his "two great points"), Sedgwick, and other British geologists during the late 1820s provides an excellent example. When accumulating empirical evidence suggested they were wrong, they admitted it and adopted other approaches to the same phenomena. As C. C. Gillispie has observed, the catastrophists "accorded complete philosophic validity to whatever results Baconian induction might bring them."[68] Given Buckland's wary approach to caves and his generally straightforward approach to data from the earth, it does seem appropriate to wonder exactly what he would have done had he known of the open site at Hoxne.

Indeed, if anything retarded the acceptance in Britain of a tremendous human antiquity, it was the uniformitarians themselves. The uniformitarian geologists agreed completely with Buckland on the issue of human antiquity: people were recent arrivals on earth. But not only did their direct influence far outlast that of Buckland and other British catastrophists, but the uniformitarians also tended to be somewhat more impervious to empirical data. The greatest of all British uniformitarian geologists, Charles Lyell (1797–1875), was as opposed to a deep human antiquity as was Buckland, and, in Britain, it was Lyell who forcefully continued Buckland's critique of all evidence for a deep human antiquity.

Although trained as an attorney, Lyell also took geology from Buckland at Oxford and spent the rest of his life as a geologist. The first edition of his three-volume *Principles of Geology, Being an Attempt to Explain the Former Changes of the Earth's Surface by Reference to Causes Now in Operation,* appeared between 1830 and 1833. This remarkable and influential work was to go through 12 editions, the last appearing in the year of Lyell's death.

The subtitle indicates the main thrust of Lyell's *Principles* well. In these volumes, Lyell argued continually against the use of processes that had never been observed in action, or of processes working at rates much more rapid than have ever been observed, to explain past events in the history of the earth. Lyell was a uniformitarian geologist in the sense that he felt that the laws of nature worked uniformly through time, and in the sense that he felt that processes observable in the modern world should be called upon to explain earth history. These were matters with which the catastrophists fully agreed. Buckland, for instance, had attributed the Deluge to secondary laws in his *Reliquiae Diluvianae,* whereas Cuvier called upon large-scale flooding to explain aspects of earth history only after reviewing and rejecting the power of modern processes to explain these events. But Lyell was also a uniformitarian in the sense that he felt that earth history should be explained *solely* in terms of processes observable in the modern world *and* operating in the past at the same rate at which they now operate. This was a view the catastrophists did not accept.

Lyell combined these positions to produce a view of earth history that clashed significantly with the views of contemporary geologists. To Lyell, the earth was a system in dynamic equilibrium, changing while remaining the same, as it had been for Hutton. Although the catastrophists tended to see earth history as directional and life history as progressive, with, for instance, a continually cooling earth and the development of higher organisms through time, Lyell saw instead a nondirectional and nonprogressive steady-state system. In order to maintain these positions, Lyell had to explain away those aspects of the fossil record that appeared to demonstrate direction and progression, and he did this by arguing that all such evidence was produced by gaps in the fossil record and in our knowledge of the past. Indeed, he even predicted that if the conditions of existence were to return, so would the extinct organisms of the Mesozoic, and "the pterodactyle might flit again through umbrageous groves of tree-ferns."[69]

This was a view of geology and earth history markedly different from that held by the catastrophists. Lyell had begun his geological career as a student of Buckland but soon ended up in a very different place. As he wrote in an 1837 letter to the Reverend William Whewell (1794–1866) (Whewell had coined the terms *uniformitarian* and *catastrophist* in an 1832 review of the second volume of *Principles*[70]), "I was taught by Buckland the catastrophical or paroxysmal theory, but before I wrote my first volume, I had come round, after considerable observation and reading, to the belief that a bias towards the opposite system was more philosophical."[71]

Given the nature of his system, Lyell had two choices when it came to dealing with the issue of human antiquity. He could have treated the human species as just another kind of organism, and argued that our species was truly ancient. Such a position would have avoided the difficulty of dealing with the otherwise apparently abrupt arrival of people in relatively recent times on an earth whose history was quite uniform. In the late 1820s, he could have supported this argument fairly easily by using evidence recently available from France. Indeed, Lyell could have made this argument in the absence of such evidence, and simply attributed the lack of ancient human remains to the incomplete and poorly explored fossil record.

Lyell, however, had every reason to believe that this was not the case. He recognized full well where the notion of the progressive development of life through time might lead if people were seen as simply another, albeit the highest, animal. To Lyell, as Michael Bartholomew has made clear, such a notion could lead directly to the loss of any kind of special status for human beings, and to a view in which people were seen as merely the current end product in the progressive development of life through time. Lyell did not appreciate Buckland's attempts to reconcile geological fact directly with scriptural word, but he was nonetheless a man of deep religious beliefs. And he felt that the progressionist approach to earth history, no matter how well in accord with the temporal development of a designed earth it might be, held within it the seeds of destruction of the idea that human beings were something special, that our species had originated as the result of "special, independent creative attention."[72]

As a result, Lyell took the second choice, and maintained that the appearance of people on earth had been recent. The late appearance of our species in what was otherwise a nonprogressive life history achieved the special status for people that Lyell wished to preserve. On the one hand, the appearance of nonhuman life on earth was not progressive; earth historians only thought it was, and mistakenly took the incomplete fossil record as implying that progression. On the other hand, the appearance of humankind on earth represented a distinct break with the rest of the animal kingdom, a special event in earth history. In this view, the more recent people were, the more discontinuous their arrival would seem and the less they would have in common with other animals. Here was a position in which the human species could not be taken to represent merely "one step in a progressive system by which, as some suppose, the organic world advanced slowly from a more simple to a more perfect state.''[73] It was also a position that could not be reconciled with Lamarck's, or anybody else's, transformationist views of life on earth.

Did this approach not violate Lyell's own principles of analysis? Lyell did not deny it: "there was a considerable departure from the succession of phenomena previously exhibited in the organic world, when so new and extraordinary a circumstance arose, as the union, for the first time, of moral and intellectual faculties capable of indefinite improvement, with the animal nature.''[74] Nonetheless, Lyell retained his uniform physical world by stressing that the appearance of the human species was remarkable only as a spiritual, moral, and intellectual event. "The superiority of man," he argued, "depends not on those faculties and attributes which he shares in common with the inferior animals, but on his reason by which he is distinguished from them.''[75] The introduction of the human species, as a result, did not represent the violation of fixed and constant *physical* laws. Further, he noted that while he did not assert absolute uniformity through all time in the first place, there was also no reason to believe that such an event had ever occurred before. As a result, although the human arrival did represent a violation of the uniform succession of things, it did not represent a violation that weakened his strict application of uniformity to the early history of the earth. In this fashion, Lyell managed to allow a spiritual deviation from uniformity that maintained the special nature of humankind, while preserving the absence of divine intervention during prehuman earth history and the uniformity of physical law through all of it.

In this framework, the recency of the human species held a position of great importance. How, then, did Lyell deal with the accumulating evidence that people had coexisted with extinct mammals, evidence that was then being gathered and published on the other side of the English Channel? In the first volume of the *Principles* (1830), he argued most generally that

> we need not dwell on the proofs of the low antiquity of our species, for it is not controverted by any geologist; indeed, the real difficulty which we experience consists in tracing back the signs of man's existence on the earth to that comparatively modern period when species, now his contemporaries, began to predominate. If there be a difference of opinion respecting the occurrence in certain deposits of the remains of man and his works, it is always in reference to strata confessedly of the most modern order; and it is never pretended that our race co-existed with assemblages of animals and plants of which *all the species* are extinct. . . . Of caves now open to the day in various parts of Europe, the bones of large beasts of prey occur in abundance; and they indicate, that at periods extremely modern in the history of the globe, the ascendancy of man, if he existed at all, had scarcely been felt by the brutes.[76]

Since the only point of contention regarding human antiquity revolved around those relatively recent deposits that contained the remains of animals that still existed as well as those that did not, and not around more ancient deposits in which all the animals were extinct, it followed that if people were old, they were not *that* old. In addition, the fact that the bones of carnivores are abundant in the geologically recent faunas provided by caves demonstrated that if people existed when those faunas were deposited, there could not have been very many of them. Had they been abundant, the number of brutes would have been less. This was an argument that Buckland must have liked. After all, it was his argument.

In noting that human remains had never been found in association with assemblages of organisms in which all the species are extinct—a point with which no one would have disagreed—Lyell had gone far toward establishing his position. He did, however, leave open the possibility that small numbers of people may have coexisted with the most recent of the extinct mammals. Since Lyell's goal was to make people as recent, and therefore as distinct, as he could, it is not surprising that in the second volume of the *Principles* (1832), he shut the door on all evidence that implied such contemporaneity. He followed Buckland in rejecting the associations between human remains and extinct mammals in British caves, and then reviewed the evidence provided by a series of French sites for such associations (see Chapter 6). After summarizing this information, he then asked if we must "infer that man and these extinct quadrupeds were contemporaneous inhabitants of the south of France at some former epoch?"[77] His answer was firm: "we should unquestionably have arrived at this conclusion if the bones had been found in an undisturbed *stratified* deposit . . . but we must hesitate before we draw analogous inferences from evidences so equivocal as that afforded by the mud, stalagmites and breccias of caves, where the signs of *successive* deposition are wanting."[78] Such criteria were not met by the caves that had been examined so far, and the evidence available to date did not support the conclusion that human beings and extinct Pleistocene mammals had coexisted. He pointed out that many such deposits seemed to have accumulated at least in part as a result of flooding, and he concluded that

> more than ordinary caution is required in reasoning on the occurrence of human remains and works of art in alluvial deposits, since the chances of error are much greater than when we have the fossil bones of the inferior animals only under consideration. For the floor of caves has usually been disturbed by the aboriginal inhabitants of each country, who have used such retreats for dwelling places, or for concealment, or for sepulture. . . . To decide whether certain relics have been introduced by man, or natural causes, into masses of transported materials, must always be a task of some difficulty, especially where all the substances, organic and inorganic, have been mixed together and consolidated into one breccia; a change soon effected by the percolation of water charged with carbonate of lime. It is not on such evidence that we shall readily be induced to admit either the high antiquity of the human race, or the recent date of certain lost species of quadrupeds.[79]

"It is not on such evidence that we shall readily be induced to admit either the high antiquity of the human race, or the recent date of certain lost species of quadrupeds" (emphasis added): this was a position from which Lyell was not to be moved for nearly 30 years. The same phrase appears in every edition of the

Principles from the first through the ninth (1853). Lyell had accomplished his goal of demonstrating the great recency of the human species, and had also made it clear that he was not about to be moved from this position by the usual kind of cave data. His cautious, and in fact valid, arguments about the difficulties of cave stratigraphy were, of course, similar to Buckland's, and Lyell cited and discussed his teacher's work in the course of his presentation. Here, in a very different theoretical and methodological framework, is precisely the same opinion on human recency that Buckland held, and one that used the same kinds of arguments to dismiss the evidence supporting the contemporaneity of human remains and extinct Pleistocene mammals as Buckland had used.

Because of Lyell's insistence on the slow and uniform movements of nature, neither the mammals nor the diluvium provided the same precise time marker for him that they had provided for Buckland in 1823. For Buckland, the deposition of the diluvium and the extinction of the mammals had occurred rapidly and only a few thousand years ago. For Lyell, the deposits that Buckland had attributed to the Flood had been formed by the operation of normal geological processes operating over a very lengthy period of time, while the extinctions had similarly occurred over the millennia. The argument Lyell made in 1859 as to the causes and timing of these extinctions did not differ from those he had been making since the appearance of the first edition of the *Principles:* "all the species, great and small, have been annihilated one after another in circumstances in the organic world which are always in progress, and which are capable in the course of time of greatly modifying the physical geography, climate, and all other conditions on which the continuance upon the earth of any living being depends."[80] Thus, he felt that the extinctions had occurred slowly and one by one. In addition, the fact that the appearance of people on earth postdated these extinctions did not necessarily imply a human existence that was brief in terms of absolute numbers of years. In the 1850s, for instance, Lyell was thinking in terms of tens of thousands of years for this existence, while at the same time denying all evidence that people and the extinct mammals had coexisted.

However, even though Lyell saw the extinctions and the deposition of the diluvium as having been spread across a large series of years, they still retained their relative temporal significance in relation to human antiquity for him. That no human remains had been found with the extinct mammals documented the recent appearance of human beings in geologic time, an appearance that took place on an earth modern in form. Such recency carried the clear implication that people were a distinctly different kind of animal.

Lyell and Buckland thus took very similar positions on the issue of human antiquity. Not only were the specific reasons that Lyell gave for rejecting the cave data based on Buckland's approach, but Buckland's statements in his *Geology and Mineralogy* on the weak nature of the evidence available for a great human antiquity were virtually interchangeable with the statements that Lyell made on this question in all editions of the *Principles* through the ninth (1853). Indeed, Lyell's denial of human antiquity was taken in the face of stronger obstacles than those that Buckland faced. Buckland's denial created only a minor and easily reconciled strain with his equation of the diluvium with the Flood. In Lyell's system, however, the late appearance of human beings had a decidedly nonuniform cast. In order to support this late appearance, Lyell had to take an approach to the fossil record that he did not apply to other major kinds of organisms. While he routinely called on the incompleteness of the fossil record to explain away the apparent progression shown by that record, he relied heavily on negative evidence to support human recency, and he explained away positive evidence of the sort that he would have quickly seized for any other animal. Buckland's early biblical bias, in fact, proved far weaker than Lyell's commitment to a steady-state earth, and Buckland had a far easier time abandoning his Flood than Lyell had in abandoning notions he held equally dear.

From the time that Cuvier demonstrated the extinction of a set of mammals whose remains were to be found in the distinctive superficial deposits of the earth until well into the 1850s, the British position on human antiquity remained the same. People had not appeared on this wisely designed earth until after the earth had become fully modern in form, after the gravels had been deposited and the mammals had become extinct. Very few natural historians took exception to this view, and those who did, like Godwin-Austen, made no substantial converts. Not only did the British position remain the same through these years, but the arguments used to discount any association between human remains and extinct mammals or the "superficial deposits of loam and gravel" remained the same as well. Since the vast majority of the asserted associations had come from caves, some from England, Germany, and Belgium but most from France, these arguments depended on the ease with which cave deposits could be disturbed and on the difficulty of detecting such disturbance. It was clear that no change in the belief in human recency was going to come about in Britain as a result of data derived from a cave unless that cave possessed outstandingly well-stratified deposits, and unless the excavation of those deposits was carried out by someone outstandingly well qualified to make the case. Since those who were sufficiently well qualified to make the case did not believe there was a case to be made, the chances of combining the right cave with the right person were slim.

While the British position on human antiquity remained the same through these years, however, the specific reasons for asserting recency differed across investigators and across the decades. For Parkinson, human recency helped combat the possibilities inherent in any system that portrayed earth history as "a regularly recurring system of similar mutations," and helped confirm the literal accuracy of the written word of God. The threat of an eternal earth was not a major concern to Buckland, but the accuracy of the written word of God was, and human recency became for him one of the "two great points" on which he

hinged the accuracy of Scripture. Although he abandoned his equation of the
Deluge with the diluvium, and allowed the possibility that human remains might
be found with diluvial deposits yet to be explored, there is no reason to believe
that he abandoned his belief in the accuracy of the biblical chronology during the
years he published his views on the question of human antiquity. For Lyell,
human recency underlined the distinctive and special nature of our species;
combined with his nonprogressive earth history, such recency made it unlikely
indeed that people could represent merely the current and passing result of a
progressive series of creations, or that they could have been derived by transformation from some earlier form. Indeed, had Lyell argued for a deep human
antiquity, he would have produced just such a human history that Parkinson was
at pains to deny.

Given these strong and theologically derived reasons for doubting that people could have existed with the extinct mammals, it is not surprising that so few
British scientists made any arguments in favor of the ancient origin of humankind. It is also not surprising that while the British were arguing against any valid
associations between human remains and extinct mammals or diluvium, most of
the evidence they had to discount had been gathered on the other side of the
English Channel.

Notes and References

1. Frere 1800:204–205; Frere's life is discussed in Moir 1939.
2. Prestwich 1861.
3. Lyell 1863b.
4. See, for instance, Daniel 1950, 1963, 1976, 1981; Heizer 1962.
5. Cuvier 1813; Cuvier and Mitchill 1818.
6. For a valuable discussion of the history of these phrases, see Eisenstein 1979, chapter 5.
7. Jameson, in Cuvier 1813:[v]–ix.
8. Cuvier 1841.
9. Parkinson 1811:xiv. Parkinson's discussion of vertebrate extinctions and of the extinct mammals
   themselves appeared a year before Cuvier's *Recherches sur les ossemens fossiles* was published.
   Parkinson's discussion depended heavily on Cuvier's publications in the *Annales du Muséum
   d'Histoire Naturelle,* including Cuvier 1806a and 1806b.
10. Parkinson 1811:451.
11. Parkinson 1811:451–452.
12. Parkinson 1811:450–451.
13. Parkinson 1811:451.
14. Parkinson 1811:xiii.
15. Parkinson 1811:455.
16. Compare Parkinson 1811:418 with Jameson's notes in Cuvier 1813:255–256.
17. Buckland 1820:28.
18. Buckland 1820:21.
19. Buckland 1820:24.

20. Buckland 1820:24.
21. Buckland 1823:iii.
22. Buckland 1823:228.
23. Buckland 1823:183–184.
24. Buckland 1823:169.
25. Buckland 1823:83.
26. Buckland 1823:90.
27. North 1942:109.
28. Sollas 1913; Oakley 1968; Falconer 1860a.
29. Buckland 1823:169.
30. Buckland 1823:170.
31. Gordon 1894.
32. Sedgwick 1834b:191.
33. Sedgwick 1834c:313.
34. Sedgwick 1834c:313.
35. See, for instance, Buckland 1842; detailed discussions of Buckland's acceptance of glacial theory are found in Davies 1969 and Woodward 1907; see also Agassiz 1885, Volume 1:306–312 and Woodward 1883.
36. Murchison 1839.
37. Murchison 1839:576.
38. Buckland 1836, Volume 1:x.
39. Buckland 1836, Volume 1:44.
40. Buckland 1836, Volume 1:103.
41. Buckland 1836, Volume 1:104–106.
42. Buckland 1836, Volume 1:103.
43. Campbell and Sampson 1971.
44. Biographical information on MacEnery is taken from Clark 1925 and Clark 1961.
45. Vivian 1859:7.
46. Vivian 1859:7.
47. Vivian 1859:7.
48. Vivian 1859:61.
49. Vivian 1859:63.
50. Campbell and Sampson 1971.
51. Vivian 1859:49.
52. Vivian 1859:65.
53. Vivian 1859:64.
54. Vivian 1859:50–51.
55. Pengelly 1869:149.
56. Pengelly 1869:149.
57. Pengelly 1869:146.
58. Clark 1925.
59. Vivian 1859; Pengelly 1869.
60. Buckland 1836, Volume 1:95.
61. Clark 1925.
62. Austen 1842:444.
63. Austen 1842:446.
64. Anonymous 1841:626.
65. Anonymous 1841:626.
66. Anonymous 1841:626; see Clark 1961 for a valuable discussion of Godwin-Austen's work at Kent's Cavern.
67. Daniel 1950, 1976, 1981.

68. Gillispie 1959:146–147; important analyses of "catastrophist" and "uniformitarian" approaches to earth history are found in Gould 1979, Hooykas 1963 and 1970, and Rudwick 1972.
69. Lyell 1830:123.
70. [Whewell] 1832.
71. Lyell 1881, Volume 2:6–7.
72. Bartholomew 1973:284; see also Bowler 1976.
73. Lyell 1830:155.
74. Lyell 1830:156.
75. Lyell 1830:155.
76. Lyell 1830:153–155.
77. Lyell 1832:225.
78. Lyell 1832:225–226.
79. Lyell 1832:226–227.
80. Lyell 1859:164.

6

The Treatment of Human Antiquity in Early Nineteenth-Century Continental Europe

When Cuvier wrote in 1812 that "there are no human fossil bones," he had no difficulty in supporting this statement. On the one hand, this was because earlier assertions of the discovery of ancient human remains had been based on bones that were not human at all. On the other hand, his position could be readily supported because he himself had provided the framework within which potentially ancient human relics were to be evaluated; those who worked before him simply had not collected the relics of our species in such a way that they could be securely associated with either the gravels or the extinct mammals. Of the discoveries that fell into these categories, the best known to contemporary scholars had been provided by Johann Jacob Scheuchzer and Johann Friedrich Esper.

Scheuchzer (1672–1733), a Swiss physician who had studied medicine at both Altdorf and Utrecht, was an active natural historian who focused on the study of fossil vertebrates and, especially, fossil plants. He was deeply influenced by John Woodward, with whom he carried on an active correspondence for a quarter of a century; at Woodward's suggestion, Scheuchzer translated the *Essay toward a Natural History of the Earth* into Latin (1704), giving it wide currency on the continent.[1]

As a Woodward convert, Scheuchzer had strong reason to hope for the discovery of pre-Deluge human remains, since such remains would support the positions Woodward had taken in the *Essay*. In 1808, 4 years after the *Essay* had appeared in Latin, Scheuchzer made his first discovery of such material. At the base of the gallows in Altdorf, at the southern end of Lake Lucerne, he found a series of eight fossilized vertebrae of which he retrieved two. These bones, Scheuchzer argued, were human. Subsequently, the Oeningen quarries, near Lake Constance, yielded a more complete skeleton that Scheuchzer also identified as human. These remains, he argued, were of an individual who had both seen and been drowned by the biblical Deluge: *Homo diluvii testis,* the man who witnessed the Flood.

Scheuchzer discussed his human remains in a series of publications that appeared between 1725 and 1731, though his position on the meaning of this material did not change. In 1726, for instance, he observed that

> to the present, very few remains of men drowned in the Flood have been found. Perhaps the reminders of such innocent creatures as plants, testacea, fishes, and even lowly insects are more abundant, because these are more deserving of remembrance than men—all of whom, except some (though not all) of Noah's family, had taken to paths of infernal, as well as physical, corruption, and had richly deserved to be assigned to eternal oblivion. These human corpses floated on the waves and their flesh rotted. As a consequence we cannot always, or even easily, judge whether the bones that have been submerged are human. Many persons have been astonished at the two dorsal human vertebrae which I found immersed in extremely hard rock in the field of Altorf—vertebrae which were lustrous black and petrified, and which measured up exactly to the specifications of dorsal vertebrae in the structure of their osseus fibres, the position of their processes and in their overall form. They were joined to six others which I presented to a friend. . . . Should someone contend that these are Icththyospondyls, I would decline to join issue with him, were he first to show me that they are more congruously associated with the back of a fish than with that of a man. Quite otherwise is the case of the stone presented to my museum a short time ago—a stone which incontrovertibly pertains to the family of man. . . . We have here not merely some vague, general outlines which a fertile imagination could sketch into a head . . . but rather parts which are as similar to parts of a head as one egg is to another. . . . I venture to say that no-one who would even direct a passing glance, not to say an attentive study, upon this stone would fail to recognize it as a real and authentic relic of the Flood.[2]

Scheuchzer then went on to describe the partial cranium and cervical vertebrae of his human victim of Noah's Deluge.

Scheuchzer's *Homo diluvii testis* was considered a fossilized Flood victim through much of the eighteenth century. In 1787, however, the Dutch anatomist Petrus Camper (1722–1789) reanalyzed Scheuchzer's specimens and concluded that, far from being human bones, they were instead the remains of a "petrified lizard that had passed for an anthropolith."[3] Cuvier himself, though, dispensed with Scheuchzer's fossil human remains most convincingly.

Cuvier first addressed Scheuchzer's material in 1809 in the *Annals of the Museum of Natural History,* and then included his discussion of "the supposed Fossil Man from the Oeningen quarries, described by Scheuchzer"[4] in the first edition of his *Researches on the Fossil Bones of Quadrupeds* (1812). These discussions noted that even a superficial examination of the Oeningen specimen showed that it was not human. If it was not human, what was it? Cuvier provided an illustration of Scheuchzer's material as well as of a more recently discovered and more complete skeleton of the same animal, both reduced to one-sixth of their actual sizes. Next to these, he illustrated the skeleton of a salamander at its natural size. He then compared the osteology of these specimens in some detail, and concluded that the Oeningen fossils had come from large, aquatic salamanders. Cuvier also illustrated the Altdorf vertebrae and observed that these had come from a crocodile (Figure 6.1). Scheuchzer, Cuvier added in 1824, must have been blinded by his own theoretical system. Only this could account for the fact that Scheuchzer, "who was a physician and who must have seen human skeletons, was so grossly misled."[5] No one was to be misled by the Altdorf vertebrae or by the Miocene Oeningen materials again.

The work of Johann Friedrich Esper falls into quite a different category. Esper worked with Pleistocene deposits rich in fossil vertebrates, but conducted this work several decades before Cuvier's assessment of such deposits. Born into a religious family near Bayreuth, Germany, Esper (1732–1781) followed his father into a theological calling, studying theology as well as mathematics, physics, history, philosophy, and languages at the University of Erlangen between 1749 and 1752. A number of years after completing his studies, Esper became pastor to a group of communities east of Erlangen. In common with other educated professionals in the Bayreuth area, he combined his professional duties with science, publishing works on astronomy, agriculture, and earth history. He is remembered by paleontologists and archaeologists today, however, for the results of his exploration of fossil-rich caves in the vicinity of Bayreuth. He published the results of this work in German in 1774; in the same year, a French translation by Jakob Friedrich Isenflamm (1726–1793), professor of medicine and anatomy at the University of Erlangen, was published in order to gain a wider circulation for the volume.[6]

Why would an ecclesiastic bother with the study of such ancient material? In the preface to his *Description of the Newly Discovered Zooliths of Unknown Quadrupeds, and of the Caverns that Contain Them,* Esper provided a set of reasons that would have been received warmly by English natural theologians.

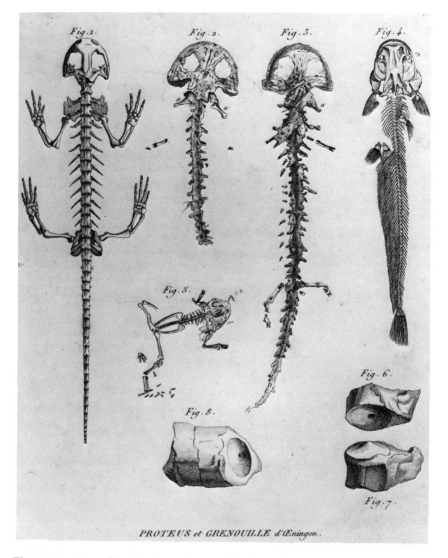

Figure 6.1. *Homo diluvii testis*, as illustrated by Cuvier (1812). Cuvier's Fig. 1 displayed the skeleton of a salamander at natural size; his Fig. 2, Schuechzer's *Homo diluvii testis* at one-sixth size; and his Fig. 3, Cuvier's more complete skeleton of the same animal at one-sixth size. The Altdorf vertebrae are illustrated in Cuvier's Figs. 6, 7, and 8. Cuvier's comparisons ended speculation concerning the human nature of Scheuchzer's material (Negative 337128, Courtesy of American Museum of Natural History).

"We know God by his works," Esper pointed out, and without knowledge of natural history we can never "understand the first page of the holy Writings, either to defend the history of the Creation and of the Deluge, such as Moses told it, against the objections of the incredulous, or to explain perfectly the several Psalms, the Book of Job, or a hundred other passages of revelation."[7]

By zooliths, Esper meant "the bones of unknown animals, calcined and become as hard as stone."[8] And by unknown Esper meant that either these animals still existed somewhere but had yet to be discovered, or, much more likely, that the animals "since many centuries, have disappeared from Nature . . . and . . . are no longer found on land or in the sea."[9] Esper, of course, was working at a time when the notion of extinction was not a popular one. He was well aware of this fact:

> To say that it impugns the wisdom of the Creator to allow races of animals to become extinct is to make an objection that does not prove what it is meant to prove. It seems to me that it is a proof of the greatest wisdom and providence of he who is also the Master and Conservator of the Animal Kingdom, to have created animals with a certain purpose for a certain time, and to cause their kind to disappear as soon as these purposes are filled.[10]

Parkinson, as I have discussed, was later to take a very similar approach to the reconciliation of the fact of extinction with the goodness and wisdom of the Creator.

Esper spent most of his *Description* discussing Gailenreuth Cave and its contents (Figure 6.2). In this multichambered cavern, located above the Weiser River some 50 kilometers northeast of Nuremberg, Esper had discovered a rich deposit of animal bones, so many that "several hundred wagons would not suffice to transport them"[11] and including many that did not belong to animals known from the area. He described some of these remains, but was unable to identify most of the species represented, although he did observe that the remains of lions, hyenas, and bears were present. Esper also discussed two distinct sets of human relics that he had extracted from this cave. The first consisted of a set of ceramic vessels, some containing animal bones, that he felt had been deposited in the cavern about eight to ten centuries ago, well after the bones of the unknown animals had been deposited there.

The second set of human remains, however, was quite a different issue. This set involved two human bones found alongside the remains of unknown and probably extinct animals, and Esper carefully noted that they had come from a bed that appeared undisturbed. Esper's original account of this discovery is expressive:

> Completely unexpectedly, we finally came upon a human maxilla in which, on the left side, were fixed two molars and a front tooth, which brought forth tremendous joy. Not far from there we found a shoulder blade so perfect that the coracoid was undamaged. I do not judge whether both pieces belonged to a single individual. However, it is these two human bones which, because of their structure, have the least in common with the comparable

Figure 6.2.   The entrance to Gailenreuth Cave, as illustrated by Esper (1774). The nonhuman fossils from this site gained wide attention during the late 1700s and early 1800s, but Esper's assertion of associated human bones was rarely discussed.

> bones of animals, and are most recognizably those of man. Did both pieces belong to a Druid, or an Antediluvian man, or to a more recent citizen of the earth? Since they lay under the animal bones with which Gailenreuth Cave is filled, and since in all probability they were found in the original bed, I conclude, not without sufficient grounds, that these human petrifactions are of the same age as the remaining animal fossils. The same accident must have placed them here.[12]

Esper knew that he had found human bones with the remains of unknown and probably extinct mammals.

How old was this material most likely to be? Esper felt that the topography of the globe, or at least of that part of the globe with which he was familiar, demonstrated that the earth had suffered a universal catastrophe, a flood, at some time in the past. This inundation was, he felt, the Deluge: "If we want to deny the reality of the inundation that Moses reported, and whose tradition is preserved among peoples who did not know this historian, we would be obliged . . . to invent another."[13] Esper felt that the Deluge accounted for many aspects of the current state of the earth, including the caverns themselves and the bones in them, and certainly "the Deluge of Moses supplies us with enough water to cause a destruction of the surface of the earth such as we see it today."[14] His human bones were, therefore, most likely to be antediluvian in age.

Working decades before Cuvier, Esper had no reason to see the presence of human remains with the bones of probably extinct mammals in a setting that suggested the individuals involved had lived before the Deluge as unwelcome information. Since people had existed before the Deluge, this was as it should have been, and Esper noted that his discovery caused him "tremendous joy." It was Cuvier's work that firmly established the framework within which such associations were to be questioned; the ease with which Esper accepted the Gailenreuth associations at face value is an indication of the impact that Cuvier was to have some 30 years later.

I stress this because Esper's opinion on the nature of the associations between the Gailenreuth human bones and those of the extinct mammals is known to archaeologists almost entirely as a result of Glyn Daniel's various discussions of Esper's work. Daniel has noted that the crucial sentences of Esper's work were translated for him.[15] That translation came from the German edition of Esper's *Description,* since it includes Esper's query as to whether the human bones had come from a Druid, an antediluvian man, or some more recent individual. Although Isenflamm's translation generally follows the German quite closely, it does not include this sentence.[16] Unfortunately, the translation that Daniel used is incorrect, interpreting Esper as saying that the association between the human remains and the remains of the unknown animals was accidental. However, by "the same accident must have placed them here," Esper meant not that the association was accidental, but that the same geological event that deposited the one set of materials had also deposited the other. Esper's original German is quite clear on this issue, as is Isenflamm's translation.[17] Esper stressed that the deposit was "primitive" and in its "original situation."[18] In addition, he entertained the possibility that people themselves had created the caverns and had accumulated the bones of the animals in them. He rejected both of these possibilities in favor of the Deluge, but not because he felt that people had not existed here at that time. Indeed, Daniel's analysis of Esper is of historical interest. Without recognizing the impact that Cuvier had on the interpretation of such associations, it is easy to project the well-known early nineteenth-century beliefs back in time, and to assume that Esper must have denied the contemporaneity of people and the unknown animals. Esper, however, did not deny such contemporaneity, and neither his contemporaries nor those who followed him during the coming decades thought that he had.

During the decades after Esper's *Description* appeared, a substantial literature grew around Gailenreuth Cave, but Esper's human bones did not attract much attention. One of the reasons was that Esper was clearly no anatomist, as the difficulty he had in identifying his fossil remains shows. His volume presented two major pieces of information that his contemporaries, and those who followed him, found valuable: the descriptions of Gailenreuth and the other caverns he had explored, and the 14 superb illustrations he had included (Figure

6.3). His written descriptions and identifications proved to be of little value, and were often noted simply to point out that they were weak. Later analyses of Gailenreuth fossils depended either on actual bones gathered from the site itself or, at times, on Esper's illustrations. None depended on, or trusted, Esper's descriptions themselves. "I do not understand why Esper took these incisors for canines" noted the young German anatomist Johann Christian Rosenmüller (1771–1820) in his 1795 analysis of the bear remains from Gailenreuth Cave, and his problem was typical.[19]

Unfortunately, the illustrations in Esper's *Description* displayed only the remains of unknown animals, including extinct bears and hyenas, and did not depict the two human bones he maintained he had found. Lacking illustrations of these two elements, there was enough internal evidence in Esper's volume to doubt that he had the anatomical knowledge to accurately identify parts of the human skeleton. Thus, Cuvier's 1812 study of the carnivores from Gailenreuth Cave was based not on anything Esper had said but on a collection of fossils that he had at hand. He also discussed the material Esper had displayed in his illustrations, pointing out that Esper had incorrectly identified many of the bones

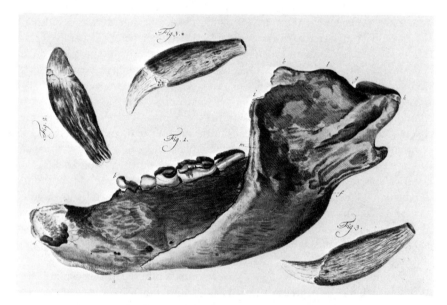

Figure 6.3. Cave bear mandible illustrated by Esper (1774). Esper's illustrations of the Gailenreuth fossils were excellent, but the discussions of the fossils in the text were weak. These weak discussions, and the fact that Esper did not illustrate his human bones, provide two of the reasons the human bones Esper retrieved from Gailenreuth attracted little attention after his publication appeared.

he had pictured and had done so because he had worked "in the absence of knowledge of comparative anatomy."[20] With an abundance of such problems and no clear indication that Esper's human bones really were human bones, there was little reason to treat Esper's claims seriously. In addition, work conducted at Gailenreuth Cave after the *Description* appeared demonstrated that there were undoubtedly recent human bones here, leaving open the possibility that even if Esper had found such bones with the remains of extinct mammals in this frequently disturbed cave, the association was fortuitous.[21] The main difficulty, however, was that there was no compelling reason to think that Esper had actually found what he said he had found. As a result, Cuvier did not mention Gailenreuth Cave in his 1812 analysis of sites that had been alleged to contain remains of ancient human beings.

In short, Scheuchzer's well-known *Homo diluvii testis* proved to be a salamander, and Esper's widely read *Description* did not provide the information needed to make the Gailenreuth human bones an issue. Flaws of this sort marked all the potentially ancient human remains that had been gathered before 1812, including Frere's stone tools. As a result, Cuvier had an easy time in the first edition of his *Researches* in arguing that "human bones have never been found among the fossils,"[22] including with those fossils even the relatively recent remains of extinct elephants and rhinoceroses in Europe.

He did not have a much more difficult time of it in 1821 in the second edition of the *Researches,* where he repeated the arguments against the reality of ancient human remains he had made in 1812. Now, however, his section on human fossils was much longer, dealing fairly extensively with the human bones that had been retrieved from Guadeloupe.

In 1805, human skeletal remains had been discovered in lithified sand near the port of Le Moule, on the northeast coast of Grand-Terre, Guadeloupe, in the Leeward Islands. A large block of this material, incorporating a human skeleton, was removed and eventually came to rest in the British Museum in London. In 1814, the mineralogist Charles Konig (1774–1851) discussed this block and its contents in the *Philosophical Transactions* of the Royal Society of London. Konig was properly cautious in his treatment of this material, dedicating the bulk of his paper to a description of the composition of the block and of the skeleton itself.

There could be no doubt about the human nature of the Guadeloupe skeleton. It was nearly complete, though lacking the skull, and Konig appended an excellent illustration of it to his report (see Figure 6.4). Its age, however, was a totally different matter; as Konig noted, "the human bones from Guadeloupe are unquestionably the only bones we are acquainted with that have ever been found in a hard stony mass, that does not appear to belong to common stalactical calcareous depositions."[23] Even though the bones themselves were not petrified, the situation in which they had been discovered was suggestive of great antiq-

Figure 6.4.   The Guadeloupe skeleton, as illustrated by Konig (1814). Although the skull was lacking, the Guadeloupe skeleton was otherwise quite complete. The fact that such a skeleton could come from lithified deposits yet be fairly recent shed doubt on other human remains found in a matrix suggestive of great antiquity.

uity. Konig, however, followed Cuvier in thinking that the appearance of people on earth had followed the extinction of the great mammals:

> All the circumstances under which the known depositions of bones occur, both in alluvial beds and in the caverns and fissures . . . tend to prove, that the animals to which they belonged met their fate in the very places where they now lie buried. Hence it may be considered as an axiom, that man, and other animals whose bones are not found intermixed with them, did not co-exist in time and place. The same mode of reasoning would justify us in the conclusion that, if those catastrophes, which overwhelmed a great proportion of the brute creation, were general, as geognostic observations in various parts of the world render probable, the creation of man must have been posterior to that of those genera and species of mammalia, which perished by a general cataclysm, and whose bones are so thickly disseminated in the more recent formations of rocks.[24]

Although the Guadeloupe skeleton did not seem to be of very recent age, Konig argued, it was unlikely to be of sufficient age to invalidate the idea that the appearance of people on earth postdated the extinction of the mammals. Nonetheless, it quite clearly had the potential of being very old.

The Guadeloupe skeleton proved to be very easy picking for Cuvier, not only because Konig had questioned an age as great as that of the extinct mammals, but also because he was able to point out that such deposits were known to grow rapidly—to accrete daily, in fact. He pointed this out in the *Preliminary Discourse* to the second edition of his *Researches* (1821), and noted as well that other such deposits with human remains were known. He repeated these arguments in the third edition of the *Researches* (1825), but he was now armed with an additional fact. He had been able to examine a newly extracted Guadeloupe skeleton, had identified the associated molluscs, and was able to point out that all of these molluscs belonged to species that still lived in the area. Clearly, the Guadeloupe skeletons were not very old.[25]

The same conclusion followed for Ernst von Schlotheim's human bones from the Elster Valley in East Germany. Although Schlotheim (1764–1832) is now most frequently remembered for his paleobotanical work, he was also an active contributor to vertebrate paleontology.[26] His work in this latter area included the description and analysis of fossil bones found in limestone fissures in the vicinity of Köstritz, some 50 kilometers southwest of Leipzig, bones initially discovered as a result of quarrying activities. Although relatively few of these remains pertained to the large, extinct mammals that Cuvier had described, both hyena and rhinoceros were represented, and the bones of these animals were intermingled with human bones. At one of the quarries, for instance, "human bones were discovered at the depth of 26 feet from the surface, lying eight feet below the bones of the rhinoceros there also deposited."[27] In 1820, Schlotheim felt that these human bones were true fossils, and indicated that "*man already existed at the time of the formation of the alluvial terrain that resulted from the last great revolution that changed the surface of the globe.*"[28] At the same time, however, he also noted that this view required further study, and that it was possible that these fossil assemblages represented animals that had lived at different times and whose bones had become commingled by natural causes subsequent to their deposition. Schlotheim returned to this question 2 years later. Noting that the bones of both recent and extinct mammals were intermixed in the Köstritz fissures and that there was no stratigraphic order to the deposits, he now concluded that

> it is highly probable that animals of the ancient world, belonging to very different repositories and very different eras, reaching in part even to the remotest antiquity, have been repeatedly brought together, and commingled in later periods with the remains of recent animals, and the bones of man. . . . At present, I consider it as most probable, that the human bones thus found belong to a much later epoch than the large land animals of the ancient world.[29]

Thus the respected Schlotheim concluded that although these remains were old, they were not extremely old. This conclusion, it turns out, was correct: in 1971, a human bone found at a depth of 15 meters in the Pleistocene gravels at Köstritz was radiocarbon dated to approximately A.D. 470.[30]

Some did, in fact, ignore Schlotheim's final opinion and treat the Köstritz material as implying a valid association between people and extinct mammals. The Scottish zoologist John Fleming (1785–1857), for instance, took this approach in 1824 in the course of an argument with Buckland over the causes of deposition of diluvium: for Fleming, though, the implication was not that people were ancient, but that the extinctions were very recent and thus could not have been caused by the Deluge.[31] Nonetheless, the fact that Schlotheim first questioned, then denied, the validity of the association removed Köstritz as a site that could be convincingly used to argue for the coexistence of people and the extinct mammals. All Cuvier had to do was to mention Schlotheim's initial hesitation to make the point that Köstritz provided no firm evidence for the existence of ancient human beings, and this is exactly what he did in the *Preliminary Discourse* to the second edition of his *Researches* (1821). Soon after, Buckland used Köstritz as an example of the accidental intermixture of human remains with those of extinct mammals.[32]

As the years passed, however, the list of sites that Cuvier had to argue against grew longer. It was no accident that the sites on this list were primarily from continental Europe. Although the prevailing view held by early nineteenth-century continental scientists concerning human antiquity was much like that held in Great Britain—that the human species was a recent arrival both in terms of absolute numbers of years and in terms of having appeared only on a fully modern earth—it was also true that the continental approach to human antiquity differed in an important way from the British approach. On the continent, the question of human antiquity was not as thoroughly charged with theological overtones as it was in England, because it was the British who stressed external evidence in addressing questions relating to the factual nature of events discussed in the Bible.[33] Few continental Europeans perceived the possibility that people had been on earth at the time the diluvium had been deposited or the Pleistocene mammals had become extinct as one that threatened the moral underpinnings of their society, or that represented an irreconcilable blow to the special nature of our species. Such concerns certainly existed, but not to the extent that they existed for British workers. As a result, the question of human antiquity was often treated as much more of a straightforward empirical issue on the continent. Indeed, even Cuvier's forceful stand against ancient human beings was driven by his desire to defend the reality of extinction, and not directly by any need to support Genesis through geology. Cuvier maintained this position throughout his lifetime, but the issues that led Cuvier to this position in the first place also remained alive during those years. Although Cuvier's opinion carried tremendous weight in and of itself in continental Europe, especially among French workers, evidence that seemed to imply contemporaneity between either the gravels or the mammals and human relics was frequently treated as such, instead of being explained away. The situation was very different in Great Britain during the same years. Thus, the number of asserted cases of ancient human remains proliferated on the continent between the first appearance of the *Preliminary Discourse* in 1812 and the late 1850s, when a new resolution of the question of human antiquity was reached.

Prior to Cuvier's death, the strongest of these assertions were forwarded on the basis of a series of sites in southern France. Cuvier was fully aware of the claims that had been advanced on the basis of the work done here, but, in the fourth edition of his *Researches* (1834), dismissed them summarily: "people made a great deal of noise, several months ago, about certain human fragments found in bone caverns in our southern provinces, but that they were found in caverns is sufficient to bring them under the rule."[34] The rule, of course, was that "there are no fossil human bones."

Although Cuvier did not bother to mention who the people were who had found these human remains, there can be no doubt that he was referring to a group of researchers who had been actively excavating bone-filled caverns in southern France and who, beginning in the late 1820s, had begun to publish the results of their work extensively. Of this group, the most active was Marcel de Serres (1780–1862). A resident of Montpellier, de Serres spent much of his active life practicing law, but he was also extremely interested in both geology and paleontology. In 1807 he had attended the lectures of Cuvier and Lamarck, among others, in Paris, and he also became friends with both Alexandre Brongniart and William Buckland. These interests led to his appointment as professor of mineralogy and geology at the Faculty of Sciences in Montpellier. Brongniart's work strongly influenced de Serres's approach to deeper earth history; however, his interest in bone caverns seems to have been stimulated by Buckland himself, and many of de Serres's more than 300 publications dealt with the fossil remains of the bone caverns and fissures of southern France.[35]

De Serres was, in turn, the driving force in involving others in these investigations. Of those who were so influenced, Paul Tournal (1805–1872) and Jules de Christol (1802–1861) took the lead in publishing the results of their work. Christol began working with de Serres in the caverns of southern France during the mid-1820s; he acted as de Serres's "constant second"[36] in those investigations. In 1837 Christol became professor of geology at the Faculty of Sciences in Dijon, though the reputation he gained as a vertebrate paleontologist had little to do with his single detailed publication that asserted the contemporaneity of human remains and the remains of extinct mammals.

A native of Narbonne, Tournal left for Paris at the age of 16 to become an apprentice to a pharmacist, then returned home in 1825 where he took over the direction of his father's pharmacy. Like Christol, Tournal was introduced to bone caverns by de Serres, and he published a series of papers on those caverns between 1827 and 1833. Tournal's last scientific publication on the caves of southern France appeared in 1833; after this time, he dropped his geological research to write popular articles on a wide variety of social and political issues, and was in addition deeply involved in the establishment of the Narbonne Museum. He became conservator of historic monuments in the department of Aude in 1834, and remained extremely active in the Narbonne Museum for the rest of his life. Only late in the 1860s did he return to geological studies, and these did not deal with the question of early human remains.[37]

Although de Serres may have introduced Christol and Tournal to the analysis of cave deposits and strongly encouraged them in their work, it was Tournal who made the crucial discovery in 1828. In addition, it was Tournal who, between 1828 and 1833, made the most meaningful attempts to overcome the opposition of Cuvier and others to accepting the evidence gathered by the entire group for the association of human remains with the remains of extinct mammals.

Indeed, prior to Tournal's 1828 discovery, both de Serres and Christol accepted Cuvier's position on human antiquity. In 1823, for instance, de Serres reviewed the evidence for possibly ancient human remains and dismissed such sites as Guadeloupe and Köstritz as providing any such evidence; in 1826, he reviewed the discoveries that had been made in the bone caverns of southern France, passing over the question of human remains in silence.[38] As late as 1828, Christol was supporting Cuvier's position fully. In his coauthored review of the hyena fossils from the cavern of Lunel-Viel, 25 kilometers northeast of Montpellier, Christol noted that this site helped prove, "as M. Cuvier has observed, that man did not exist at the epoch when these carnivores occupied caverns such as those in the vicinity of Montpellier, because one finds no human bones in those sites."[39]

Tournal's work changed the minds of both of these men. Tournal made his discovery in two caverns located about 3 kilometers north of the town of Bize, near Narbonne in the department of Aude. His initial discussion of these caverns appeared in 1827, but he did not mention human remains.[40] By the end of that year, however, he had found human bones here, a discovery that was announced by de Serres. In a paper read to the Linnaean Society of Normandy on 7 January 1828, de Serres noted that "recent stalagmites have attached several human bones to the rock" within the Bize caverns.[41] De Serres, however, did not argue that these bones were the same age as the bones of the extinct mammals found here; indeed, he did not even mention the possibility. Instead, he concluded simply that the condition of the human remains from Bize suggested an age older than those from the cavern of Durfort. Because the Durfort specimens were universally agreed to be extremely recent (see page 116), de Serres's conclusion was anything but startling.

Tournal provided the startling conclusion late in 1828. The caverns of Bize, he announced, contained the bones of extinct mammals intermingled not only with the bones of people, but also with pottery. Here he had found "in the same beds the bones of man and the bones of extinct animals, both showing the same physical and chemical characters. . . . The generally admitted proposition, that human bones in the fossil state do not exist on our modern continents, can thus be put in doubt."[42] De Serres, as I will discuss, concurred immediately.

In his third paper on the Bize caverns, published in 1829, Tournal observed that although these sites contained the remains of extinct mammals, some of which "bear the very characteristic marks of cutting tools,"[43] none were of clearly antediluvian species. The overall impression given by the faunal content of these sites, he felt, was that the Bize caverns were temporally transitional between the geological epoch, marked by such animals as the rhinoceros and the hyena, and the historical epoch, marked by only fully modern species. He also noted that this was not the case with the caverns that his colleague Christol had studied to the north.

Christol's work had been conducted in the caverns of Pondres and Souvignargues, near Sommières, northeast of Montpellier in the department of Gard. He published the result of this work in his *Notice on the Fossil Human Bones of the Caverns of the Department of Gard* in 1829, pointing out that, unlike the situation in the Bize caverns, his sites contained the remains of such antediluvian species as rhinoceros, bear, and hyena. In addition, the bones of these animals were found intermixed not only with human bones, but also with pottery, "veritable *geognostic equivalents* of human bones."[44] The antediluvian nature of the fauna indicated that these deposits were older than those in the Bize caverns. Mixture, he argued, could not account for the associations, since he "paid the greatest attention in examining to see if the earth had been accidently disturbed, and saw that the different beds . . . offered no interruption in continuity."[45] Although the implications of his discovery were clear, Christol decided to

> abstain, for the moment, from full reflections on this discovery of fossil human bones, the only ones of this type that, up to now, have satisfied the conditions of placement and condition indicated by the geologists; I restrict myself to reporting the facts, in remembering, always, that the opinion of the nonexistence of man in the fossil state was above all founded on negative facts, whose value has sometimes been exaggerated, that science rests on legitimate deductions from secure principles.[46]

Tournal was much less reticent to reflect. To him, the discoveries in the caverns of Bize and Gard presented a very coherent picture. The Bize deposits, with extinct but not antediluvian species (de Serres later indicated that these faunas included horse, goat, and antelope), postdated the deposits in the caverns of Gard, which included extinct and antediluvian species (de Serres listed rhinoceros, lion, hyena, and cave bear).[47] Both sets of sites contained undoubtedly contemporary remains of people:

> Indeed, the animals met in the caverns of Bize, while offering some species actually extinct, do not indicate to us a population very different from that which actually occupies our countries, since the same population, or at least closely related species, still live in the Pyrenees, while the caverns of Gard offer . . . species that I call essentially antediluvian, not only because they do not exist any longer on the surface of the globe, but because they must have, for their reproduction and well-being, different circumstances than those that are found today in the department of Gard.[48]

"Thus," he concluded, "man was not only contemporary with several species of extinct animals . . . but, at an earlier time, he was equally contemporary with several species of animals that have disappeared from the earth, and that characterize the antediluvian population."[49]

Tournal and Christol were fully aware of Buckland's opinion of their arguments, since Buckland had made a point of visiting many of the caverns of southern France. They disagreed fully with him on the meaning of what they had found. They stressed both the undisturbed nature of the deposits they had examined and the validity of the associations provided by these deposits. Tournal also agreed with what had by now become the mainstream British view that no universal deluge could account for the diluvium.

Indeed, Tournal's confidence that no catastrophe was involved in the deposition of the diluvium grew as the years went by, paralleling the decline of the Deluge equation in England. In 1829, he argued that no catastrophic or supernatural cause was needed to interpret the bone cave data, but hinged his argument mainly on the extinct mammals. Since human intervention had caused such extinctions in recent times, he observed, no great catastrophe was required to account for the earlier ones. At the same time, he characterized the human remains from the Gard caverns as antediluvian and was careful to note that his "observations are in accordance with the book that forms the basis of the beliefs of civilized Europe, since man lived before the event to which the words ante or post diluvian allude, an event some geologists see as coincident with the extinction of several races of mammals."[50] The following year, Tournal took a much tougher stance. He noted, just as Sedgwick was then doing, that the nature of diluvium varied locally, that in some places tranquil deposition was clearly indicated, that a lengthy period of time must have passed while this material was being laid down, and that as a result the diluvium could not have resulted from a universal flood. The early human remains from southern France, however, were still "antediluvian."[51]

Finally, in his last paper on the issue of human antiquity (1833), Tournal tackled the intertwined issues of diluvium, early human remains, and Genesis forcefully. He repeated his arguments that the nature of diluvium was such that an equation with the Deluge was impossible. In addition, although he had discussed the biblical implications of his work 4 years earlier, he now noted that he would rather avoid this issue, "because it has always seemed to me that one must avoid introducing the authority of religious traditions into scientific discussions."[52] He could not ignore the issue, however, because those who had equated the diluvium with the Deluge had committed "grave heresies." Tournal mentioned only one such heresy, but it was telling: how could one possibly argue that the Deluge deposited the diluvium, while arguing that human remains were not to be found in this material? The available facts, he suggested, divided the history of the globe into two unequal periods: one of vast length prior to the appearance of our species, and one of much shorter duration subsequent to that appearance. The latter, modern, geological period he also divided in two: the "periode ante-historique" began with the first human beings and extended to the earliest traditional histories; the historic period, lasting not much more than 7000 years, covered the rest. The word *antediluvian* does not appear in this sequence.

Tournal had thus grappled with the issues that were perplexing MacEnery during the same years and had solved them to his satisfaction.

De Serres's first major discussion of the evidence for the contemporaneity of extinct mammals and human remains appeared in 1829 as the bulk of a 92-page introduction to his *Geognosy of Tertiary Formations, or Description of the Principal Invertebrate Animals of the Tertiary Formations of Southern France*. As the title suggests, a lengthy discourse on the vertebrate remains from bone caverns was out of place in this work. Separately signed, separately paginated, and largely extraneous to the main theme of the volume, this introduction seems to have been prepared and submitted after production of the rest of the volume was well under way. Such timing would seem to reflect the impact of the discoveries that had been made by Tournal and Christol on de Serres. De Serres,. however, took a markedly different approach to the evidence provided by the bone caverns of southern France than that taken by either Tournal or Christol.

In his *Geognosy,* de Serres argued that the course of earth history had witnessed vast changes across the surface of the globe but had primarily been characterized by the slowness with which those changes had occurred. There were, he felt, three principal causes that modified the earth's surface and that drove animals to extinction (causes that he derived, in part, from Alexandre Brongniart, de Luc, and Buckland, respectively): the decrease of the temperature of the earth through time, the retreat of the seas from the modern continents, and floods. He allowed only one major exception to the slowness with which modifications of the earth's surface had occurred, a massive inundation that had deposited the diluvium in so many areas: "the phenomena presented to us by the external surface of the globe . . . do not announce violent revolutions, with the exception of the last and great inundation preserved in the memory of all peoples."[53] This flood had caused the death of thousands of terrestrial mammals and had also destroyed "a large part of mankind in the areas where they were established."[54]

De Serres carefully distinguished between the historic epoch, marked by the presence of the human species and during which the diluvium had been deposited, and the geologic epoch, which had ended after the seas had retreated from today's continents and which was antediluvian. It was, he stressed, often extremely difficult to distinguish between materials that had been deposited during these crucially different periods of time because the deposits of the geologic epoch are uninterruptedly linked with those of the historic epoch. Such historic examples as the dodo showed that the mere presence of extinct beasts in a set of deposits was no necessary marker of vast age, and it was, therefore, simply wrong to assume that the remains of rhinoceros, hippopotamus, elephant, and other extinct mammals implied an antediluvian age for the deposits in which they were embedded. On the other hand, the data recently provided by the caverns of Bize and Gard allowed two undeniable conclusions:

1. That since the appearance of man on the earth, certain species of terrestrial mammals have been completely destroyed, or at least have ceased to exist in the different parts of the globe that have been explored to the present;

2. That the debris of our species is incontestably mixed, and is found in the same geologic circumstances, with certain species of terrestrial mammals, considered to the present as antediluvian.[55]

Such terrestrial mammals included the extinct bears of Bize, and the rhinoceroses and hyenas of Pondres and Souvignargues. In fact, he noted, there were other sites that led to the same conclusion, and he offered Köstritz, a site he had rejected just 6 years earlier,[56] as an example. Thus, far from indicating the antediluvian nature of the extinct mammals, "the discovery of human bones and of objects of human manufacture in the same muds and osseus breccias that contain the remains of mammals of extinct species or of species considered until now as antediluvian, proves only that during historic times, or since the appearance of man on the earth, certain races of animals have been completely destroyed."[57] Even the superficial stratigraphic position of the deposits in which human remains had been found indicated that they could readily have been deposited during relatively recent times, and there was absolutely no evidence that "one had finally discovered the true remains of antediluvian men."[58]

De Serres was also careful to observe that none of the discoveries made to date implied that still earlier, antediluvian, human remains would ever be found. The arrival of people on earth, he argued, was associated with "a state of stability in the march of nature, and this stability did not occur until the seas withdrew into their respective basins."[59] Human beings did not appear until the globe had reached its modern condition of geological stability, and the antediluvian earth had been anything but stable.

Thus, de Serres used the presence of human remains in association with extinct mammals to argue for the recency of the mammals themselves, an argument he was to continue for some 25 years. Having demonstrated that the extinct mammals found with human remains could not be antediluvian, or to pertain to the geologic epoch as he defined it, he argued that these associations did not imply an unacceptable antiquity for the human species. In the same year Tournal and Christol were taking the very different position that the extinct mammals from the caverns of Gard were, in fact, both antediluvian and ancient. De Serres's conclusion was one with which Buckland would have agreed 6 years earlier, but certainly disagreed with in 1829:

Since the existence of man, it appears that rhinoceroses, hyaenas, bears, and unknown species of deer lived in our regions, and that their races witnessed the last and great inundation which caused members of our species to perish, and dispersed the *diluvium* over a great part of the surface of the globe.[60]

De Serres had been trained to practice law, and it is perhaps no surprise that much of his argument depended on the careful, and often subtle, redefinition of terms and concepts. His use of the term *antediluvian* is a prime example. Standard contemporary usage applied this term to deposits that lay beneath the diluvium. De Serres, however, used the term to refer to the period of time prior to the onset of the historic epoch, an epoch he in turn defined in terms of the joint appearance of the human species and of modern environmental conditions. As a result, in de Serres's scheme, the appearance of the human species could be postdiluvian, thus avoiding the negative connotations associated with the discovery of antediluvian human remains, yet still predate the deposition of the diluvium. Such arguments were bound to make his position seem "exceedingly complicated,"[61] as his English translator noted. They were essential, though, to de Serres's attempt to accept the evidence from the caves of southern France—which he had seen with his own eyes and excavated with his own hands—while at the same time trying to reconcile this information with the view that people had first appeared on a modern earth and at a time that was not extremely ancient.

De Serres used the same definitional approach to the question of whether any fossil human bones had been discovered. He was understandably reluctant to apply the term fossil to any human bones found associated with extinct mammals, or for those mammals themselves. Cuvier's repeated denial of the existence of human bones in the fossil state had erected formidable barriers to any conjunction of the words *human* and *fossil* not directed toward arguing against the possibility. In addition, de Serres himself had earlier defined a fossil as any remnant of an organism that had been found in a situation indicating that it had been deposited at a time "anterior to those causes now acting on our continents."[62] Since an integral part of de Serres's position was that the human remains in question postdated the appearance of a modern earth, such remains could not be fossil. To get around these two problems, in 1832 de Serres coined a new term, *humatiles,* to refer to organic materials deposited after the onset of the operation of solely modern geological processes. Since he maintained that this onset had occurred at the end of the Tertiary, he used the term for all post-Tertiary organic remains, and continued this use to the end of his life.[63] This semantic shift helped de Serres avoid what would otherwise have been a serious contradiction in his own system. However, it did not avoid the stigma attached to *human fossils.* Because no one else accepted de Serres's new term, he had to define it each time he used it; in so doing he explicitly raised the specter of human fossils again and again.

Tournal, Christol, and de Serres routinely communicated the results of their research to the Academy of Sciences in Paris, the heart of French science. The year 1829, for instance, saw the presentation of Christol's discoveries at Pondres and Souvignargues (29 June), Tournal's theoretical considerations on the bone caverns of Bize (28 September), and de Serres's analysis of materials found in the cavern of Fauzan (30 November).[64] In response to these communications, and apparently at Tournal's request, the Academy appointed a commission headed by Cuvier to examine and report on the work of "the different authors who believe they have found human debris mixed with the remains of extinct species."[65]

The report was not quick in coming. With clear annoyance, Cuvier noted in December 1829 that the "report would already be done, if the authors of the different memoirs sent to the commission, had paid attention to sending them specimens of bones and rocks."[66] Only Christol, he said, had taken the trouble to send in human bones. Cuvier's annoyance may have been partially feigned, however, and one can only wonder at Tournal's response to this statement, since he had sent Cuvier specimens from Bize in 1828 but received no response. In addition, one month earlier, Christol had transmitted a collection of Bize fossils whose arrival was formally acknowledged by the Academy at that time. Only de Serres had failed to comply with the commission's request. Had the real issue been the lack of human bones, Cuvier would not have hesitated to point out that not a single human bone was included among the fossils he had received. Instead, Cuvier was implying lack of cooperation by all, when only de Serres was at fault.

The commission's report finally came on 3 May 1830. Cuvier began by repeating his charge that none of the specimens required by the commission had arrived. Tournal clearly could not win, since he had sent yet a third set of Bize materials to Cuvier in January of that year. The real culprit was still de Serres, who did not get around to sending in his materials until late in June, nearly 2 months after the report had been issued.[67] Despite the specimens, given Cuvier's position on the reality of human fossils, which he had repeated as recently as 1829,[68] the results of the report were no surprise. Although many cases of ancient human debris had been forwarded, "as to true Anthropoliths, that is to say, as to human bones that exist in the rocks of regular formations, one has yet to find a single example,"[69] and there was no reason to believe any of the associations between human remains and the bones of extinct mammals reported to date.

This conclusion was very much preordained. Cuvier's general annoyance with the whole affair is indicated by his false implication of noncooperation by all the investigators involved. De Serres's intransigence did not help, and even Tournal lost patience with him.[70] To make matters worse, in 1829 de Serres had claimed that some of the mammals from Bize showed the effects of domestication, the very possibility that led Cuvier to so strongly deny the existence of human fossils in the first place.[71] Clearly the commission did not take the question seriously; the issue was to be resolved by reading the memoirs and examining materials taken from the sites, but not by inspecting the sites themselves. Had the commission, and in particular Cuvier, felt that there really might be something to all these claims, surely they would have taken the effort to examine the sites. Only if the claims were not taken seriously in the first place could the commission reach a conclusion in Paris, which is exactly what happened. It is significant that Tournal, Christol, and de Serres were not members of the Academy. Intellectual outliers, they could not provide evidence that assailed one of the most firmly established facts in life history and be taken seriously.

Nonetheless, they and others were compiling a lengthy list of asserted associations between human remains and the bones of extinct beasts. The simple enumeration of cases never led to a change in attitude concerning human antiquity by itself, but the growing size of the list clearly required an explanation more detailed and more encompassing than that provided by Cuvier's generally piecemeal approach. That explanation was established in France in 1832 by Jules Desnoyers (1800–1887), then secretary to the Geological Society of France. Once established, it formed the mainstay of the rejection of cave data in continental Europe until the late 1850s.

Desnoyers began his argument by observing that there were three principal points of view on the question of the associations between human remains and extinct mammals in the caves of southern France. One set of theorists speculated that the cooccurrences were valid, and that both the human materials and such extinct mammals as rhinoceros and cave bear were antediluvian in age. Tournal and Christol, he noted, held this position. A second set of theorists also held that the cooccurrences were valid, but maintained that the associations implied the recency of the extinctions; in this view, the extinctions had occurred during historic times, and one could say that the early Gauls had hunted hyena and rhinoceros. This, of course, was de Serres's view. Finally, there was a third opinion: the mixture of human remains and extinct mammals in the caverns and fissures was fortuitous, and that people and the mammals had not coexisted. This, Desnoyers emphasized, was his position.[72]

He supported his argument in two ways. First, he pointed out that the kinds of artifacts found associated with the bones of extinct mammals in the caverns included some that were very similar to those found in such clearly postdiluvian archaeological sites as dolmens in France, Germany, and Great Britain. Such stylistic similarities, he argued, implied temporal similarities as well. As a result, the human remains from the bone caverns must be postdiluvian. This argument alone, however, was not enough, since it could still be reconciled with de Serres's view. To remove that possibility and to deny further the validity of the associations, Desnoyers argued just as Buckland had argued before him. People, he noted, had used caves throughout historic times for shelter, for burial places, and for many other purposes. These recent uses had caused the intermixture of human remains with the bones of extinct mammals; indeed, even if all the materials left by people in these caverns simply sat on the surface, the disturbing action of water and other natural phenomena would soon introduce them to deeper levels within those caverns, and produce accidental associations with more ancient items. "The essential fact," he pointed out, "is to show intimate connections; to prove that no subsequent cause could have operated to mix debris and animals whose existence could have been separated by a long period of time, and without doubt by one of those revolutions that has powerfully modified the topography of continents.''[73] It was precisely this intimate association in an undisturbed context that had yet to be demonstrated, and that could not be demonstrated in sites with such ''discordant stratigraphy''[74] as caverns.

Here was an argument that both Buckland and Lyell could appreciate. Desnoyers's paper was translated and published in English in 1834,[75] and Lyell's appreciation of Desnoyers's position is shown by the fact that he discussed his arguments in every edition of the *Principles* from the third (1835) to the ninth (1853). Lyell used Desnoyers's discussion to emphasize the treacherous nature of cave stratigraphy and of the meaning of the associations between human remains and extinct mammals in caves. In fact, even Tournal saw the merit in Desnoyers's logic, arguing that while his observations clearly applied to many cave sites, they did not apply to the caverns of Bize and Gard. Tournal also realized that Desnoyers's approach posed a real threat to the use of bone caverns to resolve the issue of human antiquity: ''if one admits in principle that every time human bones and pottery are observed in bone grottos, the mixture occurred accidentally and after the fact, this would be . . . to announce *a priori* that the problem of contemporaneity that has been discussed for so long can never be resolved.''[76]

Both Desnoyers and Tournal were right in this dispute. Desnoyers was fully correct in stressing the tricky and unreliable nature of cave deposits.[77] Tournal was right in thinking that Desnoyers's reasoning meant that cave data alone would not be accepted as resolving the issue by those who were convinced that human beings and extinct Pleistocene mammals had not been contemporary occupants of the earth. Indeed, while directed toward the caves of southern France, Desnoyers's arguments were clearly meant to apply to all caverns. Tournal was wrong, however, in thinking that there was no source of information other than caves that could be brought to bear on the question.

In 1832, Desnoyers was aware of a new set of sites being examined near Liège at the time he was writing, and he noted the work of P.-C. Schmerling at those sites. Schmerling's work, however, did not begin to appear until the following year.

Phillipe-Charles Schmerling (1791–1836) was born in Delft, studied medicine in Holland, and in 1821 moved to Liège, where he completed his medical studies and established a successful practice as a physician. Part of his practice involved treating the poor who lived in the vicinity of Liège, treatment he often provided free. During an 1829 visit to the home of one of his impoverished patients, a quarry worker who lived in the village of Chokier near Liège, Schmerling became interested in fossils. While at Chokier, Schmerling saw the children of his patient playing with large bones; he asked where they had come from and was told by his patient that he had found them during the course of his work in the quarries. Schmerling asked the worker to save such things for him, and he soon after launched a massive program of exploration of the bone caverns in the vicinity of Liège.[78] By the time he published his *Researches on the Fossil Bones Discovered in the Caverns of the Province of Liège* in 1833 and 1834, he had discovered more than 40 caverns, a number of which proved to contain vertebrate fossils.

Schmerling described seven groups of caverns in the vicinity of Liège that contained such fossils; the animals represented in those caverns included elephants, rhinoceroses, hyenas, and cave bears, as well as a wide variety of species that were still to be found in the area. How had these caverns come to be filled with such a disparate set of creatures? Schmerling believed, with Tournal and de Serres, that his fossils had been deposited as a result of flooding. While Tournal had postulated a series of tranquil floods scattered through time, Schmerling's opinion was much closer to that of de Serres and his massive inundation. He felt that the bones that filled his caverns had been deposited as a result of "a violent eruption of water."[79] These flood waters had washed in a large number of local animals, but had also been sufficiently powerful to transport the carcasses of such nonlocal mammals as elephants and rhinoceroses from afar. The catastrophic flooding had caused the extinction of many creatures, but many had also survived to repopulate the earth after the inundation had ended: "this catastrophe could have completely destroyed species, even genera, but a part escaped, and continued to propagate themselves. The gradual and regular march of nature does not authorize us to adopt phenomena appearing too brusquely in the succession of organized beings."[80]

In several of the caverns that he explored, Schmerling found not only the remains of extinct mammals, but also both human bones and artifacts. He had made such a discovery, for instance, at two caverns near Engis, approximately 13 kilometers southwest of Liège. In the first of these caverns, located on a nearly perpendicular cliff and reached by clambering down a rope attached to a tree, both scattered human bones and "several worked flints of triangular form"[81] were found intermingled with the bones of animals, including hyenas. In the second Engis cave, two human skulls and a variety of postcranial human bones were discovered "mixed with those of elephant, rhinoceros, and carnivores of species unknown in the modern creation."[82] This phenomenon was repeated at Engihoul, some 11 kilometers southwest of Liège, while Schmerling noted in general that

a very singular fact among all the singularities resulting from excavations in the bone caverns, is the presence of fragments of flint whose regular form struck my attention immediately. In all the caverns of our province where I found fossil bones in abundance, I also found a more or less considerable quantity of these flints. . . . All reflections made, it must be admitted that these flints were worked by the hand of man.[83]

The caverns of Engis, Engihoul, Chokier, and Fond-de-Forêt having provided human bones or artifacts, or both, along with the remains of extinct mammals, Schmerling quickly surmounted the problems that were then confusing MacEnery. He insisted that these remains had not become intermingled by accident. At Engis, for instance, "the earth that contained the human skulls showed no disarrangement,"[84] and none of the caverns showed any evidence of recent human burials. The implications were clear: "these human remains were incorporated in these caverns at the same time and as a result of the same causes that buried a mass of bones of different extinct species."[85] Indeed, he observed, "even if we had not found human bones in situations completely favorable for considering them as belonging to the antediluvian epoch, these proofs would have been furnished us by the worked bones and fashioned flints"[86] (Figure 6.5).

Even the human bones themselves bespoke primitive times to Schmerling. Two human skulls had been retrieved from the second, lower Engis cave. One was that of a child, found in the deepest deposits of the site and found adjacent to an elephant tooth. Schmerling could not analyze this specimen because it had fallen apart upon being removed. The other skull, however, could be examined in detail. This skull, recovered at a depth of 1.5 meters, had lain alongside the remains of rhinoceros and hyena and was adult. Schmerling compared the morphology of this specimen to the descriptions of human racial forms provided by

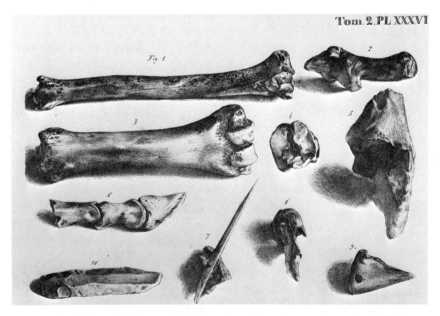

Tom. 2. PL XXXVI

Figure 6.5. Unmodified bones and artifacts from the caverns in the vicinity of Liège, as illustrated by Schmerling (1834). Schmerling's Figs. 7 and 9 depict bone artifacts from Engis and Chokier; his Fig. 10, a stone tool typical of those found in many of his caverns. (Negative 337129, Courtesy of American Museum of Natural History.)

Johann Friedrich Blumenbach (see Chapter 7), and found it most similar to Blumenbach's Ethiopian type. The adult skull from Engis, he concluded, "belonged to a man whose degree of civilization could have been but little advanced."[87]

All of these facts fit together tightly for Schmerling. People, he pointed out,

> have long denied the existence of these bones and have heatedly maintained that the remains of our species are never found in the regular strata. This assertion supported the gratuitous hypothesis that man appeared on earth only at a time when our globe took its modern form; that, having no precise facts on human remains found either with those of bear, hyaena, etc., either in caverns or in fissures, one concluded that their presence here was accidental. If it is necessary to believe those who admit that the appearance of man occurred since the earth took its modern form, this would be after the destruction of several species [of mammals]; but however MM de Luc and Cuvier positively deny the existence of fossil human bones, the latter of these experts does not contest the existence of man in the epoch when gigantic species peopled the earth, species which have been totally destroyed since the last catastrophe. But if, on the one hand, we know that naturalists have often been obliged to renounce erroneous opinions, opinions due to false stories and fabulous descriptions, on the other hand we cannot be astonished to see newly discovered facts concerning fossil bones destroy theories marked by grave errors and that have been in favor much too long.[88]

It was, he said to the Geological Society of France, time to let the facts put an end to the "reign of chimeras and of hypotheses."[89] And, he noted, he was not the only one to have provided such facts. Not only had de Serres and others working in southern France forwarded such discoveries, but Esper had provided identical evidence some 60 years earlier. He was, he said, "very surprised that no modern author had mentioned the discovery of human fossils made by Esper"[90] at Gailenreuth Cave.

Schmerling's discoveries became widely known, and Lyell visited Liège in 1833 in order to examine the collections Schmerling had made. In a letter to the geologist Gideon Mantell (1790–1852) written in September of that year, Lyell noted that he had been deeply impressed:

> I have just arrived from Dover, having passed through Belgium in my way. I saw there at Liege the collection of Dr. Schmerling, who in *three years* has, by his own exertions and the incessant labour of a clever amateur servant, cleared out some twenty caves untouched by any previous searcher, and has filled a truly splendid museum. He numbers already thrice the number of fossil cavern mammalia known when Buckland wrote his 'Idola specûs;' and such is the prodigious number of the individuals of some species . . . that several entire skeletons will be constructed. Oh, that the Lewes chalk had been cavernous! And he has these and a number yet unexplored, and shortly to be investigated holes, all to himself. But envy him not—you can imagine what he feels at being far from a metropolis which can afford him sympathy; and having not one congenial soul at Liege, and none who take any interest in his discoveries save the priests—and what kind *they* take you may guess more especially as he has found human remains in breccia, embedded with the extinct species, under circumstances far more difficult to get over than any I have previously heard of.[91]

Although these were difficult circumstances for Lyell to get over, get over them he did. In all editions of the *Principles* published after Schmerling's work appeared, up to the ninth (1853), Lyell carefully noted Schmerling's opinion that "the human remains were washed in at the same time as the bones of extinct quadrupeds, and that these lost species of mammalia co-existed on earth with man."[92] But he followed this mention with a discussion of the caves of southern France, with Desnoyers's opinion of these caves, and with his general refutation of the validity of cave data.

Buckland also visited Liège and examined Schmerling's collection. He, too, was unswayed. The human bones appeared better preserved than those of the extinct mammals to him, and he felt that both the bones and the artifacts derived from later peoples who utilized the caves for one purpose or another. Buckland discussed these materials in his *Geology and Mineralogy* (1836) and left no doubt that Schmerling's opinion that the associations were valid was one from which he "entirely dissents."[93]

Schmerling's data came from caves, and caves were not going to convince a wide range of geologists of the contemporaneity of human beings and extinct animals because of the stratigraphic difficulties posed by such sites. Schmerling's sites took their place as yet another set of caves that had provided interesting, but far from compelling, data on human antiquity. In hindsight, Engis is especially compelling because, of the two skulls recovered here by Schmerling, one was that of a Neanderthal child.[94] Schmerling had been the first to discover demonstrable Neanderthal remains. But that is hindsight. Not all the copies of Schmerling's *Researches* were sold during his lifetime; those that were not were purchased by a grocer who used the pages as wrapping paper.[95]

Desnoyers's early articles attacking the validity of cave associations had appeared in the *Bulletin* of the Geological Society of France. One of the rules of this society required that a summary of the progress of geology during the preceeding year be prepared by one of its members. The summary for 1833 was written by Ami Boué (1794–1881). Boué was one of the founding members of the society (Desnoyers was another) and, at one time, a student of Cuvier's annotater, Robert Jameson. In his review, Boué noted a marked difference between the treatment of geological discoveries in England and in continental Europe:

> Certain English theologians ridiculously persist in their mania of wanting to make the results of geology agree with Genesis. England is so pervaded with the spirit of sect that everyone is obliged, by force or by will, to enroll under a religious banner; in such a way that in the midst of the marvels of industry and an advanced civilization, the most elevated minds are too often mired in theological disputes that recall the middle ages, and of which continental Europe offers no more than rare examples.[96]

Although Boué was specifically criticizing English theologians who were then grossly reinterpreting the geological record in order to bring it in line with

Scripture, it is also true, as I have noted, that the distinction applied up and down the line.

But the distinction did not apply completely, and in 1835 de Serres began to develop a reconciliation of Scripture with the data bearing on the question of human antiquity that could well have appeared in England. This he did in two separate works, one addressing the question of absolute human chronology, the other analyzing the bone cavern data and its implications in great detail.

His brief *Discourse on the Differences between the Dates Given by Monuments and Historic Traditions and Those Resulting from Geologic Facts*[97] accepted the position that the earth would have taken millions of years to cool from its original molten state to its current temperature. This position had been developed much earlier by Buffon but was now gaining increasing popularity in France.[98] He coupled this view of an ancient earth with a series of arguments meant to demonstrate that the human species was no older than Scripture suggested. To accomplish this, he simply borrowed a set of themes that had been presented by another reconciler, Jean André de Luc, many years before. De Serres repeated his earlier assertion that people had not appeared until the earth had assumed its modern, stable form. He noted that because this was the case, the absolute time of the human appearance could be judged by examining the results of those processes that could only have begun to operate when the continents became as they are now. To derive this date, de Serres took the same set of natural chronometers that de Luc had used. The magnitude of alluviation, of dune formation, of the growth of peat bogs and talus slopes, and numerous other phenomena that could be used as geological clocks all led to the same result: the modern continents were at most 6000 or 7000 years old. He emphasized that this fact in no way contradicts the association of human remains with those of extinct mammals, and he restated the arguments he had made in his *Geognosy* to make the point. The many examples of historic extinctions showed that neither long periods of time nor such extraordinary causes as massive catastrophes are needed to account for the complete loss of any species of animal. People, he concluded, had appeared on earth at the time the earth took on its modern stability and form, some 7000 years ago, and as long as one accepts the Mosaic day as allegorical, the facts of geology and the facts of Genesis are in full accord.

De Serres's detailed analysis of the cave data appeared in the same year in his *Essay on Bone Caverns*. He now had available a much larger set of materials to work with than in 1829, and he was able to list some 15 sites or groups of sites that had provided evidence for the association of human remains with the remains of extinct mammals. Some of these, such as the caverns of Sallèles and Fauzan in southeastern France, he had described himself.[99] Others, including the caverns of Bize, Pondres, and Souvignargues, had been described by his colleagues. Still others, including Schmerling's caverns and the Köstritz fissures, had been described by men working outside of his circle. The associations provided by all, however, had been rejected by Desnoyers, Lyell, and, in the case of Köstritz, even by Schlotheim himself.

The structure of de Serres's position, however, remained the same as it had been 6 years before. Buffon would have recognized his own thoughts in de Serres's belief that the presence of elephants and rhinoceroses in an earlier Europe resulted from the fact that the slowly cooling earth had not reached its modern temperature, but de Serres was able to incorporate an additional discovery into this view. Schmerling, he observed, had found the bones of the Ethiopian race mixed with those of extinct mammals in Belgium, and this, too, reflected the warmer climates of those times. It was not, he felt, until after the deposition of the diluvium that modern temperatures were reached. Those deposits had been laid down by a series of floods that had occurred at different times during the same epoch; those floods not only explained the diluvium but also explained how the caverns and fissures had come to be filled with gravel, mud, and organic debris. "Violent and terrible inundations alone appear to have been able to cause the extraordinary mixture"[100] of materials seen in the caverns and fissures.

One of de Serres's main goals in his *Essay,* however, was to reconcile what he saw as the undoubted contemporaneity of extinct mammals and people with the Mosaic account of human history. To achieve this reconciliation, de Serres had to take two steps. He had to demonstrate that people had not existed prior to some 6000 to 7000 years ago, and he had to show that their appearance had occurred after the earth became modern in form. He attempted to reach the second of these two positions by simply defining the onset of modern environmental conditions in terms of the retreat of the seas into their basins at the end of the Tertiary, a view derived in large part from de Luc. As a result of this definition, any human remains found in post-Tertiary settings had to have been deposited on an earth characterized by the operation of modern processes. De Serres was thus able to date the onset of modern environmental conditions through de Luc's natural chronometers, arriving at a date of 6000 to 7000 years ago. This approach still left him with a serious problem, since virtually everyone else defined the onset of an environmentally modern earth at least in part through the extinctions themselves. To solve this problem, de Serres continued to develop his arguments on the chronological and environmental meaning of the extinct mammals. He repeated his observations that many animals had become extinct during historic times, that such recent extinctions demonstrated both that the extinct mammals of the caverns and fissures might be very recent, and that no extraordinary catastrophic causes were needed to account for the demise of those mammals. His list of historic extinctions had, in fact, become quite long by now, since he had recently maintained that many of the strange animals depicted by the early Egyptians, Greeks, and Romans had once existed, but were now lost to the world.[101] Followers of Cuvier were not likely to accept this conclusion, since

Cuvier had rejected the very same possibility in his *Preliminary Discourse* (1812). De Serres bolstered his arguments that the extinct mammals of the caverns and fissures were likely to be quite recent by stressing the similarity of those animals to modern forms; he even used the associations of the animal remains with human debris to argue for the recency of the extinctions. All available evidence, he emphasized, indicated that the extinctions had not occurred very long ago and that, far from indicating a world not yet modern in form, were part of the normal course of nature. The human species had, in short, arrived on earth no more than 7000 years ago, and had arrived only after the earth had become geologically modern and stable.

Such facts were in accord with Genesis, but there was also one other piece of information from the caverns that meshed fully with the Mosaic account. Many of the bones of such animals as horses and cattle that had come from these sites, de Serres noted, showed so much morphological variability that they must have been domesticated. He was thus able to point out the correlation between the presence of these domesticated forms in the bone caverns and the statement in Genesis that animals had been domesticated prior to the Deluge. Indeed, de Serres argued that people must have existed at the time the bones in the cavern of Lunel-Viel had accumulated because the remains of horses here appeared to belong to a domesticated form. Thus he included Lunel-Viel in his list of sites that demonstrated the contemporaneity of people and extinct mammals, even though neither human bones nor artifacts had been found here.[102] To de Serres, all of this evidence was consistent: "the appearance of man, which coincided with the intensity that we now see in the operation of modern causes, goes back scarcely six or seven thousand years,"[103] and all that was known of earth and life history was in complete accord with Scripture, including the history of our own species, the "object and end of creation."[104]

To accept both the cave data and the recency of the human species was to run a tight course, and de Serres knew it from the first. One of the two major aspects of his arguments concerning the meaning of the extinctions would not have fallen on deaf ears. In England, for instance, Lyell was then taking a similar position concerning the normality of extinction in his *Principles,* and was using the data John Fleming had provided on the recent extirpation of British birds and mammals to do it.[105] But to say that extinction was a part of the modern world was one thing. It was quite another to say that the extinction of such beasts as the mammoth and rhinoceros in Europe was extremely recent, and that such mammals had been part of a modern fauna. It was here that de Serres's position was fatally weak. It was clear that the recently exterminated English beaver was a creature of the modern world, but all the data indicated that this was simply not the case for the ancient mammals of the caverns. This position was not a secure stronghold, and de Serres was not able to occupy it very long.

No matter how de Serres interpreted his information, and no matter how many caves were dug that provided human remains intermixed with the bones of extinct mammals, the criticisms voiced by Buckland, Lyell, Desnoyers, and others were compelling. Cave data were not to be trusted. It was, in fact, easy to find case illustrations to make the point. In 1821, for instance, Louis Auguste d'Hombre-Firmas had reported the remains of human bones encrusted in calcium carbonate discovered in a cavern near Durfort, in southeastern France. D'Hombre-Firmas argued that the bones were recent, just as were the Guadeloupe skeletons, a view that was fully accepted. The fact that a set of clearly recent bones were encrusted, however, showed that materials from caverns could give the appearance of antiquity when they were not at all old, and helped shed doubt on the antiquity of such deposits in general.[106] More damaging was the fact that even when a single cave was examined by several investigators, the interpretations of those observers could differ in serious ways. The cavern of Mialet, near Anduze in southeastern France, provides a case in point. First discussed in detail in 1833 by J. B. A. Buchet, a pastor from the nearby town of Mialet, this cavern provided human bones and artifacts intermixed with the remains of extinct mammals. Buchet argued that the associations were accidental, caused by disturbance subsequent to the deposition of both sets of remains. De Serres visited this cavern with Jules Teissier, a physician from Anduze. Teissier agreed with Buchet that the association was accidental and published that view; however, de Serres included Mialet on his list of caverns that had provided valid evidence for the contemporaneity of people and extinct mammals.[107] The same fate befell the cavern of Nabrigas, which was examined both by de Serres and by Nicolas Joly. Later to become well known for his zoological and anthropological work, the young Joly (1812–1885) made Nabrigas the subject of his first publication, concluding that "man was *perhaps* contemporaneous" with the extinct mammals found at this site and denying de Serres's claim that human bones had been found here.[108] De Serres included Nabrigas as a cavern that had provided both human bones and artifacts with the remains of extinct species.[109] Certainly, a firm argument for contemporaneity was not going to be made from such disputable data, no matter how often the undisturbed nature of a set of cave deposits was emphasized and no matter how many caves were dug.

Desnoyers was certainly not impressed by any of the cave associations forwarded during the 1830s and 1840s. He repeated his arguments against the validity of such associations in detail in 1849. His own work had led him to support the hypothesis that most ancient bones in caves had been water deposited.[110] This in turn led him to emphasize the effects of running water in reworking cave deposits more than he had in 1832, but the results were the same. The cave associations neither implied that people had existed prior to the events that "gave our continents their modern form"[111] nor that the extinctions were recent. They were, instead, accidental, "the results of several fortuitous causes"[112] including the effects of flowing water and of recent human activities.

If cave sites could not provide convincing evidence for the coexistence of people and extinct mammals, where was such evidence to be found? Tournal's response to Desnoyer in 1832 indicates that he felt that the question could not be resolved at all if caves were removed from consideration. Discoveries of human remains associated with the bones of extinct mammals had, however, been made in diluvium in open settings prior to Desnoyers's initial discussion of the caves of southern France. In 1823, for instance, Ami Boué had made such a discovery in the valley of the Rhine near Lahr. Here, Boué had extracted a series of human bones that had been embedded in loess at a great depth. Because this deposit also contained the remains of extinct mammals, Boué assumed that his bones were not human, and sent them to Cuvier. "My astonishment was great," he noted, "when Cuvier . . . decided one after another that the bones were human."[113] Boué felt that the bones had not come from recent burials, and that they could not represent reworked younger materials; Cuvier felt that either of these two explanations could easily account for them. Although his discovery made Boué sympathetic to the notion of ancient human beings, he never pressed the issue. Since the bones were not tightly associated with the remains of extinct animals, and since Cuvier had offered plausible alternative explanations, Boué's materials were not accepted as providing a serious contender for an ancient age.[114]

Nonetheless, open sites of this sort held the potential of providing another source of data on human antiquity, a source whose stratigraphy might be less complex than that provided by caves and that might at least be used to verify the cave associations. During the 1840s this second source of information on human antiquity began to be more fully developed. In 1844, for instance, human bones were found embedded in volcanic debris from the mountain of Denise, near Le Puy in central France. Auguste Aymard (1808–1889) and his colleague Félix Robert published the facts of this discovery in a series of papers that began to appear in 1845.[115] The simple fact that these bones had been embedded in volcanic debris implied the possibility of great antiquity, but the fact that they could not be linked stratigraphically with diluvial deposits made the issue of relative age difficult to solve. However, such extinct mammals as elephant and rhinoceros had been found in morphologically similar deposits and in a stratigraphically similar position in the vicinity of the human bones. Accordingly, both Aymard and Robert argued that if the human remains were not as old as the bones of those mammals, they were close to it. Although some felt that these investigators had been duped and that the association was fradulent[116] and debate on the Denise bones continued well into the 1850s (see Chapter 8), this episode helped focus attention on the potential of sites other than caves to provide information on the deeper human past.

During these years, however, the use of archaeological data from open sites that appeared markedly ancient was most fully exploited by Jacques Boucher de Perthes (1788–1868). At the time he conducted his excavations, Boucher de

Perthes was director of customs at Abbeville, in northwestern France, a position he had held since 1825 and one that his father had held before him. His ambitions, however, went far beyond those of being a competent civil servant. He wrote prolifically on an astounding variety of topics. Among other things, he produced plays, novels, poetry, travelogues, pamphlets on free trade and on the place of women in society, political satires, and a five-volume work on the nature of God and life.[117] But Boucher de Perthes is known today for his archaeological investigations.

These investigations were stimulated by the work of Casimir Picard (1806–1841). Picard, a physician and native of Amiens, came to Abbeville in 1828 after studying both natural history and medicine in Paris. Extremely active, Picard served as administrator of the Abbeville museum and both founded the Linnean Society of Northern France (1838) and acted as its secretary-general.[118] Beginning in the early 1830s, he also became involved in the study of stone and antler tools discovered in the valley of the Somme near Abbeville. The first of these implements, he noted in 1835, had been found by workers in 1830 during the course of canal construction.[119] By the late 1830s, Picard was able to describe a fairly sizable series of such implements in the *Memoirs* of the Société d'Emulation d'Abbeville.

Picard's work was to lead directly to Boucher de Perthes's excavations in the same deposits and to Boucher de Perthes's discovery of stone tools in association with the remains of extinct mammals in the Somme River valley. But Picard's research had little in common with the explorations conducted by such men as Esper, Tournal, de Serres, Schmerling, and MacEnery. These latter men had begun their excavations for reasons that were strictly paleontological and geological: they were interested in the fossil bones that lay within their caverns, and in the information these bones could provide on life and earth history. It so happened that some of their sites also contained human bones and artifacts, and their interests became at least partially channeled into those materials as a result. Their archaeological discoveries were, in short, fortuitous, and occurred as a result of work initially conducted for very different reasons.

Picard's curiosity, however, was piqued by the artifacts themselves; his work focused on those tools, not on the question of human antiquity as it might be assessed by the nature of the deposits in which the implements were found. This was a very different orientation from that which characterized the labors of a MacEnery or a Schmerling. Picard was not alone in having interests that centered on the nature of Paleolithic and Neolithic stone tools, since interest in that direction had already been generated by the work of François Jouannet (1765–1845).

Born in Rennes, Jouannet came from a long line of printers; his father was both an attorney and printer to the King and to Parliament. After a stay in Paris, where he pursued interests in the arts and literature, Jouannet left for Perigueux in south-central France in 1803 to join a printing firm. He became a teacher in

1810, moved to the nearby town of Sarlat in 1815 and then to Bordeaux in 1817, where he remained for the rest of his life. He began archaeological research in 1810, working at the open site of Ecorne-Boeuf where he found both stone and metal tools, and then at the caves of Combe Grenal (then Combe Grenant), Pech de l'Azé (they Pey de l'Azé), and Badegoule (then Badegol). Although his cave work provided stone tools in association with mammal bones, Jouannet concluded in 1834 that those organic remains ''have nothing in common, as regards their age, with the bones that fill the cavities that geologists call *bone caverns*.''[120] While arguing that the artifacts from these sites were of high antiquity, he did not consider them to be of an extraordinary age. He was wrong about this assessment,[121] but Jouannet's real interest was in the stone tools themselves. He paid fairly detailed attention to the methods by which his stone axes had been made, concluding in 1819 that the polished stone axes of Ecorne-Boeuf had been manufactured by striking flakes from a piece of raw material, and then by polishing the resulting object.[122]

He thus saw his flaked stone axes as one step in the manufacture of the polished versions, and not as an earlier member of a chronological series. Later, however, he came to recognize that the stone implements of Ecorne-Boeuf and other open sites were quite different in form and to some extent in raw material from those that he had retrieved from the caves. These differences led him to conclude that two different time periods might be represented:

> [The stone tools] of the grottos are of flint and of a form given by an initial blow, repaired by light blows repeated almost indefinitely. . . . At Ecorne-Boeuf, on the contrary, as at several other localities, there is more skill, more variety in the products: not only flint was worked, but also jasper, Lydian stone, porphyry, basalt, hard serpentine; also, they were often given a polish as alive, as brilliant as could today be obtained by our best workers. . . . The projectile points [armures de flèche] . . . are treated with an astonishing perfection, which demands more taste, more intelligence, and more skill than is ever required by the knives and fashioned darts of the grottos. These latter seem to indicate the infancy of an art. . . . The others, on the contrary, better made and at times of stone transported from afar, seem to pertain to an epoch of improvement, even indicating social communication between peoples, and consequently a greater degree of civilization. But what amount of time separates these two epochs? Is it even certain that we are not taking for a difference of time what is only a difference in the use of these instruments? I do not know.[123]

Jouannet's work thus focused on the artifacts, not on the paleontological and geological indicators of age. In this way it differed greatly from the contemporary work of Tournal and de Serres, for whom the prime importance was the age of the material itself. Although many of Jouannet's discussions appeared in the very local *Almanac of Dordogne,* knowledge of his work spread, in large part because it formed the basis of the discussion of the Celtic Era that Arcisse de Caumont (1801–1873) provided in the first volume (1830) of his *Course of Monumental Antiquities.*[124]

Picard certainly knew of Jouannet's work through this volume,[125] and his work was similar to Jouannet's in that it was the nature of the artifacts themselves that occupied most of Picard's attention. Indeed, Picard's "Notice on some Celtic Instruments" (1836–1837) took issue with Jouannet over the nature of the flaked stone axes, Picard arguing that these were, in fact, finished implements and not simply unfinished versions of polished forms.[126]

Because his interests were oriented toward the artifacts, Picard did not offer detailed discussions of the age of the implements he had discovered. In 1835, he did, however, point out that the woody peat in which these artifacts were found also yielded the remains of such animals as the aurochs and beaver, species "now extinct or far removed"[127] from the region. Although Picard went no further than this, F.-P. Ravin discussed the geological history of the Somme River valley in the same volume of the *Memoirs* of the Société d'Emulation d'Abbeville in which Picard's paper appeared. Ravin noted that "the bones of mammals buried in our peats belong to species less ancient than those in our marly deposits,"[128] but also pointed out that these species also characterize the diluvial formations and must, as a result, be quite old. While Picard did not mention the possible diluvian age of the peats and Ravin did not mention the artifacts that these peats contained, it was not difficult to put the two papers together and reach the obvious conclusion.

Intrigued by these discoveries, Boucher de Perthes encouraged Picard to continue his work and "in order to assist him . . . had several excavations made which were not unproductive."[129] Although Boucher de Perthes rewrote his own history fairly liberally, he does give Picard credit in stimulating his observations. According to Boucher de Perthes, those observations began in 1837: "from 1837 to the present, there has been no removal of earth of any consequence around Abbeville which I have not assisted."[130]

Although his work was stimulated and influenced by that of Picard, Boucher de Perthes went much further than the young Picard was able to go before his death in 1841 at the age of 35. Unlike Picard, Boucher de Perthes maintained that he had discovered artifacts associated with the remains of such extinct mammals as elephant and rhinoceros in gravels that Ravin argued predated the formation of the peat deposits.

The first discoveries of this sort were made in the gravel pits at Menchecourt, in the valley of the Somme near Abbeville (see Figure 6.6). These gravels had long been productive sources of the bones of extinct mammals; in 1835 Ravin had noted that the Menchecourt gravels had yielded the remains of elephants, rhinoceroses, and cave bears, among others. According to Boucher de Perthes, the first ancient artifact was found at Menchecourt in 1840.[131] Similar finds were then made in 1844 in gravel beds adjacent to the hospital in Abbeville and at nearby Moulin Quignon.

Boucher de Perthes published the results of his initial decade of excavation in the first volume of his *Celtic and Antediluvian Antiquities*. The second and

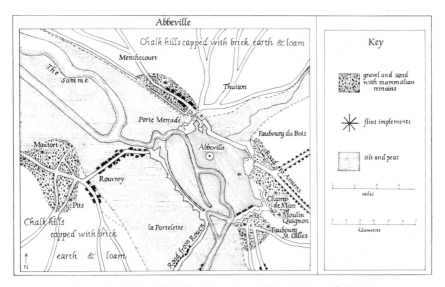

Figure 6.6. Location of the Abbeville sites, adapted from Prestwich (1861).

third volumes of this trilogy appeared in 1857 and 1864, but the first has a relatively complex publication history. Although the completed version of this volume was ready for the bookseller in 1847, Boucher de Perthes wanted the support of the Academy of Sciences for his work prior to its issuance. In 1846 he requested the Academy to prepare an evaluation of that work. In response, the Academy appointed a five-member commission to prepare the evaluation, the second commission the Academy had formed during the century to deal with matters relating to the question of human antiquity. Indeed, the chair of Boucher de Perthes's evaluation committee was Pierre Cordier (1777–1861), the same Cordier who had transmitted the works of Tournal, de Serres, and Christol to the Academy in 1829.[132]

This commission's report, however, was not to come. In February 1849, Cordier informally transmitted the commission's opinion to Boucher de Perthes:

> All the members recognized that among the angular flints that you have represented in your plates, there are a certain number that evidently carry the traces of human industry, but they do not think that is the case with all the rest. As to the nature and geological age of the superficial loose gravel in which you have found the flints and as to the manner in which they were introduced into this material, the commission recognizes that it does not have good reason . . . to manifest an opinion. The publication of your work probably coming to excite lively opposition under those different points of view and to provoke further observation, the solution will very probably come from debate; it is from time and the public that it is necessary to await a solution. In this state of things, Sir and Dear compatriot, I do not think that you will have interest in making demands on the Commission in order to obtain a report, since this report would not be what you hoped for and would be truly injurious to the sale of your work.[133]

As a result, the first volume of *Antiquities* went on sale in 1849, 2 years after the date indicated on the title page. A small notice was affixed facing the title page that noted that "this work, printed in 1847, could not, because of circumstances, be published until 1849." The circumstances to which the note referred were Boucher de Perthes's decision to await the report of the commission, and the 3 years that passed before he got his answer.

Thus, this volume did not gain wide circulation until 1849, even though ready for sale in 1847. Nonetheless, an earlier edition was printed and distributed in 1846. In that year, Boucher de Perthes had an apparently very small edition of his work bound. Some of these he distributed privately, although his biographer, Alcius Ledieu, noted that fewer than 100 were also sold. A copy of this edition went to the Academy of Sciences for their evaluation.[134]

The first volume of *Antiquities* was a curious work, and it is important to understand just how curious it was in order to understand its reception. In it, Boucher de Perthes described his excavations in some detail, including both those that dealt with the ancient gravels as well as those that dealt with more recent materials. He discussed the Menchecourt gravels in detail, incorporating Ravin's earlier observations on this site and including the list of extinct mammals that Ravin had published in 1835. He also provided a stratigraphic profile that showed not only the strata observed at Menchecourt, but also the location of the stone tools that had been found there, some of which had reportedly been discovered at a depth of over 6 meters. He provided a similar discussion for the excavations made at the Hospital site, again including stratigraphic profiles depicting the location of stone tools. Finally, he described and discussed the deposits at Moulin Quignon (Figures 6.7 and 6.8).

He was also careful to describe how his work was conducted. Pointing out that since many of the excavations and discoveries were made by workers, he would be sure to distinguish between those things he had found himself and those things retrieved by others. Further, he emphasized that while "each barbaric people is . . . characterized by its utensils, by the form and materials of its arms,"[135] it was nonetheless true that artifacts "absolutely similar in form can have an age very different"[136] because items whose use has become traditional or which are made to serve an unchanging function will not change form through time. It was, then, essential to use stratigraphic criteria to determine the age of a set of artifacts:

Figure 6.7. Boucher de Perthes's profile of the Menchecourt strata (1847). Boucher de Perthes's work combined the artifact-oriented approach of Jouannet and Picard with the concern for stratigraphy that characterized contemporary geology. His concern with stratigraphic relationships shows both in his profiles of the Menchecourt and Hospital strata (see Figure 6.8) and in his discussions of those sites. The black bars mark the positions of artifacts.

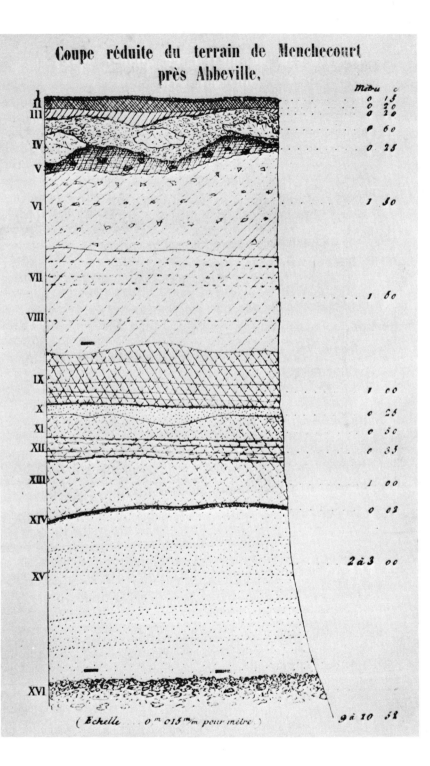

Coupe réduite du terrain de Menchecourt
près Abbeville.

(Echelle   0^m.015^mm pour mètre.)

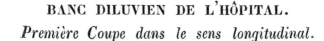

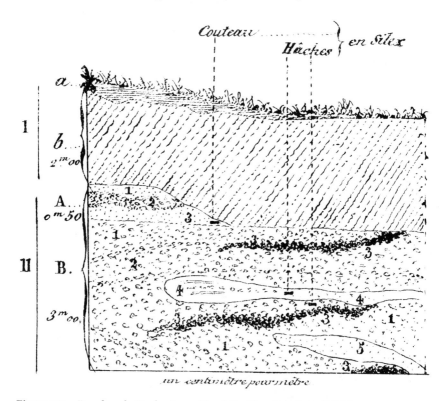

Figure 6.8. Boucher de Perthes's profile of the Hospital strata (1847).

> It is not only the form and the raw material of the object that serve to establish its high
> antiquity, and thus of the people from which it came; it is also the place where it is; it is the
> distance from the surface; it is the nature of the deposits, and also that of the superposed
> beds and of the debris that composes them; it is finally the certainty that this is its original
> soil, the earth walked on by the worker who made it.[137]

Stratigraphic position and stratigraphic integrity, in short, were the prime
criteria for establishing the age of a set of buried artifacts. In line with this
position, Boucher de Perthes stressed the undisturbed nature of the Menchecourt
and Hospital strata. At Menchecourt, for instance, he observed that "the aspect
of the deposits and of these superposed gravel beds, gravel that is compact and
lacking all appearances of modern detritus, does not allow the belief that these
axes reached this depth by an accident after the formation of the bank, or by the

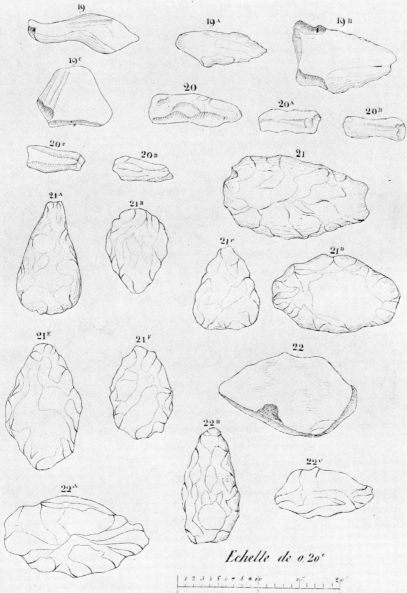

tiers de Grandeur

Echelle de 0,20ᶜ

Figure 6.9. Antediluvian stone tools from the vicinity of Abbeville illustrated by Boucher de Perthes (1847). These illustrations of stone implements from the Moulin Quignon and Hospital sites were poor, yet were as good as any in the first volume of *Antiquities* and allowed easy rejection by nonbelievers. Compare these illustrations with Frere's much earlier depiction of a Hoxne handaxe (Figure 5.2) and Prestwich's later depictions of stone implements from Abbeville (Figure 8.7).

infiltration of superior beds, for one would see the vestiges of this."[138] And, he emphasized, his stone tools had been found in beds that also contained the remains of extinct mammals: elephant and rhinoceros at Menchecourt, and elephant at both the Hospital and Moulin Quignon sites. Whatever had deposited the bones of extinct mammals at these spots, he concluded, had also deposited the artifacts.

These arguments were sound and insightful ones. The theoretical context in which he embedded his archaeological discoveries, however, was not one that was likely to impress his scientific contemporaries.

He did not feel that all of his stone implements were tools of the everyday sort (Figure 6.9). He believed that many were symbolic items, operating as a means of exchange or within religious contexts. As regards many of the stone handaxes that he had found, for instance, he argued that "this form, consecrated by use, necessity, politics, or religion, was a representative sign, a means of exchange, a sort of money, or as well a myth whose meaning is no longer known, a religious symbol like the crescent among the Turks, the cow among the Indians."[139] These were arguments that Picard had made before him, though in much more moderate form, and Picard himself felt that the chipped stone axes were weapons, meriting the name of "skull-breakers."[140] In addition, Boucher de Perthes felt that he had discovered many "figured stones," stones purposefully fashioned by people into the shape of animals—horses, cattle, elephants, rhinoceroses, ducks, even human beings—and dedicated a lengthy part of his work to discussing and illustrating these ostensible artifacts. No doubt, these figured stones were among those questioned by the Academy's commission (Figure 6.10).

He also had a view of life and earth history that was quite out of date. A committed catastrophist, he argued that there had not only been "a last deluge, that of scripture and of tradition,"[141] but that this had been preceded by other, more terrible catastrophes whose results had been the immediate dissolution of all life, after which new life forms had been created. This in itself was standard catastrophism of a form still acceptable in France, though fully rejected by nearly all contemporary English-speaking geologists. However, it was not standard to argue that these earlier catastrophes had destroyed "the human species, as well as all the races of which fossil debris is found,"[142] and that this occurred "as many times as there were geological revolutions."[143] Bold enough to hypothe-

Figure 6.10. Figured stones illustrated by Boucher de Perthes (1847). Boucher de Perthes's identifications of artifacts were also questioned because of his figured stones. In this figure, those numbered 9 were felt by Boucher de Perthes to be depictions of horses. There were many figured stones which he felt depicted animals but was unsure of the kinds of animals involved. Those numbered 10 in this figure begin his illustrations of such problematic figured stones.

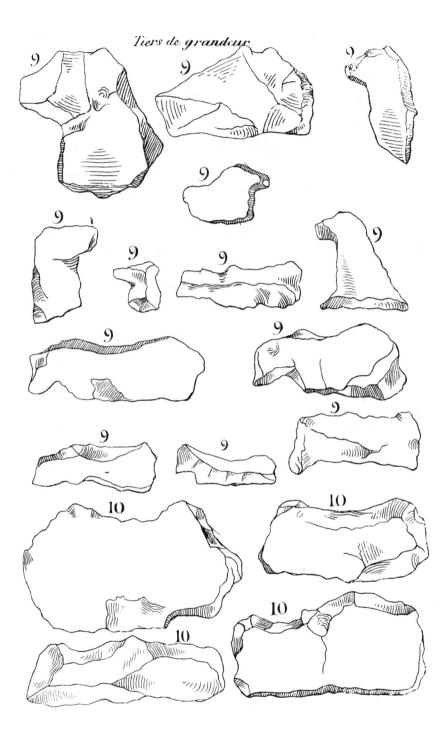

Tiers de grandeur

size such a series of catastrophes and the associated destructions and recreations of people, Boucher de Perthes suggested that the earliest members of the human species may have walked the earth thousands of centuries ago. Indeed, this view of human antiquity was mild compared to the millions of centuries he assigned to that antiquity in the draft of the first volume of *Antiquities*.[144]

The stratigraphic relationship he had found between stone tools and the bones of extinct mammals during the course of his excavations convinced him of the contemporaneity of the two. Although he had not found the bones of the makers of his artifacts, he was certain that they would be found. Because each catastrophe had destroyed all life and had also changed the surface of the globe, new organisms had to be created after each revolution and had to be created in a morphologically different form in order to be in harmony with the new environment. Thus, it was clear to him that "postdiluvian men are no more descended from antediluvian men than today's elephants are descended from those found in the clysmien deposits, and that if someday one discovers the bones of these antediluvian men one will find in them nuances of form which will prove what I assert."[145]

Boucher de Perthes's last major catastrophe, that which had deposited the diluvium, was not Noah's flood. Although he stipulated an unknown number of destructions and recreations of people, he was explicit about two such creations. There had been, he said, an antediluvian human race contemporary with extinct animals that had been completely annihilated by a massive flood "anterior to the biblical deluge."[146] After an unknown but lengthy period of time, a new human race appeared, that of Adam and his descendants. It was this new line of people that had been ravaged by the flood described in Genesis, though not completely destroyed by it.

To grasp the full context of Boucher de Perthes's speculations, it is important to realize that his approach to earth and life history was much more similar to that of some late eighteenth century *philosophes* than it was to any contemporary scientific approach. In 1770, for instance, Paul Henri Thiry, Baron d'Holbach (1723–1789) had presented a model of earth history in his *System of Nature* similar in a number of ways to that presented by Boucher de Perthes though developed in somewhat less detail. Holbach suggested that "there may have been, perhaps, men on the earth from all eternity, but in different periods they may have been destroyed, together with their monuments and their sciences; those who survived these periodic revolutions each time formed a new race of men."[147] Holbach suggested, as did Boucher de Perthes, that the world would have been a different place after such a revolution, and as a result, the new races of people would have been different in form from those before them. In fact, he suggested that "primitive man differed, perhaps, more from modern man than the quadruped differs from the insect."[148] Catastrophes, tremendous human antiquity, and the periodic destruction and subsequent reappearance of morphologically distinct races of people all formed part of Holbach's system; they formed as well the basis of Boucher de Perthes's model of earth, and within it human, history. Differences between the two systems certainly exist. Holbach was a militant atheist, and his *System of Nature* was an unremittingly atheistic work. Indeed, Denis Diderot noted that when some foreign religious work appeared, Holbach would hire some "imbecile tartar" to translate it badly.[149] Boucher de Perthes's history assumed a God and assumed as well the general accuracy of Genesis from Adam onward, and in this was quite different from Holbach's approach. Nonetheless, the similarities are so great that it appears likely that the general outline of Boucher de Perthes's speculative history was derived, if not from Holbach, then from one of his contemporaries. At the least, Boucher de Perthes's earth and life history demonstrates his isolation from the contemporary scientific community. In a very real sense, however, Boucher de Perthes's early work represents Holbach's system put to the empirical test.

It is also true that at this point, Boucher de Perthes's approach was an antitransformationist one. His repeated catastrophic destructions of life in effect denied the possibility of descent with modification for those forms that had been totally destroyed. Those totally destroyed explicitly included the antediluvian peoples whose remains he had found. Working in a place that had produced the now fully scorned transformationist speculations of both Lamarck and Étienne Geoffroy Saint-Hilaire (1772–1844), Boucher de Perthes built into his theoretical structure a denial of any transformationist possibilities relating to his discovery of ancient human beings.

Although his antitransformationist views were in line with most contemporary thought, Boucher de Perthes's speculative earth and life history was far removed from mainstream midnineteenth-century views. Other aspects of his approach, including his interpretation of stone tools and his figured stones, seemed equally preposterous. It is no wonder, then, that British and continental scholars alike did not receive his views favorably. From the point of view of these scientists, Boucher de Perthes was a provincial amateur whose work read in part as if it had been produced in a different century. Thus the negative results of his attempt to gain a favorable review from the Academy of Sciences are not at all surprising, nor is it surprising that Charles Darwin looked at Boucher de Perthes's work at the time and "concluded that the whole was rubbish."[150]

Nevertheless, it is also true that the first volume of *Antiquities* contained a notable innovation in its treatment of early stone tools. Boucher de Perthes's knowledge of artifact-oriented studies had come not only from Picard, but also from Arcisse de Caumont, whose work he cited in 1847. He was also aware of some of the work that had been done in the bone caverns, since he asserted that the human remains from those caves, while ancient, were not as old as those he had discovered. In addition, he had worked closely with local geologists in his excavations, and had taken their concern with stratigraphy to heart. As a result of these very different influences, his treatment combined the detailed, artifact-oriented approach of Jouannet and Picard with the concern for precise stratigraphic position that marked the work of the geologists and to some extent of such natural historians as Tournal and de Serres. Historically, these concerns had been derived from the antiquarians on the one hand and the geologists on the other; Boucher de Perthes's innovation was to combine them in his investigation of the deep human past.[151]

Although he did not make the job any easier by embedding his evidence for human antiquity in an interpretive framework virtually guaranteed to cause its rejection, Boucher de Perthes was confident that his arguments would eventually be accepted. "It is not lightly," he noted, "that one can put in doubt a generally admitted order of things and a system established on the basis of long experience."[152] "How many things which were impossible a half-century ago," he asked, "are today proven, and how many others that are rejected as absurd today will, before another half-century passes, be recognized as logical and incontestable"?[153]

In preparation for that day, Boucher de Perthes adopted the habit of rewriting his own history fairly extensively. As a result, much of what he said about the development of his ideas on human antiquity cannot be taken at face value. The rewriting began in the preface of the first volume of *Antiquities* (1847). Here, one finds a brief history of Boucher de Perthes's ideas:

> As is known, the research done to discover human fossils has, to date, been without success. In his book entitled *On creation*, M. Boucher de Perthes posed in principle that sooner or later such remains would be found. He supported this opinion:
>
> 1st. On the tradition of a race of men destroyed by the deluge;
>
> 2nd. On the geological proofs of the deluge;
>
> 3rd. On the existence, at this time, of mammals close to man and that could live only in the same atmospheric conditions;
>
> 4th. On the certainty thus acquired that the earth was habitable by man;
>
> 5th. On the fact that in all regions . . . where one finds these great mammals, man lived or had lived; from which one could conclude that if the animals had appeared on the earth before the human species, people would have followed soon after, and that at the epoch of the deluge, they were already sufficiently numerous to leave signs of their existence;
>
> 6th. Finally, on the fact that these human remains could have escaped the investigation of geologists and naturalists because the difference in conformation seen between fossil individuals and their living analogues could have existed between fossil men and those of today; consequently they could have been confused with these other animals.[154]

In this earlier work, the Preface went on to say, Boucher de Perthes had concluded that "evidently a race of men anterior to the last cataclysm that changed the surface of the earth, lived here at the same time and probably in the same place as the great quadrupeds whose bones have been discovered."[155]

However, as Louis Aufrère has observed in his indispensable analysis of Boucher de Perthes's work,[156] *On Creation* contains no such passages. What that earlier, 1841 publication says on the issue of human antiquity is very different from that which the Preface to the first volume of *Antiquities* would have us believe:

> All announces that this globe had existed for many years before becoming inhabitable by any creatures, and that men did not appear until long after the animals. This opinion, in accord with the sacred books, is accompanied by the evidence of our senses and also by the experience of knowledgeable people of all countries: what tradition says, geology proves. . . . If the animals and above all the plants have a high antiquity, all tends to show that it is not thus with our species. Human debris is found only superficially and in the beds belonging to the last revolutions of the ground.[157]

Clearly, the positions in *On Creation* and in the first volume of *Antiquities* are irreconcilably different.

Boucher de Perthes went further in rewriting his history in the second volume of *Antiquities* (1857). The version presented in 1847 still left room for the source of his field observations, and some of his ideas, to lie in Picard. In 1857 he removed that possibility: "it was on a spring evening in Abbeville . . . that the idea came to me that these worked flints could be found in the tertiary deposits. . . . This was in 1826."[158] The year 1826 was not only well before Picard had begun his work, but it was also 2 years before Picard had even arrived in Abbeville. Boucher de Perthes was, as Aufrère has pointed out, presenting himself not as the follower of Picard, but as a prophet.

Unfortunately, Boucher de Perthes not only rewrote his history to serve himself, but he also rewrote his discoveries, a very different matter altogether. Aufrère has documented this fact decisively from his examination of Boucher de Perthes's manuscripts. The most serious of the documented instances deals with a set of fossil teeth discovered during the Hospital excavations. In his manuscript, Boucher de Perthes described this discovery in the following words:

> The 26th of August, I found in the first bed of yellow clayey-ferruginous gravel the teeth of a large mammal—cattle or aurochs—these teeth were at 2½ meters from the surface.[159]

But in the first volume of *Antiquities,* this passage has been significantly altered:

> The 26th of August, we found the teeth of a large mammal. . . . These teeth, fragments of molars of an elephant, were at 2½ meters from the surface.[160]

Boucher de Perthes clearly did this because, without the elephant, the Hospital beds would lack convincing faunal evidence of great antiquity. Clearly, there are aspects of Boucher de Perthes's work that are not to be trusted.

It is somewhat ironic, then, that while Boucher de Perthes was providing a series of deceptions, he was in turn being deceived by the workers who were providing him with artifacts. Aufrère has reexamined the artifacts from Menchecourt that Boucher de Perthes described in the first volume of *Antiquities* and has convincingly argued that many represent frauds that Boucher de Perthes apparently unknowingly accepted. Some of the bone tools that he was given, for instance, seem to have been cut by the knives of the workers, while the stone tools include Neolithic implements that the workers said came from the lower Menchecourt gravels. Indeed, this latter fact is clear from the illustrations provided by Boucher de Perthes himself.[161] Boucher de Perthes, Aufrère argues, had no demonstrably ancient stone tools from Menchecourt; the first valid discovery was made during the Hospital excavations. It seems, then, that the workers did to Boucher de Perthes what Boucher de Perthes did at least occasionally to his readers.

It was impossible to know all this from the first volume of *Antiquities* itself, however, and Boucher de Perthes' work was rejected on the basis of that volume. The book was filled with curious interpretations of stone tools, including illustrations of presumed artifacts that could be validly questioned as representing objects worked by human hands and including poor illustrations of true artifacts. Not a single human bone had been discovered, and human bones were the prime evidence of the prior presence of people. Even more important was the fact that the theoretical structure in which all this was embedded was that of a different century. As hard as Boucher de Perthes worked, and he worked hard, and as much as he argued, and he argued a lot, this was not convincing stuff, and people were not convinced.

Thus, as the sixth decade of the nineteenth century opened, many sites had been excavated and described from western Europe that provided stratigraphic associations between human remains, extinct mammals, and diluvium. Some thought that these associations indicated the recency of the extinctions. A greater number thought that the associations indicated the tremendous antiquity of the human species. Nearly all continental scholars, however, saw the associations as accidental or at best as unproven. This third position was one with which almost all British scientists entirely agreed, as Lyell's rejection of the evidence for the contemporaneity of human beings and extinct Pleistocene mammals in edition after edition of the *Principles* underscores. In 1850, people were still seen by nearly all as recent arrivals on earth, that recency being measured in terms of the absence of undoubted human remains in secure association with geological deposits indicative of an earth not yet modern in form. Although infrequently discussed in print by scientists during these years, the reaction to the establishment of a great time depth for our species in 1859 shows that many continued to believe the human antiquity was also to be measured in terms of the biblical chronology. However, the number of scientists who adhered to that short chronology by 1850 was substantially less than it had been 20 years before. Diverse influences had led to weakened adherence to the biblical chronology, but one of the main blows had come from a surprising source: the analysis of human morphological diversity in conjunction with the depiction of human forms on Egyptian monuments.

Notes and References

1. Eyles 1971, Jahn 1972; see also Jahn 1969 and 1974.
2. Jahn 1969:207–209.
3. Jahn 1969:205.
4. Cuvier 1809, 1812d.
5. Cuvier 1824:432.
6. Biographical information on Esper is from Geus 1978.
7. Esper 1774:[v].
8. Esper 1774:4.
9. Esper 1774:75.
10. Esper 1774:76.
11. Esper 1774:15.
12. Esper 1968[1774]:25–26.
13. Esper 1774:81.
14. Esper 1774:81.
15. Daniel 1950; see also Daniel 1963, 1976, 1981.
16. Isenflamm's French translation of Esper's comments on the Gailenreuth human bones reads as follows: "Against all expectations we found, at last, a human jaw in which there were still two molar teeth and an incisor. Very near this spot we found a perfectly well preserved scapula, to the point that even the coracoid process was not at all damaged. I do not want to maintain that these two pieces had formed part of the same body. But it is precisely these two bones of the human skeleton that, by their structure, have the least resemblance to the corresponding bones of animals, and can thus be easily recognized as human bones. As they were found among the bones of animals, with which the caverns of Gailenreuth are filled, and in this bed which, following all probability, is primitive, I believe I have reason to suppose that these human bones are as ancient as the other bones of animals, and that the same accident placed them here" (Esper 1774:21). Isenflamm thus also eliminated Esper's comment that his discovery had brought forth "tremendous joy," but left the rest of the statement unaltered. I am unable to account for the changes he did make. Certainly, Druids were popular among contemporary French readers (Piggot 1968), and I can only suggest that Isenflamm may have detected the inconsistency in suggesting the presence of a post-Deluge Druid or even more recent individual in beds that were argued to be both "original" and to have been deposited as a result of the Deluge itself.
17. The crucial sentences in the original German and French passage dealing with the human bones from Gailenreuth Cave are as follows: "Ganz unerwartet, kam endlich eine *Maxilla* von einem Menschen, in welcher noch auf der linken Seite, zwey Stockzähne und ein vorderer, stacken, zu einem in der That, ganz schröckhaften Vergnügen hervor. . . . Haben beede Stücke aber einem Druiden, oder einem Antediluvianer, oder einem Erdenbürger neuerer Zeiten gehört? Da sie unter denen Thiergerippen gelegen, mit welchen die Gailenreuther Hölen ausgefüllt sind; da sie sich in der nach aller Wahrscheinlichkeit, ursprünglichen Schichte gefunden, so muthmaße ich wohl nicht ohne zureichenden Grund, daß diese menschlichen Glieder, auch gleiches Alters, mit denen übrigen Thierverhärtungen, sind. Sie müssen durch einen Zufall, mit selbigen hieher gekommen senn" (Esper 1968[1774]:26); "Contre toute attente nous avons trouvé à la fin la machoire d'un homme, dans laquelle il y avoit encore au côté gauche deux dents molaires et une incisive. . . . Comme ils se sont trouvés parmi les os d'animaux, dont les cavernes de Gailenreuth sont remplies, et dans cette couche qui, suivant toute probabilité, est primitive, je crois pouvoir supposer de raison, que ces os humains sont aussi anciens que les autres ossemens d'animaux, et que le meme accident les a placés ici" (Esper 1774:21).
18. Esper 1774:20–21.

19. Rosenmüller 1795:41.
20. Cuvier 1824:432; see also Cuvier 1812c:20.
21. See the discussion in Geus 1978.
22. Cuvier 1812a:82.
23. Konig 1814:119.
24. Konig 1814:110.
25. Cuvier 1821a and 1825. The high antiquity of the Guadeloupe skeleton was uniformly rejected; for examples, see Brongniart 1814, Desmarest 1816, d'Hombres-Firmas 1821a and 1821b, and de Serres 1823.
26. Schlotheim's paleobotanical work is discussed in Andrews 1980.
27. In Weaver 1823:29.
28. Schlottheim [sic] 1820:184.
29. In Weaver 1823:31–32.
30. Barker, Burleigh, and Meeks 1971.
31. Fleming 1824; for Buckland's response and Fleming's answer, see Buckland 1825 and Fleming 1826; see also the discussion in Rudwick 1972 and Grayson 1980 and 1983.
32. Cuvier 1821a; Buckland 1823. Cuvier repeated his arguments on Köstritz in the later editions of the preliminary discourse, which in 1825 was retitled *Discourse on the revolutions of the surface of the globe, and on the changes they have produced in the animal kingdom* (Cuvier 1825, 1834).
33. See the discussion in Frei 1974.
34. Cuvier 1834:216.
35. Bourdier 1975; Gervais 1861–1863[1862].
36. De Serres 1826:201.
37. Gervais 1861–1863[1861]; Rouville 1876–1877. A general discussion of de Serres, Tournal, and Christol appears in Lyon 1970.
38. De Serres 1823, 1826.
39. Christol and Bravard 1828:143.
40. Tournal 1827.
41. De Serres 1828:38.
42. Tournal 1828:348–349.
43. Tournal 1829:244. Tournal's discoveries were widely announced; see, for instance, [Tournal] 1829.
44. Christol 1829:15.
45. Christol 1829:23.
46. Christol 1829:25.
47. De Serres 1838 and 1855–1857[1855]. A review of the Bize material was later provided by Gervais and Brinckmann 1864–1866[1864].
48. Tournal 1829:243–244.
49. Tournal 1829:244.
50. Tournal 1829:251–252.
51. Tournal 1830.
52. Tournal 1833:168. This article appears in English translation in Elsasser 1959 and in Heizer 1962.
53. De Serres 1829a:xlj.
54. De Serres 1829a:xxx.
55. De Serres 1829a:lxxxv–lxxxvj.
56. De Serres 1823. De Serres continued to reject Guadeloupe. An English translation of de Serres's discussion of the caverns of Bize and Gard in *Geognosy* appears in de Serres 1830a, though the translation does not include de Serres's reevaluation of Köstritz or any other material not pertaining to the caverns of Bize and Gard themselves.

57. De Serres 1829a:lix–lx.
58. De Serres 1829a:lij.
59. De Serres 1829a:xc–xcj. When Félix Robert later brought de Serres human bones from Tertiary debris excavated during railway construction, de Serres noted that "we dare not suppose" them to be of such ancient age, and argued that they were reburied during historic times (de Serres 1844).
60. De Serres 1829a:lxxxix; see also de Serres 1830b and 1831–1832[1832].
61. In de Serres 1830a:122.
62. De Serres 1823:280.
63. The term was first used in de Serres 1831–1832[1832]; to my knowledge, his last published paper in which he used the term appeared 2 years before his death in 1862 (de Serres 1860c).
64. [Christol] 1829; [Tournal] 1829; [de Serres] 1829a; see also [de Serres] 1829b.
65. In [de Serres] 1829a:149. I infer that Tournal suggested the commission from correspondence in Aufrère 1936a.
66. In [de Serres] 1829b:155.
67. Tournal's efforts to provide Cuvier with specimens have been reconstructed from his published correspondence (Aufrère 1936a), and from [de Serres] 1829a. De Serres's transmittal of specimens was noted in [de Serres] 1830.
68. Cuvier 1829.
69. In [Fontenelle] 1830:76.
70. See Tournal's correspondence in Aufrère 1936a.
71. Tournal 1829.
72. Desnoyers 1831–1832[1832]a.
73. Desnoyers 1831–1832[1832]b:251.
74. Desnoyers 1831–1832[1832]b:252.
75. [Desnoyers] 1834.
76. Tournal 1831–1832[1832]; Tournal repeated these arguments the following year (Tournal 1833).
77. The tricky nature of these deposits is well indicated by the ceramics noted by Tournal, de Serres, Christol, and many others during the early nineteenth century in the Pleistocene strata of caves. If this pottery was real, its association with the extinct mammals was fortuitous.
78. Morren 1838.
79. Schmerling 1834:95.
80. Schmerling 1833:69.
81. Schmerling 1833:31.
82. Schmerling 1833:63.
83. Schmerling 1834:178–179.
84. Schmerling 1833:60.
85. Schmerling 1833:65–66.
86. Schmerling 1834:79.
87. Schmerling 1833:61.
88. Schmerling 1833:53–54.
89. Schmerling 1835:171.
90. Schmerling 1833:58.
91. Lyell 1881, Volume 1:401–402.
92. Lyell 1857:737.
93. Buckland 1836, Volume 1:598.
94. Fraipont 1936; Twiesselmann 1958.
95. De Laet 1981.
96. Boué 1834:166.
97. De Serres 1835a.

98. Rudwick 1972.
99. For Sallèles, see de Serres and Pitorre 1831; for Fauzan, see de Serres 1829b and 1832.
100. De Serres 1838:104. At least three editions of the *Essay on Bone Caverns* appeared: the first was published in 1835 in Haarlem; the second, 1836, in Montpellier; the third, 1838, in Paris. I have not seen the first two editions and have used the third here. De Serres noted in this edition that the prime difference between the third and earlier editions involved his addition of a discussion of transformation to the 1838 version (his views were antitransformationist and followed those of Cuvier).
101. See de Serres 1832–1833, 1833–1834; an English translation of these papers is found in de Serres 1834–1835.
102. Buckland visited Lunel-Viel with de Serres, but saw no evidence to support de Serres's assertion of an ancient human presence here (Buckland 1834).
103. De Serres 1838:333.
104. De Serres 1838:340; see also de Serres 1835b.
105. Lyell 1832; Lyell drew on Fleming 1824 for many of his examples.
106. D'Hombres-Firmas 1821a and 1821b. In 1823, de Serres not only agreed that the Durfort human bones were recent, but strongly objected to D'Hombres-Firmas's use of the term *fossil* to describe them (de Serres 1823). For examples of the negative impact Durfort had on the interpretation of human remains from caverns in general, see Boué 1830 and Renaux 1830. Renaux not only suggested that Durfort threw doubt on many or all such sites, but also mistakenly thought that de Serres had argued the Durfort human bones to be true fossils. De Serres denied both points immediately, and noted that he had never called *any* human bones fossils (de Serres 1830c). Soon after, he introduced the term *humatile*.
107. Buchet 1833, 1834; Teissier 1831–1832[1831]; de Serres 1838.
108. Joly 1835:363. After a great human antiquity had been established, Joly rewrote his own history to make it appear as if he had argued for such an antiquity in 1835. In 1874, for instance, he claimed that his 1835 paper had asserted "the contemporaneity of man with certain species now completely extinct" (Joly 1874:16; see also Joly 1862), although his actual conclusion had been that "l'homme était *peut-être* contemporain des espèces dont nous retrouvons aujourdhui les débris" (Joly 1835:363).
109. De Serres 1838.
110. Desnoyers 1842a,b.
111. Desnoyers 1849:402.
112. Desnoyers 1849:402.
113. Boué 1829:151.
114. Boué discussed these materials in a number of places (e.g., Boué 1825 and 1830), but his most informative early discussion appeared in Boué 1829, which also includes Cuvier's opinion of his material; for a typical later rejection, see d'Orbigny 1849–1852, Volume 1 (1849). In England, Boué's discovery was soon forgotten. When Lyell published the first edition of his *Geological Evidences of the Antiquity of Man* (1863b), Boué was not included. He appended a discussion of Boué's discovery to the second edition of *Antiquity of Man*, after Boué reminded him of it (Lyell 1863c).
115. Aymard 1845, 1847, 1848, 1850; Robert 1848.
116. See the discussion in Aymard 1847 and 1848, and in Lyell 1863b.
117. Ledieu 1885 presents a detailed discussion of Boucher de Perthes's publications; biographical information on Boucher de Perthes is derived from Aufrère 1940 and Ledieu 1885.
118. Morgand 1841–1843.
119. Picard 1834–1835, 1836–1837.
120. Jouannet 1834, "Notes sur quelques antiquités du département de la Dordogne," *Calendrier de la Dordogne* 1834, 232–237. The *Calendrier de la Dordogne* is not, to my knowledge, found

in any North American library, and I have depended on the reprints found in Cheynier 1936. The quotation is from Cheynier 1936:63. All biographical information on Jouannet is also taken from Cheynier.

121. A recent, detailed account of Combe Grenal and Pech de l'Azé is provided by Laville, Rigaud, and Sackett 1980; for an earlier, more popular account, see Bordes 1972.

122. See Jouannet 1819, "Antiquités Gauloises," *Calendrier de la Dordogne* 1819:3–12, in Cheynier 1936:42–48.

123. Jouannet 1834, "Notes sur quelques antiquités . . .," in Cheynier 1936:63–64.

124. See the discussion in Aufrère 1935. Laming-Emperaire 1964 provides a valuable discussion of Caumont's work.

125. Aufrère 1935.

126. Picard 1836–1837; Aufrère 1935.

127. Picard 1834–1835:112.

128. Ravin 1834–1835:206.

129. Boucher de Perthes 1847:2.

130. Boucher de Perthes 1847:2.

131. For a discussion of the Menchecourt gravel pits, see Aufrère 1936c.

132. Cordier's transmittal is noted in the references provided in Note 57.

133. Cordier's letter has been published in Aufrère 1940:105–106, and Ledieu 1885:223–224.

134. Boucher de Perthes 1846; the history of this volume is discussed in Aufrère 1940 and Ledieu 1885. The only copy of this edition that I have seen was printed to be a presentation copy, and includes a leaf preceeding the title page that reads *"Offert par l'auteur à____Abbeville, le____184—"*.

135. Boucher de Perthes 1847:35.

136. Boucher de Perthes 1847:35.

137. Boucher de Perthes 1847:37–38.

138. Boucher de Perthes 1847:228.

139. Boucher de Perthes 1847:124.

140. Picard 1836–1837:237. Jouannet had used the term before him (Jouannet 1819, "Antiquités Gauloises"; see Cheynier 1936:47), and it had been applied to prehistoric stone tools discovered in the Somme River valley near Abbeville as early as 1815 (Aufrère 1936b).

141. Boucher de Perthes 1847:244.

142. Boucher de Perthes 1847:244–245.

143. Boucher de Perthes 1847:496.

144. Aufrère 1940.

145. Boucher de Perthes 1847:245.

146. Boucher de Perthes 1847:579.

147. [Holbach] 1770, Volume 2:29.

148. [Holbach] 1770, Volume 1:85.

149. Kors 1976:252.

150. Darwin 1887, Volume 3:15–16.

151. Laming-Emperaire 1964 contains an excellent discussion of the development of the artifact-oriented approach in France; for Boucher de Perthes's discussion of the bone caverns, see Boucher de Perthes 1847:241.

152. Boucher de Perthes 1847:227.

153. Boucher de Perthes 1847:267.

154. Boucher de Perthes 1847:iii–iv.

155. Boucher de Perthes 1847:iv–v.

156. Aufrère 1940.

157. Boucher de Perthes 1841:316–317.

158. Boucher de Perthes 1857:361.
159. Aufrère 1940:85–86.
160. Boucher de Perthes 1847:255.
161. See, for instance, Boucher de Perthes 1847, Plate XVII, numbers 1–4; Aufrère 1940 contains photographs of the artifacts Boucher de Perthes had depicted in these illustrations.

7

The Implications of
Human Morphological
Diversity

In the *Antiquity of Man* (1863), Charles Lyell noted that the great physical diversity among the peoples of the world had long seemed to indicate that human beings must have been on earth for a much greater time than the biblical chronology allowed. The diversity itself became hard to explain if this were not the case, Lyell observed, since it did not seem possible for such divergence to develop rapidly. In making this statement, Lyell was repeating a position he had first published in 1847. In retrospect, the statements are logical, and the debate over the origins of human diversity has been presented as having provided a serious challenge to the notion of human recency.[1] However, although Lyell's comments were true in 1863, they were not true in 1847. Most of those who dealt with the issue of the origins of human diversity during the eighteenth and nineteenth centuries, up to about the year 1840, saw no such challenge.

Genesis, of course, is explicit about the earliest years of human history. It relates that after God created Adam and Eve, but before they were banished from

Eden, the human species consisted of just two people. Created in God's own image, the members of the original pair presumably looked very much alike. But by the beginning of the nineteenth century, there were approximately one billion people on earth—people who were well known to come in a surprising diversity of sizes, shapes, and colors. How had this come about? Genesis is much less explicit here. It tells us that God blessed Noah and his three sons after they left the ark, that they were told to "be fruitful and increase in number and fill the earth," and that from Noah's sons "came the people who were scattered over the earth."

Taken at face value, Genesis supplies a full picture of the peopling of the earth. In this account, all peoples have the same origin; close adherence to this account requires that the differences among people today be interpreted as being due to morphological change subsequent to the Flood.

The hypothesis of monogenesis, that all peoples share a common origin, has always been associated with the assignment of those peoples to a single species, however a species might be defined. The hypothesis of polygenesis, that morphologically distinct groups of people had separate origins, however, was not necessarily connected with an argument that those groups belonged to different species. Some who favored polygenesis also asserted that human populations of separate origin belonged to different species, however they defined that term, while others did not. The defining characteristic of the polygenist position is simply the assertion of separate origins for different groups of people, regardless of how those groups are treated taxonomically.

While Genesis derives all people from a single, original pair, arguments for multiple origins can be found at least as early as the twelfth century, as J. S. Slotkin has discussed.[2] Nonetheless, the possibility of polygenesis was not a major issue until the publications of Isaac de la Peyrère raised the question in a way that could not be ignored.

La Peyrère (1594–1676) was born in Bordeaux and raised a Calvinist in Catholic France. He became librarian to the Prince of Condé and was apparently friendly with many of the prominent literary people of the day. His modern reknown comes from two books on similar themes published anonymously in 1655, *Men Before Adam* and *A Theological Systeme*. Both books dealt with original sin, but both had at their heart the argument that Adam was not the first man: "out of opinion, as many times it comes to pass, and common consent rather than naked truth, it seems to be believed that *Adam* was the first man that was ever made, for Holy writ never affirms it, nor ever intends it, nay, on the contrary it is gathered out of them, which we shall easily prove, that there were men before *Adam*."[3] This was so evident, he noted, that he had realized it as a child, but withheld making his opinion known for fear that he would be thrown "headlong into some deep Heresie."[4]

La Peyrère's thesis that there had been men before Adam, contentious in itself, was accompanied by a large number of controversial arguments. Adam, he felt, was the father of the Jews and the Jews alone, while the Gentiles had been created "altogether in a huddle"[5] long before Adam and are thus completely different in origin from the Jews:

> You shall finde the species of the Jews peculiarly made and formed by God in Adam; you shall finde the species of the Gentiles promiscuously created with the rest of the creatures in the same day of Creation, which is diligently to be observed, that a day did not distinguish them whom the nature of their Creation did not distinguish.[6]

The Pentateuch, he asserted, dealt only with the history, laws, and chronology of the Jews. Moreover, internal analysis of the books themselves suggested that they are not originals, set down at or soon after the events described, but are instead the works of different people through time. "The first five books of the Bible," he maintained, "were not written by *Moses,* as is thought. . . . they are a heap of Copies confusedly taken."[7] The Deluge described in Genesis had not been a universal flood, but a localized one, affecting the lands of the Jews alone. Further, and even more inflammatory, the chronology of the Bible applied only to the Jews; the Gentiles had been created "innumerable ages ago upon all the earth."[8] La Peyrère did not know how long ago this had been. Indeed, he argued that not only was this fact unknown, it was unknowable: "if the Son of God, as he was man, knew not the end of the world, why should we, poor men, search for the beginnings of it?"[9] But there was no doubt in La Peyrère's mind that the beginning had occurred deep in the past, so long ago that it could be considered to have been "laid from eternal times, or from eternity, in regard of us."[10] The world was not eternal, but it was so old that, from our perspective, it might as well be. Our only access to deeper time, he observed, relates to the biblical chronology and the history of the Jews, but that information just scratches the surface.

La Peyrère's books, with the separate origins of different groups of people and their suggestions of eternalism, proved popular. *Men Before Adam* went through four Latin editions in 1655, while his *Theological Systeme* went through three. In 1656, *Men Before Adam* was translated into English; in the same year an English edition of both books was printed and published together, although bearing a 1655 date. A Dutch edition of *Men Before Adam* appeared in 1661. La Peyrère's books were well read but they were not popular with the authorities. The work was ordered to be burned in Paris, and La Peyrère was imprisoned in either Brussels or Antwerp for six months, released on the condition that he retract his statements. This he did, publishing disavowals in 1657 and 1663; not only did he publicly retract his thesis, but he also converted to Catholicism, entered a seminary near Paris in 1659, and remained there until his death in 1676. As David McKee has discussed, however, there is little reason to think that he ever changed his beliefs, and his decision to enter a Catholic seminary did not cost him his income as the Prince of Condé's librarian.[11]

La Peyrère's two volumes became a target not only for the official fires, but also for many other authors. At least seven refutations had been published by the end of 1656; Andrew White asserted, without support, that 36 responses had appeared within a generation of the publication of La Peyrère's works.[12]

One of the lengthiest responses to the issues raised by La Peyrère was Matthew Hale's *Primitive Origination of Mankind,* published in 1677. Hale (1609–1676), an influential jurist who served as chief justice of England under King Charles II and who was knighted in 1660, wrote *Primitive Origination* to destroy the notion that human beings could have been in existence for vast periods of time, and to destroy along the way all the arguments that La Peyrère had made that cast doubt on the accuracy of Scripture. One of those arguments was La Peyrère's assertion that, as Hale put it, "*Adam* was not the first man that was created. . . . And consequently, though *Adam* was the common Parent of the Inhabitants of Palestine and many of the countries adjacent, yet those that peopled the far greater part of the World . . . were not descended from him."[13] He felt that suggestions of this sort could have only one effect, to "not only weaken but overthrow the Authority and Infallibility of the Sacred Scriptures."[14] Throughout *Primitive Origination* Hale argued that all peoples were descended from Adam and Eve. In answer to one of the more difficult questions posed by La Peyrère, that American natives could not have been descended from the original pair because there was no way for them to get from the Old World to the New, Hale suggested that there may have been a land passage between northern North America and the Old World that allowed human migration. Therefore, he concluded, "though the Origination of the common Parents of Mankind were in *Asia,* yet some of their Descendants did come into *America.*"[15] These and similar problems solved, there was no stumbling block to accepting the Mosaic account of the single origin of all peoples.

In this interchange, Hale was clearly arguing on the side of the majority. In fact, during the following century, the prevailing view firmly remained that of a single origin for all peoples, followed by their spread across the surface of the earth and their physical diversification. The real problem during most of that century became explaining how such diversity could have arisen from a morphologically homogeneous pair of progenitors. As John C. Greene has discussed, the assumption of a single origin led to much speculation during the 1700s on the causes of variability of organisms.[16] Such speculations usually included a consideration of the rate of morphological change, but at the time no one saw the development of human physical diversity through time as in any conflict with the notion of human recency.

The relationship between a short human chronology and the explanation of human diversity in a monogenist framework can be seen clearly in Buffon's work. In the third volume of his *Natural History* (1749), Buffon reviewed the morphology, customs, and distribution of a wide variety of peoples, and concluded that every circumstance concurs in proving, that mankind are not composed of species essentially different from each other; that on the contrary there was originally but one species, who, after multiplying and spreading over the whole surface of the earth, have undergone various changes by the influence of climate, food, mode of living, epidemic diseases, and the mixture of dissimilar individuals; that at first, these changes were not so conspicuous, and produced only individual varieties; that these varieties afterwards became specific, because they were rendered more general, more strongly marked, and more permanent, by the continual action of the same causes; that they are transmitted from generation to generation, as deformities or disease pass from parents to children; and that, lastly, as they were originally produced by a train of external and accidental causes, and have only been perpetuated by time and the constant operation of these causes, it is probable that they will gradually disappear, or, at least, that they will differ from what they are at present, if the causes which produced them should cease, or if their operation should be varied by other circumstances and combinations.[17]

Buffon believed not only that the earliest peoples had lived in central Asia, but also that they had been white in color. This homogeneous set of progenitors occupying a circumscribed portion of the globe became the widespread and physically heterogeneous populations now occupying the earth through migration, and through physical degeneration caused by the action of different climates, diets, and modes of life. These three sets of factors caused morphological change, and these changes were then inherited. Buffon shared the common belief in the inheritance of acquired characters, and felt that such inheritance allowed the development of physically diverse human populations. Just as "dogs who, for a few generations, have had their ears and tail cut, transmit these defects, in a certain degree, to their descendants,"[18] so could "the heat of the climate"[19] cause a white human population to become black and this blackness be transmitted to future generations.

Buffon had an empirical test for species-level divergence: the ability to interbreed and produce fertile offspring. This test clearly showed that all of humanity belonged to the same species, while biblical evidence pointed to the same conclusion. The changes human beings had undergone since their origin, he observed, had been

so great and so conspicuous, as to give room for suspecting, that the Negro, the Laplander, and the White, were really different species, if, on the one hand, we were not certain, that one man only was originally created, and, on the other, that the White, the Laplander, and the Negro, are capable of uniting, and of propagating the great and undivided family of the human kind.

Hence, it followed that "those marks which distinguished men who inhabit different regions of the earth, are not original, but purely superficial."[20]

Positing morphological change from a set of homogeneous progenitors did not require considering the speed with which that change had occurred. Buffon, however, was a uniformitarian not only in his approach to earth history, but also in his approach to the development of physical diversity, and he did not miss the opportunity to maintain that such divergence developed slowly. Indeed, one of his best-known statements about the slowness of change was embedded in a discussion of the morphological differences shown by single species of wild animals:

> If we examine each species in different climates, we shall find sensible varieties both in size and figure. These changes are produced in a slow and imperceptible manner. Time is the great workman of Nature. He moves with regular and uniform steps. He performs no operations suddenly; but by degrees or successive impressions, nothing can resist his power; and those changes which, at first, are imperceptible, become gradually sensible, and at last are marked by results too conspicuous to be misapprehended.[21]

He did feel that because wild animals are less exposed to changes in climate, diet, and mode of life, they are also less subject to morphological change. Nonetheless, he still believed that changes in human morphology required lengthy periods of time. The conspicuous differences that had led some to believe that "the Negro, the Laplander, and the White" belonged to different species had, he suggested, taken "many ages" to develop, and he argued that "many centuries would perhaps be necessary"[22] for a black population to become white once transported to a northern climate. The large number of centuries required was, in fact, indicated by the lack of change in skin color that had occurred during the 200 years since black slaves had been brought to the New World.

Even so, Buffon's emphasis on the slowness with which physical diversity developed did not conflict with his acceptance of the biblical chronology for human antiquity. This was true simply because the inheritance of acquired characters allowed substantial morphological change across six millennia within a fully uniformitarian framework. Thus, in 1749 Buffon suggested that black peoples transplanted into northern districts might become as white as northern natives in eight to twelve generations, and his later speculations on such change was couched in terms of hundreds, not thousands, of years. For Buffon, monogenesis, the environmental induction of morphological variability in human populations, and a short human chronology formed a coherent and consistent package.

While in France Buffon was arguing for monogenesis and the external causation of human physical diversity, the anatomist and physiologist Johann Friedrich Blumenbach (1752–1840) had begun to do so in Germany. Blumenbach's *On the Natural Variety of Mankind* (1775; third edition, 1795) presented a position on human origins and on the development of human diversity that was similar to Buffon's. He agreed with Buffon that all human beings belonged to a single species, although he did not feel that the ability to interbreed and produce fertile offspring provided a sufficient criterion for species membership. Instead, he argued that our genus is monotypic because the physical diversity seen among human populations is no greater than that found among the most variable of all mammals, the domestic forms, and because "one variety of mankind does so sensibly pass into the other, that you cannot mark out the limits between them."[23] There was, he felt, absolutely no evidence that human beings were divided into several species: "only ill-feeling, negligence, and the love of novelty have induced persons to take up the latter opinion. The idea of the plurality of human species has found particular favor with those who made it their business to throw doubt on the accuracy of Scripture."[24] Not only did Blumenbach see all peoples as forming a single species, but he also saw that species as having a single origin. Because Caucasians have the most perfect skulls from which all others diverge, he argued, and because it is relatively easy for a white skin to degenerate into a brown one, but much more difficult for a dark skin to become white, he speculated that the first people must have been Caucasian.

For Blumenbach, as for Buffon, three major factors accounted for modern human physical diversity: climate, diet, and mode of life. Such causes, acting "by long and daily action, continued through many series of generations, are sufficiently strong, slowly, and little by little, to change the primeval character of animals and produce varieties."[25] Thus, like Buffon, Blumenbach argued for single origins, for an environmental cause of human diversity, and for the slow development of that diversity through time. But Blumenbach also accepted the inheritability of acquired characters, stressed the speed with which domesticated animals could change form, and argued that the human species was to be considered the most domesticated mammal of them all. Although he did not address the chronology of deeper human history, his call for the environmental causation of human variability coupled with his assumption of the inheritability of acquired characters and his knowledge of the rapidity of morphological change in domesticated animals meant that his belief in monogenesis did not require any notion of great antiquity for people.

Not all eighteenth-century monogenist positions accepted the external environment as the prime force in causing human diversification. In his *Physical Venus* (1745) and *System of Nature* (1751), Pierre de Maupertuis (1698–1759), for instance, argued that "we are not permitted to doubt"[26] a single origin for all of the world's peoples, and emphasized the importance of internal factors in causing the physical diversity displayed by those peoples. Since there were known cases of white children being born to black parents, but none of white children born to black parents, Maupertuis felt that the human originals were white, and that the varied human skin colors had developed through time from initial whiteness.

How had such diversification come about? One of the reasons for Maupertuis's fame today results from the fact that he saw inheritance as particulate. He argued that particles drawn from the body parts of each parent were transmitted to their seminal fluids, and that these particles then united to form the developing fetus. As a result, offspring tend to resemble their parents. In addition to particles that would form traits identical to each parent, however, there were other, less

numerous particles that had the potential for producing characters possessed by
neither parent. Normally, the more numerous particles, containing the developmental background for parental characters, would combine to produce offspring
that looked like the parents. Nonetheless, at times "chance, or the scarcity of
familial traits, will sometimes cause other assemblages to occur; and one will see
a white child born from black parents, or perhaps even a black one from white
parents, although this latter phenomenon must be much rarer than the former."[27]
Because minority particles representing far-removed ancestors are present in the
seminal fluids of parents, children can even resemble those early ancestors.
Thus, since Maupertuis's earliest human beings were white, he left open the
possibility that black parents could give rise to white offspring, regardless of the
fact that no such instances were known. To Maupertuis, such an event would
simply represent the historical reality of the whiteness of the first members of our
species.

Maupertuis knew from breeding experiments and from his own study of
polydactyly in a Berlin family that newly appearing traits could disappear
through time as well as appear. Therefore he had to address the issue of how
traits could be preserved to form the basis of new varieties. Animal breeders
accomplished these results by ensuring that only those animals with the desired
traits mated with one another. In nature, he suggested, a similar result could
occur by chance; as individuals with the traits in question interbred, the characters of the original parents would become less frequent through time.

He did think that more directional, external forces could bring about the
same results. The first of these forces was provided by climate and diet: "It
seems that the heat of the torrid zone is more likely to foment particles that render
the skin black, than those that render it white: and I do not know where this
influence of climate or of diet might lead, after a long series of centuries."[28] He
also felt that a very different external cause might account for the distribution of a
number of human physical varieties. After having originated by chance, he
suggested, such morphologically distinct individuals as those who were black or
excessively tall might have been forced out of the more congenial portions of the
world by others into the areas in which they are now found.[29]

Nonetheless, Maupertuis's emphasis was on the role of internal hereditary
mechanisms in producing morphological variety, and he combined this emphasis
with a belief in monogenesis. This approach to the development of human
physical diversity demanded even less time than did that of the environmental
monogenists. Variant individuals could arise in a single generation, and, in the
proper setting, could quickly form a morphologically distinct population.
"Black," he observed, "is only a variety that has become inherited over the
course of several generations."[30]

Monogenesis was the prevailing opinion held during the eighteenth century.
Some, like Maupertuis and Immanuel Kant (1724–1804), called on internal

forces to account for human diversity. But most, including Buffon, Blumenbach, Johann Albert Fabricius (1668–1736) in Germany, Petrus Camper (1722–1789) in the Netherlands, and Samuel Stanhope Smith (1750–1819) in the United States, called solely or primarily on external factors, and especially on climate, diet, and mode of life, as the cause of human physical diversity.[31]

The monogenists assigned all peoples to a single species, though the empirical criteria used to support this assignment varied. The ability to interbreed and produce fertile offspring; the possession of diversity no greater than that seen in well accepted, and usually domestic, species of mammals; the difficulty of subdividing human beings into well-defined varieties or races—all these were used singly or in combination to argue for the specific unity of humankind. Most explanations of the diversity displayed by that single species used terminology suggesting that substantial periods of time were required to allow the development of such variety, but there was no strain between the time needed and a short human existence on earth. There was empirical evidence that some physical attributes that at least mimicked the development of racial characters, such as the appearance of albino children to black parents and the birth of polydactylous infants to normal parents, could occur virtually instantaneously. In addition, the widespread belief in the inheritance of acquired characters allowed for the relatively rapid physical divergence of groups in different physical or cultural settings, divergence whose development was to be measured in centuries, not millennia. Lacking any dated, ancient evidence as to how long such changes might take or how long the diversity now displayed by modern peoples had been in existence, those arguing for a single origin for all peoples saw no conflict between this position and a short existence of people on earth. In fact, there was no conflict to be seen.

It is, perhaps, evident that those who argued for the separate origins of physically different human populations also did not have to deal with the question of chronology. Since those populations had been placed on earth in their current, distinct form, the question of how long it had taken for modern divergence to arise simply did not exist. While such a view was now less heretical than it had been in La Peyrère's time, it still did not seem in accord with Genesis. It was, nonetheless, possible to argue for the truth of both the Mosaic account and polygenesis by maintaining that Genesis referred to only one set of people that existed at that time, or to only the first people that had been created. Alternatively, one could argue that Genesis was a divinely inspired allegory.

Henry Homes, Lord Kames (1696–1782) took the second of these approaches in his *Sketches of the Natural History of Man* (1774). Kames argued that "were all men of one species, there never could have existed, without a miracle, different kinds, such as exist at present."[32] His lengthiest discussion was reserved for native Americans. He felt these people must represent a separately created species, because they were so physically and linguistically distinct and because there seemed to be no route by which they could have entered the New World. Following Buffon, Kames suggested that America had emerged from the sea later than any other region, and that "supposing the human race to have been planted in America by the hand of God later than the days of Moses, Adam and Eve might have been the first parents of mankind, *i.e.* of all who at the time existed, without being the first parents of the Americans."[33]

Charles White (1728–1813), on the other hand, took the other two approaches in reconciling Genesis and polygenesis in his *Account of the Regular Gradation in Man* (1799). White observed that just as "nature descends by gradual and imperceptible steps from man down to the least organized beings,"[34] so too do people grade from the highest and best formed, represented by Europeans ("where shall we find, unless in the European, that nobly arched head, containing such a quantity of brain?"[35]), down to the most brute-like peoples, represented by the Hottentots, and from there down to the highest of apes. Climate, he argued, was insufficient to account for the physical differences among human groups, as were all other suggested causes of human diversity through time. The major morphological divisions of humankind had to represent separate species, originally created in the graded sequence in which we now find them. Indeed, to suggest that all peoples had descended from a single pair was to open the door to the possibility that all animals had descended from two progenitors: "a more degrading notion certainly cannot be entertained."[36] White was not sure of the exact number of human species, but felt that at least Americans, some Asiatic groups, black Africans, Europeans, and Hottentots had been created separately. Such a notion did not conflict with Genesis, he noted. Not only was revelation not meant to teach us natural history, but many good Christians accepted the Mosaic account as allegorical. Even if it were factual, Genesis implies the existence of peoples other than those descended from Adam. Were this not the case, he asked, where did Cain get his wife?

The pieces that went together to form the argument for polygenesis in the late eighteenth century can be seen well in the *Natural History of Mankind* (1801) by Julien-Joseph Virey (1775–1846). To Virey, the changes in human form that could be caused by such external factors as climate, diet, and mode of life were only superficial and did not affect the true nature of human groups: "nature does not prostitute the beauty of her works."[37] That these changes are only superficial can be seen, he argued, from two related facts: that people of different color are found in comparable climates, and that people who have migrated retain the physical attributes of their ancestors. Jews, he observed, had been in Germany for 800 years, yet they still looked like Jews. He divided human beings into five named principal races that could not be more than superficially altered by external circumstances. Among these races, he felt that at least three, Americans, black Africans, and Europeans, represented true species that had been created in different homelands. The fact that these separate species can interbreed and produce fertile offspring was not an issue, since many different species can interbreed. Instead, they formed different species because they breed true in spite of external circumstances. Like White, he also arranged the various human races into a graded series, with the most perfect Europeans at the head and the least perfect forms, including the Hottentots, closest to the highest of the apes.

Virey's positions are representative of late eighteenth-century polygenists in a number of important ways. All those who argued for separate origins of morphologically different human groups, both in the eighteenth century and through much of the nineteenth, either had to deny the validity of the ability to interbreed and produce fertile offspring as a test of species identity, or had to deny that the offspring resulting from matings between members of those groups were fully fertile. White, for instance, made both arguments, denying the validity of interfertility as a criterion and asserting that the offspring resulting from mixed matings are less fertile than those produced by members of the same physical variety.[38] In the place of interbreeding as a species criterion, polygenists tended to employ the ability to maintain morphological distinctiveness through an indefinite series of generations, the ability to breed true and remain distinct, as the mark of a real species. Thus, the different varieties of dogs, treated as separate species, became a favored analogue in arguing that the human genus was polytypic. However, eighteenth-century polygenists, just like eighteenth-century monogenists, felt that physical change could occur rapidly, and thus used examples like Virey's German Jews or the lack of physical change across generations of American slaves as proof of the unchanging nature of human morphology. Because of the belief in the possibility of rapid morphological change, those who also believed in the separate origins of different human groups never argued that the short chronology of human existence posed problems for those who believed in monogenesis. In fact, some of those who believed in plural origins—de Maillet and Voltaire, for example—provided arguments for great antiquity.[39]

Thus, during the eighteenth century, the question of single or multiple origins of physically different groups of people was not integrally related to the question of the length of existence of those groups on earth. The common belief in the inheritance of acquired characters and the known instances of rapid morphological change, including albinism, polydactyly, and alterations provided by animal breeding, allowed the monogenists to derive distinct human populations in a relatively brief period of time. However, since both monogenists and polygenists accepted the possibility of such rapid change, neither side saw any conflict between single origins and the recent appearance of people on earth. If Lyell was correct in his opinion that naturalists "have long felt" that a single origin was in conflict with the short chronology of human existence, that conflict must have developed after this time.

In expressing this opinion in *The Antiquity of Man* (1863), Lyell was, as I have noted, repeating an argument he had first made nearly 20 years earlier in the seventh edition of the *Principles* (1847):

> Naturalists have long felt that to render probable the received opinion that all of the leading varieties of the human family have sprung from a single pair, (a doctrine against which there appears to me to be no sound objection,) a much greater lapse of time is required for the slow and gradual formation of races . . . than is embraced in any of the popular systems of chronology. The existence of two of these marked varieties can be traced back 3000 years before the present time, or to the painting of pictures, preserved in the tombs or on the walls of buried temples in Egypt. In these we behold the Negro and Caucasian physiognomies portrayed as faithfully and in as strong contrast as if the likenesses of those races had been taken yesterday. When we consider therefrom the extreme slowness of the changes, which climate and other modifying causes have produced in modern times, we must allow for a vast series of antecedent ages, in the course of which the long-continued influences of similar external circumstances give rise to peculiarities, probably increased in many successive generations, until they were fixed by hereditary transmission.[40]

Lyell had made his argument for a single species of human beings, and for a single origin of that species, earlier in the same volume: "the varieties of form, colour, and organization of different races of men, are perfectly consistent with the generally received opinion, that all the individuals of the species have originated from a single pair."[41] In support of this statement, he cited the work of Blumenbach, William Lawrence, and James Cowles Prichard. Blumenbach saw no conflict between monogenesis and a brief existence of people on earth. Did Lawrence or Prichard?

Lawrence (1783–1867), professor of anatomy and surgery at the Royal College of Surgeons, presented his thoughts on human physical diversity in a series of lectures delivered at that college between 1817 and 1819. He began by posing the main question plainly:

> We may suppose that different kinds of men were originally created; that the forms and properties, of which the contrast now strikes us so forcibly, were impressed at first on the respective races; and consequently that the latter, as we now see them, must be referred to different original families, according to which supposition they will form, in the language of the naturalists, different *species*. Or, we may suppose that one kind of human beings only was formed in the first instance; and account for the diversity, which is now observable, by the agency of the various physical and moral causes to which they have been subsequently exposed; in which case they will only form different *varieties* of the same species.[42]

Lawrence chose the second, monogenetic alternative. Rejecting the production of fertile offspring as a criterion for species membership because members of different species are known to interbreed, he depended instead on three other criteria to assign all people to the same species: that, taken as a whole, people retain their distinctive human characteristics across indefinite series of generations; that all varieties of human beings grade insensibly into one another; and, that the amount of variation within the human species is matched by variation in single species of domestic mammals.

Although this was very similar to Blumenbach's position, to whom the published version of Lawrence's lectures was dedicated, Lawrence did not feel that climate, diet, or mode of life could directly account for the heritable characters that distinguished human populations. The changes caused by such factors affected only individuals, not their offspring:

> The permanency of the characters, of any race, when it has changed its original situation for a very different one, when it has passed into other climes, adopted new manners, and been exposed to the action of these causes for several generations, affords the most indisputable proof that these characteristics are not the offspring of such adventitious circumstances.[43]

In support of this view, he noted that Europeans had been living in Asia and America for three centuries but had undergone no physical change. Similarly, he observed that Africans had been in the New World for nearly the same length of time and they, too, looked the same as they had looked originally. Difference in variety, he argued, could be explained only by two principles: "the occasional production of an offspring with different characters from those of the parents, as a native or congenital variety; and the propagation of such varieties by generation."[44] How this occurred he did not know, but he did know that it occurred most often in domestic animals, perhaps because of the "unnatural causes" to which they are exposed, and that human beings are the most domesticated of all animals. As a result, the great diversity shown by the human species was to be expected.

That Lawrence used the lack of physical change across three centuries of generations of Europeans in Asia and America and across an even smaller series of generations of Africans in the New World shows that he assumed that any effects of external factors on human morphology would have become evident during a brief period of time. His own explanation of diversification did not make any greater temporal demands. The physical effects of domestication could be rapid, as evidenced by "the formation of new varieties, by breeding from individuals in whom the desireable properties exist in the greatest degree."[45] Among people, major new traits could arise in a single generation, as, for instance, polydactyly showed. In addition, such traits could rapidly come to mark an entire population if that population were small, or if the trait itself promoted breeding between like individuals, as with an attribute that imparted greater beauty. Given these views, there was no reason for questions of chronology to arise for Lawrence. Although a major participant in the debate over the origins of human diversity, he was not one of the naturalists to whom Lyell was referring.

Lawrence's views on human diversity were influenced not only by Blumenbach, but also by James Cowles Prichard (1786–1848). Trained as a physician,

Prichard earned lasting fame as a result of his work on both insanity and on ethnology. After submitting a thesis on the nature of variation within the human species in completing his medical studies in 1808, he published his *Researches into the Physical History of Man* in 1813, a work that went through three editions and became the most influential work on human races published in nineteenth-century England before Darwin.

Prichard observed that he had become interested in the nature and origin of human physical diversity "by happening to hear the truth of the Mosaic records implicated in it,"[46] and he was, as George W. Stocking has discussed, deeply committed to revelation as the basis of moral behavior.[47] Accordingly, he was strongly opposed to the view that human beings were divided into several species, and that different peoples stemmed from different origins.

For Prichard, a species was a real entity, marked by "constant and perpetual"[48] differences from other such entities, and whose fixed and permanent boundaries prevented the organic world from lapsing into confusion. Like Blumenbach, Prichard felt that the ability to produce fertile offspring did not provide a sufficient criterion for the definition of a species; the best such criterion was provided instead by analogy with well-accepted species (a conclusion he reached, Prichard said, independently of Blumenbach). Since human beings were no more diverse than well-accepted species of mammals, it followed that all must belong to the same species.

Prichard realized that even if this were the case, it was still "uncertain, whether all the races, into which the genus is separated, derive their origin from one stock, or are the progeny of the same first parents."[49] He solved this problem by analogy as well. Since there are no known instances of a single species of animal being found on separate parts of the earth without there also being a clear migratory route available to allow such a distribution, it followed that each species must have had a single place of origin: that "a single stock of each species was first produced, which was left to extend itself, according as facilities of migration lay open to it, or to find a passage by various accidents into countries removed at greater or less distances from the original point of propagation."[50] Human beings could be no exception; they had been created in a single region, from which they had subsequently dispersed. Analogy, which had served to establish a single species of people, thus served as well to establish a single origin for that species. The problem now became explaining the physical diversity displayed by our species.

In 1813, Prichard was unimpressed with the evidence suggesting that the physical environment could cause human diversity, and equally unimpressed with the evidence for the inheritance of acquired characters. "If an instance be wanting to prove that repetition effects no difference in the results," he appropriately observed, "we have one in the Jews, and in the other nations who have practiced circumcision invariably during many thousand years, yet the artificial state has not become natural."[51]

On the other hand, the most powerful cause of the production of varieties in the animal and plant kingdom was domestication, and people seemed to be no exception to this rule. He found the human analogy to domestication in civilization, and the process of civilization became for him the cause of the development of the major human races. The correlation between degree of civilization and physical attributes showed that this must be the case: the more civilized people were, the more they looked like Europeans. Thus, the most savage peoples were darkest in color; the most civilized, lightest.

Since this was so, it also followed that "the process of Nature in the human species is the transmutation of the characters of the Negro into those of the European, or the evolution of white varieties in black races of men," and that "the primitive stock of men were Negroes."[52] This conclusion was supported by the fact that other species of animals were also known to change from darker to lighter hues, and by the fact that while there were known examples of black people giving birth to lighter colored offspring, there were none in the other direction (William Charles Wells was to provide one 5 years later[53]).

Prichard paid a great deal of attention to chronological issues in the first edition of *Researches,* attention that was directed toward showing that the Septuagint version of the biblical chronology was not put in doubt by the chronologies available for early Egyptian and Indian civilizations. He placed the early Egyptians at about 2500 B.C., and agreed with the dating of the origins of Indian civilization at 2250 B.C., rejecting Indian claims to a greater antiquity as "extravagant pretensions."[54] In 1819, he published a lengthy analysis of Egyptian mythology and chronology that supported the origins of Egyptian civilization in the middle of the third millennium before Christ and no earlier.[55] Clearly, Prichard saw no conflict between monogenesis and a short human chronology at this time. Indeed, his defense of Scripture depended on both points.

Nor was there any reason for such a conflict to develop for him during these years, since his explanation of the development of human diversity at this time allowed for rapid morphological change. He used Maupertuis's polydactylous family as an example of the origin of a physical difference greater than those that distinguished between different varieties of people, and noted that dark peoples who had advanced toward civilization during the past few hundred years have also become lighter in color. In addition, he used an example of physical change through time taken from the archaeological record, one that was later to be used against him with great success.

In 1794, Blumenbach had described the physical attributes of Egyptian mummies and of human depictions on Egyptian monuments, and had observed that the latter illustrated three different kinds of people: Egyptians, Hindus, and a mixed group having attributes of both.[56] Prichard argued that these three physical groups were sequential, with the Ethiopians representing the original Egyptian stock and developing into the Hindu form through time, passing through a mixed phase along the way. For Prichard, this process represented the progressive effects of civilization. Blumenbach, however, had not ordered his physical types in time, nor did Prichard present any evidence that the depictions really were sequential. Instead, he derived the order from the assumption that increasing civilization led to the development of lighter forms from darker ones, and then used the developmental sequence itself to support his argument for single origins. Although Prichard later came to regret the use of Egyptian monuments, in 1813 he saw no difficulty in the evolution of Hindu from Ethiopian morphology within a very short period of time.

The problems that Prichard addressed in the third edition of his *Researches*, published in five volumes between 1836 and 1847, remained the same:

> If a person previously unaware of the existence of such diversities . . . after surveying some brilliant ceremony or court–pageant in one of the splendid cities of Europe, were suddenly carried into a hamlet in Negroland, at the hour when the sable tribes recreate themselves with dancing and barbarous music, or if he were transported to the saline plains over which bald and tawny Mongolians roam, differing but little in hue from the yellow soil of their steppes, brightened by the saffron flowers of the iris and tulip;—if he were placed near the solitary dens of the Bushman, where the lean and hungry savage crouches in silence, like a beast of prey, watching with fixed eyes the birds which enter his pitfall, or greedily devouring the insects and reptiles which chance may bring within his grasp; if he were carried into the midst of an Australian forest, where the squalid companions of kangaroos may be seen crawling in procession, in imitation of quadrupeds;—would the spectator of such phenomena imagine the different groupes which he had surveyed to be the offspring of one family? and if he were led to adopt that opinion, how would he attempt to account for the striking diversities in their aspect and manners of existence?[57]

But while the problems remained the same, and Prichard held as firmly as ever to the belief that all peoples belonged to a single species and shared a common origin, he had now modified many of the arguments he had made in 1813. He still assigned human beings to the same species because the amount and kind of variation they display is analogous to that seen in domestic animals, but now also emphasized the ability of all peoples to interbreed and produce fertile offspring and deemphasized the physical intergradation of human varieties. In addition, he stressed the fact that the very characters that serve to distinguish the best-marked varieties of people can be shown to vary across time and space within a single population, and thus did not distinguish different species of human beings.

He still discussed the correlation between degree of civilization and morphological type, as in noting that "the tribes in whose prevalent conformation the Negro type is discernable in an exaggerated degree, are uniformly in the lowest stage of human society. . . . Whenever we hear of a Negro state, the inhabitants of which have attained any considerable degree of improvement in their social condition, we constantly find that their physical characters deviate considerably from the strongly-marked or exaggerated type of the Negro."[58] But such arguments were now much less important than those that asserted the correlation between physical environment and morphology. Thus, he also observed that "those races who have the Negro character in an exaggerated degree, and who may be said to approach deformity in person . . . are in many instances inhabitants of low countries, often of swampy tracts near the sea-coast."[59] In contrast to his position in 1813, he routinely argued that the external physical environment could alter human morphology, and at the same time he downplayed the effects of civilization in producing such change. People who had changed environments yet remained in the same cultural state, he emphasized, changed form nonetheless, as had Arabs who had emigrated to Africa 1100 or 1200 years ago. Indeed, as Stocking has discussed,[60] his emphasis on the physical environment as a cause of morphological change at times implies a belief in the inheritance of acquired characters, a belief he had strongly denied in 1813.

His argument for the single origin of the one human species remained similar to that used in 1813: the distribution of all species implied a single seat of creation, and there was no reason to believe people exempt from this rule. Gone, however, was the assertion that the original human stock had been black. While he still pointed out that black people could become lighter over the course of generations, but that there were no authenticated cases of comparable change in the opposite direction, he remained silent on the color of the human originals. Stocking has suggested that Prichard abandoned the argument that the first people were black because the idea was poorly received by his European audience.[61] An additional reason may be found in the fact that this position had been embedded in the argument that the process of civilization itself caused morphological change, including the lightening of skin color. Now, with the effects of civilization no longer a central part of his argument, the idea that the first people were black could be abandoned.

Throughout the third edition of *Researches*, Prichard spoke in terms suggesting that changes in human morphology could occur relatively rapidly. Indeed, one of his main props for assigning all peoples to one species was drawn from the fact that changes in the most pronounced physical attributes distinguishing human varieties "have actually arisen in repeated instances, and have generally displayed themselves under the influence of similar external agencies;—that their origination may be historically proved."[62] Thus, he observed that "transitions from one physical character to another strikingly different have sometimes taken place suddenly or in a single generation, as in the occasional appearance of the xanthous variety among the dark-coloured races."[63] More frequently, however, he saw those changes as taking place over "many successive gradations,"[64] as with Arabs in Africa.

The assertion of rapid change notwithstanding, in 1847 Prichard came to believe that the biblical chronology did not provide enough time to allow the development of modern human physical diversity. In a "Note on the Biblical Chronology" appended to the very end of the last volume of the last edition of *Researches* (1847), he abandoned that chronology as revealed fact.

"I might have avoided the discussion," Prichard said, "had it not been pointed out as one which is necessary for the support of my argument, and for establishing the probability of the main conclusion that all mankind are the offspring of one family.''[65] He gave the impression that this necessity had been driven home to him by an anonymous review of the first four volumes of the new edition of *Researches,* which had appeared in the *New Quarterly Review* in 1847. Although the analysis actually impaled Prichard on a number of crucial issues, its closing sentence addressed the problem of time:

> We may add, that he hardly avows to himself, what we think he must feel, that the lapse of time requisite to bring about such changes as he maintains, is far greater than the limits of received history allow. Viewing, therefore, his work as an exceedingly valuable contribution, we are unable to think that the argument is as yet exhausted.[66]

This simple criticism hit home because it was now widely accepted that the depictions of sub-Saharan Africans, Egyptians, and Asians on Egyptian monuments were not sequential, as Prichard had assumed about similar evidence in 1813, but were instead synchronous and dated to at least 1000 or 1500 B.C. Here was a fact Prichard could not evade. Since his own interpretation of the biblical chronology allowed him less than 900 years between the destruction of nearly all peoples in the Deluge and the depictions on the Egyptian monuments, there simply did not seem to be enough time to allow for the development of human diversity displayed on those monuments. Although Prichard had suggested in 1837 that the cause of morphological change ''may have been more powerful in the early stage of the existence of each tribe, than it is now known to be,''[67] it was still clear that something had to give. What gave was the biblical chronology.

Using the same critical approach to the Bible that he had used almost 30 years before in his examination of Egyptian chronology, Prichard argued that the Pentateuch consisted of a series of documents of ancient date but written by unknown persons, not by Moses himself ''solely from the dictates of revelation.''[68] Indeed, ''the Biblical writers had no revelation on the subject of chronology, but computed the sucession of times from such data as were available to them.''[69] Not only were the initial lists of generations in these books incomplete, leading later chronologists to compute a misleadingly short series of years for human existence on earth, but this problem was compounded by the fact that there had been errors introduced into the Pentateuch as it was copied and preserved by later peoples. The omission of generations did not represent a flaw in the Pentateuch, since it was not the purpose of the authors of these books to allow us to construct a chronology but simply to inform us of lines of succession. Prichard did not feel that these difficulties affected later genealogies, but they did mean the early genealogies could not be used to tell time. This, in turn, meant that there was no chronology for the earliest ages of human existence. Prior to the date for the arrival of Abraham in Palestine, ''we can never know how many centuries or even chiliads [thousands] of years may have elapsed since the first man of clay received the image of God and the breath of life."[70] Nonetheless, he concluded, "the whole duration of time from the beginning must apparently have been within moderate bounds."[71]

Prichard had long felt that the separate days of the Mosaic cosmogeny were to be interpreted as indefinite periods and that vast eras of time were to be allowed for the history of the earth prior to the creation of human beings.[72] Now, although he still kept human history within "moderate bounds," he had abandoned entirely the biblical chronology as it pertained to the earlier years of human existence. Clearly, Prichard was one of those naturalists to whom Lyell referred in 1847 as feeling conflict between monogenesis and the received chronology. The anonymous author in the *New Quarterly Review* was another.

That reviewer did not make it clear whether or not he believed in plural origins. Although he stated that "we have no doubt ourselves of the unity of our species,"[73] the firmest of pluralists usually made a pitch for unity at some level, even while arguing for separate origins, differential intelligence, and the like. In addition, the reviewer criticized some of Prichard's most crucial arguments so convincingly that the editor of the *New Quarterly Review* appended a note saying that all tradition and religion supported Prichard's position. It is clear, however, that if time were perceived as a problem, one would expect to find the strongest statements of the problem among the polygenists.

During the decades that Prichard was writing and rewriting *Researches,* arguments for plural origins began to be made with increasing frequency. It is certainly no coincidence that this occurred as Europeans came into closer and closer contact with a wide variety of non-Western peoples, and as relationships among racial groups were becoming the focus of deepening social and political problems.[74]

In France, for instance, Virey continued to develop his position, publishing a lengthy discussion of human variation in the *New Dictionary of Natural History* in 1817, and a second edition of the *Natural History of Mankind* in 1824.[75] He now divided people into two species on the basis of both morphological and cultural attributes, and then subdivided these into three races each. Arguing that climate could not cause such differences, he maintained that each race had dispersed from a separate homeland. He felt that natural history could not tell us if "people had been created thus, or if they were drawn from a single man,"[76] but since he also argued that the differences among human races were "fundamental and original,"[77] the implications were quite clear. While pointing out the absence of human remains in association with the remains of extinct mammals, however, Virey did not use this fact to attack the hypothesis of single origins.

Jean Baptiste Bory de Saint Vincent (1778–1846) went even further in subdividing human beings. In his *Zoological Essay on Mankind* (1827), he defined 15 separate human species, organized into two subgenera and speculated on the separate homelands of each of these species. He doubted that all of the kinds had been created synchronously and suggested that "the degree of civilization or of barbarity of each of these can provide a sufficiently exact fact for establishing the comparative degree of their antiquity."[78] He subdivided humankind much more than had Virey, and he also pointed out that none of his human types could be very old because no truly ancient human remains had been found. However, he followed Virey in not using this fact to implicate the monogenist position.

In America, where polygenism came to be most strongly developed and most influential, the chronological issue gained most play by pluralists. The scientific development of the American pluralist position began with the publication of Samuel G. Morton's *Crania Americana* in 1839. A native Philadelphia physician and anatomist, Morton (1799–1851) based the analysis of human variation presented in *Crania Americana* on the large collection of human skulls that he had amassed and housed at the Philadelphia Academy of Natural Sciences. Unlike many earlier writers, the author of this study had a data base from which to work.

Morton began *Crania Americana* by observing that the prevalent belief as to the origin of human beings was derived from Scripture, but he then made a statement that seemed to indicate that he did not ascribe to that belief:

> We may inquire, whether it is not more consistent with the known government of the universe to suppose, that the same Omnipotence that created man, would adapt him at once to the physical, as well as to the moral circumstances in which he was to dwell upon the earth? It is indeed difficult to imagine that an all-Wise Providence, after having by the Deluge destroyed all mankind excepting the family of Noah, should leave these to combat, and with seemingly uncertain and inadequate means, the various external causes that tended to oppose the great object of their destination: and we are left to the reasonable conclusion, that each Race was adapted from the beginning to its peculiar local distribution. In other words, it is assumed, that the physical characteristics which distinguish the different Races, are independent of external causes.[79]

In addition, Morton made a chronological assault on the monogenist position, pointing out that the earliest available records show different peoples to look as exactly as they look today: "the characteristic features of the Jews may be recognised in the sculptures of the temples of Luxor and Karnak, in Egypt, where they have been depicted for nearly thirty centuries."[80] And, to drive home the point, he also observed that

> the recent discoveries in Egypt . . . show beyond all question, that the Caucasian and Negro races were as perfectly distinct in that country, upwards of three thousand years ago as they are now: whence it is evident that if the Caucasian was derived from the Negro, or the Negro from the Caucasian, by the action of external causes, the change must have been effected in at most a thousand years; a theory which the subsequent evidence of thirty centuries proves to be a physical impossibility.[81]

Although Morton denied the power of external agencies in causing human diversity and although he pointed out the serious conflict between the argument for single origins based upon such causes and the biblical chronology, he left his own views as to the single or multiple origins of different human varieties up in the air. Following Blumenbach, he divided humanity into five races, but did not argue that they had been separately created: such a conclusion was up to the reader to draw. That one did not have to draw a conclusion of separate origins is clear from Prichard's 1841 review of *Crania Americana*. Prichard was clearly wary of where Morton was heading but could not determine Morton's stand on this issue. His review was primarily a synopsis of Morton's data and conclusions, and ended with the observation that *Crania Americana* "well deserves to be generally known and to find a place in every library connected with natural science."[82]

Morton had, however, raised the chronological question in an important way, and he was not about to let the issue slide. During an 1842 lecture to the Boston Society of Natural History, for instance, he stressed the distinctiveness of all American Indians, took a strong stand on the original distinctiveness of each human variety, and once again used the Egyptian monuments to box the monogenists into a corner:

> Where others can see nothing but change, we can perceive a wise and obvious design, displayed in the original adaptation of the several races of men to these varied circumstances of climate and locality which, while congenial to the one, are destructive to the other. The evidence of history and the Egyptian monuments go to prove that these races were as distinctly stamped three thousand five hundred years ago as they are now; and, in fact, that they are coeval with the primitive dispersion of our species.[83]

At the same time Morton was delivering these words, he was also preparing a major analysis of the physical types evidenced by early Egyptian skulls and by depictions on early Egyptian monuments. The results of this study were presented to the American Philosophical Society in 1842 and 1843, and published as *Crania Aegyptica* in 1844. Here Morton gathered all the data he needed to demonstrate that many human races were fully in existence by as early as 2000 or 2500 B.C. His detailed review of the cranial and monumental data left no doubt that "the physical or organic characters which distinguish the several varieties of men, are as old as the oldest records of our species."[84] Morton, whose abilities could be denied by none, had presented the proof to back up his earlier statements as to the existence of Caucasians, Negroes, and other human physical varieties in modern form some two millennia or more before Christ—less than 1000 years after the Septuagint date for the Flood.

It was this argument that got Prichard in trouble. He could not deny Morton's evidence, since Morton had made his case impeccably. He could not deny Morton's chronology, since it agreed with his own; indeed, Morton had cited Prichard as one of the sources for his dates. Here were varieties of people looking just as they look now, but dating to less than a millennium after the Flood. Prichard's discussion of the biblical chronology in the last volume of the *Researches* was no response to the anonymous critic in the *New Quarterly Review*:

it was a response to Morton. Prichard abandoned the biblical chronology in order to provide himself with enough time for the development of Morton's ancient races.

Here, then, was the pressure on the received chronology imparted by the debate over human physical diversity. The pressure began in the late 1830s, but came primarily in the early 1840s, particularly as a result of the 1844 publication of Morton's *Crania Aegyptica*. It was this book that made the difference. Although Morton asserted the full development of human races nearly 3 millennia ago in Egypt in his *Crania Americana* (1839), Prichard could ignore that assertion, and did ignore it in his review of 1841. He could not ignore *Crania Aegyptica* with its full documentation. The problem, of course, was a problem only for the monogenists. Morton showed that single origins could not be reasonably accommodated within the biblical chronology, but that the origins of human physical diversity "coeval with the primitive dispersion of our species"[85] could be so accommodated.

The reviews that appeared of Prichard's completed *Researches* make it clear that the point had been made to others as well. The physician Henry Holland (1788–1873) provided such a review in the *Quarterly Review* for 1850, also analyzing Prichard's more popular *The Natural History of Man,* Baron Bunsen's "Results of Egyptian Researches," and those chapters of the seventh edition of Lyell's *Principles* that dealt with transmutation, species concepts, and organic diversity.[86] Holland was a staunch monogenist, and emphasized the evidence for rapid morphological change. "Climate, food, and other contingencies"[87] caused human physical diversity, and the proof of the power of these causes was to be found in the fact that changes in human morphology have occurred during the past few centuries in the absence of interbreeding. The mechanism that allowed such rapid change was the inheritance of acquired characters: "qualities or instincts artificially acquired, but which, so transmitted and maintained by use, tend to become hereditary in the breed."[88] At one time, arguments of this sort sufficed to reconcile the monogenist position with the biblical chronology, but no longer. "A more momentous and difficult question," Holland noted, "is that of the time involved in the early part of man's history, and requisite to explain his dispersion and multiplication on the globe. . . . We must postpone its consideration till the whole topic is more completely before us."[89] What did not have to be postponed, however, was the question of the biblical chronology, because that chronology could no longer be felt to apply to all of human history. Other means of measuring time were needed and, to explain the development of modern human physical diversity from a common source, "time is manifestly an element of the greatest importance."[90]

The physiologist William B. Carpenter (1813–1885) provided a similar analysis for the *Edinburgh Review* in 1848. Carpenter, with Holland, believed that all peoples shared a single origin, that external conditions could cause fairly rapid physical change, and that the historical records demonstrated such change. Like Prichard, he believed that the most rapid physical diversification would have occurred during the earliest years of human existence. Again, these positions would not have been in conflict with the biblical chronology as recently as a dozen years earlier. Now, however, "the lapse of time necessary to bring about such changes as those required in any hypothesis of the single origin of the human races, is far greater than the received chronology admits; the evidence of extreme diversity of races being at least coeval with the earliest records."[91] Those earliest records, of course, were the Egyptian monuments. He observed that geological researches were continually extending the length of the modern epoch, during which people had been in existence, so that "we are quite free to assign any moderate number of thousands of years that we may think necessary, for the diffusion of the race, and for the origination of its varieties."[92] But with bitterness he noted that "an objection founded upon the authenticity of the Mosaic chronology comes with an ill grace from those who refuse their assent to the Mosaic account of the origin of the human race from a single pair."[93]

The point made, some American polygenists soon dropped any pretense of belief in the scriptural chronology. The most vocal attacks came from the Mobile physician and medical scholar Josiah C. Nott (1804–1873) and from George R. Gliddon (1809–1857). Gliddon had been appointed United States vice-consul in Cairo in 1832, but he subsequently became interested in Egyptian antiquities, studied under some of the best Egyptologists, and launched a popular lecture series on Egypt in the United States.[94] Although the two began to publish on issues dealing with human origins, chronology, and Egyptian antiquities in the 1840s, it was their joint production of *Types of Mankind* in 1854 that spread their views most widely.

Although the often inflammatory writing styles of Nott and, especially, Gliddon, did not help to give their book an aura of scientific respectability, the book could not be ignored in Europe because of the contribution made to it by Louis Agassiz.

Agassiz came to the United States from Switzerland in 1846, and remained here for the rest of his life. Although he had argued in 1845 for the unity of the human species,[95] his views on this issue changed soon after his arrival in the United States. Edward Lurie has suggested two reasons for this shift that certainly seem correct.[96] First, his move to America acquainted Agassiz with Americans of African descent, an acquaintance that impressed him negatively. "The more pity I feel at the sight of this degraded and degenerate race," he wrote to his mother in 1846, "the more . . . impossible it becomes for me to repress the feeling that they are not of the same blood as we are."[97] Second, Agassiz was strongly opposed to all transmutationist theory. His view of the unfolding of life saw that unfolding as progressing toward humanity in discontinuous steps and as representing the realization of the Divine plan. New creations following mass extinctions were an important part of this view, and Agassiz used the ice and cold of the glacial age to explain one such catastrophic set of extinctions.[98] Had the great physical diversity displayed by human beings developed through time as a result of variations on an original morphological theme, it might also have been possible for other creatures to so vary, and for related organisms to have been derived from one another through time. "A more degrading notion certainly cannot be entertained," as Charles White said in 1799.

In a series of articles published in the *Christian Examiner* in 1850 and 1851,[99] Agassiz used the Egyptian data to show that the passage of time does not see change in human morphology. He argued that the distribution of human physical types is not well correlated with such external factors as climate and observed that the location of human varieties coincides with zoogeographic provinces defined on the basis of other organisms. These facts implied to him that the "assertion of the common descent of all races of men from a common stock is a mere human construction,"[100] and that "men were primitively located in the various parts of the world they inhabit, and . . . arose everywhere in those harmonious numeric proportions with other living beings, which would at once secure their preservation and contribute to their welfare."[101]

In these articles, Agassiz did not assert that different human varieties formed different species. He was concerned only with showing that the differences among these varieties were original, not derived, and that this view did not conflict with Scripture. In his contribution to *Types of Mankind,* however, he not only repeated these positions, but went a step further. A few years earlier, Morton had argued that interfertility was no proof of conspecificity.[102] In 1851, the year of his death, Morton suggested that a species be defined as a "primordial organic form,"[103] a group of organisms whose defining characters had been impressed upon them at the time of their origination and that did not change through time. Morton's primordial organic forms varied from proximate species, which could produce fully fertile offspring, to remote species, which could not produce hybrids at all. In *Types of Mankind,* Agassiz adopted Morton's species definition, and concluded that "what are called human races, down to their specialization as nations, are distinct primordial forms of the type of man.[104] That is, they are in Morton's sense different species. Were it otherwise, Agassiz was careful to point out, the consequences would "run inevitably into the Lamarckian development theory."[105]

Although Nott and Gliddon were not internationally known scientists, Agassiz was; the inclusion of his paper ensured that *Types of Mankind* would be noticed by the European scientific community. Agassiz did not deal with the issue of chronology, but that issue was impossible to avoid elsewhere in the volume. Nott made much of Prichard's abandonment of the biblical chronology, and concluded that "it is now generally conceded that there exist no data by which we can approximate the date of man's first appearance on earth; and, for ought we yet know, it may be thousands or millions of years beyond our reach."[106] While Nott's phraseology was often intemperate, it never matched Gliddon's venom. Regarding the use of the biblical chronology to date early events, Gliddon spouted that "it is far worse than folly: it is an absolute disregard of every principle of rectitude; an impudent mockery of educated reason; a perpetualized insult to honest undertakings. . . . Ignorance, abject ignorance."[107] Nott and Gliddon cited the work of Boucher de Perthes, Schmerling, and others to support their argument for a great human antiquity. In addition, they included a chapter by William Usher, a Mobile physician, on "Geology and paleontology, in connection with human origins." Usher listed a number of instances in which human remains had been found in association with extinct mammals, including Kent's Cavern, Engihoul, Bize, and Gailenreuth, and dedicated a full 15 pages to Boucher de Perthes and his *Antiquities* alone. The conclusion was inevitable: "human fossil remains have now been found so frequently, and in circumstances so unequivocal, that the facts can hardly be denied; except by persons who resolutely refuse to believe anything that can militate against their own preconceived notions."[108] The position of the majority of American polygenists on the biblical chronology was clear. That chronology was, as H. S. Patterson wrote to Nott in 1850, a broken reed.[109]

Not all polygenists took this position. In 1848, for instance, Charles Hamilton Smith (1776–1859) accepted the association of human remains with extinct mammals, but he followed de Serres in inferring the recency of the extinctions from this association and argued that the Egyptian depictions of Caucasians and Negroes allowed insufficient time for the development of these forms since "the last great cataclysis."[110] But the general picture is clear. During the 1840s, Morton's arguments had created an irreconcilable conflict between the received chronology and monogenesis, forcing the monogenists to abandon that chronology. Most polygenists soon dropped that chronology themselves. By the early 1850s, the debate over the origin of human varieties had seriously weakened the belief that the absolute antiquity of our species could be extracted from the Bible.

Where does this leave us in regard to Lyell's statement that "naturalists have long felt that to render probable the received opinion that all the leading varieties of the human family have originally sprung from a single pair . . . a much greater lapse of time is required . . . than is embraced in any of the popular systems of chronology?"[111] In 1863, this statement was clearly true. But just as clearly, it was not true in 1847: only 3 years had passed since *Crania Aegyptica* had been published. There is no need to infer the impact of this work on Lyell. Just 7 years earlier, in the sixth edition of *Principles* (1840), he had included that same statement on human unity that he was to include in the seventh edition, that "all the individuals of the species have originated from a single pair,"[112] but he did not mention that monogenesis and the received chronology were in conflict. Something happened between 1840 and 1847 that led Lyell to discuss this conflict. The fact that Lyell followed his 1847 comment on the received chronology with his discussion of the "Negro and Caucasian physiognomies" depicted on Egyptian monuments shows that what happened was *Crania Aegyptica*.

While it is true that Lyell's statement in 1847 was incorrect, it is very likely that the statement was true for him. Lyell's species journals, although written between 1855 and 1861, show that he was much more impressed by the differences between human varieties than he ever suggested in his publications. In 1856, for instance, he noted that "the creation of a true species will be a very rare event. . . . The appearance of man may have been a recent exemplification and the Negro a sub-species which in one of the Quadrumana might have been described as a species."[113] Comments of this sort, comparing human varieties to full species among other mammals, are found throughout Lyell's journals on transmutation, as are statements calling for considerable amounts of time for the formation of such varieties. In 1856, he used 20,000 years, 50,000 years, and 2,000 and 4,000 generations as possible figures for the time depth of existing human races. In the same year, and in direct reference to the Egyptian data, he noted that

> the most orthodox creed must assign an antiquity to the human race so great that 3000 or 4000 years tells for little in the formation of a distinct race and in ascending the stream of time, we must reach an era of tens of thousands of years to revert to the departure from a common stock.[114]

It seems likely, then, that in 1847 Lyell's comment about the difficulties "naturalists" had long felt about the relationship between monogenesis and the biblical chronology referred mainly to himself. Lyell was using an editorial "we," a device he used on other occasions.[115] Other naturalists had only recently come to feel that way and to publish such feelings, and the issue now had to be addressed. Lyell addressed it, and did so in such a way as to make the issue appear more routine than it really was. By 1853, when he repeated the statement in the ninth edition of the *Principles,* it was entirely true, and it was truer still in 1863.

Notes and References

1. Daniel 1950, 1976.
2. Slotkin 1965.
3. [La Peyrère] 1656:21–22.
4. [La Peyrère] 1655:[ii].
5. [La Peyrère] 1655:140.
6. [La Peyrère] 1655:122.
7. [La Peyrère] 1655:208.
8. [La Peyrère] 1655:126.

9. [La Peyrère] 1655:163.
10. [La Peyrère] 1655:261.
11. McKee 1944; biographical information I have presented on La Peyrère is from this source and from Bendyshe 1865.
12. White 1896.
13. Hale 1677:184.
14. Hale 1677:185.
15. Hale 1677:189.
16. Greene 1959.
17. Smellie 1791, Volume 3:206–207.
18. Smellie 1791, Volume 7:403.
19. Smellie 1791, Volume 3:165.
20. Smellie 1791, Volume 7:392–393.
21. Smellie 1791, Volume 4:70–71.
22. Smellie 1791, Volume 7:395.
23. Blumenbach 1865[1775]:98–99.
24. Blumenbach 1865[1775]:98.
25. Blumenbach 1865[1795]:200.
26. Maupertuis 1974[1768], Volume 2:106. All citations are to *Vénus Physique* (1745). See Glass 1959 for a discussion of Maupertuis's biological work.
27. Maupertuis 1974[1768], Volume 2:121–122.
28. Maupertuis 1974[1768], Volume 2:123.
29. See Maupertuis 1974[1768], Volume 2:129–130.
30. Maupertuis 1974[1768], Volume 2:125.
31. For Kant, see the discussion in Greene 1959; Fabricius 1865[1721]; for Camper, see Cogan 1821; Smith 1965[1810].
32. Kames 1774–1775, Volume 1:41.
33. Kames 1774–1775, Volume 3:86.
34. White 1799:10.
35. White 1799:135.
36. White 1799:133.
37. Virey 1801, Volume 1:74.
38. White 1799.
39. De Maillet 1748; Voltaire 1963.
40. Lyell 1847:634.
41. Lyell 1847:583.
42. Lawrence 1828:213.
43. Lawrence 1828:462.
44. Lawrence 1828:438.
45. Lawrence 1828:392.
46. Prichard 1813:ii.
47. Stocking 1973. Stocking's analysis must be consulted by anyone interested in Prichard's work; the biographical information I have presented on Prichard is from this source.
48. Prichard 1813:8.
49. Prichard 1813:86.
50. Prichard 1813:145.
51. Prichard 1813:199.
52. Prichard 1813:233.
53. Wells 1818.
54. Prichard 1813:433.

55. Prichard 1819.
56. Blumenbach 1794.
57. Prichard 1836:1–2.
58. Prichard 1837:338.
59. Prichard 1837:337.
60. Stocking 1973.
61. Stocking 1973.
62. Prichard 1847:549.
63. Prichard 1847:549–550.
64. Prichard 1847:550.
65. Prichard 1847:553.
66. Anonymous 1847:134.
67. Prichard 1837:108.
68. Prichard 1847:562.
69. Prichard 1847:557.
70. Prichard 1847:570.
71. Prichard 1847:570.
72. See, for instance, Prichard 1815 and 1816; see also the discussion in Stocking 1973.
73. Anonymous 1847:97.
74. Lurie 1954; Stocking 1968.
75. Virey 1817, 1824.
76. Virey 1817:174.
77. Virey 1817:174.
78. Bory de Saint Vincent 1827, Volume 1:161.
79. Morton 1839:2–3; see Gould 1978 for a discussion of subtle biases in Morton's analysis. The best discussion of the American polygenists is found in Stanton 1960.
80. Morton 1839:2.
81. Morton 1839:88.
82. Prichard 1841:561.
83. Morton 1844a:36.
84. Morton 1844b:66.
85. Morton 1844a:36.
86. Prichard 1843; Bunsen 1848; Lyell 1847 (the title of Holland's review incorrectly indicates that it was Lyell's *Elements of Geology* that was under discussion). Holland's paper also examined Smith 1848.
87. [Holland] 1850:21.
88. [Holland] 1850:27.
89. [Holland] 1850:33.
90. [Holland] 1850:25.
91. [Carpenter] 1848:485.
92. [Carpenter] 1848:486.
93. [Carpenter] 1848:485.
94. Stanton 1960.
95. See the discussion in Stanton 1960.
96. Lurie 1954, 1960; see also Marcou 1896.
97. Lurie 1960:257.
98. See the discussion in Bowler 1976 and Grayson 1983.
99. Agassiz 1850a, 1850b, 1851.
100. Agassiz 1850b:135.
101. Agassiz 1850b:137–138.
102. See, for instance, Morton 1847a, 1847b, and 1850.

103. Morton 1851:275.
104. Agassiz 1854:lxxvi.
105. Agassiz 1854:lxxvi.
106. Nott 1854:59.
107. Gliddon 1854:662.
108. Usher 1854:343.
109. Patterson 1854:lii.
110. Smith 1848:130.
111. Lyell 1857:660.
112. Lyell 1840, Volume 3:79.
113. Wilson 1970:92.
114. Wilson 1970:98; see also pp. 84, 97, and 115.
115. Bartholomew 1973.

8

A New Resolution
Reached: 1850–1860

Analyses of human morphological diversity did not stand alone in mid-nineteenth century scientific thought. Increasingly detailed information concerning the tremendous linguistic and cultural diversity of the world's peoples also suggested that our species had been on earth far longer than the biblical chronology would allow, though the results of the morphological studies were certainly most visible.[1] By about 1850, analyses of all this diversity had greatly weakened adherence to the Mosaic chronology. "It makes no difference to our argument," wrote the Reverend William Whewell in 1853, "whether we accept six thousand or ten thousand years, or even a longer period, as the interval which has elapsed since the creation of man took place, and the peopling of the earth began."[2]

While studies of modern diversity could strongly imply that the biblical chronology was wrong, however, this was all they could do. They could not address the crucial issue of whether human beings were geologically ancient, whether they had appeared on earth prior to the time the globe had taken on its modern form. Only archaeological data could do that, because only archaeological data could be tightly associated with deposits that were geologically ancient.

"The present state of things is that to which the existence and history of Man belong," said Whewell, and there is no evidence that our species existed alongside the mastodon and the mammoth, no vestige of man "previous to the deposits and changes which we can trace as belonging obviously to the present state of the earth's surface, and the operation of causes now existing."[3] And, Whewell noted, that present state extends back an unknown but clearly vast amount of time. The resolution of this aspect of human antiquity had to come from the earth itself.

When Pierre Cordier informally transmitted the opinion of the commission appointed by the Academy of Sciences to report on the first volume of *Antiquities* to Boucher de Perthes, he noted that the publication of this work would probably come to "excite lively opposition . . . and to provoke further observation." The solution, Cordier suggested, would probably result from the ensuing debate. The commission's opinion about lively opposition may have been an obvious one, but it was nonetheless correct.

Boucher de Perthes's work attracted attention not only on both sides of the English Channel, but on both sides of the Atlantic Ocean. I have mentioned that the initial reaction to the first volume of *Antiquities* was largely negative. Although that reaction cut across national boundaries, the response of the English geologist Gideon Mantell was typical.

Mantell's review of the data that seemed to suggest a great human antiquity was delivered to the Royal Archaeological Institute in Oxford in June 1850. It was, in fact, "a perusal of the treatise of M. Boucher de Perthes"[4] that suggested to him that such a review was necessary. His approach to the evidence for ancient peoples was generally Lyellian in its cautious and even-handed nature. Mantell gave examples of such clearly modern materials as coins and nails embedded in breccia to show that geological settings that seemed to imply great antiquity might be extremely misleading, and he used Kent's Cavern as a prime example of a misleading site of this sort. Here, he argued, human remains had sunk through the travertine layer before it had hardened, and had thus become accidentally mixed with the remains of extinct mammals. As a result, it could be concluded that "the occurrence of the remains of man with those of extinct species of animals, in a deposit that is covered by a thick layer of solid rock, must not be regarded as a certain proof that the human bones are of as high antiquity as those of the quadrupeds with which they are associated."[5] Although he felt it possible that human remains might someday be found with the remains of mammoth and other ancient, extinct mammals, he also felt that the associations to date "have generally, upon a rigid examination, failed to establish the synchronism of the human and quadrupedal remains."[6]

But Mantell abandoned his even-handed approach when it came to Boucher de Perthes and his *Antiquities*. Boucher de Perthes had, he correctly observed, "deteriorated the value of his antiquarian labours by vague and erroneous conclusions, which but a slight acquaintance with the elements of geology would have enabled him to avoid.''[7] Moreover, one could ''perceive at a glance that the so-called antediluvian works of art, figured and described by M. Boucher de Perthes, are nothing more than accidental forms of pebbles and stones . . . which can never have been fashioned by the hand of man.''[8] While the idea of reviewing the evidence for human remains discovered in possibly ancient contexts had been suggested to Mantell by Boucher de Perthes's book, that book itself did not merit serious consideration, and Mantell did not consider it.

Mantell was not pleased with his experience at the Royal Archaeological Institute: ''Most of the leading members of the Institution were absent! dining out. . . . Very great mismanagement and enough to deter me from undergoing so much trouble again for so little purpose.''[9] Nonetheless, because his critique was published it did not go unnoticed. In France, Alfred Maury (1817–1892) translated and paraphrased Mantell's review, added a more detailed discussion of French sites, and published the results in the *Memoirs* of the National Society of Antiquaries of France in 1852. Maury agreed with virtually everything that Mantell had to say, though he felt that the problem of accidental admixture in caves had been overstated. Many sites, Maury felt, had contained human relics stratigraphically above those of extinct mammals but had not been dug with sufficient care to keep those materials separate. Excavators themselves had intermingled debris from upper strata containing human remains with debris from lower strata that lacked them. This, he thought, was what had led de Serres astray.

It was not, however, what had led Boucher de Perthes astray, for Maury was convinced that Boucher de Perthes had carefully distinguished the various beds with which he had worked. The problem with Boucher de Perthes's work stemmed from his heavy dependence on his workers to find human relics. On matters of such a crucial nature, the workers were not to be trusted, and there was good reason to entertain serious question as to where the artifacts had really been found: ''It is very possible, after having read M. Boucher de Perthes's book, to have doubts on the precision of the observations relating to the elevations at which the axes were discovered.''[10] In addition, Maury felt that many of the stone tools illustrated by Boucher de Perthes were not stone tools at all. Instead, they seemed to be naturally occurring flints whose shape recalled those of modern implements. Only the preoccupation of an antiquarian, Maury thought, could have ''made him interpret as products of art that which was only the work of nature.''[11] Finally, Maury asserted that those aspects of Boucher de Perthes's results that could not be interpreted as due either to the mistakes of the workers or to the misinterpretation of naturally occurring objects had resulted from accidental admixture. In short, he felt that nothing Boucher de Perthes had presented to support a great human antiquity was of any value.

Between them, Mantell and Maury voiced the major criticisms that were to be made during the initial wave of reaction to the first volume of *Antiquities*.

Boucher de Perthes had been deceived by his workers, he had mistaken natural items for items worked by human hands, he had missed stratigraphic evidence for accidental admixture, and he clearly had little knowledge of contemporary geology. Many of these were reasonable responses because many of them were, in fact, correct. But these responses at least helped make Boucher de Perthes's work better known. A second way of handling his work—ignoring it entirely— did not accomplish this.

This second route was taken by many scientists, including the Swiss paleontologist François-Jules Pictet (1809–1872). In the second edition of his *Treatise on Paleontology* (1853), Pictet addressed a short but meaty section to the question of whether "man appeared on the surface of the earth before the modern epoch."[12] He reviewed the older and generally rejected evidence for ancient people, including Scheuchzer's salamander and the Guadeloupe skeleton, and then turned to the real issue. Pictet felt that the question was a straightforward empirical one, that there was no a priori reason to believe people had not coexisted with the extinct mammals whose remains had been found in the diluvium. He carefully reviewed the cave data, and included a lengthy series of references to the work of de Serres, Tournal, Christol, Teissier, Schmerling, and others. He observed that Schmerling, in particular, had presented information that was "difficult to contest,"[13] and then summarized potentially ancient human remains from open sites, including Boué's material and the human remains from Denise. He had visited Denise with Aymard and was convinced of the integrity of the association here, suggesting that while the human bones were old, they were not as old as the deposits in the caves of Belgium or southern France. He concluded that some of the evidence forwarded for the contemporaneity of human beings and extinct mammals was valid: "the first men who entered Europe perhaps saw the cave bear, the elephants, and the contemporary animals; some among them were victims of the same inundations. . . . The definitive establishment of man in Europe and the occupation of this continent by a large population probably took place after the great inundation, which deposited the rolled pebbles in the caverns and on the plains of our continents."[14]

Here, in a major work, was a sympathetic view of the argument that people and extinct mammals had coexisted. Pictet not only provided a concise review of the evidence but also concluded that some of the associations were real and that people had lived and died with the extinct mammals. But what of Boucher de Perthes and his evidence? Of the more than 50 references Pictet provided, none referred to Boucher de Perthes's *Antiquities*.

Not everyone who discussed Boucher de Perthes's work during the early 1850s discussed it unfavorably. Those who responded positively, however, were hardly influential scientists. One of the favorable responses came from Abraham Hume (1814–1884), a Liverpool cleric. In 1851, Hume published his discussion "On Certain Implements of the Stone Period" in the *Transactions* of the Historic

Society of Lancashire and Cheshire, a society he had helped found 3 years earlier. Here, Hume accepted most of Boucher de Perthes's arguments concerning the early stone tools from Abbeville: they were real artifacts, including the figured stones (some of which Hume illustrated), they had been used as symbolic items, and they were probably antediluvian in age. Indeed, Boucher de Perthes saw Hume's acceptance of his work as a real coup, and used Hume's paper to contrast the rejection he had received in France with the acceptance he had gained in England.[15] What Boucher de Perthes did not point out in this overstatement was that Hume did not agree with all that he had argued in 1847. Hume not only felt that the difficulties of assessing the age of these artifacts were insurmountable, a point with which Boucher de Perthes would have agreed, but also felt that "man has been on the face of the earth nearly 6000 years,"[16] a position very different from that which Boucher de Perthes had taken. Although Hume agreed that Boucher de Perthes had discovered antediluvian implements, that term had a very different meaning for the Liverpool cleric than it had for the Abbeville antiquarian.

The most extensive discussion of Boucher de Perthes's work published during the early 1850s, however, came not from Europe but from America, and was provided by William Usher in Nott and Gliddon's *Types of Mankind* (1854). Usher's 15-page discussion of Boucher de Perthes was dedicated to providing translations of parts of the first volume of *Antiquities,* reproducing illustrations from that volume, and emphasizing the great antiquity of Boucher de Perthes's antediluvian artifacts. Usher, of course, had nothing but praise for all those who had provided evidence for ancient peoples, including Boucher de Perthes, since such evidence helped make the case for an extremely long human existence on earth, an existence that was part of the attack Nott and Gliddon were then making on the monogenist position (see Chapter 7).

In short, the initial reaction of influential scientists to the first volume of *Antiquities* was to reject or ignore it. Acceptance came from those working on the fringes of the scientific community, a place that Boucher de Perthes himself unwillingly occupied. Cordier's prediction of lively opposition had come true.

Cordier's prediction of further observations also turned out to be accurate. The most important of those observations during the early 1850s resulted from the work of Marcel-Jérôme Rigollot (1786–1854). Rigollot was a physician from the town of Amiens, 40 kilometers upstream from Abbeville in the Somme River valley. He had broad antiquarian interests, and was an active participant in, and frequent president of, the Society of Antiquaries of Picardy. Rigollot's experience in geological and paleontological matters was much more extensive than Boucher de Perthes's; as early as 1819, he conducted research on the extinct mammals known from the valley of the Somme and provided Cuvier with materials that were incorporated into the second edition of Cuvier's *Researches.*[17]

In 1849, Rigollot wrote to Boucher de Perthes to inform him that "the

Academy of Amiens has also received your volume and has charged me with
making a report for them, a report that will also serve for the Society of Antiquaries.''[18] At the time, Rigollot was by no means disposed to agree with
Boucher de Perthes's arguments and conclusions. According to one of Rigollot's
colleagues, his visit to examine Boucher de Perthes's collection was not one he
was highly motivated to make: "Dr. Rigollot was led into M. Boucher de
Perthes's gallery to examine his collection of antediluvian artifacts. *He did not
want to come here,* and it was almost necessary to do him violence to get him to
do it; he treated these discoveries as impossible, even as absurd.''[19]

In 1853, however, Rigollot was told that at St. Acheul, near Amiens, stone
tools had been found in deposits that had also yielded elephant bones. As a
result, he excavated both here and at St. Roch, about 2.5 kilometers distant
(Figures 8.1 and 8.2). At St. Acheul, Rigollot discovered stone implements in
gravels that also held the remains of elephant, horse, cattle, and deer; at St.
Roch, he found stone tools associated with the remains of rhinoceros. Of these
two sites, St. Acheul was by far the most productive. Workers here found over
400 stone implements, while Rigollot himself retrieved over 150. To confirm the
antiquity of his discoveries, Rigollot brought in two geologists: Charles-Joseph
Buteux (1794–1876), who had written major works on the geology of the valley
of the Somme, and Edmond Hébert (1812–1890), professor of geology at the
Sorbonne. These geologists confirmed that the deposits at St. Acheul and St.
Roch were, indeed, of diluvial age.

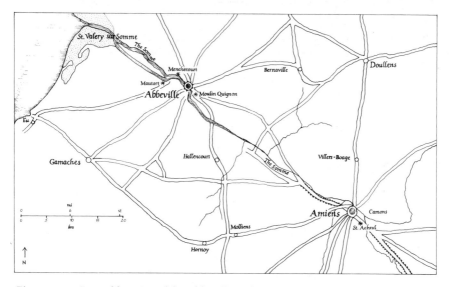

Figure 8.1. General location of the Abbeville and Amiens sites, adapted from Prestwich
(1861).

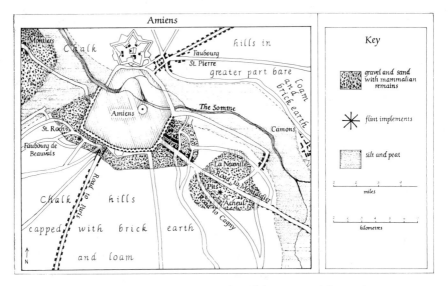

Figure 8.2.   Location of the Amiens sites, adapted from Prestwich (1861).

Only recently an adversary of Boucher de Perthes, Rigollot was now converted. On 28 November 1854, he wrote to Boucher de Perthes that

> I have just written, in some haste, a memoir on the discovery of axes made at Saint-Acheul. In this work, I can scarcely do more than follow your traces and my only ambition is to prove that you had reason in being the first to announce that our country was occupied by men before the cataclysm that destroyed the elephants and rhinoceroses that lived here. What you have said with all the arguments necessary to convince, I have restated more briefly and, without a doubt, not as well. But I was pressed to make the best of the work I had witnessed. I am going to have my memoir printed immediately, and I will be eager to pay you homage.[20]

This letter was not meant to be a private one. It was published in the *Bulletins* of the Society of Antiquaries of Picardy in 1855, read to the Société d'Emulation d'Abbeville, and later published by that society as well.[21]

Rigollot had, in fact, read his memoir to the Picardy society on 14 November, 2 weeks before his letter to Boucher de Perthes.[22] His report was then published twice, as a separate pamphlet in 1854 and in the *Memoirs* of the Society in 1856.[23] In his *Memoir on the Flint Implements Found at Saint-Acheul,* Rigollot was emphatic about what it was he had found: "at Abbeville as at Amiens, worked flints are found exclusively in the lower parts of the excavation, in the midst of gravels and pebbles."[24] No question could be entertained about the age of these materials, since they had been found in the "veritable diluvium," that is, "in the deposit enclosing the remains of animals of the epoch immediately preceeding the cataclysm that destroyed them. There can be no doubt in this regard."[25] Unlike Boucher de Perthes, Rigollot shied away from any interpretation of what he had found, including any discussion of the function of the implements he had retrieved: "I content myself with presenting the facts in all their simplicity."[26] Those facts plainly indicated that "men existed here at the same time as the great animals whose species were destroyed by a cataclysm."[27]

Rigollot's short, descriptive paper was impressive. He included stratigraphic profiles for his excavations, with the locations of the artifacts clearly indicated, as Boucher de Perthes had done. In addition, he provided excellent illustrations of the tools he had found, including a classic set of handaxes; his illustrations were far better than any Boucher de Perthes ever published. He appended Buteux's report on the geology of the area, and had as well Hébert's opinion on the antiquity of the gravels at the St. Acheul and St. Roch sites. In Rigollot, Boucher de Perthes had found an extremely competent ally—but an ally who died in December 1854.

Geologists were generally unmoved by Rigollot's discoveries. The influential Hébert, for instance, was less than fully supportive. In 1855, he noted that he had visited both the Amiens and Abbeville localities, and that the St. Acheul deposits did belong to a period generally considered to predate the appearance of people on earth.[28] He also noted that all the workers gave the same answer as to where the tools had been found: they came from the diluvium. But this was not enough, because Hébert himself had not found any of the flints in place. As a result, he could not personally confirm their stratigraphic placement. His opinion of the question was that it was "worthy of examination,"[29] but not that Rigollot was right. Buteux was much more supportive, but he was much less influential.[30] During the discussion of Rigollot's *Memoir* held by the Geological Society of France in 1855, the St. Acheul and St. Roch data were questioned by a series of geologists: the flints might have been naturally shaped, they might have reached their deep position by accident, and they had been found by workers, not by geological specialists.[31] As the geologist Joseph Prestwich (1812–1896) said later, "geologists admitted the antiquity of the beds, and antiquarians admitted the workmanship of the implements; but neither would own to a conjoint interest and belief in them."[32]

Three years after Rigollot's description of the Amiens discoveries was published, the second volume of Boucher de Perthes's *Celtic and Antediluvian Antiquities* appeared. Boucher de Perthes was now able to point to Rigollot's work as corroboration of his own, as well as to further discoveries in the vicinity of both Abbeville and Amiens. He also spent a good deal of time answering his critics. The deposits he worked in were clearly diluvian in age, they were undisturbed, the tools were real, and he had certainly not been defrauded by his workers. His general conclusions were the same as they had been in 1847: he, and now others, had found the remains of antediluvian people in ancient strata of the Somme River valley associated with the remains of such extinct mammals as elephant and rhinoceros.

What is remarkable about the second volume of *Antiquities*, however, is not the presentation of new data on the same issue, but the theoretical framework in which the data were now embedded. Between the time he wrote his initial monograph and the time he wrote the second, Boucher de Perthes had traveled extensively in Europe and had also corresponded with many of the leading earth scientists in England and on the continent.[33] He was no longer the isolated provincial amateur, and he was now in much better command of contemporary geological approaches to the more recent aspects of earth history. As a result, the arguments he made concerning that history were vastly different than they had been 10 years before.

He now felt that the effects of glaciation or of events that had accompanied glaciation could account for the deposition of much of the diluvium, a position then much in favor among geologists. He also felt that global cooling accounted for the extinction or extirpation of the large mammals, also an argument in favor among some major earth scientists. Louis Agassiz was one such scientist. "A Siberian winter established itself," Agassiz wrote in 1837, "on ground previously covered by rich vegetation and occupied by great mammals, similar to forms that today occupy the warm regions of India and Africa. Death enveloped all nature in a shroud."[34] Although he did not mention Agassiz's opinion, Boucher de Perthes now asked "will we one day see again the earth covered by a shroud which, for centuries to follow, will throw the earth into the sleep of death?"[35] While Agassiz's catastrophic explanation of Pleistocene extinctions was not widely followed during the 1850s,[36] it was certainly no mark of ignorance to side with this respected scientist.

Boucher de Perthes also drastically changed his views on the relationship between the floods that had deposited the diluvium in western Europe and the human beings that had been affected by those floods. No longer had the entire antediluvian human population been destroyed by those waters. Some, though not many, escaped, and the catastrophe itself became "that of which tradition remains with us."[37] Indeed, the tradition itself became support for his position:

> All traditions speak of a deluge that caused the death of both men and animals, with the exception of a few. But, in order for the memory to remain, men must have been witnesses and men must have survived it. Science recognizes and geology proves that almost all mammals disappeared in the great catastrophe: how could men alone have escaped? And if there were no men, how could those of today have the revelation of the event? Be consistent and do not divide the question: either the deluge of Noah is a fiction or it is true. If it is true, it is necessary to admit it with all the consequences: it is necessary to believe, with our fathers and after Scripture, that the same cataclysm struck both the throng of terrestrial creatures and the men among them.[38]

Gone were the separate races of human beings, each destroyed by a separate catastrophe; gone was the notion that antediluvian people were not the ancestors of modern ones. Yet Boucher de Perthes still felt that "not only is modification of the human form possible, it is probable. The modern species must show differences at least as great as those which exist between the antediluvian animals and the living races."[39] It was not impossible, he noted, that one of the reasons the bones of antediluvian people had not been reported was that they had been mistaken for those of apes.

He was, in fact, able to present evidence that such morphological change had occurred. In 1853, Frédéric-Antoine Spring (1814–1872), a physician and professor at the University of Liège, had reported the discovery of human bones and the remains of clearly postdiluvian mammals from a cavern located in the mountain of Chauvaux, near Namur, southcentral Belgium, in the Meuse River valley. Spring had actually made the discovery in 1842, but withheld publication, he said, because he was unable to decide how old his material was. Now, however, he was sure that it was postdiluvian, and he made the results of his work known. Spring argued that the bones he had found did not pertain to any race of people native to modern western or central Europe; he saw them as much more similar to both American Indians and Africans.[40] Although Spring asserted that the people represented by the Chauvaux bones had been replaced by a wave of immigrants from the east, Boucher de Perthes assumed that they were ancestral to modern Europeans. This assumption made, Boucher de Perthes then used this material to support his argument that change in human morphology through time did occur, while agreeing with Spring that the Chauvaux remains were postdiluvian.

In 1847, Boucher de Perthes had linked catastrophic extinctions of human beings, their subsequent recreation, and morphological change into a single antitransformationist package. Now, however, he was arguing that some peoples had escaped the last catastrophe, while retaining the notion of morphological change through time. Since he could no longer call on the formation of a new set of human beings to create the physical change he believed had occurred, he needed a new mechanism to explain that change. The mechanism he used was transformation:

> We doubt the possibility of the modification of animated forms and of the transformation of what we call one species into another, and our most distinguished experts affirm that this transformation is impossible. I agree, if we are dealing with a sudden change or even with change limited to a time that can be embraced by our ordinary calculations, but I am convinced that this metamorphosis can take place in the long run. Forms change not only as a result of needs, passions, customs, habits, but also in so far as variation in the elements and location requires this modification.[41]

To Boucher de Perthes, it now seemed possible that postdiluvian mammals were descended from antediluvian ones. Why, he asked, would God destroy something simply to remake it? It was far easier to believe that "the existing races descend, in spite of these differences, from the primitive and antediluvian races."[42]

The human species was no exception to this transformationist rule. In fact, Boucher de Perthes observed, one did not even need the fossil record to know that changes in mode of life and climate could cause morphological change over long periods of time. Only such change could account for the tremendous physical diversity seen among modern peoples, diversity that must have developed from a single, original pair of human beings.

However, while Boucher de Perthes now argued in favor of descent with modification and used evidence drawn from modern human physical diversity and from Spring's work to support this position, his approach was still a fairly mild one. His strongest statement on the transformation of species appeared in a note, not in the body of the text itself, and even that statement was a sober one. In addition, his discussion of the magnitude of morphological change through time in human beings was primarily confined to variation within the species; his comment that antediluvian human bones might have been mistaken for the bones of a nonhuman primate was also in a note. In the text itself, Boucher de Perthes's arguments did not sound much stronger than Prichard's.

It is telling that Boucher de Perthes chose Spring to provide his fossil example, since human bones from potentially ancient European deposits that had been assigned to non-European races had been reported years before the first volume of *Antiquities* appeared. Not only had Boué reviewed such finds in 1830 and 1832,[43] but Schmerling's attribution of the Engis skull to a member of the Ethiopian race was widely known. Boucher de Perthes seems to have relied on Spring's discussion because he had not read the earlier reports of these discoveries. He knew of Spring's work because, as he noted, Spring had sent him a copy of his paper. Much of Boucher de Perthes's discussion of prior discoveries of fossil human bones in the second volume of *Antiquities* was drawn directly from Spring's review of those finds. While Boucher de Perthes was now much less intellectually isolated than he had been in 1847, he was still not fully versed in the literature on ancient human remains.

Even though he clearly had not read the voluminous literature dealing with human remains from ancient deposits, Boucher de Perthes nonetheless took a strong stand on the meaning of those associations that had been reported from caves and of which he was aware. He argued that many of these caves were filled with deposits that were entirely postdiluvian in age, and that even those containing antediluvian materials were not to be trusted:

These caverns have sometimes presented a mixture of highly disparate objects belonging to markedly distinct ages. Thus, these sites have provided the bones of great carnivores and of other families that have not lived in our climates for many centuries, mixed with polished stone axes, projectile points, pottery whose paste is indicative of recent manufacture, finally gallic or roman coins. It is thus neither in the osseus breccias nor in the post-diluvian caverns that one will find irrefutable proof of the existence of antediluvian man, for the age or the origin of the bones found there will always remain surrounded by doubt.[44]

Boucher de Perthes took this highly critical stand for two reasons. First, his position on this issue aligned him with the contemporary conservative approach to the meaning of cave data, and gave his discussion an aura of caution that helped highlight the care with which he worked and the validity of his results. Second, and probably more important for him, it underlined the significance of his own contribution. If the human remains from caves were not ancient, then he was the first to prove the case for antediluvian people. "You will remember my efforts"[45] he said, and the less one trusted the cave discoveries, the more novel and important his work became.

His figured stones were still real and many of his stone tools were still symbolic items (Figures 8.3 and 8.4). But the overall impression provided by the second volume of *Antiquities* is very different from that provided by the first. Boucher de Perthes was no longer the totally isolated provincial working completely outside of contemporary science. Nonetheless, it is also true that the second volume did not provide the detailed exposition of the crucial Menchecourt and Hospital data. That information was to be found only in the first volume, where it was surrounded by very odd statements on earth and life history. To understand precisely what Boucher de Perthes had found that led him to argue for ancient peoples in the first place, one had to read his initial monograph. As a result, it was difficult to separate the old Boucher de Perthes from the new one.

Thus, the new resolution that was to be reached on the question of human antiquity stemmed from work done in England. This work enabled Boucher de Perthes's discoveries to be extracted from the theoretical framework in which he had initially placed them and to be recognized for what they really were. The crucial step in reaching this resolution was the excavation of Brixham Cave.

Located near Torquay in southwestern England, Brixham Cave was discovered in January 1858, during limestone quarrying operations that revealed not only the cave but also the fossil bones within it. Soon after, the geologist and educator William Pengelly (1812–1894) visited the site and realized that it might provide an excellent source of specimens for the Torquay Museum.[46] As Pengelly was attempting to gain access to the site from the owner, the paleontologist Hugh Falconer (1808–1865) arrived to examine the cave for himself. Falconer and Pengelly agreed to cooperate in the examination of the site; on his return to London, Falconer appealed to the Geological Society of London for the financial support needed for the work to proceed. The nature of Falconer's appeal makes it clear that he saw the potential value of Brixham Cave in the light of the information it could provide on the sequence of Pleistocene faunal change in England.[47] Brixham Cave was, as Jacob W. Gruber has noted in his invaluable discussion of these events, to be "explored by *geologists* with a view toward the solution of certain *geological* problems."[48]

The Geological Society of London responded to Falconer's appeal by assist-

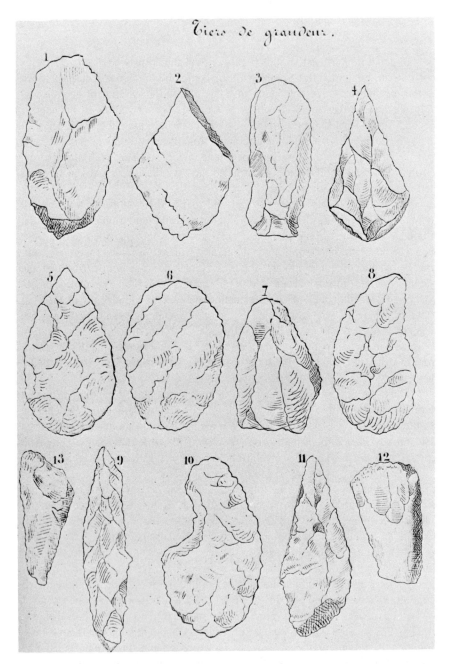

Figure 8.3. Antediluvian stone tools from the vicinity of Abbeville illustrated by Boucher de Perthes (1857). The artifact illustrations in the second volume of *Antiquities* were little better than those in the first. These particular specimens came from various sites in the Abbeville area.

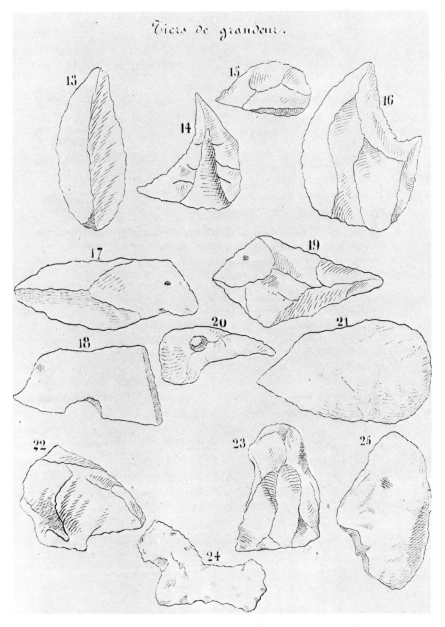

Figure 8.4. Figured stones illustrated by Boucher de Perthes (1857). In this series, Boucher de Perthes identified number 13 as the depiction of a leaf, number 14 as the tooth of a shark or crocodile, number 20 as the head of a bird, and number 25 as a human face.

ing him in obtaining the necessary funding, and by establishing a committee of prestigious British scientists to oversee the work. Among others, that committee included Charles Lyell, Joseph Prestwich, R. C. Godwin-Austen, the famed anatomist and paleontologist Richard Owen (1804–1892), and both Falconer and Pengelly.

Brixham Cave was thus to be excavated for the same general reason that Tournal, de Serres, and Schmerling had excavated their caves. But there were significant differences between those earlier excavations and those that were to take place in this new site. Those differences resulted from the scientific stature of the individuals involved in the Brixham Cave work, and from the detailed nature of the questions being asked of the deposits here. Since those questions dealt with faunal change through time, it was clear that precise stratigraphic information was required. The excavators were quite explicit about this point:

> The Committee, fully impressed with the probability of remains of different periods being met with at the different levels in the cavern floor, determined from the outset on working the upper deposits horizontally inwards, as far as might be practicable, in the same horizon, and then of working the lower deposits successively in the same manner. In this manner they considered that they would avoid the risk of confounding the remains of different levels, which is apt to take place when excavating cave-bottoms vertically down to the rock floor, and which has vitiated the results obtained in many other cave-explorations, more especially in regard of the contested position of human industrial remains.[49]

In addition, "whenever a bone or other article worthy of preservation was found, its situation (that is to say, its distance from the mouth or entrance of the gallery in which it occurred, as well as its depth below the surface of the bed in which it lay) was carefully determined by actual measurement."[50] After being so measured, each item was then numbered and catalogued.

Even with this relatively slow method of excavation, designed to guarantee that proper stratigraphic context would be preserved for all significant objects, the work quickly proved productive. Pengelly stated that about 1500 bones were removed during the first 6 weeks of excavation, including the remains of extinct mammals. And, on 29 July 1858, a flint implement was found beneath a continuous calcareous layer 7.5 centimeters thick. The antiquarian John Evans (1823–1908) later described this artifact as a "portion of a flake, 2¾ inches long and 1¼ wide . . . obtusely pointed, and truncated at the butt-end. . . it bears evident marks of wear."[51] By the time the excavations were completed in the summer of 1859, 36 flint objects had been discovered in Brixham Cave, of which 15 were felt to be undeniable artifacts. Many of these had been found in sealed strata that also contained the remains of such extinct mammals as elephant, rhinoceros, cave bear, and hyena (Figures 8.5 and 8.6).

The results of the Brixham Cave excavations were first made public at the 1858 meeting of the British Association for the Advancement of Science. Here two papers on the site were presented, one by Pengelly, the other prepared by

Figure 8.5. The entrance to Brixham Cave, as illustrated by Prestwich (1873). The excavation of this site under the direction of some of England's finest geologists and paleontologists led directly to the reexamination of Boucher de Perthes's sites.

Falconer but representing the report of Geological Society's committee. Although Pengelly's presentation simply mentioned the flint implements, the other observed that

> several well-marked specimens of the objects called 'Flint Knives' and generally accepted at the present day as the early products of Keltic or pre-Keltic industry, have been exhumed from different parts of the cavern, mixed in the ochreous earth indiscriminately with remains of *Rhinoceros*, *Hyaena*, and other extinct forms. One of these so-called 'Flint Knives' was brought up . . . from a depth of 30 inches below the superficial stalagmite . . . We failed in detecting evidence that these so-called 'Flint-Knives' were of different age, as regards the period of their introduction, from the bones of extinct mammals occurring in the same stratum of cave-earth, or that they were introduced into the cavern by different agencies.[52]

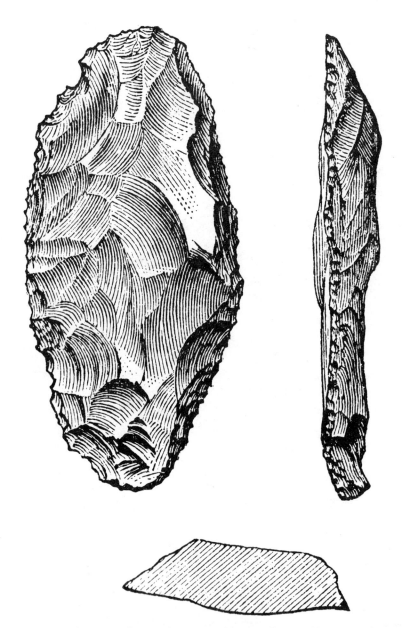

Figure 8.6. Brixham Cave flint implement number 7, as illustrated by Prestwich (1873). According to the Brixham Cave report, artifact number 7 (8.3 cm long, 4.4 cm wide) was discovered on 17 August 1858 in the Flint-knife Gallery of Brixham Cave, 42 feet (13 m) from the entrance of this gallery, and at a depth of 42 inches (1.1 m) from the top of the third bed. Such precision in excavation and note-taking characterized the excavation of this site.

Neither of these presentations was published in the *Reports* of the British Association for 1858 but, as Pengelly noted, "all the great geologists"[53] were there. Brixham Cave was opening the question of human antiquity in Britain in a way that it had not been opened since Cuvier provided his time markers. These were the results of a carefully conducted excavation made by individuals whose qualifications could not be reasonably doubted.

The results of the Brixham Cave excavations, however, were not published in any detail until 1873. In addition the site was still a cave, no matter how carefully it had been excavated. Although Prestwich, for instance, visited Brixham Cave with Pengelly and was impressed by what he saw, he was not fully convinced by the artifacts because he "considered that cave evidence alone was not sufficient."[54] The real significance of the work here stemmed from the fact that the status of the individuals who had made the discoveries opened people's eyes and that it led to the immediate reexamination of the discoveries made by Boucher de Perthes and Rigollot.

In October 1858, Falconer wrote to Boucher de Perthes, noting that "next Saturday, I will be travelling to Paris, when I will stop at Abbeville for two hours in the hope of finding you there. During the last three months, we have found flint knives in English bone caverns that are probably of great antiquity."[55] Boucher de Perthes was in, and Falconer examined his collection and came away favorably impressed. On 1 November, while still in Abbeville, he wrote to Prestwich that Boucher de Perthes had shown him

'Flint' hatchets which *he had dug up* with his own hands mixed *indiscriminately* with the molars of *Elephas primigenius* [mammoth]. . . . Abbeville is an out-of-the-way-place, very little visited, and the French savants who meet him in Paris laugh at Monsieur de Perthes and his researches. But after devoting the greater part of a day to his vast collection, I am perfectly satisfied that there is a good deal of fair presumptive evidence in favour of many of his speculations regarding the remote antiquity of these industrial objects, and their association with animals now extinct. . . . Let me strongly recommend you come to Abbeville. I am sure you would be richly rewarded.[56]

Prestwich followed the suggestion and spent his annual Easter geological excursion visiting Boucher de Perthes in April 1859.[57] As Aufrère has noted, Boucher de Perthes was ready for the visit. He had begun a register for visitors to his home; the very first names in that register were those of Prestwich and Evans, who joined Prestwich after his arrival in Abbeville.

While here, Prestwich not only saw Boucher de Perthes's collection, but also visited Menchecourt, Moulin Quignon, and other sites that had provided both stone tools and the remains of extinct mammals. Although three possible flakes were found while he was at Menchecourt, no undoubted implements were found during his tour of the Abbeville locations. He continued on to Amiens to examine St. Acheul, where he again failed to find any artifacts in place. After returning to Abbeville, however, he received a message from Amiens informing him that what he wanted to see had now been found. He returned to St. Acheul, where he was joined by Evans, and both were able to observe a flint implement in place about 6 meters below the original surface level, in deposits that also contained the remains of extinct mammals.[58]

Prestwich, who had been sceptical, was now convinced, as was Evans. Early in May, Prestwich wrote to Boucher de Perthes that "I have the conviction that the opinion you advanced in 1847 in your work on the Celtic and antediluvian antiquities, that the axes are found in undisturbed gravel and associated with the bones of the great mammals is just and well founded."[59] Other visits to Abbeville and Amiens by British scientists followed. Prestwich returned in June 1859 with the antiquarian John W. Flower (1807–1873), the geologist Robert W. Mylne (1817–1890), and R. C. Godwen-Austin; on this trip, Flower excavated a handaxe at a depth of 5 meters from the surface at St. Acheul. In July, Lyell made the trip, afterwards visiting Le Puy to inspect the site of the Denise discoveries. All came away convinced of the validity of the finds that had been made by Boucher de Perthes and Rigollot.

The visitors presented and published a flurry of papers on their observations. Prestwich's paper was delivered to the Royal Society of London in May 1859; a lengthy abstract was published in the Society's *Proceedings* in 1860, and the full version appeared in the Society's *Transactions* in 1861. Evans's paper was presented to the Society of Antiquaries in June 1859 and published in *Archaeologia* in 1860. Flower gave his in the same month to the Geological Society of London, which published it in 1860. Lyell's presentation was made in September 1859 at the meeting of the British Association for the Advancement of Science, which carried it in their *Reports* in 1860. All of these papers agreed on one essential point: the artifacts found at Abbeville and Amiens did, indeed, prove that people had coexisted with the now-extinct mammals.[60]

Of all these publications, the most symbolic was certainly Lyell's. Britain's most influential geologist, Lyell had argued against the contemporaneity of human beings and the extinct beasts in every edition of the *Principles* through the last to have been published (1853). In addition, his belief in the geological recency of humankind was tightly linked to his belief that people occupied a special place on earth, a place that was in part indicated by their very recency. His trip to France had, however, shown him that he had been wrong. His presentation to the British Association in September, some 2 months after he had left for Abbeville, was delivered from a powerful position, for he was then president of the geology section of that association.

Lyell was succinct and clear about his new opinion of human antiquity. He began by discussing the earlier scepticism:

For the last quarter of a century, the occasional occurrence, in various parts of Europe, of the bones of man or the works of his hands, in cave-breccias and stalactites associated with the remains of the extinct hyaena, bear, elephant, or rhinoceros, has given rise to a suspicion that the date of man must be carried further back than we had heretofore imagined. On the other hand, extreme reluctance was naturally felt on the part of scientific reasoners to admit the validity of such evidence, seeing that so many caves have been inhabited by a succession of tenants, and have been selected by man, as a place not only of domicile, but of sepulture, while some caves have also served as the channels through which the water of flooded rivers flowed, so that the remains of living beings which have peopled the district at more than one era may have subsequently been mingled in such caverns and confounded together in one and the same deposit. The facts, however, recently brought to light during the systematic excavation . . . of the Brixham Cave, must, I think, have prepared you to admit that scepticism in regard to the cave-evidence in favour of the antiquity of man has previously been pushed to an extreme.[61]

Recent work at Denise, he noted, still left the antiquity of human bones from that site in doubt. While that was the case, however, he also noted that he was

fully prepared to corroborate the conclusions which have recently been laid before the Royal Society by Mr. Prestwich, in regard to the age of the flint implements associated in undisturbed gravel, in the north of France, with the bones of elephants, at Abbeville and Amiens. These were first noticed at Abbeville, and their true geological position assigned to them by M. Boucher de Perthes, in 1847, in his "Antiquités Celtiques," while those of Amiens were afterwards described in 1854, by the late Dr. Rigollot. . . . I have myself obtained abundance of flint implements . . . during a short visit to Amiens and Abbeville. . . . The stratified gravel resting immediately on the chalk in which these rudely fashioned implements are buried, belongs to the post-pliocene period. . . . The great number of the fossil instruments which have been likened to hatchets, spear-heads, and wedges is truly wonderful. . . . Although the accompanying shells are of living species, I believe the antiquity of the Abbeville and Amiens flint instruments to be great indeed if compared to the times of history or tradition. . . . The disappearance of the elephant, rhinoceros, and other genera of quadrupeds now foreign to Europe, implies . . . a vast lapse of ages, separating the era in which the fossil implements were framed and that of the invasion of Gaul by the Romans.[62]

Flower's presentation dealt with his excavation of a handaxe at St. Acheul; Evans focused on the undoubtedly artifactual nature of the tools involved. Although it might appear that the names of Pengelly and Falconer were missing from this set of papers, in fact they were not. In May 1859, Pengelly presented a synopsis of the Brixham Cave discoveries to the Royal Institution of Great Britain, noting that "whatever was the antiquity of the bone-earth in the cavern, the human period is as ancient."[63] After his trip to Abbeville, Falconer had gone to Italy where he excavated in Maccagnone Cave, near Palermo, and found stone tools with the remains of hippopotamus, elephant, and hyena. He presented these discoveries at the same meeting of the Geological Society in which Flower discussed his work, and both papers were published in the same volume of the Society's *Quarterly Journal*.[64]

Although Lyell's paper was clearly the most symbolic of the lot, Prestwich's was the most detailed and carried the empirical evidence for what the others were arguing. Prestwich's paper began by recalling a "few highly probable instances" of earlier, rejected discoveries of ancient human remains—those by Schmerling, MacEnery, Boucher de Perthes, and Rigollot—and by noting that the entire issue had been revived by the discoveries at Brixham Cave. He discussed the sections he had examined at Abbeville and Amiens in detail, providing stratigraphic profiles and lists of animals for Menchecourt, Moulin Quignon, and St. Acheul. He argued that the flint implements were real, and that they had not reached the positions in which they were found by accident (Figure 8.7). Prestwich also directed attention to Hoxne. Evans had called his notice to Frere's paper, and Prestwich had visited Hoxne as a result.[65] He found no stone tools here, but workers assured him that they were to be found, and Prestwich concluded that Hoxne provided a situation analogous to the Somme Valley sites.

Prestwich's view of the implications of these discoveries for human antiquity was more restrained than Lyell's. People, he observed, had existed "anterior to the surface assuming its present form, so far as it regards some of the minor features."[66] Yet this did not mean that our species was extremely ancient:

> It might be supposed that in assigning to Man an appearance at such a period, it would of necessity imply his existence during long ages beyond all exact calculations; for we have been apt to place even the latest of our geological changes at a remote, and, to us, unknown distance. The reasons on which such a view has been held have been, mainly,—the great lapse of time considered requisite for the dying out of so many species of great Mammals,—the circumstance that many of the smaller valleys have been excavated since they lived,—the presumed non-existence of Man himself,—and the great extent of the later and more modern accumulations. But we have in this part of Europe no succession of strata to record a gradual dying out of the species, but much, on the contrary, which points to an abrupt end, and evidence only of relative and not of actual time. . . . The evidence, in fact, as it as present stands, does not seem to me to necessitate the carrying of man back in past time, so much as the bringing forward of the extinct animals towards our own time.[67]

But the conservative Prestwich made his position on the major issue clear: people had been associated with the extinct mammals, and this association predated the time the earth had taken on its modern form. Although his position may appear somewhat similar to de Serres's earlier stand, the similarities are only superficial: de Serres's point was that the co-occurrence of human remains and extinct mammals implied the extreme recency of the mammals and that the deposits involved had been laid down after the earth acquired its modern form. Indeed, Prestwich soon clarified his position. In 1863, he observed that while the actual amount of time that had passed since the flint implements had been deposited cannot be calculated, it is "obvious, however, that our present chronology with respect to the first appearance of Man must be greatly extended; but, like a mountain-chain in the distance, its vast magnitude is felt before an exact measurement of its height and size can be taken."[68]

This entire set of papers has the appearance of a coordinated onslaught. In the space of a few months during the middle of 1859, Pengelly and Prestwich (May), Evans, Falconer, and Flower (June), and Lyell (September) had presented their views to the five British scientific associations whose opinion counted

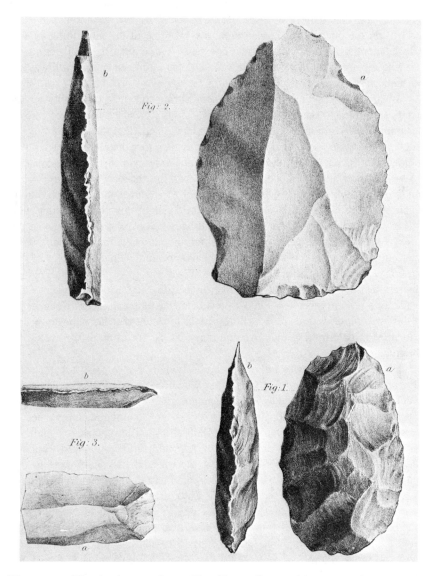

Figure 8.7. Flint implements from Abbeville, as illustrated by Prestwich (1861). The artifact illustrations provided by Prestwich left no doubt as to the nature of the items depicted. Such was not the case with Boucher de Perthes's earlier figures.

the most: the British Association for the Advancement of Science, the Geological Society of London, the Royal Institution of Great Britain, the Royal Society of London, and the Society of Antiquaries. Clearly a new resolution had been reached on the question of human antiquity by some of the most influential of British scientists. Human beings had coexisted with extinct mammals at a time that was ancient in terms of absolute years, and at a time when the earth was not yet modern in form.

What was happening on the continent during this rush of activity in England? In France, the issue was complicated by the presence of Léonce Élie de Beaumont (1798–1874). A geologist, mathematician, and disciple of Cuvier, Élie de Beaumont was a firm opponent of the view that the human species was geologically ancient. He followed de Luc and Cuvier, for instance, in equating the onset of formation of modern sand dunes with the onset of modern geological conditions, in inferring from the magnitude of these dunes that such conditions began only a few thousand years ago, and in equating this period of time with "all of human history."[69] In 1853, he had become one of the perpetual secretaries of the Academy of Sciences, a position that allowed him some latitude in determining the nature of publications that appeared in the *Accounts* of the Academy's weekly meetings. He was not above using his political strength to suppress aspects of work he did not like; indeed, he had been a member of the Academy's commission appointed to evaluate the first volume of Boucher de Perthes's *Antiquities* and there is little reason to doubt that his opposition was influential in determining that any report issued by that commission would be negative.

Élie de Beaumont was fully opposed to the notion of a great human antiquity, and with that to anything connected with Boucher de Perthes. However, Boucher de Perthes did have two major supporters in France by 1858: the highly respected paleontologist Édouard Lartet (1801–1871) and the equally respected zoologist Isidore Geoffroy Saint-Hilaire (1805–1861). The supportive collaboration of these two scientists was clear in the publication of Alfred Fontan's discussion of the caverns of Massat, near the town of the same name in far-southern France. In one of these caverns, Fontan had found the remains of cave bear, hyena, and a large cat (later identified by Lartet as the extinct cave lion[70]) intermingled with human teeth. Fontan's report appeared in the Academy's *Accounts* for 10 May 1858, followed by Geoffroy Saint-Hilaire's discussion of Lartet's identification of some of the Massat fossils. At the same meeting, Geoffroy Saint-Hilaire also put on display some of Boucher de Perthes's artifacts, noting that they had been "found with the bones and fossil tooth fragments of elephants." In addition, he took the opportunity to "render homage to the perseverant and fortunate zeal"[71] that Boucher de Perthes had shown in conducting his work. This was high praise from a member of the elite Academy of Sciences.

It was a year later that the issue broke open in France, spurred by the reports of the British scientists. Late in the summer of 1859, the paleontologist Albert Gaudry (1827–1908) visited Amiens in response to Flower's discovery at St. Acheul. Gaudry's excavations at St. Acheul were also a success: he extracted nine handaxes from the diluvium. He communicated his results to the Academy of Sciences, which published an abstract of them in the reports for 26 September and a longer account in the reports for 3 October,[72] including the conclusion that his discovery proved "definitively that man was contemporaneous with several of the great, extinct fossil animals."[73] There was, however, no mention of Boucher de Perthes's work in Gaudry's publication.

A few weeks later, Georges Pouchet (1833–1894) of the Rouen Museum of Natural History published a similar report in the *Accounts*. Pouchet's interest in examining St. Acheul resulted from a discussion with Lyell, who had visited the Rouen Museum on 23 August 1859. Two days later, Pouchet was on his way to Amiens in hopes of retrieving specimens to display at his museum. He proved to be as lucky as Flower and Gaudry, and was able to excavate a handaxe from undisturbed deposits. He sent his results to the Academy, which published an extract of his letter on 10 October. Pouchet's communication was like Gaudry's in more than one way: not only had Pouchet found a handaxe in diluvium, but he also failed to mention Boucher de Perthes's work.[74]

The reasons that Pouchet and Gaudry did not mention Boucher de Perthes, however, were significantly different. Pouchet omitted mention of Boucher de Perthes's work because, as he noted in 1860, he simply had not read it at the time.[75] Gaudry was a different case. Not only was he fully aware of Boucher de Perthes's research, but he had credited both Boucher de Perthes and Rigollot in the communication that had gone to the Academy. That section of his report never appeared.

On the same day that Pouchet's results were communicated to the Academy, Geoffroy Saint-Hilaire decided to intervene on Boucher de Perthes's behalf. On 10 October, he wrote to Boucher de Perthes, told him that "not even your name has been uttered,"[76] and requested a summary of his discoveries that he could transmit to the Academy. Boucher de Perthes complied, and his summary, including a review of the support he had received from the English geologists, appeared in the *Accounts* for 24 October.[77] Boucher de Perthes also wrote to Élie de Beaumont, expressing dissatisfaction that his work had not been mentioned, and Élie de Beaumont took the occasion of the 24 October meeting to note that he had overseen the excision of the names of Boucher de Perthes and Rigollot from Gaudry's paper. He observed that "the memoir read by M. Albert Gaudry in the meeting of last October 3 included a paragraph concerning the flint axes found at Abbeville, in which the name and work of M. Boucher de Perthes was mentioned, so justice was done." The paragraph was dropped, he explained, because the paper had to be shortened, as was the case with most papers, and because everyone knew of Boucher de Perthes's research anyway: "the removal of the paragraph concerning the motives that brought M. Gaudry to look in the diluvium for the products of human art was essentially a tacit homage to the notorious [notoire] rights of priority of M. Boucher de Perthes."[78]

Lartet was also subject to Élie de Beaumont's power. In April 1860 he wrote to Boucher de Perthes that

> I decided several days ago to present a short note to the Academy of Sciences that started with these lines: "Of all the discoveries that tend to give a high antiquity to the appearance of the human race in the western part of the European continent, none, without exception, are more conclusive than the worked flints recovered by M. Boucher de Perthes. . . ." An omnipotent will, the same that had M. Gaudry's memoir inserted, decided, contrary to my request and also contrary to generally adopted custom, that not one line of this note would appear in the reports.[79]

Lartet did not mention the paper by name, but he was referring to his "Geologic Antiquity of the Human Species in Europe," a paper that appeared by title only in the Academy's *Accounts* for 19 March 1860.[80] He did, however, get his paper published. It appeared in 1860 in the Swiss *Archives of Physical and Natural Sciences;* a much modified version also appeared in the *Proceedings* of the Geological Society of London, altered because the fact of contemporaneity was no longer an issue among members of that body.[81] The paper sheds much light on why Élie de Beaumont suppressed it, for it would have offended any follower of Cuvier.

Lartet had begun his paper by praising Boucher de Perthes, just as his letter to Boucher de Perthes indicated. He then noted that many had questioned the validity of the associations between human remains and those of extinct mammals, and suggested that the best demonstration of contemporaneity would be provided by the bones of extinct mammals that had been worked by human hands, as long as the indicative marks could not have come long after the death of the animal. "It was this that I tried to verify in the collections of the museum of natural history, and particularly on those described or mentioned by Cuvier."[82] Lartet found exactly what he was looking for in Cuvier's material (*"Oss. foss.,* in-4°, 1822, tome IV, pl. VI, fig. 9" he carefully observed[83]). This was a nasty cut, attempting to show Cuvier wrong on such a major issue by using items that Cuvier himself had handled, a cut that probably went too far not only for Élie de Beaumont but for others in the audience on 19 March as well. As if this were not enough, Lartet then used Élie de Beaumont's own hypotheses on the effects of mountain building to date the arrival of people in Europe, and argued against Élie de Beaumont's position that the history of life had, during later geological times, been interrupted by major catastrophes. Élie de Beaumont's reaction to all this is understandable, and Lartet clearly was not the completely innocent victim of an "omnipotent will" as he suggested in his letter to Boucher de Perthes.

Soon after Élie de Beaumont rejected Lartet's paper, he accepted a series of comments by the geologist Eugène Robert (1806–1879) that maintained that the strata from which the stone tools had come were not the true diluvium, but had instead been deposited much later in time. Any association between the stone tools and extinct mammals, he asserted, was accidental, caused by the reworking of older deposits. "Between the presence of the first men of Europe and that of the great Pachyderms," he concluded, there has been "an enormous distance, of thousands of years for example."[84] Boucher de Perthes published a response to this critique, Robert answered, and Boucher de Perthes responded again.[85] The last response, however, was preceeded by Élie de Beaumont's opinion of the whole matter:

> Concerning the flint axes found in the valley of the Somme, of the Seine, and elsewhere, it does not seem demonstrated, as of the present, that any of these axes, or any other products of human industry, have been extracted from *diluvial terrain* NOT REWORKED.[86]

This comment was published in the Academy's *Accounts* for 5 June 1861. While 4 years earlier it would have been the received opinion, it now marked Élie de Beaumont as an outsider on the issue. French scientists as influential in their country as Lyell and Prestwich were in Great Britain had joined with Boucher de Perthes. Not only were Geoffroy Saint-Hilaire, Lartet, and Gaudry firmly on his side, but the 1859 English and French examinations of the Somme Valley sites had brought even such earlier opponents as Maury into the fold during that year.[87] Hébert was completely correct when he wrote to Boucher de Perthes in December 1860 that "now it is a dead issue, and the people who still question the existence of man during the quaternary epoch are evidently not up to date on the question."[88]

Symbolic of the decision by French scientists in favor of a vast human antiquity was Lartet's "New Researches on the Coexistence of Man and the Great Fossil Mammals," published in 1861. This important paper looked forward, not back. For Lartet the crucial issue was no longer whether people and mammals had coexisted, but was instead that of deriving a method for placing the many sites containing the proof of this contemporaneity in proper chronological order. This issue was to become extremely important during the following decades and, in more refined form, remains of crucial importance today. Lartet's solution to this problem was to derive a relative chronology for the human remains from the nature of the fauna with which they were associated, an approach similar to that which Tournal had taken in 1829. He defined four successive faunal ages for western Europe—the age of cave bears, of elephants and rhinoceroses, of reindeer, and of aurochs—and suggested that archaeological materials be ordered in terms of the faunal stage to which the associated mammals belonged. The only mention he gave to the old question of contemporaneity was confined to a footnote:

> It is true that some persist in objecting to Boucher de Perthes: "that it is not demonstrated, as of the present, that any of these axes, or any other product of human industry, has been extracted from *diluvial terrain not reworked.*". . . In the observational sciences, the first condition of all discussion is the impartial consideration of facts; the second, logic and good faith in objections. The moment that an adversary, refusing to examine the facts, limits himself to denying by sentiment or prejudices, the discussion must stop, for it will cease to have a scientific nature.[89]

Lartet did not mention Élie de Beaumont by name, but he did not have to.

Boucher de Perthes held his victory celebration in 1860. In that year, he published *Antediluvian Man and His Works,* much of which was dedicated to a discussion of the support that others had now provided his discoveries. He also provided a synopsis of the history of his research, implying along the way that he had been interested in the question of human antiquity since 1805.[90] In 1860, he had won and he knew it.

And where was Marcel de Serres during all of this? Now aged, he was in Montpellier publishing works that retracted nearly all he had said concerning the association of human remains with the remains of extinct mammals. By the mid-1850s it had become clear to him that his approach to the reconciliation of Genesis and the deeper archaeological record simply would not work. Many of the extinct mammals were undoubtedly older than any interpretation of the biblical chronology would allow, and no one of any scientific stature had accepted his argument that those animals belonged to a modern world. He was faced with a difficult decision. Either his religion was wrong or his geology was wrong. He found the flaw in his geology. In 1855, he published a lengthy review of bone caverns and the human remains they contained in which he surveyed virtually every cave that had provided evidence for the contemporaneity of human beings and extinct beasts, including, of course, the caverns of Bize, Pondres, and Souvignargues. He rejected all evidence of the association of human remains with animals of diluvial age. The mixtures, he argued, were "the result of purely accidental causes," of the reworking of older material upwards and of younger material downwards. People, he now argued, "were not contemporary with elephants, rhinoceroses, *Megatherium,* no more than the great lions, hyaenas, megalonyx, and gigantic bears."[91]

He soon found what seemed to be a pristine cave, a model of what the other caves must have looked like before they had been disturbed. The cavern of Pontil, in southern France, contained three separate, stratified deposits: an uppermost, recent bed; a middle group of materials holding artifacts of Gallo-Roman age; and a lowermost complex of deposits containing the remains of such extinct mammals as rhinoceros and cave bear. The human remains and extinct mammals were separated by a thick, almost impenetrable calcareous crust. Were it not for this fact, he argued, running water and other disturbing processes would inevitably have caused intermixture, producing precisely those associations seen in other caverns "where conditions like those of Pontil are not present."[92] Although de Serres was willing to accept possibly very recently extinct mammals as human contemporaries, the Pleistocene mammals were not to be included.[93] Indeed, he retooled his earlier arguments on the magnitude of recent extinctions, arguments originally forwarded to remove the troubling implications of the association of human remains with extinct mammals of diluvial age. Now, holding those associations as invalid, he used the same arguments to stress the modernity of the associations he would accept, for extinct species of such animals as horses, cattle, and deer.[94]

Thus, while Fontan was arguing for the antiquity of the human remains from the cavern of Massat, de Serres was arguing against the validity of the Massat associations.[95] In the same volume of the *Archives of Physical and Natural Sciences* in which Lartet and Pictet were arguing that biotic continuity throughout the Quaternary implied that the human species could have existed for the same length of time, de Serres was arguing that Boucher de Perthes's stone tools were not diluvian in age and that true diluvial deposits "do not contain the least vestige of tools or the products of human industry, no more.than the bones of our species."[96] And in the third edition of his *Cosmogeny of Moses Compared with Geological Facts* (1860), published 2 years before his death, de Serres maintained that the dispersal of the diluvium predated the appearance of people on earth and that human beings came into existence some 8000 years ago, about 2500 years before the biblical Deluge. In a statement that MacEnery could have written, he observed that "it is only after long and exacting study that we have recognized our mistake"[97] in interpreting the mixture of human remains with those of extinct mammals in cave deposits. The Bible is a "great scientific work,"[98] and all science is in accord with it, including the scientific knowledge gained from the bone caverns. De Serres had lost, and he knew it.

By 1860, then, a new resolution on the question of human antiquity had been reached both in Great Britain and in western Europe. It was now very generally agreed that people had coexisted with the extinct mammals, that they had been on earth prior to the time that the earth had taken on its modern form, and that they had existed for a series of millennia that could not be encompassed within the biblical chronology. Not everyone agreed, as I will discuss, but the situation was now reversed from what it had been just a few years before. Majority opinion now held that people were both geologically ancient and ancient in terms of the number of years they had been in existence. Only a very small minority held otherwise. An argument that had lasted for 60 years was now over.

Notes and References

1. In his 1858 presidential address to the British Association for the Advancement of Science, for instance, Richard Owen noted that two lines of evidence called for a higher human antiquity than "assigned to it in historical and genealogical records": Leonard Horner's deeply buried ce-

ramics from the Nile Valley (see Chapter 9), and the diversity of human languages (Owen 1859:xciv–xcv).
2. [Whewell] 1853:93.
3. [Whewell] 1853:90.
4. Mantell 1851:237.
5. Mantell 1851:249–250.
6. Mantell 1851:248.
7. Mantell 1851:238.
8. Mantell 1851:238.
9. Curwen 1940:255.
10. Maury 1852:277.
11. Maury 1852:277–278. Much later, Maury noted that the doubtful nature of many of Boucher de Perthes's artifacts had hurt his cause considerably (Maury 1867).
12. Pictet 1853:145.
13. Pictet 1853:151.
14. Pictet 1853:154.
15. Boucher de Perthes 1857:7.
16. Hume 1851:49.
17. Biographical information on Rigollot is drawn from Rembault 1855; Cuvier discussed Rigollot's specimens in Cuvier 1821b:110 and 1822, Part 1:50, 111.
18. Aufrère 1940:110.
19. Boucher de Perthes 1857:467–468.
20. Rigollot 1855:308.
21. Rigollot 1857:678–679.
22. The presentation of Rigollot's memoir on 14 November is noted in the Société des Antiquaires de Picardie *Bulletins* 5 (1855).
23. Rigollot 1854, 1856.
24. Rigollot 1854:13; 1856:33.
25. Rigollot 1854:13; 1856:34.
26. Rigollot 1854:16; 1856:36.
27. Rigollot 1854:3–4; 1856:23–24.
28. Hébert 1855a.
29. Hébert 1855b:255.
30. Buteux 1855; see also Buteux 1857.
31. See the discussion accompanying Buteux 1855.
32. Prestwich 1866:215.
33. See the correspondence and discussion in Ledieu 1885.
34. Agassiz 1837:xxiv.
35. Boucher de Perthes 1857:21.
36. Grayson 1983.
37. Boucher de Perthes 1857:32.
38. Boucher de Perthes 1857:357.
39. Boucher de Perthes 1857:444.
40. Spring 1853.
41. Boucher de Perthes 1857:373.
42. Boucher de Perthes 1857:80.
43. Boué 1830, 1831–1832[1832].
44. Boucher de Perthes 1857:69.
45. Boucher de Perthes 1857:210.
46. Biographical information on Pengelly is taken from Woodward 1895.
47. Prestwich 1873.

48. Gruber 1965:385.
49. Prestwich 1873:476–477.
50. Prestwich 1873:482.
51. Prestwich 1873:549.
52. In Murchison 1868:495–496. Pengelly's paper appeared by title only (Pengelly 1859).
53. In Gruber 1965:390.
54. Prestwich 1866:214.
55. Aufrère 1940:114.
56. In Murchison 1868:597.
57. Prestwich's Easter field trips are discussed by Woodward 1907.
58. Prestwich 1860.
59. Aufrère 1940:114.
60. Prestwich 1860 and 1861; Evans 1860; Flower 1860; Lyell 1860. Lyell also discussed the Abbeville and Amiens material in his correspondence (Lyell 1881, Volume 2:341; Wilson 1970:lvii).
61. Lyell 1860:93.
62. Lyell 1860:94–95.
63. Pengelly 1862:150.
64. Falconer 1860b.
65. Prestwich 1861.
66. Prestwich 1861:309.
67. Prestwich 1861:309.
68. Prestwich 1863d:52; see also Prestwich 1866.
69. Élie de Beaumont 1845:219.
70. Lartet 1861.
71. Fontan 1858; Geoffroy Saint-Hilaire 1858:902–903.
72. Gaudry 1859a,b.
73. Gaudry 1859a:454.
74. Pouchet 1859.
75. Pouchet 1860a; see also Pouchet 1860b.
76. Ledieu 1885:246. Geoffroy Saint-Hilaire also raised the issue directly to Pouchet (Geoffroy Saint-Hilaire 1860).
77. Boucher de Perthes 1859; Prestwich announced his support in the *Accounts* of the Academy of Sciences the following week (Prestwich 1859).
78. Élie de Beaumont 1859:582.
79. Aufrère 1940:118; see also Ledieu 1885:256–257.
80. Lartet 1860d; see also Lartet 1860a.
81. Lartet 1860c, 1860b.
82. Lartet 1860c:194.
83. Lartet 1860c:195.
84. Robert 1861b:64; see also Robert 1860.
85. Boucher de Perthes 1861c; Robert 1861a; Boucher de Perthes 1861b.
86. Élie de Beaumont 1861:1133–1134; see also Boucher de Perthes 1861a and Robert 1863.
87. Maury 1859; Pictet 1859, 1860a.
88. Ledieu 1885:266. General agreement with Boucher de Perthes can also be seen in the comments of various individuals in the ''Discussion of Diluvial Axes'' held by members of the Anthropological Society of Paris on 17 November 1859 (Société d'Anthropologie de Paris *Bulletins* 1:60–78, 1860).
89. Lartet 1861:216. The first section of this paper, on Aurignac, was translated into English and published the following year (Lartet 1862).
90. Boucher de Perthes 1860; see also Boucher de Perthes 1864a:1–107. Boucher de Perthes's new

version of the history of his interest in the question of human antiquity quickly made its way into the literature (see, for instance, Anonymous 1863c).

91. De Serres 1855–1857[1855]:87; see also de Serres 1855–1857[1856].

92. De Serres 1857a:650.

93. De Serres 1857a,b.

94. De Serres argued this point in a number of very similar papers. The lengthiest version is de Serres 1860b; see also de Serres 1859, 1860c, and 1860d.

95. De Serres 1858.

96. Lartet 1860c; Pictet 1860a; de Serres 1860d:114; see also Collomb 1860 and Gaudin 1860.

97. De Serres 1860a, Volume 2:lxxii.

98. De Serres 1860a, Volume 2:376.

9

A Great and Sudden Revolution

"No subject has lately excited more curiosity and general interest among geologists and the public than the question of the Antiquity of the Human Race,—whether or no we have sufficient evidence in caves, or in the superficial deposits commonly called drift or 'diluvium,' to prove the former co-existence of man with certain extinct mammalia." So began Charles Lyell's *Geological Evidences of the Antiquity of Man*, published in 1863. This work addressed not only the antiquity of the human species, but also the origin of species through descent with modification. The first of these topics had been raised by the events I discussed in the previous chapter; the second, by the publication of Charles Darwin's *Origin of Species* in 1859. Lyell did not support evolution by natural selection in the way Darwin hoped he would, and Darwin was "greatly disappointed" that he had not even spoken decisively on the more general issue of transmutation.[1] Lyell did, however, throw his full weight behind the evidence for human antiquity.

Lyell began by resurrecting the cave data. Noting that his earlier writings had given "no small weight to the arguments of M. Desnoyers, and the writings of Dr. Buckland on the same subject"[2] and that it was clear that accidental mixtures of ancient and recent materials had occurred in some caves, he now argued that these strictures did not apply to all such sites. His prime example came from Schmerling, who had, in fact, "accumulated ample evidence to prove that man had been introduced into the earth at an earlier period than geologists were then willing to believe"[3]:

> One positive fact, it will be said, attested by so competent a witness, ought to have outweighed any amount of negative testimony, previously accumulated, respecting the non-occurrence elsewhere of human remains of the like antiquity. In reply, I can only plead that a discovery which seems to contradict the general tenor of previous investigation is naturally received with much hesitation.[4]

One by one, Lyell reviewed the sites that had provided what now appeared to be solid evidence for the presence of human remains in deposits of great antiquity in general, and with the remains of extinct mammals in particular. Engis, Engihoul, Kent's Cavern, Brixham Cave, Denise, Hoxne, St. Acheul, St. Roch, Menchecourt, Moulin Quignon, and others all came under favorable scrutiny. There could no longer be any doubt that people and the extinct mammals had coexisted. Indeed, Lyell suggested that human activities might even have played a role in causing the demise of those animals.[5]

The *Antiquity of Man* proved extremely popular. First issued in February 1863, the second and third editions appeared in April and November of the same year. "I am reading your book on the Antiquity of Man," wrote William Whewell to Lyell in February, "as all the world has done or is doing."[6] A flood of books that summarized and interpreted some or all of the evidence for a deep human antiquity followed during the next two decades, each with its own purpose. Great Britain alone saw the publication of John Lubbock's *Pre-Historic Times* (1865), destined to go through seven editions by 1913; John Evans's *Ancient Stone Implements, Weapons, and Ornaments of Great Britain* (1872); Hodder M. Westropp's *Pre-Historic Phases* (1872); the much-revised fourth and last edition of Lyell's *Antiquity of Man* (1873); James Geikie's *Great Ice Age and its Relation to the Antiquity of Man* (1874) and *Prehistoric Europe* (1881); and W. Boyd Dawkins's *Cave Hunting* (1874) and *Early Man in Britain* (1880). But as important as some of these books were—and Lubbock's *Pre-Historic Times* and Geikie's *Great Ice Age* were extremely important—the most powerful of them all was Lyell's *Antiquity of Man*. Lyell's discussion of the evidence for human antiquity was, as he made clear, more of a postgame summary than an argument for things not then believed, but his summary introduced a wide readership to the new view and to the facts that supported it, thus laying the synthetic foundation for future work.[7]

Over 50 years had passed since Cuvier had provided an objective means by which human antiquity could be assessed, and had provided such an assessment himself. Cuvier had followed earlier belief in seeing people as recent arrivals on earth in two different senses, and his twin time markers were to be applied to both. The human species was a recent arrival in terms of absolute chronology, a chronology whose 6000-year date had been derived from Scripture, no matter how independent of revelation de Luc's natural chronometers might appear. Our species was also a recent arrival in terms of the development of the earth itself, appearing only after the earth had taken on its modern form. This idea was also theological in origin, derived from the pervasive notion that the prehuman history of the earth was the history of the preparation of the earth for humankind by a providential God. An earth modern in form was an earth ready for our species, and this view had no place for geologically ancient human beings.

In the years immediately following the publication of Cuvier's *Preliminary Discourse* in 1812, these two themes remained tightly linked. Thus Buckland, while altering aspects of Cuvier's interpretation of the mammals and gravels in major ways, treated the issues of absolute chronology and geological antiquity as inseparably as Cuvier had treated them. But as soon as the Deluge and the diluvium were uncoupled during the late 1820s, empirical arguments as to absolute chronology became very difficult to make, unless one wished to fall back on de Luc's natural chronometers. As a result, the two themes separated, with the biblical chronology relegated to a dim and often unmentioned background. Any reference to the Mosaic chronology indicated faith, not science, on the part of the author. As such, this chronology retained its role in theology, but was only occasionally discussed in the scientific literature between about 1830 and 1859.

Indeed, those who did utilize the biblical chronology during these years did so because their interests lay in reconciling the Mosaic chronology with indications of a human presence deep in the past. De Serres's attempt to reconcile what he saw in the caves of southern France with what was revealed to him in Scripture, MacEnery's discussion of the absolute chronology of Kent's Cavern, Hume's compression of Boucher de Perthes's data into 6000 years, and Prichard's final submission in 1847 all fall into this category.

The loss of the diluvium as an absolute time marker and the associated retreat of discussion of the Mosaic chronology into the background does not mean that all scientists who dealt with the issue of human antiquity had given up faith in the chronology. It simply means that the biblical chronology as applied to the human species had become an issue that could no longer be compellingly addressed in a scientific fashion. That the issue remained of some importance is seen not only through the work of such people as de Serres and Prichard who did discuss it, but also from the reaction after a great human antiquity had been established. In and after 1859, many observed that the biblical chronology needed modification or had been overturned. Thus, the anti-Darwinian and very conservative geologist John Phillips (1800–1874), William Smith's nephew and Buckland's successor at Oxford, observed in his review of the *Antiquity of Man* that "geological evidence might support some extension of the ordinary chronology"; Prestwich noted that it was obvious that "our present chronology with respect to the first appearance of Man must be greatly extended"; and Pictet was careful to note in 1859 that the new evidence did not controvert Genesis.[8] In the *Westminster Review,* the anonymous reviewer of Lyell's 1863 volume not only agreed that "the Human Race is much older than the ordinary chronology admits," but also felt it "remarkable how chary Geologists have until recently been of disturbing the popular notion that the creation of *Man* took place in the year 4004 B.C. It has seemed as if they had purchased their right to speculate freely on the anterior history of the Earth, by promising to leave untouched that which the Theologian claims as his proper province, the origin and early history of the Human Race."[9] While the biblical chronology had been greatly weakened by the end of the 1840s, it had not been totally abandoned.

Unlike questions relating to absolute age, questions of relative age or of geological antiquity could be addressed directly with the tools of science. Here, the focus of interest was whether or not people had appeared on earth prior to the time the globe had taken on its modern form. Indeed, Frere had this issue in mind in 1797 when he was tempted to assign his stone tools to a period so remote that it might even be "beyond that of the present world." This aspect of human antiquity loomed largest in the literature produced during the decades between Cuvier's establishment of the reality of extinction and Lyell's *Antiquity of Man.*

Those who focused on geological antiquity and were explicitly concerned only with that issue might or might not have cared about the short absolute chronology. Those who were concerned with scriptural chronology had to care about geological antiquity, because they all agreed that a high geological antiquity seemed irreconcilable with Scripture. Thus, Lyell could state in 1847 that human physical diversity required more time to have developed than any of the "popular systems of chronology" allowed, while at the same time denying the association of extinct mammals and human remains. Similarly, Richard Owen could become convinced of an impressive human antiquity by human linguistic diversity, while remaining aloof on the question of the associations. Because the blade did not cut both ways, scriptural geologists like Buckland, who denied the associations, and de Serres, who accepted them, were in a much tighter bind than scientists such as Lyell and Owen whose stated concerns were only with geological antiquity. When analyses of human physical diversity suggested that the biblical chronology could not be correct if the monogenist position were sound, those who were concerned with that chronology found themselves in a difficult situation, but those for whom the question was geological antiquity alone were unshaken. Accordingly, Prichard had to shift positions in 1847, while Lyell was not required to move until a dozen years later. Early in 1858, Leonard Horner (1785–1864) announced his discovery of pottery at a depth of 12 meters in Nile Valley sediments and calculated an age of over 13,000 years for this material.

Those who adhered to the biblical chronology had reason to worry, but those who defined the problem solely in terms of geological age did not, because this discovery did not suggest that the earth was not then modern in form.[10]

The most basic of the two issues, then, was geological age, because this issue had to be addressed by all. A stone tool or human bone found in deposits laid down prior to the onset of modern environmental conditions implicated not only the biblical chronology, but also the interpretation of the history of the earth as a history of the earth in preparation for the advent of the human species.

Exactly what "modern form" meant, however, was a point of some contention. For de Serres, modern form meant the appearance of the modern continents, and thus of the onset of the alteration of those continents by the processes now seen operating around us. Accordingly, he linked the appearance of human beings with the appearance of those continents, and used observed rates of earth-modifying phenomena to date those events to 6000 or 7000 years ago, just as de Luc had done before him. That our lands were once the home of now-extinct beasts did not imply a lack of modernity to him since, as he argued over and over, extinctions were known to have occurred during very recent times and were clearly an attribute of the earth as it is today.

Although some, including John Fleming, would have agreed with de Serres on the issue of extinction, most did not. Schmerling was explicit about the meaning of modern form to him: "if it is necessary to believe those who admit that the appearance of man occurred since the earth took its modern form, this would be after the destruction of several species [of mammals]." When Pictet asked in 1853 whether "man appeared on the surface of the earth before the modern epoch," he meant before the extinctions. And when Prestwich concluded that people had existed "anterior to the surface assuming its present form," he was including both modification of the earth's topography and the extinctions as his criteria of modernity.

There was, then, general agreement that an environmentally modern earth had not come into existence until after the extinctions had occurred. The existence of the great mammals themselves showed that the globe could not then have been fully modern in form. It was this general agreement that gave associations between human relics and extinct mammals their great importance. It was also this agreement, as well as the high antiquity implied for the extinct beasts, that eventually lead de Serres's tightrope to snap.

Discussions of the great antiquity of our species at and after the time of its acceptance are instructive here as well, since it was only then that the issue had to be dealt with by all concerned. The providential history of the earth and the nature of our planet at the time of the earliest human remains loom large in these discussions. William Whewell's concern with these matters, for instance, was clear in the letter he wrote to the geologist James D. Forbes (1809–1868) in 1864, prompted by Forbes's discussion in the *Edinburgh Review* of the *Antiquity of Man:*

I will not conceal from you that the course of speculation on this point has somewhat troubled me. I cannot see without some regrets the clear definite line, which used to mark the commencement of the human period of the earth's history, made obscure and doubtful. There was something in the aspect of the subject, as Cuvier left it, which was very satisfactory to those who wished to reconcile the providential with the scientific history of the world, and this aspect is now no longer so universally acknowledged. It is true that a reconciliation of the scientific with the religious view is still possible, but it is not so clear and striking as it was. But it is weakness to regret this; and no doubt another generation will find some way of looking at the matter which will satisfy religious men. I should be glad to see my way to this view, and am hoping to do so soon.[11]

Prestwich was also deeply concerned with such questions, observing that while our species had appeared prior to the surface of the earth assuming its modern form, this was merely in regard to "some of the minor features." But Prestwich went beyond deemphasizing how different that former world was, and attempted to show that the presence of ancient human beings in a world not yet modern in form was not antithetical to a belief in a providential God preparing the earth for His highest creation. "The special nature of the glacial period," he argued in 1863, suggests "its effect has possibly been to give increased rigidity and immobility to the flexible crust of the earth, and to produce a state of equilibrium which might otherwise have been a long and slow attainment, whereby it has been rendered fit and suitable for the habitation and pursuits of civilized man."[12] Prestwich was already seeking the solution Whewell felt was needed to satisfy religious men.

Prestwich also stressed the uninterrupted succession of life from the Pleistocene to modern times in 1863. This was an important issue, since the smooth succession of organisms through time helped to account for the presence of people with extinct mammals. There was continuity from those times to ours; the differences that existed resided in the piecemeal extinction of animals, not in the addition of new ones, and our species clearly belonged to the last creation. This was, in fact, a common argument, though it had to be made more forcefully in France, where catastrophism still had a sizable following. In his "suppressed" paper of 1860, for instance, Lartet maintained that the Quaternary had been characterized by successive, not catastrophic, extinctions, and that there had been no break in the continuity of life throughout this period. Pictet followed Lartet's paper with an attempt to demonstrate that so many of the terrestrial vertebrates of modern western Europe were known from diluvial deposits that it was clear that continuity was the rule. Indeed, Pictet argued, the extinctions seemed to have been so piecemeal that it was difficult to know where the diluvial period ended and the modern one began. C.-T. Gaudin followed in turn with an identical argument for plants and left no doubt as to the meaning of all this for the human species: "a great part of the vegetal population of our continent continued across all the phases of the quaternary, and man could have continued to exist as well as the plant world of our continent."[13] These arguments for the continuity of life and for the lack of new additions to the faunal and floral list of western Europe during Quaternary times did not change the fact that human beings had appeared before the earth had taken on its modern form. However, they most certainly did help to diminish the impact of this fact by stressing the aspects of those early times that seemed modern and that still allowed our species to be the last to appear on earth. In fact, the argument that people had caused the extinctions became routine after 1859, and this causal agent also helped make the ancient world seem more modern in form.[14]

Even though theological concerns were at the heart of the beliefs that people were only 6000 years old and that they had not appeared until the earth had become fully modern in form, the reasons that Cuvier, Buckland, Desnoyers, and Lyell gave for rejecting the associations were good ones. Until Boucher de Perthes, the only evidence of any magnitude that had been forwarded to support the coexistence of people and extinct mammals had come from caves. As I have emphasized, the stratigraphy of caves can be tremendously, even imposssibly, complex. As Laville and his colleagues have recently noted, the Pleistocene sediments of the rock shelters of southwestern France represent "some of the most complex and heterogeneous deposits encountered by archaeologists anywhere in the world."[15] The point made by Lyell in 1832 was a valid one: one could accept cave data if that information had been derived from "an undisturbed *stratified* deposit . . . but we must hesitate before we draw analogous inferences from . . . caves, where the signs of *successive* deposition are wanting." Caves, as Desnoyers observed in the same year, are often characterized by "discordant stratigraphy" and are thus not to be trusted. Indeed, this was a position that continued to seem sound even after the acceptance of a vast human antiquity. "We coincide," said Lyell's anonymous reviewer in the *Westminster Review,* "with those who hesitate to base so important an inference as the contemporaneousness of Man with the great extinct Pachyderms, upon the association of their remains in the stalagmitic incrustrations of the floors of caves."[16] To Prestwich, the value of Brixham Cave was that it led him to the French sites: "cave evidence alone," he said of Brixham, "was not sufficient."

The arguments made by Lyell, Desnoyers, and others against the validity of cave associations may have been arguments in the service of a particular belief, but they were nonetheless sound ones. Because the belief they served was so generally held and so important in terms of contemporary views of the human place in nature, these arguments were especially compelling. As a result, Boucher de Perthes's impression of the importance of his own work in open sites was an appropriate one. Lyell, in fact, stressed the significance of this aspect of Boucher de Perthes's work in the *Antiquity of Man:*

> It has naturally been asked, if man coexisted with the extinct species of the caves, why were his remains and the works of his hands never embedded outside the caves in ancient river-gravel containing the same fossil fauna? Why should it be necessary for the geologist

to resort for evidence of the antiquity of our race to the dark recesses of underground vaults and tunnels, which may have served as places of refuge or sepulture to a succession of human beings and wild animals, and where floods may have confounded together in one breccia the memorials of the fauna of more than one epoch? Why do we not meet with a similar assemblage of the relics of man, and of living and extinct quadrupeds, in places where the strata can be thoroughly scrutinized in the light of day? Recent researches have at length demonstrated that such memorials, so long sought for in vain, do in fact exist, and their recognition is the chief cause of the more favorable reception now given to the conclusions which MM. Tournal, Christol, Schmerling, and others, arrived at thirty years ago respecting the fossil contents of caverns. The first great step in this direction was made . . . by M. Boucher de Perthes.[17]

Although the relative stratigraphic simplicity of the river terrace sites provided major advantages over caves in documenting the validity of the associations, such sites also provided an advantage in assessing the age of the associations. What was known of the general sequence of Quaternary earth history during the mid-nineteenth century had been extracted primarily from deposits that could be traced over vast expanses. The artifact-bearing river terrace sites could be correlated with this sequence with relative ease. In contrast, caves presented geographically isolated sediments that often proved difficult to relate to the general sequence in ways that did not depend largely on their faunal content. As a result, the artifacts from open sites could be dated on the basis of both the geological *and* paleontological nature of the beds in which they were found, but the cave deposits could generally be dated only by their faunas. This situation allowed some latitude with caves even if the associations were accepted, since it could always be argued that the animals represented had simply survived longer than had previously been thought. As Lyell's anonymous reviewer in the *Westminster Review* observed, cave associations "might as well be explained by the prolongation of the period of the great extinct Pachyderms into the human period, as by carrying back the origins of Man to the epoch specially marked by their prevalence."[18] De Serres's arguments, of course, were based on exactly this possibility. While such an approach could also be applied to open sites, the results were much less convincing. Here, one had to bring not only the extinct mammals forward in time, but also the depositional events represented by the sediments—events of great magnitude that were registered over huge regions. To most, there seemed little chance that events of such scope could have occurred during the relatively recent past. Thus, in dealing with Boucher de Perthes's data, de Serres could neither deny the associations (the first advantage provided by the river terrace sites) nor deny the antiquity of the events represented at those sites (the second advantage). His only way out was to agree with Robert that these deposits were not the true diluvium, and were therefore not that old. Many, including Prestwich in 1861 and Forbes in 1863, felt that the vast expanse of ages called for by Lyell and others was inappropriate and that the extinct mammals and geological events were more recent than had been supposed, but such recency was still well beyond anything suggested by the biblical chronology.

Even though the terrace sites carried these major advantages, Boucher de Perthes's data were at first rejected. While this rejection can reasonably be attributed to the theoretical framework in which he embedded his evidence—as Evans noted in 1860, Huxley in 1869, and Geikie in 1881, among others[19]—the same cannot be said for Rigollot's cautious and solid presentation of the data from Amiens. Here, rejection stemmed from the sheer belief that such things could not be. In addition, however, there was the problem that the right person had not made the discovery.

With almost no exceptions, the people arguing for a great human antiquity were not influential scientists whose word alone could convince. Boucher de Perthes was a customs official, Rigollot and Schmerling physicians, Tournal a pharmacist, and so on. Unlike, for example, Lyell, who was trained for the law but did geology, these men worked full time at their chosen professions; their geological studies were done as time allowed. Christol became a competent and known paleontologist, but this was after his publication on the bone caves. Godwen-Austen was an exception, but he argued over a site that had already been discredited. De Serres comes close to being an exception, but his geological pronouncements were often controversial, even when they had nothing to do with the issue of human antiquity.[20] Most importantly, those who were most emphatic about the associations were not members of the scientific elite of the countries in which they lived. Because these men were scientific outsiders, their word did not carry much weight among the elite on such a crucial matter. The catch, of course, is that those on the inside generally did not believe that human beings were ancient, and so were not conducting the work that men such as Schmerling and Tournal were conducting. If they did conduct such work, they explained away any evidence for a great human antiquity by using the arguments provided by other members of the elite—for instance, by Cuvier, Buckland, or Desnoyers. Spring provides an example. He discovered the Chauvaux materials in 1842, but withheld publication for over a decade while pondering their age.[21] The real problem, however, was not that he did not know how old they were, but that they might have been ancient. A de Serres would have published such a discovery immediately, but Spring, a member of the Belgian scientific elite, waited until he was convinced his material was postdiluvian in age. Boué provides another example. While thinking that his human bones were ancient, he did not press the issue after Cuvier announced his opposition.

Members of the inner circle did not believe, and only the word of a member of that circle would be accepted at face value or at least listened to seriously. Outsiders did the work and published the arguments, but their word was not trustworthy. Science still works this way, and the situation is not all bad. After all, one of the reasons that the elite reach their position is that they are, generally, highly accomplished scientists. Although Élie de Beaumont's actions during the late 1850s were not particularly admirable, it is nonetheless true that he had reached his position of power through genuine scientific achievements.

It was not until members of the elite saw for themselves that the situation changed. Hébert made the point well in his discussion of Rigollot's work: the St. Acheul and St. Roch deposits were ancient; all the workers, as well as Rigollot, said that the implements had come from the ancient deposits, but he had not seen any tools come from those deposits himself. Accordingly, Hébert concluded that although Rigollot's work was provocative and the question worthy of examination, nothing had been solved.

"The great and sudden revolution in modern opinion, respecting the probable existence at a former period of man and many extinct mammalia," Charles Murchison said in 1868, "has been universally attributed to the results of the exploration of Brixham Cave."[22] Although Murchison's statement would have been more accurate if he had pointed out that the universal attribution was a particularly British affair, it is true that Brixham Cave changed the situation dramatically. Here, members of the British scientific elite were integrally involved in the excavations and saw for themselves. Once that had happened, they became willing to believe what many outsiders had been saying for decades. And, influenced by their British counterparts, members of the French inner circle were stimulated to see for themselves. There was, indeed, a "great and sudden revolution in modern opinion," a revolution that began because this time the right people had made the discovery.

In his autobiography, the physicist Max Planck repeated the old observation that "a new scientific truth does not triumph by convincing its opponents and making them see the light, but rather because its opponents eventually die, and a new generation grows up that is familiar with it."[23] David L. Hull and his colleagues have argued that Planck's principle does not accurately describe the acceptance of evolutionary theory after the publication of Darwin's *Origin of Species* in 1859.[24] Does it, as Kenneth P. Oakley has suggested,[25] accurately characterize the acceptance of the evidence for human antiquity, the other burning issue of the day?

It does not. The British scientists who played the crucial role in 1859 were not young. Lyell was 62, Flower 52, Falconer 51, Pengelly 47, Prestwich 47. Evans was the exception, and even he was 36. In France, the situation was no different. Rigollot was 68 when he announced his conversion in 1854. Pictet was 50 in 1859, Hébert 47, Maury 42. Geoffroy Saint-Hilaire was 53 when he voiced his praise of Boucher de Perthes at the Academy of Sciences in 1858, and Édouard Lartet was 58 in that year. These were not young men. Among those making the discoveries, de Serres was 49 when he published his *Geognosy,* and Schmerling was 39 in 1830; Boucher de Perthes may not count since he certainly had not been properly socialized scientifically, but he was 49 in 1837 when he began his work. There were, of course, young men involved: Tournal was 23 in 1828 and Christol was 27 in 1829; in 1859, Gaudry was 32 and Pouchet was 26. But the influential movers, the converted members of the elite, were men of an older generation, as were many of those who had made the discoveries themselves. Indeed, had the older generation of scientists not been converted so rapidly and fully, the new resolution on the question of human antiquity would not have been so quick in coming. Planck's principle does not apply here.

Why, then, did Oakley, whose work is so excellent, suggest that it did? The answer is simple: the individual who led him to make the argument was Élie de Beaumont, who was 62 years old in 1859.

With the Pleistocene time barrier for human antiquity broken, only the age of the oldest known ape-like creatures limited the possible antiquity of the human species. This limit was implied by both evolutionary and creationist perspectives. In the evolutionary perspective, those ancient primates represented potential human ancestors, or had lived at a time that must have postdated the divergence of the human lineage from the ancestral primate stock.[26] In the creationist perspective, people might have appeared soon after the higher primates had been called into being. The temporal limits were well known. In 1837, Lartet reported the remains of an extinct ape-like animal, subsequently named *Pliopithecus*, from late Tertiary deposits in southern France.[27] In 1856 he followed with the discussion of another, more advanced Miocene primate, *Dryopithecus*, also from southern France, but by this time a series of such Miocene-aged pongids had been reported.[28] Once a Pleistocene age for early human beings was accepted, a flood of reports of human remains from Miocene and Pliocene deposits in both the Old World and the New were published.

One of the first such discoveries was published by Jules Desnoyers. Desnoyers had been converted in 1859 (at the age of 59) when he, too, had visited St. Acheul and seen for himself.[29] Now, in 1863, he presented the results of work conducted in Pliocene deposits at Saint-Prest, near Chartres, some 80 kilometers southwest of Paris. These deposits had yielded the remains of elephant, rhinoceros, hippopotamus, and other animals whose bones bore "numerous and incontestable traces of incisions, striations, and cuts"[30] from the work of human hands. People, he concluded, had lived in France during the Pliocene, prior to the glacial epoch. In fact, Desnoyers soon found himself arguing against the nonbeliever, Eugène Robert.[31]

Many other discoveries of Tertiary human remains followed in short order. In 1867, the Abbé Louis Bourgeois (1819–1878) added stone tools to Desnoyers's cut bones from Saint-Prest,[33] and reported the discovery of stone tools in Miocene deposits from south of Orléans, northcentral France.[34] In 1872, the geologist Carlos Ribeiro (1813–1882) published a similar find from Miocene and Pliocene deposits near Lisbon, while Franz-Fritz von Dücker (1827–1892) added the Miocene fossil deposits of Pikermi to the list.[35] The number of such sites grew to the point that a separate term was coined for the apparent implements they contained. In 1883 Gabriel de Mortillet assigned all Tertiary artifacts to the "Eolithic Period," and he included the Eolithic as his basal prehistoric unit in both his *Prehistory* (1883) and his *Prehistoric Museum* (1881) (the latter designed as a pictorial atlas to accompany the former[36]). Debate over the validity of the eoliths continued well into the twentieth century.

The reaction in the New World was little different from that in Europe. In 1872, Charles C. Abbott (1843–1919) reported the discovery of stone implements in gravels along the Delaware River near Trenton, New Jersey, and soon argued that they were glacial in age.[37] Abbott's finds were widely accepted; indeed, Alfred Russel Wallace noted that Abbott "appears to stand in a somewhat similar relation to this great question in America as did Boucher de Perthes in Europe."[38] Discovery of Tertiary human remains soon followed. The most widely discussed was the Calaveras skull, discovered in 1866 at a depth of 40 meters in a Calaveras County, California, mine shaft. In 1872, and in a series of later publications, the geologist Josiah D. Whitney (1819–1896), once a student of Élie de Beaumont, argued that this skull was Pliocene in age; this view was adopted by many, including Wallace.[39]

Wallace was clear about why he was convinced that the discoveries of human remains in Miocene and Pliocene deposits in Europe and North America were valid. Evolutionary theory led to the prediction that they would be found:

> If there is any truth whatever in the doctrine of evolution as applied to man, and if we are not to adopt the exploded idea that the Paleolithic men were specially created just when the flood of ice was passing away, they *must* have had ancestors who *must* have existed in the Pliocene period, if not earlier.[40]

Since the acceptance of human antiquity and the publication of Darwin's *Origin of Species* both occurred in 1859, it is easy to assume that these events were directly connected. The intimate temporal connection of the two can be seen from the fact that Lyell announced the forthcoming publication of Darwin's book at the same session of the 1859 British Association for the Advancement of Science meetings in which he discussed his acceptance of the Amiens and Abbeville data; his announcement concerning Darwin's work was published in the paragraph that followed his address on human antiquity in the Association's *Reports*.

That an extreme antiquity for the human species bore on the question of human evolution is obvious. Darwin made the point at the very beginning of his *Descent of Man* (1871): "the high antiquity of man has recently been demonstrated by a host of eminent men, beginning with M. Boucher de Perthes, and this is the indispensable basis for understanding his origin. I shall, therefore, take this conclusion for granted."[41] Soon after Darwin's *Origin of Species* appeared, the question of human antiquity became caught up in the question of human evolution: it was not by accident that Lyell's *Antiquity of Man* addressed both human antiquity and the origin of species. The two issues were never again to be separated.

Nonetheless, as Gruber has discussed,[42] by the time the *Origin* was published, the high antiquity of the human species was already well accepted, and the two events were not causally connected. Although some of those involved in the acceptance of a great human antiquity, including Lyell, were aware of what Darwin was about to say, most were not. Because concern with the human place in the scheme of things was so important in supporting the notion of the recency of people on earth, agreement that people were ancient would probably have been much longer in coming had Darwin published a few years earlier.

It was widely recognized at the time that although a recent origin of our species was incompatible with transmutationist theory, what had now become the fact of great time depth did not provide a crucial test for any of the available explanations of human origins. Such time depth was compatible with evolution by natural selection, with transmutationist theory that did not call upon natural selection as the driving mechanism, and with creationist approaches. Thus Sir Roderick Murchison could accept a great human antiquity while completely rejecting any form of transmutation, Pictet could accept that antiquity while accepting transmutation guided by a supernatural creative force, and Darwin could combine human antiquity, transmutation, and natural selection into a single package.[43] Pictet's opinion was the general one:

> Whether one admits with Lamarck or with M. Darwin a gradual transformation of beings, whether one believes in a general law of nature leading to new organic formations in certain epochs, whether one accepts the idea of successive creations, one will always be obliged to state the same facts in the history of the globe.[44]

Indeed, Lyell was frequently criticized by admirers and detractors alike for having needlessly drawn the issue of transmutation into the question of human antiquity in his *Antiquity of Man*. Thus, he was chided by an anonymous reviewer in the *Anthropological Review* for discussing the development theory at all: "that subject has nothing to do with the antiquity of man . . . No theory of development can be true without an enormous antiquity; but any amount of antiquity for the appearance of man or his works does not give any support to the theory of progressive transmutation."[45]

A great human antiquity did not provide a crucial test for any explanation of human origins, and a shallow time depth clearly falsified any of the proposed transmutationist theories. Therefore views on transmutation in the contemporary literature can be inferred from a denial of a deep time depth for our species, but such views cannot be inferred from its acceptance. John Dawson (1820–1899),[46] John Phillips,[47] and de Serres all argued against a great time depth, and one can correctly infer from that stance that their orientation was an antitransformationist one. W. Boyd Dawkins (1837–1929), Armand de Quatrefages (1810–1892), and Pictet all accepted a deep human antiquity, but one could not know from that fact that Dawkins was bitterly opposed to evolution by natural selection,[48] de Quatrefages unconvinced by the arguments either for or against transmutation,[49] and Pictet amenable to evolution as long as a "creative force" was recognized.[50] Darwin's *Descent of Man* was in part possible because of, and was certainly made more plausible by, the new consensus on human antiquity, but his arguments gained no support from the fact of that antiquity. People could as well have been created 100,000 years ago as 6,000 years ago, and everyone recognized that fact.

The question of human morphological change through time was a different issue, since fossil evidence held the potential of providing tremendous support for transmutationist theory. As was the case with human antiquity, this issue also became caught up in the debate over evolution after the *Origin of Species* appeared. Although Schmerling discovered the partial skull of a Neanderthal child in one of the Engis caves, not until 1936 were these remains recognized to be anything but morphologically modern.[51] The Engis skull that did become well known during the second half of the nineteenth century was the other one that Schmerling had found. At Lyell's request, Frédéric-Antoine Spring had a plaster cast made of this cranium, and that cast became widely distributed.[52] This skull, however, was modern in form. The child's skull from Engis was so fragmented that one just could not tell that it was morphologically distinct.

Thus, the first hint of significant morphological change came from the skull recovered from Neanderthal Cave, in the Neander Valley near Dusseldorf, western Germany, in 1856. Preserved as a result of the efforts of Karl J. Fuhlrott (1804–1877), this skull was described by the anatomist Hermann Schaafhausen (1816–1893) in 1858. Schaafhausen pointed out the apparently primitive characters displayed by this specimen and suggested that it represented "the most ancient memorial of the early inhabitants of Europe,"[53] a memorial that was "traceable to a period at which the latest animals of the diluvium still existed."[54] The problem with the Neanderthal skull and associated postcranial bones, however, was that they had not been found in a stratigraphic context that required great age: no extinct mammals had been found along with them. As a result, they could have been of virtually any date, and Schaafhausen's assertion of antiquity was based primarily on the fact that the skull looked primitive. It could not be demonstrated to be ancient, and thus played no role in the establishment of human antiquity.

When Thomas Henry Huxley (1825–1895), Darwin's great supporter, examined *Man's Place in Nature* in 1863, one of the questions he addressed was "how far the recent discoveries of human remains in a fossil state bear out, or oppose" the view that "the structural intervals between the various existing modifications of organic beings may be diminished, or even obliterated, if we take into account the long and varied succession of animals and plants which have preceeded those now living and are known to us only by their fossilized remains."[55]

Huxley chose to examine two human fossils in detail: the adult skull from Engis and the Neanderthal specimen. The fragmentary Engis child's skull went unexamined, since Schmerling had "not . . . been able to put [it] together again."[56] His analysis of the adult Engis skull did not reveal any markedly primitive characteristics to him: "it is, in fact, a fair average human skull, which might have belonged to a philosopher, or might have contained the thoughtless brains of a savage."[57] Such was not the case with the Neanderthal cranium, however. This skull showed "ape-like characters, stamping it as the most pithecoid of human crania yet discovered."[58] Nonetheless, the fact that its cranial capacity was large, approximately 1230 cc, suggested to him that any ape-like tendencies could not have run very deep. Huxley concluded that the features shown by this skull could be encompassed within the variation now seen among human crania. No known human fossils, he concluded, "take us appreciably nearer to that lower pithecoid form, by the modification of which he has, probably, become what he is."[59] (Figure 9.1).

In the following year, the Neanderthal skull from Gibraltar was reported, 16 years after it had been discovered, but it, too, had come from deposits whose age was equivocal.[60] In 1866, a Neanderthal mandible from the cave of La Naulette, near Dinant in southern Belgium, was described. Associated with extinct mammals, this mandible was generally agreed to be of remarkably primitive form, some seeing it as support for Darwin.[61] However, not until 1885 were Neanderthal *skulls* of clear antiquity finally discovered, at Spy near Namur in Belgium.[62] When Darwin published his *Descent of Man* in 1871, he could not turn to any undoubtedly ancient human fossils that were morphologically very different from the bones of modern human beings.

Boucher de Perthes was hopeful of contributing here as well. He had long argued that early members of the human species were morphologically different from modern people, but he had not been able to document those differences in "nuances of form" he had predicted in 1847 because the bones of the makers of his stone tools had eluded him. After having offered a reward to any of his workers who found such remains, and double the amount if they were found in place, he was shown what he wanted. On 23 March 1863, a human tooth was found in the gravels at Moulin Quignon; on 28 March, a second tooth and then a partial mandible were discovered. Prestwich, Evans, and the geologist Alfred Tylor (1824–1884) visited Moulin Quignon and immediately became suspicious, since the handaxes said to have been found with the skeletal material seemed to be counterfeits. The possibility of fraud was a real one, since the workmen were now conducting a substantial business in the manufacture of stone tools for sale to both geologists and tourists.[63] Falconer arrived the next day, after Prestwich,

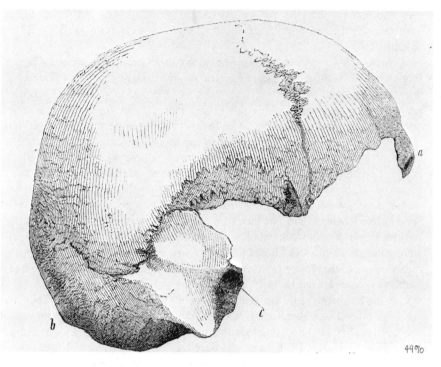

Figure 9.1. The Engis skull, as illustrated by Huxley (1863). Huxley analyzed the adult's cranium from Engis, basing his study on the cast prepared by Frédéric-Antoine Spring. Huxley was unable to analyze the Engis child's skull, identified as Neanderthal in 1936.

Evans, and Tylor had left, and examined the mandible itself. Feeling that the jaw possessed characters consistent with a possibly great antiquity, he immediately wrote to the zoologists William B. Carpenter and Armand de Quatrefages to tell them of his opinion.[64]

On 16 April, Carpenter reported the discovery to the Royal Society of London and supported its antiquity.[65] Boucher de Perthes presented the facts to the Academy of Sciences on 20 April. At the same session, de Quatrefages announced that both he and Falconer had visited Moulin Quignon and believed the association to be valid.[66] Falconer, however, had had a change of mind since his visit. Further examination of both the hand axes and the skeletal remains had convinced him that they were forgeries, and he announced this conclusion in a letter to the London *Times* on 25 April.[67] During the Academy of Sciences 27 April meeting, de Quatrefages argued that although some of the handaxes might be counterfreit, the mandible was, in fact, ancient.[68] The following week, he repeated his conviction, and noted that Desnoyers, Gaudry, Pictet, and other French scientists were of a similar mind[69] (Figure 9.2).

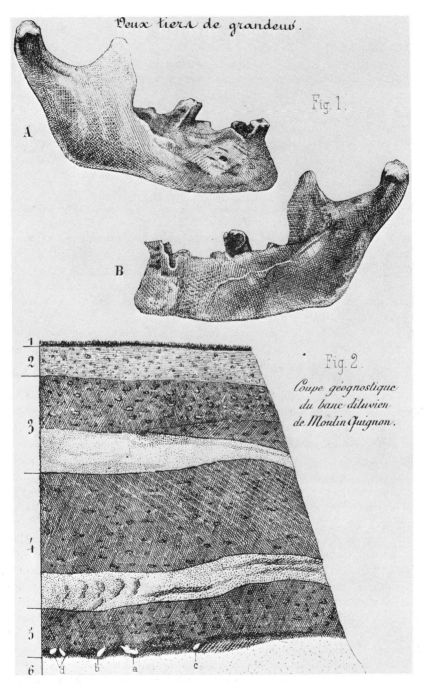

Figure 9.2. The Moulin Quignon mandible and a stratigraphic profile of the Moulin Quignon deposits, as illustrated by Boucher de Perthes (1864). Although the authenticity of the Moulin Quignon mandible was quickly rejected, no one involved implicated Boucher de Perthes.

Only a month had passed since the original discovery, yet opinions on the validity of the Moulin Quignon mandible were seriously divided along lines that strongly coincided with the English Channel. On 2 May, Lartet wrote to Falconer suggesting that a meeting be held in Paris to resolve the issue, with the English represented by Falconer, Prestwich, and Evans. At the same time, de Quatrefages wrote to the apparently less sceptical Carpenter to invite him as well.

The "trial of the jaw," as Falconer called it, began 9 May and lasted 5 days. Evans was unable to attend; his place was taken by the anatomist George Busk (1807–1886), with Carpenter, Falconer, and Prestwich (who came a day late) making up the rest of the British contingent. The French were represented by the geologist Achille Delesse (1817–1881), Desnoyers, de Quatrefages, and Lartet. The zoologist Henri Milne-Edwards (1800–1885) served as moderator; many others attended and took part, including Bourgeois, Buteux, Gaudry, and Hébert. The first sessions were held in Paris. Here the English participants maintained that many of the stone tools involved were forgeries, and that the jaw was a fraud as well. The French maintained that the facts did not support such a negative conclusion. Twenty of the participants then traveled to Abbeville to examine the Moulin Quignon deposits firsthand, a trip that Carpenter was unable to make. Excavations in these deposits provided what seemed to be undoubted stone tools in the same gravels that had provided the mandible, an observation that softened Prestwich's view, but left Falconer and Busk unmoved.[70]

The committee reached its conclusions on 13 May: the mandible had not been fraudulently introduced; it was contemporaneous with the ancient deposits; the handaxes were, at least for the most part, authentic; there was insufficient reason to doubt the contemporaneity of the tools, the mandible, and the gravels. These, however, were conclusions democratically reached: Falconer and Busk did not agree with most of them.

The summary of the committee's proceedings appeared in the *Accounts* of the Academy of Sciences for 18 May,[71] followed by comments by de Quatrefages and Élie de Beaumont. De Quatrefages repeated his support, but Élie de Beaumont was not a believer. The issue for him was not whether the mandible was a fraud: that did not matter, since he did not believe the Moulin Quignon deposits were old in the first place. These deposits, he maintained, were not the true diluvium, and any association between human remains and extinct mammals here, or anyplace else, were accidental: "I do not believe that the human species was contemporary with *Elephas primigenius*. I continue to share the opinion of M. Cuvier in this matter. The *opinion of Cuvier* is a creation of genius; it is not destroyed."[72] His French colleagues, however, did not agree.[73]

The committee had reached its conclusions but little had, in fact, been solved. Among the English, only Prestwich had been swayed. Although Falconer wrote to the London *Times* on 21 May, retracting his earlier *Times* letter, both he and Busk remained unconvinced.[74] Evans, who had not attended, was also unconvinced.[75] With Boucher de Perthes's approval, Evans sent Henry Keeping to assist in the Moulin Quignon excavations in June. Keeping was a man with a significant background: he had been in charge of the field operations at Brixham Cave. It did not take him long to discover that the workers were not to be trusted. Between 3 and 6 June, seven handaxes were found at Moulin Quignon, all of which Keeping convincingly argued had been "placed there on purpose for me to find."[76] Evans reported the results of his mission in the 4 July issue of the widely read periodical *The Athenaeum*. He was blunt:

> A regular system of imposition has been carried on by the gravel-diggers of Abbeville, that the majority of implements lately obtained at Moulin-Quignon are false and inferentially, that the human jaw which was associated with them is, probably, unauthentic. . . . I sincerely hope that the human jaw from Moulin-Quignon may from this time be consigned to oblivion: *Requiescat in Pace*.[77]

Soon after, Prestwich announced that he, too, had lost faith in the Moulin Quignon mandible.[78]

These conclusions were, as Pictet noted, in complete disagreement with the conclusions of the Moulin Quignon committee.[79] Yet, while some continental scholars continued to support the validity of the find,[80] Evans's demonstration of fraud and the strongly negative reaction of the British scientists ensured that the Moulin Quignon mandible would never be accepted as an undoubted human fossil. The same applied to additional human bones reported from Moulin Quignon in 1864,[81] and all this material quickly faded into the background.[82] Boucher de Perthes did not live to see the discovery of any widely accepted human fossils that showed his predicted differences in "nuances of form."

In 1848, the publisher John Murray had rejected Harriet Martineau's *Eastern Life Present and Past* because it contained what he found to be theologically offensive passages, among which he noted those that asserted a much greater human antiquity than that provided by Scripture.[83] Fifteen years later, he had no such difficulties in publishing Lyell's *Antiquity of Man*. John Murray's history reflects in microcosm what had happened in the few years between Martineau's search for a different publisher and the appearance of Lyell's synthesis.

"There is something dreary in the indefinite lengthening of a savage and blood-stained past"[84] wrote Julia Wedgwood (1833–1913), Darwin's niece, in *Macmillan's Magazine* in 1863, and it was becoming clear to most that we had all sprung from savages. There were, however, those who disagreed that the beginnings of modern civilization could have been so dark. There was an alternative to this view, one drawn from Genesis. This view saw our early past as golden, and the history of humankind marked by the differential fall of various peoples into barbarism and savagery.

This was an old idea that had been revived early in the 1830s by Richard Whately, Archbishop of Dublin (1787–1863). In his *Introductory Lectures on Political Economy* (1832), Whately confessed that he had no convincing answer as to why "mankind were not placed at once in a state of society as highly civilized as it was ever destined to be,"[85] but he did believe that the development of civilization had not been as great a climb as many had suggested. "We have no reason to believe that any community ever did, or ever can, emerge unassisted by external helps, from a state of utter barbarism, into any thing that can be called civilization,"[86] Whately asserted, and although there were instances of savages rising to a higher condition because of close contacts with civilized peoples, there were absolutely no cases of such progress among base peoples left to themselves. All seemed to show that savages left alone remained savages no matter how much time passed. It followed that the original state of humankind could not have been one of savagery. Modern savages must have come "from ancestors less barbarous, and from whom they have degenerated."[87] Because human beings could not improve themselves to such a degree, there was only one possible source for the high state of the earliest people: direct revelation from God. This, Whately observed, was in accord with Genesis, which represents "mankind as originally existing in a state far superior to that of our supposed savages."[88]

For Whately, then, the earliest human generations had existed in a high cultural state, and modern savages represented people who had fallen from that condition. Although the acceptance of a deep human antiquity did not in itself make this position untenable, the nature of the artifacts that marked these early human beings seemed inconsistent with the degenerationist position. Nonetheless, there were those who attempted to reconcile the new discoveries with the biblically derived notion of the fall of savages from an earlier, more noble state.

This was, for instance, the approach taken by the eminent Canadian geologist John W. Dawson. At one time a student of Jameson in Edinburgh, Dawson went on to conduct significant geological and paleontological research in Canada. He was held in high esteem by his fellow scientists, serving as president of the American Association for the Advancement of Sciences in 1882, the British Association for the Advancement of Science in 1886, and the Geological Society of America in 1893. He received an even greater honor in 1884 when he was knighted.[89]

A devout Calvinist, Dawson was as dedicated to his religion as he was to his science. His religious beliefs molded his approach to the questions of human antiquity, evolution, and the cultural condition of the earliest members of our species. He was a fervid opponent of Darwinian evolution, and felt it fortunate that such scientists as Sedgwick, Lyell, Owen, and Agassiz had been able to complete so much of their labors before Darwin's revitalization of transmutationist thought had occurred—before "the advent of those poisoned streams and mephitic vapours which threaten the intellectual obscuration of those who should be their successors."[90]

His reaction to the establishment of a great human antiquity was less violent, but no less conservative. He accepted the associations between human remains and extinct mammals, but brought the antiquity of our species in line with Genesis by arguing that these associations confirmed the recency of the extinctions and the deposition of the gravels. His position on this issue did not change between 1860 and the time of his death: "What geological evidence have we that the residence of man in Europe has been longer than 6000 years? . . . Absolutely none."[91] He also observed that the oldest known human fossils, the Engis and Neanderthal crania, fell within the ranges of modern human variation. If the earliest human skulls showed no deviation from modern ones, surely it followed that one could not find any "transition of apes to men in any period; for this great lapse of time renders the species practically permanent."[92]

To Dawson, the purpose of the glacial period was to prepare the earth for our species:

> Out of that chaos came at length an Eden. . . . The glaciers and icebergs of the Post-Pliocene were the ploughshares of God preparing the earth for the time when, with a flora and fauna more beautiful and useful, if less magnificent that that of the Tertiary, it became as the garden of the Lord, fitted for the reception of His image and likeness, immortal and intelligent Man.[93]

Only after the earth had been prepared by the ploughshares of God had the first human beings been created. Many modern scientists, he despaired, would have us believe that primeval man had been "a coarse and filthy savage, repulsive in feature, gross in habits . . . sheltering himself in damp and smoky caves with no eye heavenward."[94] But this picture was simply not true. The earliest state of our species had been the highest we had attained: "man had been a high and noble creature before he became a savage,"[95] and had fallen from here to reach the degraded stations now occupied by so many. This view was far from Julia Wedgwood's picture of a blood-stained past, and fully in accord with the paradise of Eden.

The denial of a savage ancestry fit well with an antievolutionary stance, since it was hardly likely that the immediate descendants of some ape-like creature could have been "high and noble." Not all those who combined a golden past with opposition to transmutation, however, also denied the great antiquity of our species. "I know of no one moral or religious truth which depends on a short estimate of man's antiquity" wrote George D. Campbell, Duke of Argyll (1823–1900) in 1869,[96] yet he also denied both the descent of the human species from some other primate and the lowly condition of our earliest ancestors. Indeed, he argued, the earliest inventions of our race were the most remarkable of them all. Compared to those who discovered fire and the use of corn, "Faraday and Wheatstone are but the inventors of ingenious toys."[97]

Unlike Whately, Argyll did not feel that early achievements of this sort had been made possible by direct revelation but saw them instead as the result of human instinct. But even more important than these early discoveries was the moral condition of the first peoples. Ignorance of the industrial arts, he observed, does not imply that these people were also "ignorant of duty or ignorant of God."[98] If the first human beings were not savages, why did savages exist today? Argyll advanced two explanations. On the one hand, we contain within ourselves "at all times the elements of corruption,"[99] and so tend not to progress but to fall. On the other hand, modern savages do not exist in favorable regions, but only in areas they have been forced to occupy by others, and these environments themselves have caused degradation from a higher state. People, Argyll concluded, had not begun their existence as savages.[100]

Dawson and the Duke of Argyll were not fighting a winning battle, and Julia Wedgwood's characterization was far closer to the common belief. Charles Lyell used the argument from invention and discovery to observe that if early peoples had been endowed with superior intelligence or inspired knowledge, they would have accomplished much more during the lengthy span of their existence than they had accomplished; we might be finding relics whose meaning was beyond us, "machines, perhaps, for navigating the air or exploring the depths of the ocean, or calculating arithmetical problems, beyond the wants or even the conception of living mathematicians."[101]

Whether we liked it or not, we had all sprung from savages. This was a view that was disconcerting to many, but it was also a view that could be comforting. It was clear that we had come a long way from our rude beginnings, and there was little reason to think that the progress had ended. John Lubbock's vision was a grand one:

> In reality we are but on the threshold of civilisation. Far from showing any indications of having come to an end, the tendency to improvement seems latterly to have proceeded with augmented impetus and accelerated rapidity. Why, then, should we suppose that it must now cease? . . . It is surely unreasonable to suppose that a process which has been going on for so many thousand years, should have now suddenly ceased; and he must be blind indeed who imagines that our civilization is unsusceptible of improvement, or that we ourselves are in the highest state attainable by man. . . . Utopia, which we have long looked upon as synonymous with an evident impossibility, which we have ungratefully regarded as "too good to be true," turns out on the contrary to be the necessary consequence of natural laws, and once more we find that the simple truth exceeds the most brilliant flights of the imagination.[102]

Notes and References

1. Darwin 1887, Volume 3:11; for a discussion of Darwin's response to Lyell's treatment of evolution by natural selection in *Antiquity of Man*, see Bartholomew 1973, Ellegård 1958, and Ruse 1979.
2. Lyell 1863b:62.
3. Lyell 1863b:68.
4. Lyell 1863b:68.

5. See Grayson 1980 and 1983.
6. Todhunter 1876, Volume 2:429.
7. Lyell's summary was sufficiently powerful that Falconer immediately accused him of attempting to usurp the credit that belonged to others: "The day has long gone by when scientific work could be written in the style of Louis Quatorze: *La Géologie; c'est moi!—l'Ancienneté d'Homme; c'est moi aussi!*" (Falconer 1863d:586). "Awfully severe" was Darwin's opinion of this (Darwin 1887, Volume 3:101). Prestwich, however, agreed with Falconer's complaint (Prestwich 1863a). Lyell responded that his summary would have been more easily accomplished had the Brixham Cave data been fully published (Lyell 1863a). See also Falconer 1863e and the contemporary account of the dispute provided by [Forbes] 1863.
8. [Phillips] 1863:417; Prestwich 1863d:52; Pictet 1859. See also Phillips 1860.
9. Anonymous 1863a:518.
10. Horner 1859a, 1859b. Horner's estimates of absolute age were based on the assumption that the rate of deposition of Nile Valley sediments had been completely uniform through time, an assumption for which he was frequently, and at times severely, criticized (see, for instance, [Phillips] 1863 and Anonymous 1863b). Even Horner's son-in-law, Charles Lyell, approached Horner's estimation of age with great caution (Lyell 1863b).
11. Todhunter 1876, Volume 2:435–436.
12. Prestwich 1863d:52.
13. Lartet 1860c; Pictet 1860a; Gaudin 1860:283.
14. Grayson 1983.
15. Laville, Rigaud, and Sackett 1980:51.
16. Anonymous 1863a:521; see also [Forbes] 1863.
17. Lyell 1863b:94.
18. Anonymous 1863a:522.
19. Evans 1860; Huxley 1869; Geikie 1881.
20. See, for instance, the editor's comments in de Serres 1829c.
21. Spring 1853.
22. Murchison 1868:486.
23. Planck 1949:33–34.
24. Hull, Tessner, and Diamond 1978.
25. Oakley 1964b.
26. To Lyell, the early apes represented potential ancestors (Wilson 1970); to Darwin, the known fossils of nonhuman higher primates postdated the time of divergence (Darwin 1871). É. Littré noted the relationship I have discussed here in 1858 (Littré 1858).
27. Lartet 1837a,b.
28. Lartet 1856.
29. See the discussion accompanying Gaudry 1860.
30. Desnoyers 1863a:1082.
31. Robert 1863; Desnoyers 1863b.
33. Bourgeois 1867.
34. Bourgeois 1873; see also Anonymous 1873. Bourgeois's work is discussed in Houssay 1902.
35. Ribeiro 1873; von Dücker 1873.
36. De Mortillet 1883; de Mortillet and de Mortillet 1881.
37. Abbott 1873, 1876, 1877, 1881.
38. Wallace 1887:673; this paper was reprinted in Wallace 1891.
39. Whitney 1879; Wallace 1887, 1891.
40. Wallace 1887:667; see also Wallace 1864 and 1891.
41. Darwin 1871:3.
42. Gruber 1965.

43. For Murchison's views, see the discussion following Crawfurd 1863. Pictet expressed his views on Darwin in Pictet 1860b; an English translation of most of this paper appears in Hull 1973. Darwin provided his views in Darwin 1871.

44. Pictet 1860a:268.

45. Anonymous 1863b:136. For similar critiques, see Anonymous 1863a, Hunt 1863, and [Forbes] 1863.

46. See, for instance, Dawson 1863 and 1880.

47. Phillips 1860; [Phillips] 1863.

48. [Dawkins] 1871.

49. See the discussion of de Quatrefages in Stebbins 1972.

50. Pictet 1860b.

51. Fraipont 1936.

52. Spring 1864.

53. Schaafhausen 1861:172.

54. Schaafhausen 1861:155.

55. Huxley 1863:119.

56. Huxley 1863:123.

57. Huxley 1863:156.

58. Huxley 1863:156.

59. Huxley 1863:159; Huxley had presented these conclusions to the Royal Society in 1862 (Huxley 1862).

60. Busk 1865.

61. Pruner-Bay 1866; Dupont 1871.

62. Twiesselmann 1958.

63. Many of the visitors to Abbeville and Amiens commented on the lively market in counterfeit artifacts. See, for instance, Evans 1866, Pictet 1863a, and Pouchet 1860a. A. Tylor, older brother of the anthropologist E. B. Tylor, discussed both the forgeries and his trip with Prestwich and Evans in Tylor 1863.

64. The general outline of events discussed here are taken from Falconer, Busk and Carpenter 1863, Falconer 1868, and Milne-Edwards 1863a. An excellent discussion of the Moulin Quignon controversy is provided by Oakley 1964b.

65. Carpenter 1863.

66. Boucher de Perthes 1863; de Quatrefages 1863c.

67. Falconer 1863f; this letter also appears in Falconer 1863a.

68. De Quatrefages 1863a.

69. De Quatrefages 1863f.

70. Prestwich's changed opinion is noted in Prestwich 1863b.

71. Milne-Edwards 1863a.

72. De Quatrefages 1863d; Élie de Beaumont 1863:937.

73. De Quatrefages 1863d; Garrigou 1863; Hébert 1863; Milne-Edwards 1863b; Pictet 1863a. De Quatrefages 1863e provides English translations of Boucher de Perthes 1863 (de Quatrefages 1863e:318–321), and of several of his own contributions to the dispute (1863a, translated in 1863e:321–327; 1863b, translated in 1863e:330–332; 1863c, translated in 1863e:312–318; 1863f, translated in 1863e:327–330).

74. Falconer 1863c,b.

75. Evans 1863a.

76. Evans 1863b:20.

77. Evans 1863b:19–20.

78. Prestwich 1863c.

79. Pictet 1863b.

80. See the sympathetic views in Cartailhac 1903, de Quatrefages and Hamy 1882, and Maury 1867.

81. De Quatrefages 1864; see also Anonymous 1864. Boucher de Perthes discussed the Moulin Quignon human bones in Boucher de Perthes 1864a and 1864b. As discussed by Oakley (1964b) the Moulin Quignon mandible is certainly post-Pleistocene in age.
82. Rejection by French scientists is shown well by Pruner-Bay 1866.
83. Martineau 1848; the rejection, and the reasons for it, are discussed in Martineau 1877, Paston 1932, and Pichanick 1980.
84. [Wedgwood] 1863:486.
85. Whately 1832:103.
86. Whately 1832:106–107.
87. Whately 1832:117.
88. Whately 1832:111.
89. Biographical information is from O'Brien 1971; see also Trigger 1981.
90. Dawson 1873:250.
91. Dawson 1880:278; Dawson published this view as early as 1860 and as late as 1901 (Dawson 1860, 1901); after 1869, he used the arguments provided by Andrews (1869) as support.
92. Dawson 1863:55.
93. Dawson 1873:280–281.
94. Dawson 1873:377.
95. Dawson 1894a:66. He expressed similar views in Dawson 1882 and 1894b.
96. Argyll 1869:127; see Argyll 1862 for his initial reaction to Darwin's *Origin of Species*.
97. Argyll 1869:154.
98. Argyll 1869:132–133.
99. Argyll 1869:200.
100. Argyll's *Primeval Man* was written in response to positions taken by John Lubbock; for a discussion of the argument, see Gillespie 1977.
101. Lyell 1863b:379.
102. Lubbock 1865:490–492.

Literature Cited

Brackets are used in literature citations as follows:

1. Bracketed authors: authors' names have been bracketed to indicate (i) brief summaries of papers presented at scientific meetings and written by persons other than the authors themselves (e.g., [Christol] 1829, [Fontenelle] 1830, [de Serres] 1829a,b, and 1830, and [Tournal] 1829); and (ii) works of known authorship that were published anonymously. All attributions of authorship for anonymous papers in Victorian periodicals (e.g., [Carpenter] 1848 and [Dawkins] 1871) are taken from the *Wellesley Index to Victorian Periodicals* (W. E. Houghton and E. R. Houghton, eds. 1966–1979, Toronto: University of Toronto Press).
2. Bracketed dates: bracketed dates are used to indicate (i) the initial date of publication for cited works which are facsimiles or reprints (for instance, Esper 1978[1774]; and (ii) the actual year of presentation of a paper in a volume with a multi-year date of publication (e.g., de Serres 1855–1857[1855]).
3. Bracketed titles: in those instances in which papers were untitled, I have provided titles that were either taken from the index of the journal in which the paper appeared (e.g., Gaudry 1860), or that provide a brief description of the contents of that paper (for instance, Aufrère 1936a). In both situations, I have bracketed the titles supplied.
4. Bracketed inserts: in a few cases involving reviews, I have inserted [Review of] to indicate the nature of the publication when that nature might not otherwise be clear.

Abbott, C. C.
   1873   Occurrence of implements in the river drift at Trenton, New Jersey. *American Naturalist* **7**:204–209.
   1876   Traces of an American autochthon. *American Naturalist* **10**:329–335.
   1877   Report on the discovery of supposed Paleolithic implements from the glacial drift in the valley of the Delaware River, near Trenton, New Jersey. *Peabody Museum of American Archaeology and Ethnology Annual Report of the Trustees* **10**:30–43.
   1881   *Primitive industry, or illustrations of the handiwork, in stone, bone, and clay, of the native races of the northern Atlantic seaboard of America.* Salem, Mass.: Bates.

Agassiz, E. C.
   1885   *Louis Agassiz: His life and correspondence* (two volumes). New York: Houghton, Mifflin.

Agassiz, L.
   1837   Discours prononcé à l'ouverture des seances de la Société Helvétique des Sciences Naturelles, à Neuchâtel le 24 Juillet 1837. *Société Helvétique des Sciences Naturelles, Actes, 22me Session*:v–xxxii.
   1840   *Études sur les glaciers.* Neuchâtel, Switzerland: Jent and Gassman.
   1850a   Geographical distribution of animals. *The Christian Examiner and Religious Miscellany* **48**:181–204.
   1850b   The diversity of origin of the human races. *The Christian Examiner and Religious Miscellany* **49**:110–145.
   1851   Contemplations of God in the kosmos. *The Christian Examiner and Religious Miscellany* **50**:1–17.
   1854   Sketches of the natural provinces of the animal world and their relation to the different types of man. In *Types of mankind,* by J. C. Nott and G. R. Gliddon. Philadelphia: Lippincott, Grambo. Pp. lviii–lxxviii.

Aldrovandi, U.
   1648   *Musaeum Metallicum in Libros IIII Distributum,* Bologna.

Andrews, E.
   1869   Reexamination of the localities of human antiquities at Abbeville, Amiens, and Villeneuve. *American Journal of Science* **5**:180–190.

Andrews, H. N.
   1980   *The fossil hunters: in search of ancient plants.* Ithaca, N.Y.: Cornell University Press.

Anonymous
   1841   Eleventh meeting of the British Association for the Advancement of Science. *Athenaeum* **1841**:612–630.
   1847   [Review of] Researches into the physical history of mankind. By James Cowles Prichard, M.D., F.R.S., M.R.I.A. 3rd edition. London: Sherwood, Gilbert, and Piper. 1836–1844. *The New Quarterly Review; or, Home, Foreign, and Colonial Journal* **8**:95–134.
   1863a   The antiquity of man. *Westminster Review* **79**:517–551.
   1863b   Lyell on the geological evidence of the antiquity of man. *Anthropological Review* **1**:129–141.
   1863c   Notes on the antiquity of man. *Anthropological Review* **1**:60–106.
   1864   The fossil man of Abbeville again. *Anthropological Review* **2**:220–222.
   1873   Conclusions de la commission chargée de l'examen des silex de Thenay. *Congrès International d'Anthropologie et d'Archéologie Préhistoriques, Compte Rendu de la 6e Session, Bruxelles* **1872**:93–94.

[Arbuthnot, J.]
   1697   *An examination of Dr. Woodward's account of the deluge, etc., with a comparison*

between Steno's philosophy and the Doctor's, in the case of marine bodies dug out of the earth. London.

Argyll, Duke of [George Douglas Campbell]

1862 Opening address. *Proceedings of the Royal Society of Edinburgh* **4**:350–377.

1869 *Primeval man, an examination of some recent speculations.* London: Strahan.

Aufrère, L.

1935 Une controverse entre François Jouannet et Casimir Picard sur les "haches ébauchées." *Bulletin de la Société Préhistorique Française* **32**:300–302.

1936a [Deux lettres de Tournal à Cuvier.] *Bulletin de la Société Préhistorique Française* **33**:167–168.

1936b Les premières découvertes préhistoriques dans la vallée de la Somme. *Bulletin de la Société Préhistorique Française* **33**:585–592.

1936c Les sablières de Menchecourt. *Bulletin de la Société Préhistorique Française* **33**:139–149.

1940 Figures des préhistoriens. 1. Boucher de Perthes. *Préhistoire* **7**:1–134.

Austen, R. A. C.

1842 On the geology of the south-east of Devonshire. *Transactions of the Geological Society of London* **6**:433–489.

Aymard, A.

1845 Note sur une découverte de fossiles humains dans un bloc de pierre provenant de la montagne volcanique de Denise. *Bulletin de la Société Géologique de France* **12**:107–110.

1847 Résumé d'une lettre de M. Aymard sur les ossements humains fossiles des environs du Puy, et sur de nouvelles espèces de mastodontes. *Bulletin de la Société Géologique de France* **14**:412–416.

1848 Des fossiles humains trouvés sur la montagne volcanique de Denize, près Le Puy, des ossements de mammifères signalés dans divers depots de la Haute-Loire, et de l'epoque de leur enfouissement. *Bulletin de la Société Géologique de France* **5**:49–60.

1850 [Les ossements fossiles de Denise.] *Annales de la Société d'Agriculture, Sciences, Arts et Commerce du Puy* **14**:74–78.

Bagford, J.

1707 An essay on the invention of printing. *Philosophical Transactions of the Royal Society of London* **25**:2397–2407.

1770 A letter to the publisher, written by the ingenious Mr. John Bagford, in which are many curious remarks relating to the city of London, and some things about Leland. In *Joannis Lelandi Antiquarii de rebus Britannicus collectanea,* edited by T. Hearne. (2nd ed.) (Vol. 1) lviii–lxxxvi. London.

Barker, H., R. Burleigh, and N. Meeks

1971 British Museum natural radiocarbon measurements VII. *Radiocarbon* **13**:157–188.

Bartholomew, M.

1973 Lyell and evolution: an account of Lyell's response to the prospect of an evolutionary ancestry for man. *British Journal for the History of Science* **6**:261–303.

Bendyshe, T.

1865 The history of anthropology. *Anthropological Society of London Memoirs* **1**:335–458.

Berry, W. B. N.

1968 *Growth of a prehistoric time scale based on organic evolution.* San Francisco: Freeman.

Blount, C. *et al.*

1693 *The oracles of reason.* London.

Blumenbach, J. F.

1794   Observations on some Egyptian mummies opened in London. *Philosophical Transactions of the Royal Society of London* **84**:177–195.

1865   On the natural variety of mankind. In *The anthropological treatises of Johann*
[1775]   *Friedrich Blumenbach,* translated and edited by T. Bendyshe. London: Longman, Green, Longman, Roberts, and Green. Pp. 65–143.

1865   On the natural variety of mankind (3rd ed.). In *The anthropological treatises of*
[1795]   *Johann Friedrich Blumenbach,* translated and edited by T. Bendyshe. London: Longman, Green, Longman, Roberts, and Green. Pp. 145–276.

Bordes, F.

1972   *A tale of two caves.* New York: Harper and Row.

Bory de Saint-Vincent, J. B. G. M.

1827   *L'homme. (Homo). Essai zoologique sur le genre humain* (2nd ed.) (two volumes). Paris: Rey and Gravier.

Boucher de Perthes, J.

1841   *De la création. Essai sur l'origine et la progression des êtres* (Vol. 1). Paris: Treuttel and Wurtz.

1846   *De l'industrie primitive ou des arts à leur origine.* Paris.

1847   *Antiquités celtiques et antédiluviennes. Mémoire sur l'industrie primitive et les arts à leur origine* (Vol. 1). Paris: Treuttel and Wurtz.

1857   *Antiquités celtiques et antédiluviennes. Mémoire sur l'industrie primitive et les arts à leur origine* (Vol. 2). Paris: Treuttel and Wurtz.

1859   Sur les silex taillés des bancs diluviens de la Somme. *Comptes Rendus Hebdomadaires de l'Académie des Sciences* **49**:581.

1860   *De l'homme antédiluvien et de ses oeuvres.* Paris: Jung-Treuttel.

1861a   Lettre de M. Boucher de Perthes à M. Élie de Beaumont. *Comptes Rendus Hebdomadaires de l'Académie des Sciences* **52**:1133.

1861b   Réponse de M. Boucher de Perthes aux observations faites par M. E. Robert sur le diluvium de département de la Somme. *Comptes Rendus Hebdomadaires de l'Académie des Sciences* **52**:1134–1137.

1861c   Sur les silex taillés trouvés dans le diluvium de département de la Somme; remarques de M. Boucher de Perthes à l'occasion d'une communication recente sur les pierres travaillées par les habitans primitifs des Gaules. *Comptes Rendus Hebdomadaires de l'Académie des Sciences* **52**:300–302.

1863   Mâchoire humaine découverte à Abbeville dans un terrain non remanié. *Comptes Rendus Hebdomadaires de l'Académie des Sciences* **56**:779–782.

1864a   *Antiquités celtiques et antédiluviennes. Memoire sur l'industrie primitive et les arts à leur origine* (Vol. 3). Paris: Jung-Treuttel.

1864b   *De la mâchoire humaine de Moulin-Quignon. Nouvelles découvertes en 1863 et 1864.* Paris: Jung-Treuttel.

Boué, A.

1825   Memoire géologique sur le sud-ouest de la France, suivi d'observations comparatives sur le nord de même royaume, et en particulier sur les bords du Rhin. *Annales des Sciences Naturelles* **14**:125–174.

1829   Ossemens humains présumés fossiles. *Revue Bibliographique des Sciences Naturelles* **1829**:150–151.

1830   Compte rendu des progrès de la géologie. *Bulletin de la Société Géologique de France* **1**:71–75, 94–97, 105–124.

1831–1832   Compte-rendu des progrès de la géologie pendant l'année 1831. *Bulletin de la*
[1832]   *Société Géologique de France* **2**:133–318.

1834   Résumé des progrès des sciences géologiques pendant l'année 1833. *Bulletin de la Société Géologique de France* **5**:1–518.

Bourdier, F.

1975   Serres de Mesplès, Marcel Pierre Toussaint de. In *Dictionary of Scientific Biography* (Vol. 12), edited by C. C. Gillispie. New York: Scribner's. Pp. 317–318.

Bourgeois, l'Abbé

1867   Découverte d'instruments en silex dans le dépôt à *Elephas meridionalis* de Saint-Prest, aux environs de Chartres. *Comptes Rendus Hebdomadaires de l'Académie des Sciences* **64**:47–48.

1873   Sur les silex considerées comme portant les marques d'un travail humain et découverts dans le terrain Miocène de Thenay. *Congrès International d'Anthropologie et d'Archéologie Préhistoriques, Compte Rendu de la 6ᵉ Session, Bruxelles* **1872**:81–92.

Bowler, P. J.

1976   *Fossils and progress*. New York: Science History Publications.

Brongniart, A.

1814   Sur un squelette humain fossile de la Guadeloupe; par M. Ch. Koenig. *Bulletin des Sciences, par la Société Philomatique de Paris* **1814**:149–151.

Bruguière, J.-G.

1792   *Histoire Naturelle des vers* (Tome première). *Encylopédie méthodique*. Paris: Panckouke.

Buchet, J. P. A.

1833   Extrait d'un mémoire de M. J. P. A. Buchet, de Genève, Pasteur à Mialet (Basses-Cévennes), sur une caverne à ossemens fossiles, découverte à l'est de Saint-Jean-du-Gard. *Mémoires de la Société de Physique et d'Histoire Naturelle de Genève* **6**:369–378.

1834   Extrait d'un mémoire sur une caverne à ossemens fossiles, découverte a l'est de Saint-Jean-du-Gard. *Bibliothèque Universelle des Sciences, Belles-letters et Arts, Rédigée à Genève* **56**:266–275.

Buckland, W.

1820   *Vindicae geologicae; or the connexion of geology with religion explained*. Oxford.

1823   *Reliquiae diluvianae, or, observations on the organic remains contained in caves, fissures, and diluvial gravel, and on other geological phenomena, attesting the action of an universal deluge*. London: Murray.

1825   Professor Buckland's reply to some observations in Dr. Fleming's remarks on the distribution of British animals. *Edinburgh Philosophical Journal* **12**:304–319.

1834   Observations on the bones of hyaenas and other animals in the cavern of Lunel near Montpelier [sic], and in the adjacent strata of marine formation. *Proceedings of the Geological Society of London* **1**:3–6.

1836   *Geology and mineralogy considered with reference to natural theology* (two volumes). London: Pickering.

1842   On the former existence of glaciers in Scotland and in the north of England. *Proceedings of the Geological Society of London* **3**:332–337, 345–348.

Buffon, G.

1749   *Histoire naturelle, générale et particulière, avec la description du Cabinet de Roi* (Vol. 1). Paris.

1753   *Historie naturelle, générale et particulière, avec la description du Cabinet de Roi* (Vol. 4). Paris.

1775   *Histoire naturelle, générale et particulière, servant de suite à la théorie de la terre, et de préliminaire à l'histoire des végetaux, parties expérimentale et hypothétique* (Supplement, Vol. 2, *Partie hypothétique*). Paris.

1778   *Histoire naturelle, générale et particulière* (Supplement, Vol. 5). Paris.

Bunsen, C. C. J.
    1848   On the results of the recent Egyptian researches in reference to Asiatic and African ethnology, and the classification of languages. *Report of the Seventeenth Meeting of the British Association for the Advancement of Science* pp. 254–299.

Burchfield, J. D.
    1975   *Lord Kelvin and the age of the earth.* New York: Science History Publications.

Burkhardt, R. W., Jr.
    1977   *The spirit of system: Lamarck and evolutionary biology.* Cambridge, Mass.: Harvard University Press.

Burnet, T.
    1684   *The theory of the earth: containing an account of the original of the earth, and of all the general changes which it hath already undergone, or is to undergo, till the consummation of all things. The first two books concerning the Deluge and concerning Paradise.* London.
    1690a   *An answer to the late exceptions made by Mr. Erasmus Warren against the theory of the earth.* London.
    1690b   *A review of the theory of the earth, and of its proofs: especially in reference to Scripture.* London.
    1690c   *The theory of the earth: containing an account of the original of the earth, and of all the general changes which it hath already undergone, or is to undergo, till the consummation of all things. The last two books, concerning the burning of the world, and concerning the new heavens and new earth.* London.

Busk, G.
    1865   On a very ancient human cranium from Gibraltar. *Report of the thirty-fourth meeting of the British Association for the Advancement of Science, Notices and Abstracts* pp. 91–92.

Buteux, C.-J.
    1855   Silex travaillés de la Somme. *Bulletin de la Société Géologique de France* **12:**113–115.
    1857   Notions générales sur la géologie du département de la Somme. *Mémoires de la Société Imperiale d'Emulation d'Abbeville* **8:**561–574.

Cambell, J. B., and C. G. Sampson
    1971   A new analysis of Kent's Cavern, Devonshire, England. *University of Oregon Anthropological Papers* No. 3.

Carozzi, A. V. (translator and editor)
    1968   *Telliamed or conversations between an Indian philosopher and a French missionary on the diminution of the sea by Benôit de Maillet.* Urbana: University of Illinois Press.

[Carpenter, W. B.]
    1848   [Review of] Researches into the physical history of mankind, by J. C. Prichard . . . , 1836–1847, The natural history of man . . . , by J. C. Prichard, 1843, and Report of the seventeenth meeting of the British Association for the Advancement of Science . . . 1847. *Edinburgh Review* **88:**429–487.

Carpenter, W. B.
    1863   Discovery at Abbeville. *Athenaeum* **41:**523.

Cartailhac, É.
    1903   *La France préhistorique d'après les sepultures et les monuments* (2nd ed.). Paris: Alcan and Guillaumin Réunies.

Cassirer, E.
    1951   *The philosophy of the Enlightenment,* translated by F. C. A. Koelln and J. P.
            Pettegrove. Princeton, N.J.: Princeton University Press.
Cheynier, A.
    1936   *Jouannet: grand-père de la préhistoire.* Brive: Chastrusse.
[Christol, J. de]
    1829   Nouvelles cavernes à ossemens renfermant des débris humains. *Revue Bibli-
            ographique des Sciences Naturelles* **1829**:92–93.
Christol, J. de
    1829   *Notice sur les ossemens humains fossiles des cavernes de département du Gard;
            présentée à l'Académie des Sciences le 29 Juin 1829.* Montpellier: J. Martel Aîné.
Christol, J. de, and A.Bravard
    1828   Extrait d'un mémoire relatif à quelques nouvelles espèces d'hyènes fossiles dé-
            couvertes dans la caverne de Lunel-Viel près Montpellier. *Annales des Sciences
            Naturelles* **13**:141–145.
Clark, K.
    1925   A pioneer of prehistory. *Blackfriar's* **6**:603–613, 640–648, 726–728.
Clark, L. K.
    1961   *Pioneers of prehistory in England* (Newman History and Philosophy of Science
            Series No. 10). London: Sheed and Ward.
Cogan, T. (trans. and ed.)
    1821   *The works of the late Professor Camper, on the connexion between the science of
            anatomy and the arts of drawing, painting, and statuary, etc. etc. in two books* (2nd
            ed.). London.
Collomb, E.
    1860   Sur l'existence de l'homme sur la terre antérieurement à l'apparition des anciens
            glaciers. *Bibliothèque Universelle, Revue Suisse et Étrangère, Archives des Sci-
            ences Physiques et Naturelles* **8**:200–204.
Cox, L. R.
    1942   New light on William Smith and his work. *Proceedings of the Yorkshire Geological
            Society* **25**:1–99.
Crawfurd, J.
    1863   Notes on Sir Charles Lyell's "Antiquity of man." *Anthropological Review*
            1:172–176.
Curwen, E. C. (ed.)
    1940   *The journal of Gideon Mantell, surgeon and geologist.* London: Oxford University
            Press.
Cuvier, G.
    1806a   Suite de memoire sur les éléphans vivans et fossiles. *Annales du Muséum d'Histoire
            Naturelle* **8**:249–269.
    1806b   Sur différents dents du genre des mastodontes, mais d'espèces moindres que celles
            de l'Ohio, trouvées en plusieurs lieux des deux continens. *Annales du Muséum
            d'Histoire Naturelle* **8**:401–424.
    1809   Sur quelques quadrupèdes ovipares fossiles conservée dans des schistes calcaires.
            Annales du Muséum d'Histoire Naturelle **13**:401–437.
    1812a   Discours préliminaire. In *Recherches sur les ossemens fossiles de quadrupèdes, ou
            l'on rétablit les caractères de plusieurs espèces d'animaux que les révolutions du
            globe paroissent avoir détruites* (Vol. 1). Paris: Deterville.
    1812b   *Recherches sur les ossemens fossiles de quadrupèdes, ou l'on rétablit les caractères
            de plusieurs espèces d'animaux que les révolutions du globe paroissent avoir
            détruites* (four volumes). Paris: Deterville.

1812c   Sur les ossemens du genre de l'ours, qui se trouvent en grande quantité dans certaines cavernes d'Allemagne et de Hongrie. In *Recherches sur les ossemens fossiles de quadrupèdes, ou l'on rétablit les caractères de plusieurs espèces d'animaux que les révolutions du globe paroissent avoir détruites* (Vol. 4). Paris: Deterville.

1812d   Sur quelques quadrupèdes ovipares fossiles conservés dans des schistes calcaires. In *Recherches sur les ossemens fossiles de quadrupèdes, ou l'on rétablit les caractères de plusieurs espèces d'animaux que les révolutions du globe paroissent avoir détruites* (Vol. 4). Paris: Deterville.

1813   *Essay on the theory of the earth: with geological illustrations by Professor Jameson*, translated by R. Kerr. Edinburgh.

1821a   Discours préliminaire. In *Recherches sur les ossemens fossiles, où l'on rétablit les caractères de plusieurs animaux dont les révolutions du globe ont détruit les espèces* (Vol. 1) (2nd ed.). Paris: Dufour and d'Ocagne.

1821b   *Recherches sur les ossemens fossiles, où l'on rétablit les caractères de plusieurs animaux dont les révolutions du globe ont détruit les espèces.* (Vol. 1) (2nd ed.). Paris: Dufour and d'Ocagne.

1822   *Recherches sur les ossemens fossiles, où l'on rétablit les caractères de plusieurs animaux dont les révolutions du globe ont détruit les espèces* (Vol. 2) (2nd ed.). Paris: Dufour and d'Ocagne.

1824   *Recherches sur les ossemens fossiles, où l'on rétablit les caractères de plusieurs animaux dont les révolutions du globe ont détruit les espèces* (Vol. 5, Part 2) (2nd ed.). Paris: Dufour and d'Ocagne.

1825   Discours sur les révolutions de la surface du globe, et sur les changemens qu'elles ont produit dans la régne animal. In *Recherches sur les ossemens fossiles, où l'on rétablit les caractères de plusieurs animaux dont les révolutions du globe ont détruit les espèces* (Vol. 1) (3rd ed.). Paris: Dufour and d'Ocagne.

1829   Extrait de l'analyse des travaux de l'Académie Royale des Sciences, pendant l'Année 1828 (1). *Annales des Sciences Naturelles* **17**:319–386.

1834   Discours sur les révolutions de la surface du globe, et sur les changemens qu'elles ont produit dans la régne animal. In *Recherches sur les ossemens fossiles, où l'on rétablit les caractères de plusieurs animaux dont les révolutions du globe ont détruit les espèces* (Vol. 1) (4th ed.). Paris: Dufour and d'Ocagne.

1841   *Histoire des sciences naturelles, depuis leur origine jusqu'à nos jours, chez tous les peuples connus* (Vol. 1). Paris: Fortin, Masson.

Cuvier, G., and A. Brongniart
1808   Essai sur la géographie minéralogique des environs de Paris. *Journal des Mines* **23**:421–458.

1811   *Essai sur la géographie minéralogique des environs de Paris, avec une carte géognostique, et des coupes de terrain.* Paris.

1812   Essai sur la géographie minéralogique des environs de Paris. In *Recherches sur les ossemens fossiles de quadrupèdes, ou l'on rètablit les caractères de plusieurs espèces d'animaux que les révolutions du globe paroissent avoir détruites* (Vol. 1). Paris: Deterville.

Cuvier, G., and S. L. Mitchill
1818   *Essay on the theory of the earth, with mineralogical notes and an account of Cuvier's geological discoveries by Professor Jameson, to which are now added, observations on the geology of North America; illustrated by the description of various organic remains, found in that part of the world.* New York: Kirk and Mercein.

Daniel, G.
1950   *A hundred years of archaeology.* London: Duckworth.
1963   *The idea of prehistory.* Cleveland: World Publishing.
1976   *A hundred and fifty years of archaeology.* Cambridge, Mass.: Harvard University Press.
1981   *A short history of archaeology.* London: Thames and Hudson.
Darwin, C.
1859   *On the origin of species by means of natural selection, or the preservation of favoured races in the struggle for life.* London: Murray.
1871   *The descent of man, and selection in relation to sex* (two volumes). London: Murray.
Darwin, F. (ed.)
1887   *The life and letters of Charles Darwin, including an autobiographical chapter* (three volumes) (3rd. ed.). London: Murray.
Davies, G. L.
1969   *The earth in decay: a history of British geomorphology 1578–1878.* New York: American Elsevier.
[Dawkins, W. B.]
1871   [Reviews of] 1. The decent of man and selection in relation to sex. By Charles Darwin, M.A., F.R.S., 2 vols. London: 1871. 2. Contributions to the theory of natural selection. By A. R. Wallace, Second edition. London: 1871. 3. On the genesis of species. By St. George Mivart, F.R.S. London: 1871. *Edinburgh Review* **134:**195–235.
Dawkins, W. B.
1874   *Cave hunting: Researches on the evidence of caves respecting the early inhabitants of Europe.* London: Macmillan.
1880   *Early man in Britain and his place in the Tertiary period.* London: Macmillan.
Dawson, J. W.
1860   *Archaia; or, studies of the cosmogony and natural history of the Hebrew Scriptures.* Montreal: Dawson.
1863   On the antiquity of man; a review of "Lyell" and "Wilson." *Edinburgh New Philosophical Journal* **18:**40–65.
1873   *The story of the earth and man.* New York: Harper.
1880   *Fossil men and their modern representatives: an attempt to illustrate the characters and condition of pre-historic men in Europe, by those of the American races.* London: Hodder and Stoughton.
1882   *Facts and fancies in modern science: studies of the relations of science to prevalent speculations and religious belief.* Philadelphia: American Baptist Publication Society.
1894a   *The meeting-place of geology and history.* New York: Revell.
1894b   *Some salient points in the science of the earth.* New York: Harper
1901   *Fifty years of work in Canada, scientific and educational.* London and Edinburgh: Ballantyne, Hanson.
de Jussieu, A.
1725   De l'origine et des usages de la pierre de foudre. *Histoire de l'Académie Royale des Sciences. Année M. DCCXXIII. Avec les Mémoires de Mathématique et de Phisique, pour la Même Année, Memoires:*6–9.
de Laet, S. J.
1981   Phillipe-Charles Schmerling (1791–1836). In *Towards a history of archaeology,* edited by G. Daniel. London: Thames and Hudson. Pp. 112–119.

de Luc, J.-A.
1779   *Lettres physiques et morales sur l'histoire de la terre et de l'homme* (five volumes). La Haye and Paris.

de Maillet, B.
1748   *Telliamed ou entretiens d'un philosophe Indien avec un missionaire francois sur la diminution de la mer, la formation de la terre, l'origine de l'homme, &c* (two volumes). Amsterdam.

1750   *Telliamed: or, discourses between an Indian philosopher and a French missionary, on the diminution of the sea, the formation of the earth, the origin of men and animals, and other curious subjects, relating to natural history and philosophy.* London.

de Mortillet, G.
1865   Introduction. *Matériaux pour l'histoire positive et philosophique de l'homme.* Première année:5–8.

1883   *Le préhistorique* (Bibliothèque des sciences contemporaine 8). Paris: Reinwald.

de Mortillet, G., and A. de Mortillet
1881   *Musée préhistorique.* Paris: Reinwald.

[de Pauw, C.]
1771   *Recherches philosophiques sur les américains, ou mémoires intéressants pour servir à l'histoire de l'espece humaine* (three volumes). London.

de Quatrefages, A.
1863a   Deuxième note sur la mâchoire d'Abbeville. *Comptes Rendus Hebdomadaires de l'Académie des Sciences* **56**:809–816.

1863b   Mâchoire de Moulin-Quignon. *Comptes Rendus Hebdomadaires de l'Académie des Sciences* **56**:933–935.

1863c   Note sur la mâchoire humaine découverte par M. Boucher de Perthes dans le diluvium d'Abbeville. *Comptes Rendus Hebdomadaires de l'Académie des Sciences* **56**:782–788.

1863d   Observations de M. de Quatrefages au sujet de la déclaration faite par M. Élie de Beaumont. *Comptes Rendus Hebdomadaires de l'Académie des Sciences* **56**:938–939.

1863e   On the Abbeville jaw. *Anthropological Review* **1**:312–335.

1863f   Troisième note sur la mâchoire humaine d'Abbeville. *Comptes Rendus Hebdomadaires de l'Académie des Sciences* **56**:857–861.

1864   Nouveau ossements humains découverts par M. Boucher de Perthes à Moulin-Quignon. *Comptes Rendus Hebdomadaires de l'Académie des Sciences* **59**:107–111.

de Quatrefages, A., and E. T. Hamy
1882   *Crania ethnica* (two volumes). Paris: Baillière et fils.

[de Serres, M.]
1829a   Cavernes à ossemens. *Revue Bibliographique des Sciences Naturelles* **1829**:148–149.

1829b   Ossemens fossiles. *Revue Bibliographique des Sciences Naturelles* **1829**:155.

1830   Envoi des pièces fossiles. *Revue Bibliographique des Sciences Naturelles* **1830**:87–88.

de Serres, M.
1823   Observations sur les ossemens humains découverts dans les crevasses des terrains secondaires, et en particulier sur ceux que l'on observe dans le caverne de Durfort, dans le département de Gard. *Bibliothèque Universelle des Sciences, Belles-Lettres, et Arts, Redigée à Genève* **23**:277–295; **24**:11–35.

1826   Note sur les cavernes à ossemens et les brêches osseuses du midi de la France. *Annales des Sciences Naturelles* **9**:200–213.

1828   Sur les cavernes à ossements et les brèches osseuses du midi de la France. *Société Linnéenne de Normandie, Mémoires* **1828**:16–58.

1829a   *Géognosie des terrains tertiares, ou tableau des principaux animaux invertébrés des terrains marins tertiares, du midi de la France.* Montpellier and Paris: Pomathio-Durville.

1829b   Lettre addressée à M. de Ferussac sur de nouvelle cavernes à ossemens. *Bulletin des Sciences Naturelles et de Géologie* **19**:170–175.

1829c   Sur les circonstances qui paraissent avoir accompagné le dépôt des terrains tertiares. *Annales des Sciences Naturelles* **16**:145–156.

1830a   Abstracts, with occasional remarks, from a memoir regarding the human bones and objects of human fabrication discovered in solid beds, or in alluvium, and upon the epoch of their deposition. *Edinburgh Journal of Science* **3**:121–131.

1830b   Lettre addressée au President de l'Académie des Sciences de Paris. *Bulletin des Sciences Naturelles et de Géologie* **21**:33–36.

1830c   Sur les ossemens humans découverts dans certaines cavernes du midi de la France, mêlés et confondus dans les mêmes limons où existent de nombreuses espèces de mammifères terrestre, considerées jusqu'à present comme fossiles et comme anté-diluvienne. *Journal de Géologie* **2**:184–191.

1832   Letter addressed to M. Cordier, member of the Royal Academy of Sciences, on certain new bone caves. *American Journal of Science* **21**:56–59.

1831–1832 Mémoire sur les animaux découverts dans divers dépôts quaternaires. *Bulletin de la*
[1832]   *Société Géologique de France* **2**:430–432.

1832–1833 De la contemporanéité de l'homme et des espèces d'animaux perdues. *Revue en-*
[1833]   *cyclopédique* **55**:48–73; **57**:252–281; **59**:379–414.

1833–1834 Mémoire sur la question de savoir si des animaux terrestres ont cessé d'exister depuis l'apparition de l'homme, et si l'homme a eté contemporain des espèces perdues, ou du moins qui ne paraissent plus avoir de représentans sur la terre. *Bibliothèque Universelle des Sciences, Belles-Lettres et Arts, Rédigée à Genève* **53**:277–314; **55**:160–176, 231–256, 352–384.

1834–1835 Memoir on the question;—whether any land animals have ceased to exist since man's formation; and whether man has been contemporaneous with species now lost, or appearing no longer to have representatives on the earth. *Edinburgh New Philosophical Journal* **16**:160–176; **17**:268–285; **18**:59–80.

1835a   *Discours sur les différences des dates, données par les monumens et les traditions historiques et celles qui résultent des faits géologiques.* Toulouse: Paya.

1835b   On the physical facts contained in the Bible compared with the discoveries of the modern sciences. *Edinburgh New Philosophical Journal* **38**:239–271.

1838   *Essai sur les cavernes à ossemens et sur les causes qui les y ont accumulés* (3rd ed.). Paris: Baillière.

1844   Sur les ossements humains trouvés par M. F. Robert dans les environs d'Alais. *Comptes Rendus Hedomadaires de l'Académie des Sciences* **9**:116–118.

1855–1857 Des ossemens humains des cavernes et de l'époque de leurs dépôts. *Académie des*
[1855]   *Sciences et Lettres de Montpellier, Mémoire de la Section des Sciences* **3**:13–90.

1856–1857 Note supplémentaire au memoire sur les ossements humains des cavernes, et sur
[1856]   l'époque de leurs dépôts. *Académie des Sciences et Lettres de Montpellier, Mémoire de la Section des Sciences* **3**:243–248.

1857a   Note sur las caverne de Pontil, près Saint-Pons (Hérault), où l'on a découvert des objets de l'industrie, des ossements humains, ainsi que de rhinocéros et autres espèces perdues. *Comptes Rendus Hebdomadaires de l'Académie des Sciences* **45**:649–650.

1857b   Seconde note sur la caverne du Pontil, près Saint-Pons (Hérault). *Comptes Rendus Hebdomadaires de l'Académie des Sciences* **45**:1053–1055.

1858   Note sur les cavernes à ossements du Pontil (Hérault) et de Massat (Ariège). *Comptes Rendus Hebdomadaires de l'Académie des Sciences* **46**:1243–1244.

1859   De l'extinction de plusieurs espèces animales depuis l'apparition de l'homme. *Comptes Rendus Hebdomadaires de l'Académie des Sciences* **49**:860–863.

1860a   *De la cosmogonie de Moïse comparée aux faits géologiques* (two volumes) (3rd ed.). Paris: Lagny.

1860b   Des espèces perdues et des races qui ont disparu des lieux qu'elles habitaient primitivement. *Annales des Sciences Naturelles (Zoologie)* **13**:297–308.

1860c   Des espèces perdues, et des races qui ont disparu des lieux qu'elles habitaient primitivement, depuis ou avant notre existence. *Bulletin de la Société Géologique de France* **17**:262–268.

1860d   Sur les espèces perdues et les races qui ont disparu des lieux qu'elles habitaient primitivement. *Bibliothèque Universelle, Revue Suisse et Étrangère, Archives des Sciences Physiques et Naturelles* **8**:109–120.

de Serres, M., and Pitorre

1831   Notice sur de nouvelle cavernes à ossemens, situées a Sallèles-Cabardis, département de l'Aude. *Journal de Géologie* **3**:245–264.

Desmarest, [A.-G.]

1816   Anthropolithes ou anthropolites. *Nouveau dictionnaire d'histoire naturelle, appliquée aux arts, à l'agriculture, à l'économie rurale et domestique, à la médecine, etc.* (new edition, vol. 2). Paris: Deterville. Pp. 167–170.

[Desnoyers, J.]

1834   Proofs that the human bones and works of art found in caves in the south of France, are more recent than the antediluvian bones in these caves. *Edinburgh New Philosophical Journal* **16**:302–310.

Desnoyers, J.

1831–1832 [1832]a   Considérations sur les ossemens humains des cavernes du midi de la France. *Bulletin de la Société Géologique de France* **2**:126–133.

1831–1832 [1832]b   Rapport sur les travaux de la Société Géologique, pendant l'année 1831. *Bulletin de la Société Géologique de France* **2**:226–327.

1842a   Sur les cavernes et les brèches à ossements des environs de Paris. *Comptes Rendus Hebdomadaires de l'Académie des Sciences* **14**:522–528.

1842b   Sur l'existence des brèches osseuses et des cavernes à ossements dans le bassin de Paris, et plus particulièrement sur un nouveau gisement d'ossements mammifères fossiles à Montmorency. *Bulletin de la Société Géologique de France* **13**:290–297.

1849   Grottes ou cavernes. *Dictionnaire universelle d'histoire naturelle* (Vol. 6), edited by C. d'Orbigny. Paris: Renard, Martinet. Pp. 342–407.

1863a   Note sur des indices matériels de la coexistence d l'homme avec l'*Elephas meridionalis* dans un terrain des environs de Chartres, plus anciens que les terrains de transport quaternaires des vallées de la Somme et de la Seine. *Comptes Rendus Hebdomadaires de l'Académie des Sciences* **56**:1073–1083.

1863b   Réponse à des objections faites au sujet de stries et l'incisions constatées sur des ossements de mammifères fossiles des environs de Chartres. *Compte Rendus Hebdomadaires de l'Académie des Sciences* **56**:1199–1204.

236 THE ESTABLISHMENT OF HUMAN ANTIQUITY

1821a Notice sur des ossemens humains fossiles. *Bibliothèque Universelle des Sciences, Belles-Lettres, et Arts, Rédigée à Genéve* **17**:33–41.
1821b Notice sur des ossemens humains fossiles. *Journal de Physique, de Chemie, d'Histoire Naturelle et des Arts* **92**:227–233.

Diderot, D.
1875 Pensées sur l'interpretation de la nature. In *Oeuvres complètes de Diderot* (Vol. 2),
[1754] edited by J. Assézat. Paris: Garnier. Pp. 7–63.

d'Orbigny, A.
1849–1852 *Cours eléméntaire de paléontologie et de géologie stratigraphiques* (two volumes). Paris: Masson.

Dott, R. H., Jr.
1969 James Hutton and the concept of the dynamic earth. In *Toward a history of geology*, edited by C. J. Schneer. Cambridge, Mass.: M.I.T. Press, Pp. 122–141.

Dugdale, W.
1656 *The antiquities of Warwickshire illustrated; from records, leiger-books, manuscripts, charters, evidences, tombes, and armes: beautified with maps, prospects, and portraictures.* London.

Dupont, E.
1871 *Les temps antéhistoriques en Belgique: l'homme pendant les ages de la pierre dans les environs de Dinant-Sur-Meuse.* Brussels: Mucquardt.

Eisenstein, E. L.
1979 *The printing press as an agent of change* (two volumes in one). Cambridge: Cambridge University Press.

Élie de Beaumont, L.
1845 *Leçons de géologie pratique, professées au College de France, pendant l'année scolaire 1843–1844* (Vol. 1). Paris: Bertrand.
1859 [Untitled comments]. *Comptes Rendus Hebdomadaires de l'Académie des Sciences* **49**:582.
1861 [Untitled comments]. *Comptes Rendus Hebdomadaires de l'Académie des Sciences* **52**:1133–1134.
1863 Remarques à l'occasion des communications de MM. Milne-Edwards et de Quatrefages, sur les haches en silex et la mâchoire humaine trouvées à Moulin-Quignon. *Comptes Rendus Hebdomadaires de l'Académie des Sciences* **56**:935–937.

Ellegård, A.
1958 Darwin and the general reader: the reception of Darwin's theory of evolution in the British periodical press, 1859–1872. *Gothenburg Studies in English* 8.

Elsasser, A. B. (trans.)
1959 General considerations on the phenomena of bone caverns, by M. Tournal, of Narbonne. *Kroeber Anthropological Papers* **21**:6–16.

Esper, J. F.
1774 *Description des zoolithes nouvellement decouverts d'animaux quadrupedes inconnues et des cavernes qui les renferment de meme que de plusieurs autres grottes remarquables qui se trouvent dans le Margraviat de Bareith au de la des Monts*, translated by J. F. Isenflamm. Nuremberg: Knorr.
1978 *Ausführliche nachricht von neuendeckten zoolithen unbekannter vierfüsiger tiere.*
[1774] Facsimile of 1774 edition, with an introduction by A. Geus. Weisbaden: Guido Pressler.

Evans, J.
    1860   On the occurrence of flint implements in undisturbed beds of gravel, sand, and clay. *Archaeologia* **38**:280–307.
    1863a   The Abbeville human jaw. *Athenaeum* **41**:747–748.
    1863b   The human remains at Abbeville. *Athenaeum* **42**:19–20.
    1866   On the forgery of antiquities. *Proceedings of the Royal Institution of Great Britain* **4**:356–365.
    1872   *The ancient stone implements, weapons, and ornaments, of Great Britain*. London: Longmans, Green, Reader, and Dyer.

Eyles, J. M.
    1969a   William Smith (1769–1839): A bibliography of his published writings, maps and geological sections, printed and lithographed. *Journal of the Society for the Bibliography of Natural History* **5**:87–109.
    1969b   William Smith: some aspects of his life and work. In *Toward a history of geology*, edited by C. J. Schneer. Cambridge, Mass.: M.I.T. Press. Pp. 142–158.

Eyles, V. A.
    1970   Introduction. In *James Hutton's System on the earth, 1785; Theory of the earth, 1788; Observations on granite, 1794; together with Playfair's Biography of Hutton*, edited by G. W. White. Darien, Conn.: Hafner. Pp. xi–xxiii.
    1971   John Woodward, F.R.S., F.R.C.P., M.D. (1665–1728): a bio-bibliographical account of his life and work. *Journal of the Society for the Bibliography of Natural History* **5**:399–427.

Fabricius, J. A.
    1865   Dissertatio critica de hominibus orbis nostri incolis, specie et ortu inter se non
    [1721]   differentibus quam in auditorio gymnasii Hamb. ad D. viii April, translated by T. Bendyshe. *In* The history of anthropology, *Anthropological Society of London Memoirs* **1**:372–420.

Falconer, H.
    1860a   On the ossiferous caves of the peninsula of Gower, in Glamorganshire, South Wales. *Quarterly Journal of the Geological Society of London* **16**:487–491.
    1860b   On the ossiferous Grotta de Maccognone, near Palermo. *Quarterly Journal of the Geological Society of London* **16**:99–106.
    1863a   Falconer on the reputed fossil man of Abbeville. *Anthropological Review* **1**:177–179.
    1863b   The human jaw at Abbeville. *Athenaeum* **41**:682.
    1863c   The human jaw of Abbeville. *The Times* (London), May 21, p. 13.
    1863d   Primeval man. *Athenaeum* **51**:586.
    1863e   Primeval man. —What led to the question? *Athenaeum* **41**:459–460.
    1863f   The reputed fossil man of Abbeville. *The Times* (London), April 25, p. 14.
    1868   On the evidence in the case of the controverted human jaw and flint-implements of Moulin-Quignon. In *Paleontological memoirs and notes of the late Hugh Falconer, A.M., M.D. . . . with a biographical sketch of the author*. Volume II. *Mastodon, elephant, rhinoceros, ossiferous caves, primeval man and his cotemporaries*. London: Hardwicke. Pp. 601–625.

Falconer, H., G. Busk, and W. B. Carpenter
    1863   An account of the proceedings of the late conference held in France to inquire into the circumstances attending the asserted discovery of a human jaw in the gravel at Moulin-Quignon, near Abbeville; including the *procès verbaux* of the sittings of the conference, with notes thereon. *Natural History Review* **3**:423–462.

Fleming, J.
    1824   Remarks illustrative of the influence of society on the distribution of British ani-
            mals. *Edinburgh Philosophical Journal* **11:**287–305.
    1826   The geological deluge, as interpreted by Baron Cuvier and Professor Buckland,
            inconsistent with the testimony of Moses and the phenomena of nature. *Edinburgh
            Philosophical Journal* **14:**205–239.
Fletcher, W. Y.
    1898   John Bagford and his collections. *Transactions of the Bibliographical Society*
            4:185–201.
Flower, J. W.
    1860   On a flint implement recently discovered at the base of some beds of drift-gravel
            and brick-earth at St. Acheul, near Amiens. *Quarterly Journal of the Geological
            Society of London* **16:**190–192.
Fontan, A.
    1858   Sur des dents humaines et des ustensils humains trouvées dans les cavernes à
            ossements de Massat (Ariège). *Comptes Rendus Hebdomadaires de l'Académie des
            Sciences* **46:**900–902.
[Fontenelle, J.]
    1830   Ossemens humains fossiles. *Revue Bibliographique des Sciences Naturelles*
            1830:76.
[Forbes, J. D.]
    1863   Lyell on the antiquity of man. *Edinburgh Review* **118:**254–302.
Fraipoint, C.
    1936   Les hommes fossiles d'Engis. *Archives de l'Institut de Paléontologie Humaine* **16.**
Frei, H. W.
    1974   *The eclipse of biblical narrative.* New Haven: Yale University Pres.
Frere, J.
    1800   Account of flint weapons discovered at Hoxne in Suffolk. *Archaeologia* **13:**204–
            205.
Garrigou, F.
    1863   Diluvium de la vallée de la Somme. *Comptes Rendus Hebdomadaires de l'Acadé-
            mie des Sciences* **56:**1042–1044.
Gaudin, C.-T.
    1860   Sur la végétation contemporaine de l'homme primitif. *Bibliothèque Universelle,
            Revue Suisse et Étrangère, Archives des Sciences Physiques et Naturelles*
            8:280–283.
Gaudry, A.
    1859a   Os de cheval et de boeuf appartenant à des espèces perdues, trouvés dans la même
            couche de diluvium d'où l'on a tiré des haches en pierre. *Comptes Rendus Heb-
            domadaires de l'Académie des Sciences* **49:**453–454.
    1859b   Sur les résultats de fouilles géologiques entreprises aux environs d'Amiens. *Comp-
            tes Rendus Hebdomadaires de l'Académie des Sciences* **49:**465–467.
    1860   [Haches en silex d'Amiens]. *Bulletin de la Société Géologique de France* **17:**17.
Gay, P.
    1966   *The Enlightenment: an interpretation* (Vol. 1). New York: Norton.
Geikie, J.
    1874   *The great ice age and its relation to the antiquity of man.* London: Isbister.
    1881   *Prehistoric Europe, a geological sketch.* London: Stanford.
Geoffroy Saint-Hilaire, I.
    1858   [Untitled comments]. *Compte Rendus Hebdomadaires de l'Académie des Sciences*
            46:902–903.

1860   [Sur l'homme fossile]. *Bulletins de la Société d'Anthropologie de Paris* **1**:47–52.
Gervais, P.
1861–1863   Discours prononcé aux funerailles de M. Jules de Christol *Académie des Sciences et*
[1861]   *Lettres de Montpellier, Mémoire* **5**:75–78.
1861–1863   Notice sur Marcel de Serres. *Académie des Sciences et Lettres de Montpellier,*
[1862]   *Mémoire* **5**:303–308.
Gervais, P., and J. Brinckmann
1864–1866   La caverne de Bize. *Académie des Sciences et Lettres de Montpellier, Mémoire*
[1864]   **6**:65–97.
Geus, A.
1978   Einführung. In *Ausführliche nachricht von neuendeckten zoolithen unbekannter*
vierfüsiger tiere, by J. F. Esper. Facsimile of 1774 edition. Wiesbaden: Guido
Pressler. Pp. 11–30.
Gillespie, N. C.
1977   The Duke of Argyll, evolutionary anthropology, and the art of scientific controversy. *Isis* **68**:40–54.
Gillispie, C. C.
1959   *Genesis and geology: a study in the relations of scientific thought, natural theology,*
and social opinion in Great Britain, 1790–1850. New York: Harper and Row.
Glass, B.
1959   Maupertuis, pioneer of genetics and evolution. In *Forerunners of Darwin:*
1745–1859, edited by B. Glass, O. Temkin, and W. L. Strauss. Baltimore: Johns
Hopkins. Pp. 51–83.
Gliddon, G. R.
1854   Mankind's chronology. In *Types of mankind: or, ethnological researches, based*
upon the ancient monuments, paintings, sculptures, and crania of races, and upon
their natural, geographical, philological, and biblical history: illustrated by selec-
tions from the inedited papers of Samuel George Morton, M.D., by J. C. Nott and
G. R. Gliddon. Philadelphia: Lippincott, Grambo. Pp. 653–716.
Goguet, A. Y.
1761   *The origin of laws, arts, and sciences, and their progress among the most ancient*
nations (three volumes). Edinburgh.
Gordon, A. B.
1894   *The life and correspondence of William Buckland, D.D., F.R.S., sometime Dean of*
Westminster, twice President of the Geological Society, and first President of the
British Association. London: Murray.
Gould, S. J.
1978   Morton's ranking of races by cranial capacity. *Science* **300**:503–509.
1979   Agassiz's marginalia in Lyell's *Principles,* or the perils of uniformity and the
ambiguity of heroes. *Studies in History of Biology* **3**:119–138.
Gräslund, B.
1981   The background to C. J. Thomsen's three age system. In *Toward a history of*
archaeology, edited by G. Daniel. London: Thames and Hudson. Pp. 45–50.
Grayson, D. K.
1980   Vicissitudes and overkill: the development of explanations of Pleistocene extinctions. *Advances in Archaeological Method and Theory* **3**:357–403.
1983   Nineteenth century explanations of Pleistocene extinctions: A review and analysis.
In *Quaternary extinctions,* edited by P. S. Martin and R. G. Klein. Tucson: University of Arizona Press.
Greene, J. C.
1959   *The death of Adam.* Ames: Iowa State University Press.

Gruber, J. W.
      1965   Brixham Cave and the antiquity of man. In *Context and meaning in cultural anthropology*, edited by M. E. Spiro. New York: Free Press. Pp. 373–402.
Gunther, R. W. T. (ed.)
      1928   *Further correspondence of John Ray*. London: Ray Society.
Haber, F. C.
      1959   *The age of the world: Moses to Darwin*. Baltimore: Johns Hopkins.
Hale, M.
      1677   *The primitive origination of mankind, considered and examined according to the light of nature*. London.
Halley, E.
      1715   A short account of the saltness of the ocean, and of the several lakes that emit no rivers; with a proposal, by help thereof, to discover the age of the earth. *Philosophical Transactions of the Royal Society of London* **29**:296–300.
Hamy, E.-T.
      1906a   Matériaux pour servir à l'histoire de l'archéologie préhistorique. I: Le mémoire de Mahudel sur les pierres de foudre (1737). *Revue Archéologique* **7**:239–259.
      1906b   Matériaux pour servir à l'histoire de l'archéologie préhistorique. II: Mémoire inédit de Monfaucon sur les armes des anciens Gaulois et des nations voisins (1734). *Revue Archéologique* **8**:37–48.
Hébert, E.
      1855a   [Presentation of Rigollot's Memoire sur les instruments. . . .] *Bulletin de la Société Géologique de France* **12**:112.
      1855b   Silex travaillés de la Somme. *Bulletin de la Société Géologique de France* **12**:254–255.
      1863   Nouvelles observations relatives à l'existence de l'homme pendant la periode quaternaire. *Comptes Rendus Hebdomadaires de l'Académie des Sciences* **56**:1040–1042.
Heizer, R. F. (ed.)
      1962   *Man's discovery of his past: literary landmarks in archaeology*. Englewood Cliffs, N.J.: Prentice-Hall.
Hindle, B.
      1974   *The pursuit of science in revolutionary America*. New York: Norton.
[Holbach, Baron d']
      1770   *Systême de la nature. Ou les loix de monde physique et du monde moral* (two volumes). London.
[Holland, H.]
      1850   Review in one essay of Prichard's Researches (3rd edition, 1836–1847), Prichard's Natural history of man (1843), Smith's Natural history of the human species (1848), Bunsen's Results of recent Egytian researches (a discourse read before the Ethnological section of the British Association at Oxford, 1847), and Lyell's Elements [sic] of geology, ch. 34 to 40. *Quarterly Review* **86**:1–40.
Holloway, B.
      1723   An account of the pits for fuller's-earth in Bedfordshire; in a letter from the Reverend Mr. B. Holloway, F.R.S. to Dr. Woodward, Pr. Med. Gresh. S.R. and Coll. Med. Lond. Soc. *Philosophical Transactions of the Royal Society of London* **32**:419–421.
Hooykas, R.
      1963   *Natural law and divine miracle: the principle of uniformity in geology, biology, and theology*. London: Brill.

1970   *Catastrophism in geology, its scientific character in relation to actualism and uniformitarianism.* Amsterdam: North-Holland.

Horner, L.
    1859a   An account of some recent researches near Cairo, undertaken with the view of throwing light upon the geological history of the alluvial land of Egypt. *Philosophical Transactions of the Royal Society of London* **148**:53–92.

    1859b   An account of some recent researches near Cairo, undertaken with the view of throwing light upon the geological history of the alluvial land of Egypt. *Proceedings of the Royal Society of London* **9**:128–134.

Houssay, F.
    1902   Les silex tertiare de Thenay et l'oeuvre de l'Abbé Bourgeois. *Mémoires de la Société des Sciences et Lettres de Loir-et-Cher* **16**:169–219.

Hull, D. L.
    1973   *Darwin and his critics: the reception of Darwin's theory of evolution by the scientific community.* Cambridge, Mass.: Harvard University Press.

Hull, D. L., P. D. Tessner, and A. M. Diamond ,
    1978   Planck's principle. *Science* **202**:717–723.

Hume, A.
    1851   On certain implements of the stone period. *Historic Society of Lancashire and Cheshire, Proceedings and Papers, Section III* **1850–1851**:32–50.

Hunt, J.
    1863   Introductory address on the study of anthropology, delivered before the Anthropological Society of London, February 24th, 1863. *Anthropological Review* **1**:1–20.

Hunter, D.
    1978   *Papermaking: the history and technique of an ancient craft.* New York: Dover.

Hunter, M. C. W.
    1971   The Royal Society and the origins of British archaeology: I. *Antiquity* **45**:113–121.

Hutton, J.
    1788   Theory of the earth; or an investigation of the laws observable in the composition, dissolution, and restoration of land upon the globe. *Transactions of the Royal Society of Edinburgh* **1**:209–304.

    1795   *Theory of the earth, with proofs and illustrations* (two volumes). Edinburgh.

Huxley, T. H.
    1862   On fossil remains of man. *Proceedings of the Royal Institution of Great Britain* **3**:420–422.

    1863   *Evidence as to man's place in nature.* London: Williams and Norgate.

    1869   The anniversary address of the President. *Quarterly Journal of the Geological Society of London* **25**:xxviii–liii.

Jahn, M. E.
    1969   Some notes on Dr. Scheuchzer and on *Homo diluvii testis.* In *Toward a history of geology,* edited by C. J. Schneer. Cambridge: Mass: M.I.T. Press. Pp. 193–213.

    1972   A bibliographical study on John Woodward's ''An essay toward a natural history of the earth.'' *Journal of the Society for the Bibliography of Natural History* **6**:181–213.

    1974   John Woodward, Hans Sloane, and Johann Gaspar Scheuchzer: a re-examination. *Journal of the Society for the Bibliography of Natural History* **7**:19–27.

Jefferson T.
    1799   A memoir on the discovery of certain bones of a quadruped of the clawed kind in the western parts of Virginia. *Transactions of the American Philosophical Society* **4**:246–260.

Joly, N.
   1835   Notice sur une nouvelle caverne à ossemens. *Bibliothèque Universelle des Sciences, Belles-Lettres et Arts, Redigée à Genève* **58**:349–364.
   1862   *Notice sur les travaux scientifiques de M. N. Joly.* Toulouse.
   1874   *Notice sur les travaux scientifiques et sur les titres universitaires et académiques du Docteur N. Joly.* Toulouse.

Kames, Lord [Henry Homes]
   1774–1775   *Sketches of the natural history of man* (four volumes). Dublin.

Kirwan, R.
   1799   *Geological essays.* London.

Klindt-Jensen, O.
   1975   *A history of Scandinavian archaeology.* London: Thames and Hudson.

Konig, C.
   1814   On a fossil human skeleton from Guadaloupe. *Philosophical Transactions of the Royal Society of London* **104**:107–120.

Kors, A. C.
   1976   *D'Holbach's coterie: an enlightenment in Paris.* Princeton, N.J.: Princeton University Press.

Lamarck, J.-B.-P.-A.
   1801   *Système des animaux sans vértèbres, ou tableau général des classes, des ordres, et des genres de ces animaux; présentant leurs caractères essentials et leur distribution, d'après la considération de leurs rapports naturels et de leur organisation, et suivant l'arrangement établi dans les galeries du Muséum d'Histoire Naturelle, parmi leurs dépouilles conservées; précédé du discours d'ouverture du cours de zoologie, donné dans le Muséum National d'Histoire Naturelle, l'an VIII de la République.* Paris.
   1809   *Philosophie zoologique ou exposition des considérations relatives à l'histoire naturelle des animaux; à la diversité de leur organization et des facultés qu'ils en obtiennent; aux causes physiques qui maintiennent en eux la vie et donnent lieu aux mouvements qu'ils exécutent; enfin, à celles qui produisent, les unes le sentiment, et les autres l'intelligence de ceux qui en sont doués.* Paris.

Laming-Emperaire, A.
   1964   *Origines de l'archéologie préhistorique en France.* Paris: A. and J. Picard.

Lankester, R. (ed.)
   1848   *The correspondence of John Ray: consisting of selections from the philosophical letters published by Dr. Derham, and original letters of John Ray, in the collection of the British Museum.* London: Ray Society.

[La Peyrère, I. de]
   1655   *A theological systeme upon that resupposition that men were before Adam. The First Part.* London.
   1656   *Men before Adam. Or, a discourse upon the twelfth, thirteenth, and fourteenth verses of the fifth chapter of the epistle of the apostle Paul to the Romans. By which are prov'd, that the first men were created before Adam.* London.

Lartet, É.
   1837a   Note sur les ossements fossiles des terrains tertiares de Simorre, de Sansan, etc., dans le département de Gers, et sur la découverte recente d'une mâchoire du singe fossile. *Comptes Rendus Hebdomadaires de l'Académie des Sciences* **40**:85–93.
   1837b   Nouvelles observations sur une mâchoire inférieure fossile, crue d'un singe voisin du gibbon, et sur quelques dents et ossements attribués à d'autres quadrumanes. *Comptes Rendus Hebdomadaires de l'Académie des Sciences* **40**:583–584.

1856   Note sur un grand singe fossile qui se rattache au groupe des singes supérieurs. *Comptes Rendus Hebdomadaires de l'Académie des Sciences* **43**:219–223.

1860a   Addition à la note sur l'ancienneté géologique de l'espèce humaine, presentée le 19 Mars 1860. *Comptes Rendus Hebdomadaires de l'Académie des Sciences* **50**:790–791.

1860b   On the coexistence of man with certain extinct quadrupeds, proved by fossil bones, from various Pleistocene deposits, bearing incisions made by sharp instruments. *Quarterly Journal of the Geological Society of London* **16**:471–479.

1860c   Sur l'ancienneté géologique de l'espèce humaine dans l'Europe occidentale. *Bibliothéque Universelle, Revue Suisse et Étrangère, Archives des Sciences Physiques et Naturelles* **8**:193–199.

1860d   Sur l'ancienneté géologique de l'espèce humaine dans l'Europe occidentale. *Comptes Rendus Hebdomadaires de l'Académie des Sciences* **50**:599.

1861   Nouvelles recherches sur la coexistence de l'homme et des grands mammifères fossiles. *Annales des Sciences Naturelles (Zoologie)* **15**:177–253.

1862   New researches concerning the co-existence of man with the great fossil mammals, regarded as characteristic of the latest geological period. *Natural History Review* **1862**:53–71.

Laville, H., J.-P. Rigaud, and J. Sackett
1980   *Rock shelters of the Perigord: geological stratigraphy and archaeological succession.* New York: Academic Press.

Lawrence, W.
1828   *Lectures on physiology, zoology, and the natural history of man, delivered at the Royal College of Surgeons.* Salem: Foote and Brown.

Ledieu, A.
1885   *Boucher de Perthes. Sa vie, ses oeuvres, sa correspondence.* Abbeville: Caudron.

Levine, J. M.
1977   *Dr. Woodward's shield: history, science, and satire in Augustan England.* Berkeley: University of California Press.

Lhwyd, E.
1713   Extracts of several letters from Mr. Edward Lhwyd (M.A.), late keeper of the Ashmolean Museum in Oxford, to Dr. Rich. Richardson (M.D.), of North Breily in Yorkshire; containing observations in natural history and antiquities, made in his travels thro' Wales and Scotland. *Philosophical Transactions of the Royal Society of London* **28**:93–101.

Littré, É.
1858   Etudes d'histoire primitive: y-a-t-il eu des hommes sur la terre avant la dernière époque géologique? *Revue des Deux Mondes* **14**:5–32.

Lovejoy, A. O.
1964   *The great chain of being.* Cambridge, Mass.: Harvard University Press.

Lubbock, J., Lord Avebury
1865   *Pre-historic times, as illustrated by ancient remains, and the manners and customs of modern savages.* London: Williams and Norgate.

1913   *Prehistoric times as illustrated by ancient remains and the manners and customs of modern savages* (7th ed.). London: Williams and Norgate.

Lurie, E.
1954   Louis Agassiz and the races of man. *Isis* **45**:227–242.

1960   *Louis Agassiz: a life in science.* Chicago: University of Chicago Press.

Lyell, C.
  1830   *Principles of geology, being an attempt to explain the former changes of the earth's surface by reference to causes now in operation* (Vol. 1). London: Murray.
  1832   *Principles of geology, being an attempt to explain the former changes of the earth's surface by reference to causes now in operation* (Vol. 2). London: Murray.
  1833   *Principles of geology, being an attempt to explain the former changes of the earth's surface by reference to causes now in operation* (Vol. 3). London: Murray.
  1840   *Principles of geology: or, the modern changes of the earth and its inhabitants, considered as illustrative of geology* (three volumes) (6th ed.). London: Murray.
  1847   *Principles of geology; or, the modern changes of the earth and its inhabitants considered as illustrative of geology* (7th ed.). London: Murray.
  1857   *Principles of geology; or, the modern changes of the earth and its inhabitants considered as illustrative of geology* (9th ed., 1853). New York: Appleton.
  1859   *Manual of elementary geology* (6th ed.). New York: Appleton.
  1860   On the occurrence of works of human art in post-Pliocene deposits. *Report of the Twenty-Ninth Meeting of the British Association for the Advancement of Science, Notices and Abstracts* pp. 93–95.
  1863a   The antiquity of man. *Athenaeum* **41:**523–525.
  1863b   *The geological evidences of the antiquity of man with remarks on theories of the origin of species by variation.* London: Murray.
  1863c   *The geological evidences of the antiquity of man with remarks on theories of the origin of species by variation* (2nd ed.). London: Murray.
  1873   *The geological evidences of the antiquity of man, with an outline of glacial and post-Tertiary geology and remarks on the origin of species, with special reference to man's first appearance on earth* (4th ed.). London: Murray.
Lyell, K.
  1881   *Life, letters, and journals of Sir Charles Lyell, Bart* (two volumes). London: Murray.
Lyon, J.
  1970   The search for fossil man: Cinq personnages à la récherche de temps perdu. *Isis* **61:**68–84.
Mahudel, N.
  1740   Sur les prétendues pierres de foudre. *Histoire de l'Académie Royale des Inscriptions et Belles Lettres, avec les Mémoires de Littérature tirez des Registres de Cette Académie, Depuis l'Année M. DCCXXXIV. Jusques & Compris l'Année M. DCCXXXVII* **12:**163–169.
Mantell, G.
  1851   On the remains of man, and works of art imbedded in rocks and strata, as illustrative of the connexion between archaeology and geology. *Edinburgh New Philosophical Journal* **50:**235–254.
Marcou, J.
  1896   *Life, letters, and works of Louis Agassiz.* New York: Macmillan.
Martineau, H.
  1848   *Eastern life present and past* (three volumes). London: Moxon.
  1877   *Harriet Martineau's autobiography* (Vol. 1), edited by M. W. Chapman. Boston: Osgood.
Maupertuis, P. L. M. de
  1974   *Oeuvres de Maupertuis* (nouvelle édition corrigée et augmentée, Lyon). Reprinted,
  [1798]   with an introduction by G. Torrelli (four volumes). Hildesheim: Verlag.
Maury, A.
  1852   Des ossemens humains et des ouvrages de main d'homme enfouis dans les roches et

les couches de la terre, pour servir a éclairer les rapports de l'archéologie et de la géologie. *Mémoires de la Société Nationale des Antiquaires de France* **21**:251–293.

1859   La géographie zoologique. *Revue des Deux Mondes* **24**:100–123.

1867   L'homme primitif—des lumières que les découvertes paléontologiques recentes ont jetées sur son histoire. *Revue des Deux Mondes* **68**:637–663.

McKee, D. R.

1944   Isaac de la Peyrère, a precursor of eighteenth-century critical deists. *Publications of the Modern Language Association* **56**:456–485.

Meek, R. L. (ed.)

1973   *Turgot on progress, sociology and economics.* Cambridge: Cambridge University Press.

Milne-Edwards, H.

1863a   Note sur les résultats fournis par une enquête relative à l'authenticité de la découverte d'une mâchoire humaine et de haches en silex, dans le terrain diluvien de Moulin-Quignon. *Comptes Rendus Hebdomadaires de l'Académie des Sciences* **56**:921–933.

1863b   Observations de M. Milne-Edwards a l'occasion des remarques précédentes. *Comptes Rendus Hebdomadaires de l'Académie des Sciences* **56**:937–938.

Moir, J. R.

1939   A pioneer in Paleolithic research. *Royal Society of London, Notes and Records* **2**:28–31.

Montfaucon, B. de

1722   *Antiquity explained, and represented in sculptures* (Vol. 5), translated by D. Humphreys. London.

Morgand, T.

1841–1843   Extrait de la notice biographique de M. Casimir Picard, médecin, archiviste de la Société Royale d'Emulation d'Abbeville, etc. *Mémoires de la Société Royale d'Emulation d'Abbeville* **1841–1843**:449–456.

Morren, C.

1838   Notice sur la vie et les travaux de Philippe-Charles Schmerling. *Annuaire de l'Académie Royale des Sciences et Belles-lettres de Bruxelles* Quatrième Année:130–150.

Morton, S. G.

1839   *Crania Americana; or, a comparative view of the skulls of various aboriginal nations of North and South America: to which is prefixed an essay on the varieties of the human species.* Philadelphia: Dobson.

1844a   *An inquiry into the distinctive characteristics of the aboriginal race of America* (2nd ed.). Philadelphia: Penington.

1844b   *Crania Aegyptica; or, observations on Egyptian ethnography, derived from anatomy, history, and the monuments.* Philadelphia: Penington.

1846   Observations on Egyptian ethnography, derived from anatomy, history, and the monuments. *Transactions of the American Philosophical Society* **9**:93–159.

1847a   Hybridity in animals, considered in reference to the question of the unity of the human species. Part I. *American Journal of Science and Arts* **53**:39–50.

1847b   Hybridity in animals, considered in reference to the question of the unity of the human species. Part II. *American Journal of Science and Arts* **53**:203–212.

1850   [Observations on the antiquity of some races of dogs.] *Proceedings of the Academy of Natural Sciences of Philadelphia* **5**:85–89.

1851   Value of the word species in zoology. *American Journal of Science and Arts* **61**:275–276.

Murchison, C. (ed.)
    1868   *Paleontological memoirs and notes on the late Hugh Falconer, A.M., M.D.
. . . with a biographical sketch of the author.* Volume II. *Mastodon, elephant,
rhinoceros, ossiferous caves, primeval man and his cotemporaries.* London:
Hardwicke.

Murchison, R. I.
    1839   *The Silurian system, founded on geological researches in the counties of Salop,
Hereford, Radnor, Montgomery, Caermarthen, Brecon, Pembroke, Monmouth,
Gloucester, Worcestor, and Stafford; with descriptions of the coal-fields and over-
lying formations.* London: Murray.

Nichols, J.
    1812   John Bagford. In *Literary anecdotes of the eighteenth century* (Vol. 2). London.
Pp. 462–465.

North, F. J.
    1942   Paviland Cave, the "red lady," the deluge, and William Buckland. *Annals of
Science* **5:**91–128.

Nott, J. C.
    1854   Introduction. In *Types of mankind: or, ethnological researches, based upon the
ancient monuments, paintings, sculptures, and crania of races, and upon their
natural, geographical, philological, and biblical history: illustrated by selections
from the inedited papers of Samuel George Morton, M.D.,* by J. C. Nott and G. R.
Gliddon. Philadelphia: Lippincott, Grambo. Pp. 49–61.

Nott, J. C., and G. R. Gliddon
    1854   *Types of mankind: or, ethnological researches, based upon the ancient monuments,
paintings, sculptures, and crania of races, and upon their natural, geographical,
philological, and biblical history: illustrated by selections from the inedited papers
of Samuel George Morton, M.D.* Philadelphia: Lippincott, Grambo.

Oakley, K. P.
    1964a   *Frameworks for dating fossil man.* Chicago: Aldine.
    1964b   The problem of man's antiquity. *Bulletin of the British Museum (Natural History),
Geology* **9:**(5).
    1968   The date of the "red lady" of Paviland. *Antiquity* **42:**306–307.

O'Brien, C. F.
    1971   Sir William Dawson: a life in science and religion. *Memoirs of the American
Philosophical Society* **84.**

Osborn, H. F.
    1935   Thomas Jefferson as a paleontologist. *Science* **82:**533–538.

Owen, R.
    1859   Address of the President. *Report of the Twenty-Eighth Meeting of the British
Association for the Advancement of Science,* pp. xlix–cx.

Parkinson J.
    1804   *Organic remains of a former world. An examination of the mineralized remains of
the vegetables and animals of the antediluvian world; generally termed extraneous
fossils. The first volume, containing the vegetable kingdom.* London.
    1808   *Organic remains of a former world. An examination of the mineralized remains of
the vegetables and animals of the antediluvian world; generally termed extraneous
fossils. The second volume, containing the fossil zoophytes.* London.
    1811   *Organic remains of a former world. An examination of the mineralized remains of
the vegetables and animals of the antediluvian world; generally termed extraneous*

fossils. The third volume, containing the fossil starfish, echini, shells, insects, amphibia, mammalia, &c. London.

Paston, G.
1932   *At John Murray's: records of a literary circle, 1843–1892.* London: Murray.

Patterson, H. S.
1854   Memoir of the life and scientific labors of Samuel George Morton. In *Types of mankind: or, ethnological researches, based upon the ancient monuments, paintings, sculptures, and crania of races, and upon their natural, geographical, philological, and biblical history: illustrated by selections from the inedited papers of Samuel George Morton, M.D.* Philadelphia: Lippincott, Grambo. Pp. xvii–lvii.

Peake, H. J. E.
1940   The study of prehistoric times. *Journal of the Royal Anthropological Institute* **70:**103–146.

Pengelly, W.
1859   On a recently-discovered ossiferous cavern at Brixham, near Torquay. *Report of the Twenty-Eighth Meeting of the British Association for the Advancement of Science, Notices and Abstracts,* p. 106.
1862   On the ossiferous caves and fissures of Devonshire. *Proceedings of the Royal Institution of Great Britain* **3:**149–151.
1869   *The literature of Kent's Cavern. Part II. Including the whole of the Rev. J. Mac Enery's manuscript.* Reprinted from the Transactions of the Devonshire Association for the Advancement of Science, Literature, and Art.

Phillips, J.
1844   *Memoirs of William Smith, LL.D., author of the "Map of the strata of England and Wales."* London: Murray.
1860   *Life on earth: its origin and succession.* Cambridge: Macmillan.

[Phillips, J.]
1863   [Review of] The geological evidences of the antiquity of man, with remarks on theories of the origin of species by variation. By Sir Charles Lyell, F.R.S. 2nd Ed., pp. 528. 1863. *Quarterly Review* **114:**368–417.

Picard, C.
1834–1835 Notice sur des instrumens celtiques en corne de cerf. *Mémoires de la Société Royale d'Emulation d'Abbeville* **1834–1835:**94–116.
1836–1837 Notice sur quelques instrumens celtiques. *Mémoires de la Société Royale d'Emulation d'Abbeville* **1836–1837:**221–272.

Pichanick, V. K.
1980   *Harriet Martineau: the woman and her work.* Ann Arbor: University of Michigan Press.

Pictet, F.-J.
1853   *Traité de paléontologie ou histoire naturelle des animaux fossiles considérés dans leur rapports zoologiques et géologiques* (2nd ed.). Paris: Baillière.
1859   Des silex taillés trouvés par M. Boucher de Perthes dans les dépôts diluviens du département de la Somme. *Bibliothèque Universelle, Revue Suisse et Étrangère, Archives des Sciences Physiques et Naturelles* **6:**353–363.
1860a   Note sur la période quaternaire ou diluvienne considérée dans ses rapports avec l'époque actuelle. *Bibliothèque Universelle, Revue Suisse et Étrangère, Archives des Sciences Physiques et Naturelles* **8:**265–277.
1860b   Sur l'origine de l'espèce par Charles Darwin. *Bibliothèque Universelle, Revue Suisse et Étrangère, Archives des Sciences Physiques et Naturelles* **7:**233–255.

1863a   Note sur la découverte d'une mâchoire humaine fossile dans les graviers des environs d'Abbeville. *Bibliothèque Universelle, Revue Suisse et Étrangère, Archives des Sciences Physiques et Naturelles* **17**:113–137.

1863b   Nouveaux documents sur la question de l'antiquité de l'homme. *Bibliothèque Universelle et Revue Suisse, Archives des Sciences Physiques et Naturelles* **17**:340–348.

Piggot, S.

1968   *The Druids*. London: Thames and Hudson.

1976   *Ruins in a landscape: essays in antiquarianism*. Edinburgh: Edinburgh University Press.

1978   *Antiquity depicted: aspects of archaeological illustration*. London: Thames and Hudson.

Planck, M.

1949   *Scientific autobiography and other papers*. New York: Philosophical Library.

Playfair, J.

1802   *Illustrations of the Huttonian theory of the earth*. Edinburgh.

Plot, R.

1686   *The natural history of Stafford-shire*. Oxford.

Porter, R.

1977   *The making of geology. Earth Science in Britain 1660–1815*. Cambridge: Cambridge University Press.

Pouchet, G.

1859   Hache de pierre trouvée dans le diluvium. *Comptes Rendus Hebdomadaires de l'Académie des Sciences* **49**:501–502.

1860a   Excursion aux carrières de Saint-Acheul. *Actes du Muséum d'Histoire Naturelle de Rouen* **1**:33–47.

1860b   Sur les débris de l'industrie humaine, attestant l'existence d'une race d'hommes contemporaine des animaux perdus (question de l'homme fossile). *Bulletins de la Société d'Anthropologie de Paris* **1**:42–47.

Prestwich, J.

1859   Sur la découverte d'instruments en silex associés à des restes de mammifères d'espèces perdues dans des couches non remaniées d'une formation géologique récente. *Comptes Rendus Hebdomadaires de l'Académie des Sciences* **49**:634–636.

1860   On the occurrence of flint-implements, associated with the remains of extinct mammalia, in undisturbed beds of a late geological period. *Proceedings of the Royal Society of London* **10**:50–59.

1861   On the occurrence of flint implements, associated with the remains of animals of extinct species in beds of a late geological period, in France at Amiens and Abbeville, and in England at Hoxne. *Philosophical Transactions of the Royal Society of London* **150**:277–317.

1863a   The antiquity of man. *Athenaeum* **41**:555.

1863b   The human jaw of Abbeville. *Athenaeum* **41**:779–780.

1863c   On the section at Moulin Quignon, Abbeville, and on the peculiar character of some of the flint implements recently discovered there. *Quarterly Journal of the Geological Society of London* **19**:497–505.

1863d   Theoretical considerations on the conditions under which the drift deposits containing the remains of extinct mammalia and flint-implements were accumulated; and on their geological age. *Proceedings of the Royal Society of London* **12**:38–52.

1866   On the Quaternary flint implements of Abbeville, Amiens, Hoxne, etc., their geological position and history. *Proceedings of the Royal Institution of Great Britain* **4**:213–222.

1873   Report on the exploration of Brixham Cave, conducted by a committee of the Geological Society, and under the superintendence of Wm. Pengelly, Esq., F.R.S., aided by a local committee; with descriptions of the animal remains by George Busk, Esq., F.R.S., and of the flint implements by John Evans, Esq., F.R.S. *Philosophical Transactions of the Royal Society* **163**:471–572.

Prichard, J. C.

1813   *Researches into the physical history of man.* London.

1815   On the cosmogony of Moses; with some preliminary observations on Dr. Gilby's communication in number 209. *The Philosophical Magazine and Journal* **46**:285–290.

1816   On the cosmogony of Moses; in answer to the strictures of F. E. _____s. *The Philosophical Magazine and Journal* **17**:110–117.

1819   *An analysis of the Egyptian mythology: to which is subjoined, a critical examination of the remains of Egyptian chronology.* London.

1836   *Researches into the physical history of mankind* (Vol. 1). London: Sherwood, Gilbert and Piper.

1837   *Researches into the physical history of mankind* (Vol. 2). London: Sherwood, Gilbert, and Piper.

1841   [Review of] Crania americana . . . by Samuel George Morton, M.D. *Journal of the Royal Geographical Society* **10**:522–561.

1843   *The natural history of man; comprising inquiries into the modifying influence of physical and moral agencies on the different tribes of the human family.* London: Baillière.

1847   *Researches into the physical history of mankind* (Vol. 5). London: Sherwood, Gilbert and Piper.

Pruner-Bay, F.

1866   Sur la mâchoire humaine de La Naulette (Belgique). *Bulletins de la Société d'Anthropologie de Paris* **1**:584–603.

Ravin, F.-P.

1834–1835   Mémoire géologique sur le bassin d'Amiens, et en particulier sur les cantons littoraux de la Somme. *Mémoires de la Société Royale d'Emulation d'Abbeville* **1834–1835**:143–210.

Ray, J.

1692   *Miscellaneous discourses concerning the dissolution and changes of the world.* London.

1693   *Three physico-theological discourses, concerning I. The primitive chaos, and creation of the world. II. The general deluge, its causes and effects. III. The dissolution of the world, and future conflagration.* London.

Rembault, G.

1855   Notice nécrologique sur M. le docteur Rigollot. *Bulletins de la Société des Antiquaires de Picardie* **5**:253–256.

Renaux, J.

1830   Ossemens fossiles humains. *Bulletin des Sciences Naturelles et de Géologie* **21**:28–31.

Ribeiro, C.

1873   Sur la position des silex taillés découverts dans les terrains Miocène et Pliocène du Portugal. *Congrès International d'Anthropologie et d'Archéologie Préhistoriques, Compte Rendu de la 6ᵉ Session, Bruxelles, 1872*:95–100.

Rigollot, M.-J.

1854   *Mémoire sur des instruments en silex trouvés à St.-Acheul, près d'Amiens, et considérés sous les rapports géologique et archéologique.* Amiens.

1855   [Letter to Boucher de Perthes]. *Bulletins de la Société des Antiquaires de Picardie* **5**:308.

1856   Mémoire sur des instruments en silex trouvés à Saint-Acheul, près d'Amiens, et considérés sous les rapports géologique et archéologique. *Mémoires de la Société des Antiquaires de Picardie* **14**:23–60.

1857   [Letter to Boucher de Perthes]. *Mémoires de la Société Imperiale d'Emulation d'Abbeville* **8**:678–679.

Robert, E.

1860   Recherches géologiques sur les matières, notamment les pierres, qui ont eté travaillées par les premiers habitants des Gaules. *Comptes Rendus Hebdomadaires de l'Académie des Sciences* **51**:660–662.

1861a   Réponse de M. E. Robert aux remarques de M. Boucher de Perthes. *Comptes Rendus Hebdomadaires de l'Académie des Sciences* **52**:455–458.

1861b   Supplément aux recherches géologiques sur les matières, notamment les pierres, travaillées par les habitants primitifs des Gaules. *Comptes Rendus Hebdomadaires de l'Académie des Sciences* **52**:63–66.

1863   Sur l'origine récente des traces d'instruments tranchants observées à la surface de quelques ossemens fossiles. *Comptes Rendus Hebdomadaires de l'Académie des Sciences* **56**:1157–1158.

Robert, F.

1848   De l'homme fossile de Denise. *Annales de la Société d'Agriculture, Sciences, Arts et Commerce du Puy* **12**:209–225.

Rodden, J.

1981   The development of the three age system: archaeology's first paradigm. In *Towards a history of archaeology*, edited by G. Daniel. London: Thames and Hudson. Pp. 51–68.

Rosenmüller, J. C.

1795   *Beiträge zur Geschichte und nähern Kenntniss fossiler Knochen*. Leipzig.

Rouville, P. de

1876–1877   Notice biographique sur M. Paul Tournal, secrétaire de la Commission Archéologique et fondateur du Musée de Narbonne. *Commission Archéologique et Littéraire de l'Arrondissement de Narbonne* 1876–1877:5–52.

Rudwick, M. J. S.

1972   *The meaning of fossils*. New York: American Elsevier.

Ruse, M.

1979   *The Darwinian revolution*. Chicago: University of Chicago Press.

Schaafhausen, H.

1861   On the crania of the most ancient races of man. By Professor D. Schaafhausen, of Bonn (from Muller's Archiv, 1858, pp. 453). With remarks, and original figures, taken from a cast of the Neanderthal cranium. By George Busk. *Natural History Review* **1**:155–175.

Schlottheim [sic], Baron

1820   Sur les anthropolites et autres ossemens fossiles, trouvés dans le Comté de Reuss en Saxe. *Bibliotheque Universelle des Sciences, Belles-Lettres, et Arts, Redigée à Genève* **15**:173–187.

Schmerling, P.-C.

1833   Recherches sur les ossemens fossiles découverts dans les cavernes de la province de Liége (Vol. 1). Liége: Collardin.

1834   Recherches sur les ossemens fossiles decouverts dans les cavernes de la province de Liége (Vol. 2). Liége: Collardin.

1835   Annonce de la découverte faite dans deux grottes de deux os fossiles façonnés, et de fragmens de silex taillés. *Bulletin de la Société Géologique de France* **6**:170–173.

Sedgwick, A.

1834a   [Address on presenting the Wollaston Medal to Mr. William Smith.] *Proceedings of the Geological Society of London* **1**:270–279.

1834b   Anniversary address 1830. *Proceedings of the Geological Society of London* **1**:187–212.

1834c   Anniversary address 1831. *Proceedings of the Geological Society of London* **1**:281–316.

Simpson, G. G.

1942   The beginnings of vertebrate paleontology in North America. *Transactions of the American Philosophical Society* **86**(1):130–188.

Slotkin, J. S.

1965   Readings in early anthropology. *Viking Fund Publications in Anthropology* **40**.

Smellie, W.

1791   *Natural history, general and particular, by the Count de Buffon* (nine volumes) (3rd ed.). London.

Smith, C. H.

1848   *The natural history of the human species, its typical forms, primaeval distribution, filiations, and migrations*. London: Bohn.

Smith, S. S.

1965   *An essay on the causes of the variety of complexion and figure in the human species,*

[1810]   edited by W. D. Jordan. Cambridge, Mass.: Belknap.

Smith, W.

1816   *Strata identified by organized fossils, containing prints on colored paper of the most characteristic specimens in each stratum.* London.

1817   *Stratigraphical system of organized fossils, with reference to the specimens of the original geological collection in the British Museum: explaining their state of preservation and their use in identifying the British strata.* London.

Sollas, W. J.

1913   Paviland Cave: an Aurignacian station in Wales. *Journal of the Royal Anthropological Institute of Great Britain and Ireland* **43**:325–374.

Spring, A.

1853   Sur des ossements humains decouverts dans une caverne de la province de Namur. *Bulletins de l'Académie Royale des Sciences, des Lettres, et des Beaux-Arts de Belgique* **20**:427–449.

1864   Les hommes d'Engis et les hommes de Chauvaux. *Bulletins de l'Académie Royale des Sciences, des Lettres, et des Beaux-Arts de Belgique* **18**:479–515.

Stanton, W.

1960   *The leopard's spots: scientific attitudes toward race in America 1815–1859.* Chicago: University of Chicago Press.

Stebbins, R. E.

1972   France. In *The comparative reception of Darwinism*, edited by T. F. Glick. Austin: University of Texas Press. Pp. 117–163.

Steno, N.

1968   *The prodromus of Nicolaus Steno's dissertation concerning a solid body enclosed*

[1669]   *by process of nature within a solid,* translated by J. G. Winter. New York: Hafner.

Stocking, G. W., Jr.

1968   *Race, culture, and evolution: essays in the history of anthropology.* New York: The Free Press.

1973 From chronology to ethnology. James Cowles Prichard and British anthropology 1800–1850. In *Researches into the physical history of mankind, by James Cowles Prichard*, edited by G. W. Stocking, Jr. Chicago: University of Chicago Press. Pp. ix–cx.

Strachey, J.
1719 A curious description of the strata observ'd in the coal-mines of Mendip in Somersetshire; being a letter of John Strachey Esq; to Dr. Robert Welsted, M.D. and R.S. Soc. and by him communicated to the Society. *Philosophical Transactions of the Royal Society of London* 30:968–973.

1725 An account of the strata in coal-mines, etc. *Philosophical Transactions of the Royal Society of London* 33:395–398.

Teissier, J.
1831–1832 Note sur une caverne à ossemens près d'Anduze. *Bulletin de la Société Géologique*
[1831] *de France* 2:56–63.

Thackray, J. C.
1976 James Parkinson's Organic remains of a former world. *Journal of the Society for the Bibliography of Natural History* 7:451–466.

Todhunter, I.
1876 *William Whewell, D.D., master of Trinity College, Cambridge: An account of his writings with selections from his literary and scientific correspondence* (two volumes). London: Macmillan.

Toulmin, S., and J. Goodfield
1977 *The discovery of time.* Chicago: University of Chicago Press.

[Tournal, P.]
1829 Cavernes à ossemens. *Revue Bibliographique des Science Naturelles* 1829:124.

Tournal, P.
1827 Note sur deux cavernes à ossemens, découvertes a Bire [sic], dans les environs de Narbonne. *Annales des Sciences Naturelles* 12:78–82.

1828 Note sur la caverne de Bize près Narbonne. *Annales des Sciences Naturelles* 15:348–351.

1829 Considerations theoriques sur les cavernes à ossemens de Bize, près Narbonne (Aude), et sur les ossemens humains confondus avec des restes d'animaux appartenant à des espèces perdues. *Annales des Sciences Naturelles* 18:242–258.

1830 Observations sur les ossemens humains et les objects de fabrications humaine confondus avec des ossemens de mammifères appartenant à des espèces perdues. *Bulletin de la Socièté Géologique de France* 1:195–200.

1831–1832 Note sur les caverns à ossemens de Bize. *Bulletin de la Société Géologique de*
[1832] *France* 2:380–382.

1833 Considérations générales sur le phénomène des caverns à ossemens. *Annales de Chimie et de Physique* 52:161–181.

Trigger, B. G.
1981 Giants and pygmies: the professionalization of Canadian archaeology. In *Towards a history of archaeology,* edited by G. Daniel. London: Thames and Hudson. Pp. 68–84.

Twiesselmann, F.
1958 Les Neanderthaliens découverts en Belgique. In *Hundert jahre Neanderthaler: Neanderthal centenary, 1856–1956,* edited by G. H. R. von Koenigswald. Utrecht: Kemink en Zoon. Pp. 63–71.

Tylor, A.
1863 On the discovery of supposed human remains in the tool-bearing drift of Moulin-Quignon. *Anthropological Review* 1:166–168.

Usher, W.
1854   Geology and paleontology, in connection with human origins. In *Types of mankind: or, ethnological researches, based upon the ancient monuments, paintings, sculptures, and crania of races, and upon their natural, geographical, philological, and biblical history: illustrated by selections from the inedited papers of Samuel George Morton, M.D.* Philadelphia: Lippincott, Grambo. Pp. 327–372.

Ussher, J.
1658   *The annals of the world. Deduced from the origin of time, and continued to the beginning of the Emperour Vespasian's reign, and the totall destruction and abolition of the temple and common-wealth of the Jews.* London.

Virey, J.-J.
1801   *Histoire naturelle du genre humaine, ou recherche sur ses principaux fondemens physiques et moraux, et sur l'ensemble de leur physiologie. On y a joint une dissertation sur le sauvage de l'Aveyron* (two volumes). Paris.

1817   *Homme.* In *Nouveau dictionnaire d'histoire naturelle, appliquée aux arts, à l'agriculture, à l'économie rurale et domestique, á la médecine, etc.* (new edition, Vol. 15). Paris: Deterville. Pp. 1–255.

1824   *Histoire naturelle de genre humain* (2nd ed.) (three volumes). Paris: Crochard.

Vivian, E. (ed.)
1859   *Cavern researches, or, discoveries of organic remains, and of British and Roman reliques, in the caves of Kent's Hole, Anstis Cove, Chudleigh, and Berry Head: by the late Rev. J. MacEnery, F. G. S.* London: Simpkin, Marshall.

Voltaire, F. M. A. de
1963   *Essai sur les moeurs et l'esprit des nations et sur les principaux faits de l'histoire depuis Charlemagne jusqu'à Louis XIII,* edited by R. Pomeau (two volumes). Paris: Garnier.

von Dücker, Baron
1873   Sur la cassure artificielle d'ossements recuellis dans le terrain Miocène de Pikermi. *Congres International d'Anthropologie et d'Archéologie Préhistoriques, Compte Rendu de la 6ᵉ Session, Bruxelles* **1872:** pp. 104–106.

Wallace, A. R.
1864   The origin of human races and the antiquity of man deduced from the theory of "Natural Selection." Journal of the Anthropological Society of London **2:** clviii–clxxxvii.

1887   The antiquity of man in North America. *The Nineteenth Century* **22:**667–679.

1891   The antiquity of man in North America. In *Natural selection and tropical nature: essays in descriptive and theoretical biology.* London: Macmillan. Pp. 433–449.

Warren, E.
1690   *Geologia: or, a discourse concerning the earth before the deluge.* London.

Weaver, J.
1823   On fossil human bones, and other animal remains recently found in Germany. *Annals of Philosophy* **5:**17–43.

[Wedgwood, J.]
1863   Sir Charles Lyell on the antiquity of man. *Macmillan's Magazine* **7:**476–487.

Wells, W. C.
1818   *Two essays: one upon single vision with two eyes; the other on dew. A letter to the Right Hon. Lloyd, Lord Kenyon, and an account of a female of the white race of mankind, part of whose skin resembles that of a Negro; with some observations on the causes of the differences in colour and form between the white and Negro races of men.* London.

Westropp, H. M.
    1872   *Pre-historic phases; or, introductory essays on pre-historic archaeology.* London: Bell and Daldy.
Whately, R.
    1832   *Introductory lectures on political economy, delivered in Easter term, MDCCCXXXI* (2nd ed.). London: Fellowes.
[Whewell, W.]
    1832   [Review of] Principles of geology, being an attempt to explain the former changes of the earth's surface, by reference to causes now in operation. By Charles Lyell, Esq., F.R.S., professor of geology in King's College, London (Vol. II). London, 1832. *Quarterly Review* **47**:103–132.
    1853   *Of the plurality of worlds: an essay.* London: Parker and Son.
Whiston, W.
    1696   *A new theory of the earth, from its original, to the consummation of all things, wherein the creation of the world in six days, the universal Deluge, and the general conflagration, as laid down in the Holy Scriptures, are shown to be perfectly agreeable to reason and philosophy.* London.
White, A.
    1896   *A history of the warfare of science with theology in Christendom* (two volumes). New York: Appleton.
White, C.
    1799   *An account of the regular gradation in man, and in different animals and vegetables; and from the former to the latter.* London.
Whitney, J. D.
    1879   The auriferous gravels of the Sierra Nevada of California. *Memoirs of the Museum of Comparative Zoology* **6**(1).
Wilson, L. G. (ed.)
    1970   *Sir Charles Lyell's scientific journals on the species question.* New Haven: Yale University Press.
Wistar, C.
    1799   An account of the bones deposited, by the president, in the museum of the society, and represented in the annexed plates. *Transactions of the American Philosophical Society* **4**:526–531.
Woodward, H. B.
    1883   Dr. Buckland and the glacial theory. *Midland Naturalist* **6**:225–229.
    1895   Anniversary address of the president. *Quarterly Journal of the Geological Society of London* **51**:xlix–lxxxviii.
    1907   *The history of the Geological Society of London.* London: Geological Society.
Woodward, J.
    1695   *An essay toward a natural history of the earth: and terrestrial bodies, especially minerals: as also of the sea, rivers, and springs. With an account of the universal Deluge: and of the effects that it had upon the earth.* London.
    1726   *The natural history of the earth, illustrated, inlarged, and defended. Written originally in Latin: and now first made English by Benj. Holloway, L.L.B. and Fellow of the Royal Society. To which are added, physical proofs of the existence of God, his actual incessant concurrence to the support of the universe, and of all organic bodyes, vegetables, and animals, particularly man; with several other papers, on different subjects, never before printed.* London.
    1728   *Fossils of all kinds, digested into a method, suitable to their mutual relation and affinity.* London.

1774   An account of some Roman urns, and other antiquities, lately digg'd up near Bishop's-Gate, Oxford, In *The itinerary of John Leland the antiquary,* edited by T.Hearne (2nd ed.). Oxford.

Zittel, K. A. von

1901   *History of geology and paleontology to the end of the nineteenth century,* translated by M. M. Ogilivie-Gordon. London: Scott.

Index